D1740037

Auctions Law and Practice

'Ah, who can believe sellers!' said old Michael Mail in a carefully-cautious voice, by way of tiding-over this critical point of affairs.

'No one at all,' said Joseph Bowman, in the tone of a man fully agreeing with everybody.

'Ay,' said Mail, in the tone of a man who did not agree with everybody as a rule, though he did now; 'I knowed a' auctioneering feller once — a very friendly feller 'a was too. And so one hot day as I was walking down the front street o' Casterbridge, jist below the King's Arms, I passed a' open winder and see him inside, stuck upon his perch, a selling-off. I jist nodded to en in a friendly way as I passed, and went my way, and thought no more about it. Well, next day, as I was oilen my boots by fuel-house door, if a letter didn't come wi' a bill charging me with a feather-bed, bolster, and pillers, that I had bid for at Mr Tayor's sale. The slim-faced martel had knocked 'em down to me because I nodded to en in my friendly way; and I had to pay for 'em too. Now, I hold that was coming it very close, Reuben?'

''Twas close, there's no denying,' said the general voice.

Thomas Hardy *Under the Greenwood Tree* (1872).

Auctions Law and Practice

SECOND EDITION

BRIAN W HARVEY, MA, LLM (CANTAB)
Solicitor, Professor of Property Law,
University of Birmingham

FRANKLIN MEISEL, LLB
of the Middle Temple, Barrister,
Senior Lecturer in Law,
University of Birmingham

OXFORD UNIVERSITY PRESS
1995

Oxford University Press, Walton Street, Oxford OX2 6DP
Oxford New York
Athens Auckland Bangkok Bombay
Calcutta Cape Town Dar es Salaam Delhi
Florence Hong Kong Istanbul Karachi
Kuala Lumpur Madras Madrid Melbourne
Mexico City Nairobi Paris Singapore
Taipei Tokyo Toronto
and associated companies in
Berlin Ibadan

Oxford is a trade mark of Oxford University Press

Published in the United States
by Oxford University Press Inc., New York

© Brian Harvey and Frank Meisel 1995
First edition published by Butterworths 1985

All rights reserved. No part of this publication may be reproduced,
stored in a retrieval system, or transmitted, in any form or by any means,
without the prior permission in writing of Oxford University Press.
Within the UK, exceptions are allowed in respect of any fair dealing for the
purpose of research or private study, or criticism or review, as permitted
under the Copyright, Designs and Patents Act, 1988, or in the case of
reprographic reproduction in accordance with the terms of the licences
issued by the Copyright Licensing Agency. Enquiries concerning
reproduction outside these terms and in other countries should be
sent to the Rights Department, Oxford University Press,
at the address above

This book is sold subject to the condition that it shall not, by way
of trade or otherwise, be lent, re-sold, hired out or otherwise circulated
without the publisher's prior consent in any form of binding or cover
other than that in which it is published and without a similar condition
including this condition being imposed on the subsequent purchaser

British Library Cataloguing in Publication Data
Data available

Library of Congress Cataloging in Publication Data
Harvey, Brian W.
The law and practice of auctions/Brian W. Harvey, Franklin
Meisel.—2nd ed.
p. cm.
Rev. ed. of: Auctions. 1985.
Includes index.
1. Auctions—Great Britain. I. Meisel, Franklin. II. Harvey,
Brian. W. Auctions. III. Ttile.
KD1660.H37 1995
343.41'0887—dc20
[344.103887] 95–18214

ISBN 0-19-825908-5

1 3 5 7 9 10 8 6 4 2

Typeset by Best-set Typesetter Ltd., Hong Kong
Printed in Great Britain
on acid-free paper by
Bookcraft Ltd., Midsomer Norton, Avon

Foreword to First Edition

'Eureka!' Such was Archimedes' exclamation of delight when he discovered gold; or, to be more precise, when he saw the practical means of testing for purity between the real and the alloyed.

The simple test which I have been able to apply to *Auctions: Law and Practice* is to read it and, in so doing, to recognise a golden discovery of a different sort: a wide-ranging, deeply-researched and exhaustive treatise on these twin components — law and practice — of this complex pursuit, the realisation of money's worth by the auction process.

Sales by open pubic competition, by various rules, methods and styles, emerge out of the mists of time into commonplace by the early seventeenth century, when 'inch of candle' or 'hour glass' were the acknowledged means of concentrating the bargaining process within time and space, before 'fall of the hammer' gained almost universal favour as the more practical way of determining the point of sale, whether at the end of an ascending, or of a descending, pattern of bidding.

For the last two hundred years or so, therefore, there has developed in the United Kingdom a corpus of some forty statutes and perhaps a thousand cases producing a sophisticated overlapping network of law and an elaborate web of commercial and professional convention within which the machinery and skills of the auction are required to operate, for the mutual benefit of vendor, purchaser and — necessarily — practitioners, both of law and of auctioneering.

It is to the unravelling and illumination of these essential realities, in all their considerable complexity, that Brian Harvey and Frank Meisel have addressed themselves with such energy over the last two years or so and it is we, their readers, who are the beneficiaries, to their great credit. Some of their expert conclusions and commentaries will raise a few eyebrows, I think, and perhaps temperatures as well, among experienced rostrum artists whose standard procedures and interpretations of law and practice are called into serious question; but then that is what a book like this is all about and it behoves each of us to assimilate its definitive instruction whilst responding to its occasional challenge.

During this Diamond Jubilee Year of The Incorporated Society of Valuers and Auctioneers, it is my great privilege to have been given this opportunity of contributing the Foreword to what will undoubtedly become a new standard work of reference on the law and practice of auctions.

To the authors, our thanks; to the public, my recommendation.

John M Phillips FRICS FSVA ACIArb
Diamond Jubilee President of
The Incorporated Society of Valuers and Auctioneers
London
February 1985

Preface

Despite the economic recession in the UK, London can still be said to be the centre of the auction market in fine art and most other valuable commodities. Admittedly other major cities such as New York and Geneva are pressing hard on London's heels, but the whole history and development of large scale auctioneering has been and largely remains centred in London. Besides the companies who are household names operating in London there are numerous smaller firms who offer a service mainly confined to UK residents in all parts of England, Wales, Scotland and Northern Ireland. An auction sale of land can be organised by a firm which normally operates as estate agents or surveyors but which decides that on a specific occasion an auction sale of a house, and possibly the accompanying chattels, is in the best interests of the vendor. It is this situation which is most familiar to solicitors as well. But in addition to chattels sales and sales of land, there are numerous other specialised types of auction which have established a market of their own. To give an example, motor vehicle auctions have mushroomed in popularity in the UK — it being estimated that by 1982 750,000 vehicles were being sold at auction annually, and that one in five of these was bought by a member of the general public. Similarly, perhaps as a sign of the times, auctions of plant and machinery have become an important way of disposing of commercial property where companies have cashflow difficulties or need to turn their stock into cash prior to liquidation. Those trading in livestock are almost entirely dependent on the medium of the auction.

In the Preface to the first edition we remarked that there had been no monograph on the law of auctions since Bateman's *Law of Auctions* (11th edn) was published by the Estates Gazette in 1953. Modern textbooks which include a section on auction law, usually in the more general context of estate agent's work, do not normally deal with specialist auctions such as sales of motor vehicles, livestock, plant and machinery and the like. Nor could we find anywhere an examination of such matters as export licensing or, beyond a brief mention, any analysis of the increasingly important law relating to trade descriptions and obtaining property by deception in the criminal law. These matters are all of vital interest to auctioneers and the legal practitioners who advise them and we therefore hope that our readers will agree that it is opportune to endeavour to write a reasonably exhaustive treatise on this topic which examines the law as it is now. Some matters, we know from our consultations with practitioners, are controversial. We have in mind particularly potential criminal liability of auctioneers under s 15 of the Theft Act 1968 in respect of property obtained by deception. But the Trade Descriptions Act 1968 has an equally important, and often more directly threatening, bearing on auctioneers' activities and there have been recent prosecutions of auctioneers (who seem in some cases to have thought that the criminal law in this area does not apply to auctioneering activities) which have resulted in convictions. Normally problems are caused by ignorance of the law and in some cases can be obviated by adopting up-to-date Conditions of Sale or slightly altering saleroom practice. The importance of the auction in an efficiently functioning economy is such that it is vital that auctioneering practice is seen to be fair both to seller and buyer. Both are 'consumers', the seller of the auctioneer's services and the buyer, in economics if not always in law, of the property sold. Indeed, as a very recent case has shown, the buyer may be a consumer of the auctioneer's services too. We hope that our work will assist professional practitioners in these areas, and in the Appendices we have included as much material directly useful in practice for which there is space.

Since the first edition was published some ten years ago major changes have occurred in the underlying law. Land auctions have been affected more radically than some seem to realise by the Law of Property (Miscellaneous Provisions) Act 1989. A number of safety regulations affecting the sale of everyday items have both been passed and enforced through the criminal courts, to the dismay of a few unfortunate auctioneers, and it is vital to understand the basis of these provisions and how their effect can be mitigated. Legislation derived from the European Union now also affects unfair contract terms with no exception for auctions. Export licences have been recast in the European context. VAT now affects many auction sales in a complex way. A number of important decisions of the superior courts have affected, and to some extent clarified, the duties and responsibilities (particularly as to catalogue descriptions and the duty of care) of the auctioneering profession. Numerous detailed changes in the text have been required to the extent that hardly a single page of the first edition appears unamended in some respect in the second. Large portions have had to be entirely re-written.

The book is aimed to be of use primarily both to professional auctioneers and their staff and to practising lawyers. We hope that the book will also prove useful to law students and those studying for the professional examinations of the bodies to which auctioneers and estate agents belong. Professional dealers and others who make it a habit to buy at auction may also welcome a full-scale statement of the law which regulates such an important part of their business transactions.

As can be inferred from the acknowledgements which follow, the writing of the book (though inevitably hard labour) has been made exceptionally enjoyable by the very large degree of co-operation afforded to us by professional auctioneers. Whilst we both have experience in legal practice we do not pretend to be professional auctioneers, though we have observed a good many sales from the inside and from the outside. But without the help and encouragement of the auctioneering profession, together with their comments on much of our material, the book would have been the poorer. In this connection we wish particularly to thank Mr Joe Och (then of Sotheby's and an endless source of wisdom on a wide variety of auction conundrums) and both Sotheby's and Christie's for allowing us to reproduce their Conditions of Sale. The Department of National Heritage has also been most helpful in the revision of the chapter on export licences. Mr John Parsons of Phillips has been exceptionally helpful to the authors on the vexed question of VAT, now dealt with at the end of the book. The section on livestock auctions would have been the poorer without the helpful comments of John Martin, Secretary of the Livestock Auctioneers' Association. We thank also a number of other specialist auctioneers, such as those involved in the sale of motor vehicles and life policies, as mentioned in the text. The two major professional bodies, the RICS and the ISVA, have continued to be most helpful and supportive. Our student Adrian Williams assisted us with some valuable initial research. The Export Licence forms and chart in Appendix 4 are reproduced by permission of the Controller of H. M. Stationery Office.

Without the facility of the auction to reduce land or goods to often desperately needed cash, the economy would be materially stunted, as we try to make clear in chapter 1. Though we do look at the scene with critical eyes, we come to praise auctions, not to bury them.

Brian Harvey
Frank Meisel

Contents

Table of statutes

Table of cases

Table of statutory instruments

1

The Evolution and Economics of Auction Sales

DEFINITION OF AUCTIONS

It is perhaps surprising that there is no comprehensive definition of an auction in English statute law. The reason is, no doubt, that since no single statute deals with both the civil and criminal aspects of auction sales in their entirety, it has never been necessary to attempt a statutory definition. Such statutes as do relate to the topic may refer to the necessity of 'competitive bidding' (see Mock Auctions Act 1961) or may refer purely to a particular feature of auction sales, such as the general rule that the offer is made by the bidder and accepted by the auctioneer when he signifies his acceptance by fall of the hammer (see Sale of Goods Act 1979, s 57(2), Appendix 2). For present purposes, as satisfactory a definition as any is to be found in Halsbury:[1] 'An auction is a manner of selling or letting property by bids, usually to the highest bidder by public competition'.[2]

TYPES OF AUCTION

The Halsbury definition above has the virtue of making it clear that an auction 'usually' involves sale to the highest bidder by public competition. The method familiar in the British Isles, involving a system whereby prices are bid upwards until the last bidder eventually succeeds, is not the only method of auctioning. The following alternative methods also exist.

(a) The Dutch auction. This is a descending-price system whereby the auctioneer determines the starting figure and quotes prices at descend-

---

[1] 2 Halsbury's Laws (4th Edn Reissue) para 901.

[2] See also *Frewen v Hays* (1912) 106 LT 516, PC at 518, 'The prices which the public are asked to pay are the highest prices which those who bid can be tempted to offer by the skill and tact of the auctioneer under the excitement of open competition' (per Lord MacNaghten). And in *Bexwell v Christie* (1776) I Cowp 395 at 397 Lord Mansfield asked, 'What is the nature of an auction? It is, that the goods shall go to the highest real bidder.' An economist might define an auction as a market institution with an explicit set of rules determining resource allocation and prices on the basis of competing bids from market participants — see, for instance, R. Preston McAfee and John McMillan, 'Auctions and Bidding', 25 Journal of Economic Literature xxv (1987), 701.

ing intervals until a bidder is found at a particular price. Quite sophisticated methods exist to effect this scheme which may take those accustomed to the 'English' type of ascending-bid system somewhat by surprise. Whether or not the system results in a better price for the vendor is conjectural and depends upon market conditions. If a bidder is anxious to secure a lot he will not risk not being the first to shout 'mine' (or otherwise signal acceptance) for fear of losing the lot. Had the bidding been competitive in an upwards direction, competition might have been weak and he might have secured the lot at a less high price. Under this system a bid is normally made orally in the way suggested above, though a more sophisticated system of accepting the auctioneer's offer is by the pressing of electronic buttons which stops a clock at a certain point and can assist with the identification of a buyer where more than one bid is made at almost the same time. This descending-price system emanates from Holland, though the ascending-bid system is now apparently well on the way to replacing it.[3]

(b) A sub-species of the Dutch auction involves a combination of the ascending-bid and descending-bid systems. The economic justification for this hybrid system existed where a precise market level for the lots being sold (eg miscellaneous antiques) could not clearly be established. Here the auction is conducted on an ascending-bid system first, on the understanding that the highest bidder's offer is not accepted unless he remains the highest bidder in the second, or descending, phase of the auction. The method fixes the top level from which the bidding will start in a downward direction. The cumbersome and somewhat time-consuming procedures involved have made this method obsolescent if not quite obsolete on the continent of Europe.[4]

(c) In commodity markets, particularly in the Third World, there are several varieties of essentially ascending-bid systems. The variants involve the method of communicating bids to the auctioneer. Bids may be communicated privately to the auctioneer either by handshake or by a whisper, in ignorance of the competition, and the auctioneer then chooses the highest bidder. The element of open competition is thus missing. (This is also so in the case of 'postal auctions' of, for instance, stamps, but these are more akin to tenders considered below.)

---

[3] These, and other non-standard forms of auctioning, are more fully discussed in Cassady *Auctions & Auctioneering* University of California Press (1967). There is discussion of an Australian sale after sunset by Dutch auction in *Ex p Hamilton* (1882) 3 LR (NSW) 89.

[4] The Court of Appeal, Criminal Division, found it 'difficult, indeed impossible' to envisage a 'system of bidding which involved bidding up and bidding down — Dutch and English — simultaneously' in *R v Pollard* (1983) 148 JP 679, CA. See (1984) 92 Monthly Review 110 and below ch. 8 p 208.

(d) Yet another variety of the ascending-bid auction is one which is combined with a time limit. Bidding must be completed before an interval of time elapses as determined in a specified way. This may be by burning a candle of a certain length, using a sand-glass or a clock. The sale of an estate in England in 1932 was described thus: 'After supper an inch of candle is lit, and the bidding continues until it dies out, the last [and thus highest] bid before the final flicker securing the tenancy for the ensuing year'.[5] It is difficult to see what advantages the setting of a time limit in this way can confer upon the vendor. A skilled auctioneer can effectively control the time that it takes to offer each lot without this device. Its only effect would seem to be to exclude some possible higher bidders who make their offers after the candle has expired. It may now be regarded as an obsolete method, at least in Great Britain. However, a method in current use of selling commodities such as postage stamps, which perhaps evolved from 'candle' auctions, is to allow bidders using a catalogue to bid by telephone or fax over a period of, perhaps, seven days, with facilities allowing bidders to ascertain the highest preceding bid. Goods go to the highest bidder when the period expires.

(e) Sealed bid arrangements. Although 'tenders' are not, in popular parlance, regarded as 'auctions', a sale by tender to the highest sealed bidder, the property having been publicly advertised, does substantially comply with the definition advanced above. However, tenders lack the 'public' element of the true auction, an important point when considering the statutory requirements as to formatities when land is sold by tender, as discussed in chapter 9. The definition cannot apply to the type of tender which is designed to find the lowest bidder, as is the case for tenders for building construction for public authorities. Selling real property by tender is quite common and an important method of disposing of property. From the point of view of both the vendor and purchaser, there is likely to be more time for the careful consideration of a bid and for decisions as to its acceptance. Depending on the Conditions of Sale,[6] the vendor may not be obliged to accept any particular tender. The method does not, of course, involve 'competitive bidding' quite in the sense used in conventional auctions. One tenderer will not be aware of the level of the bid of his competitors. There will not, therefore, be the identification of the market price on the particu-

---

[5] Cassady (n 3 above) citing 'A curious survival . . . sale by candle' (1932) XVII Conveyancer (May) 138.

[6] See *Spencer v Harding* (1870) LR 5 CP 561, 39 LJCP 332: a circular advertised stock in trade 'for sale by tender' as one lot. It was held that there was no contract to sell to the highest tenderer.

lar day of the property sale which is a key feature of the conventional auction. On the other hand, a tenderer may well offer either more or less for the property than he would have been obliged to do at a conventional auction. (A sophisticated variation on this theme, apparently coming from the USA, is for the rules to lay down that the highest sealed bidder wins the item offered for sale but pays a price equal not to his own bid but to the second highest bid. Some psychological insight is needed to work out the possible effect of this subtlety, particularly where then is a reasonable pool of bidders.) These methods of selling property are primarily confined to sales of land (considered in further detail in chapter 9). The contractual situation is that a statement inviting tenders is normally not an offer.[7] The person submitting the tender makes the offer, and the acceptance is at the option of the person inviting such tenders.[8]

HISTORY OF AUCTIONS

What follows is necessarily a selective account of a huge subject. The auction, particularly the ascending-bid 'English' auction which is the subject matter of this book, is such a straightforward and obvious way of obtaining money for goods by matching supply and demand at a particular time, that it is not surprising that its ancestry can certainly be traced to antiquity. Herodotus writes that auctions existed at about 500 BC in Babylon, the transaction being primarily concerned with the yearly sale of women of marriageable age. These auctions could apparently work also in an inverse way, unattractive women being assigned to buyers in exchange for a donation by the seller![9]

On historically firmer ground, there has been considerable juridical investigation of auction sales under Roman law. The Roman auction proceeded in a way familiar to present-day auction-goers. The intended auction was announced publicly by a praeco (herald) and by written proscriptio (notice). The sale would be held in an atrium auctionarium (auction hall). Lots were probably available for prior inspection and the praeco acted as auctioneer, putting up the lots for sale and intimating reserve prices. Eventually the lot would be knocked down to the successful bidder. It is thought that such auctions were held under the ascending-bid

---

[7] See *Spencer v Harding* (1870) LR 5 CP 561, 39 LJCP 332, n 6 above.

[8] In June 1984 it was announced in the press that Agnews, the Bond Street picture dealers, had successfully experimented with tenders, involving sealed bids to be opened on a set date, when selling valuable paintings.

[9] In Thomas Hardy's *The Mayor of Casterbridge*, (1886), the story commences with the purported sale by auction of Michael Henchard's wife and daughter for five guineas, an incident which Hardy in his Preface suggests is founded on fact.

system, as the word 'auction' is connected to the Latin roots *augere* and *auctum* (to *increase*). Examples are known of auction sales on bankruptcy and to meet state deficits. Roman soldiers allegedly auctioned their loot *sub hasta* ('under the spear').[10]

The Roman auction sale involved four parties: the dominus, or person on whose behalf the property was sold; the argentarius who organised the sale and in some cases financed it; the praeco in charge of advertising the sale and auctioning the lots; and the emptor, the buyer whose bid was successful. How far the relationships between these parties correspond to those under current English law, particularly the law of agency, is open to some doubt. The praeco appeared to be the agent of the dominus, though the law of agency in Roman times was undeveloped. Intermediate parties are thought to have charged a low, flat-rate commission for their services. There is, however, one interesting possible divergence from English law. It is thought that all bidders in succession became conditionally bound to the vendor and could not retract their bids otherwise than in actionable breach of contract. The vendor could, however, refuse to accept a bid.[11]

In England the recorded history of auctions is much more recent.[12] Chattel auctioneering as a profession can be traced back to shortly after the Restoration. Sales of pictures and furniture were held by entrepreneurs in coffee houses, public houses and the like. An early catalogue of February 1689/90 refers to the selling of 'paintings and limnings by auction' at the Barbadoes Coffee House, and to the fact that 'of late the worthy gentlemen who comprised the buyers had both by their presence and custom, promoted and encouraged' the institution of the auction. The notice also refers to the fact that printed Conditions of Sale together with an additional one, namely 'that no Person or Persons shall be admitted to bid for his, or their own Pictures etc' are to be displayed at the place of sale. Another catalogue of a roughly similar date refers to goods being 'exposed to sale, by way of Mineing, on Thursday 12, Friday 13th and Saturday 14th of this instant March, at Mrs Smythers coffee house in Thames Street, by the Custom House'. The reference to 'Mineing' appears to relate to the Dutch-auction method of sale, ie a system of decreasing bids until someone called out 'mine' (discussed above).

---

[10] See in particular J A C Thomas 'The Auction Sale in Roman Law' (1957) I Jur R (April) 43, and T Frank (ed) *An Economic Survey of Ancient Rome* vol V: *Rome and Italy of the Empire* (1940) John Hopkins Press.

[11] See J A C Thomas (n 10 above) at 65–6.

[12] See Brian Learmont, *A History of the Auction* (Iver, 1985), and Peter Ash 'The First Auctioneer', centenary supplement to (1958) 33 E G (3 May), to which article the authors are much indebted. See also D Baldock 'Focus on Auctions — A History of the London Auction House' (1983) 268 EG 458; and A Bailey 'The Learned Babble' (1983) 268 EG 464, in which George Robbins (born 1777) is regarded as 'the father of estate-agency English' — a doubtful honour. He was a successor to Christopher Cock's practice.

In his diary for 3 September 1662, Samuel Pepys refers to the 'candle' method of limiting the time for bids (also discussed above). He states: 'After dinner, we met and sold the Weymouth Successe and Fellowship Hulkes,[13] where pleasant to see how backward men are at first to bid and yet, when the candle is going out, how they bawl and dispute afterwards who bid the most first.' Apparently the successful bidder held his fire until he observed the smoke descending, which was an indication that the candle was about to expire!

Auctions of land appear to have become established at least by 1739 when an advertisement appeared in the London Evening Post for the sale of a bankrupt's estate, including two houses at Paddington. If this indeed was amongst the first land auctions, the first such auctioneer was one Christopher Cock of the Great Piazza, Covent Garden. Certainly by 1740 he was advertising a series of landed estates to be sold 'on Whitsun Monday at Three in the Afternoon'.[14]

As already indicated, displayed Conditions of Sale were from earliest times an important feature of the auction. Typical Conditions of Sale in the eighteenth century included at least the following six points:

(a) The buyer is the highest bidder, disputes as to his identity being resolved by putting the goods up for sale again.
(b) The amount by which another's bid may be advanced is stipulated by reference to a minimum sum.
(c) There is some warranty as to the condition of the goods, in earlier times this being more absolute than is the case today.
(d) Buyers are required to give their names and make a deposit if demanded.
(e) Goods must be cleared within a stipulated period, eg three days, at the buyer's expense.
(f) The offer is made to execute bids on behalf of buyers unable to attend the sale.[15]

MAJOR BRITISH AUCTION HOUSES

It is from the middle of the eighteenth century that perhaps the three best-known auction houses in London can trace their beginnings.

---

[13] These were ships.

[14] The first reported case concerning auctions, or rather an agent's failure to hold one of real property when so instructed by the vendor, appears to be *Daniel v Adams* (1764) Amb 495. The buyer was in these circumstances held disentitled to specific performance of the privately negotiated contract (see further ch 3). Another interesting economic indication of the growth of auction sales was the introduction of an indirect tax on auctions and sales in 1779.

[15] See James Brough *Auction!* (1963), cited in Cassady (above, n 3).

At Sotheby's the first recorded auction took place in 1744. The founder was Samuel Baker, a bookseller and publisher. In 1778 on Baker's death his nephew John Sotheby was taken into partnership. Between 1861 and 1924 the firm expanded under the style of Sotheby, Wilkinson & Hodge, then becoming Sotheby & Co and then, from 1975, Sotheby Parke Bernet & Co.[16] Throughout the nineteenth century a wide variety of articles was sold, including books, pictures, jewellery, coins, wine and furniture. Removal of currency restrictions which existed until the mid-1950s enabled Sotheby's to pay the proceeds of auction sales in the consignor's own currency, and this in turn resulted in an expansion of business. As with the other great auction houses, turnover also expanded with the internationalisation of the fine arts auction market in particular. Great paintings tend to hold individual records for the sale of any type of single article. The company's revenue from the auction side of the business (there being Financial Services and Real Estate divisions as well) was as follows: 1990, $347,216,000; 1991, $193,905,000, and 1992, $200,883,000. These figures reflect the pattern of the recession in the art market.

Christie, Manson & Woods Ltd (Christie's) can be traced back to its founder James Christie (1730–1803), a Scotsman who established his auction house in Pall Mall in 1766. There were thought to be some 60 other auctioneers active in London at the time. Christie's 'Great Rooms' soon became a fashionable meeting place in London, and as he specialised in fine art auctioneering, the meeting place also for painters such as Gainsborough and Reynolds. He conducted studio sales not only of pictures by these artists but also sold many important collections belonging to British and French aristocrats. In the late eighteenth century some collections were auctioned following the execution of their ill-fated owners by the French Revolutionary Tribunal. The firm moved in 1823 to its present premises at King Street, London, while the partnerships with William Manson and Thomas Woods (1859) established the firm's present full name. In the case of both Sotheby's and Christie's, from starting as enterprises by single proprietors they became partnerships and then limited companies.

More recently these companies went public (in 1973 Christie's offered 37 per cent of its shares on the stock market),[17] though Sotheby's reverted to a private company in 1983. Its parent company is Sotheby's Holdings, Inc., registered in Michigan, USA. The company was partially refloated in 1988 and Sotheby's Class A Common Stock is listed both on the New York Stock Exchange and the London Stock Exchange.

[16] For an extensive account of Sotheby's history, see Frank Hermann *Sotheby's* (1980) Chatto & Windus. 'Sotheby's' became a private company after a successful takeover by an American consortium in 1983.

[17] Christie, Manson & Woods Ltd is one of a number of wholly-owned subsidiaries of Christie's International plc.

A third eminent firm, Phillips, Son & Neale, can also trace its ancestry back to the late eighteenth century. The founder, Harry Phillips, had been James Christie's head clerk and he established himself on his own in 1796. He, too, proved a successful entrepreneur having by the time he died in 1840 dealt with goods belonging to Beau Brummell, the Duke of Buckingham, Marie Antoinette, Napoleon, Talleyrand and, in 1823, with the sale of the contents of Fonthill Abbey, the home of William Beckford (the sale taking thirty days). The firm had somewhat mixed fortunes until after the second world war when it was once again built up by the acquisition of Glendining & Co (specialising in coins and medals) and Puttick & Simpson (a firm specialising in the sale of musical instruments). As with Sotheby's and Christie's, Phillips is now an international auction house, though a major distinctive feature is its chain of some twenty-six regional sale rooms throughout the UK. It trades as a private unlimited company and has very few shareholders.

Although these three firms have been singled out as being perhaps the best known in the UK in terms of fine art etc auctioneers, the directory in the *Auction Companion*[18] makes it clear that there is a large number of other very well-established auction-houses both in London and scattered throughout the UK, many of which can trace their history to the late eighteenth or early nineteenth century. These firms normally advertise in the local press or, on special occasions, in the national press. The *Antiques Trade Gazette* and *Art & Antiques Weekly* also carry extensive auction advertisements. Auction sales of land are described and advertised in the *Estates Gazette*, and *The Valuer* also contains much useful professional information.

Sales of Fine Art tend to dominate the discussion of auctions in the press and it is quite clear in recent years that the most spectacular sales have occurred through either Christie's or Sotheby's in New York or London. Outstanding results have been —

(a) Van Gogh, 'Portrait of Dr Gachet', £49.1 million, Christie's New York, May 1990;

(b) Renoir, 'Au Moulin de la Gallette', £46.5 million, Sotheby's New York, May 1990;

(c) Van Gogh, 'Irises', £30.5 million, Sotheby's New York, November 1987;

(d) Van Gogh, 'Sunflowers', £24.7 million, Christie's London, March 1987;

(e) Picasso, 'Acrobate', £20.9 million, Christie's London, November 1988. (The prices quoted include buyer's premium, usually at 10%.)

---

[18] Daniel and Catherine Leab *Auction Companion* (1981) Macmillan, this being a guide to the auction-houses that exist in the larger countries of the world and containing a layman's guide to selling or buying at auction. See also Klaster (ed) *Going, Going, Gone* (1982) Chartwell Books, a practical auction guide which also contains an international directory.

Paris and Geneva are also important centres — in the case of Geneva, particularly for jewellery.

This glamorous scene should not be allowed to obscure the important economic activity that goes on most weeks at about 300 auction houses throughout the UK. It is estimated that there are about 75,000 lots going under the hammer every working week of which about 60,000 are sold. Property sold includes ostensibly unglamorous objects such as those realised in sales of plant and machinery. Nevertheless, this activity is of immense economic importance to trade since the auction usually represents the only way of translating goods into money by a specific date. This is particularly the case in the livestock market which currently turns over approximately £2 billion per annum. For most producers the auction caters for the whole of their sales. The need for cash, particularly in a time of recession, can be acute. Hard pressed sellers, liquidators and receivers often take the view that although prices realisable at auction may be lower than a sale by private treaty, this discount is more than balanced by the saving in administrative effort and time which might be needed to find a suitable private purchaser. It is because of the economic significance of the everyday auction sale in converting goods into cash that it is important that the law governing the auction and the practices adopted by the auctioneer are properly understood and those practices made acceptable in modern conditions. At the top end of the market, if London is to keep its present pre-eminence, it is also important that buying and selling high value artefacts at auction are not accompanied by undue administrative problems or the activity penalised by various systems of indirect taxation and imposts. As we shall see, this ideal is presently being threatened by a number of recent developments discussed later in the book.

ECONOMIC CONSIDERATIONS IN AUCTION SALES

Our main concern here is to analyse, in layman's terms, the comparative economic efficiency of selling land or chattels by auction as opposed to the normal alternative of some variety of private treaty sale.

With regard to private treaty sales of goods, typically either they are on a take-it-or-leave-it basis, for instance in the supermarket where there is no opportunity to bargain with regard to the price, or the pricing policy may involve negotiation between buyer and seller. In the case of land to be sold by private treaty, for instance, the usual practice is for the estate agent to state either a particular price, or to use some vaguer expression such as 'offers around £50,000'. Following this advertisement there is likely to occur a series of offers and counter-offers until eventually a price acceptable to both buyer and seller is reached and a contract formed.

By contrast, if the auction is chosen as the means of disposal, competition between bidders for a particular lot is focussed at a particular time and place, supply and demand are at that time adjusted until they are in equilibrium by the emergence of the highest bid, and the sale is concluded. The price determinant here appears to be set by the buyer. The seller can have, however, a residual control by fixing a reserve price below which he is not prepared to sell. This will normally attract a penalty in the form of a commission to the auctioneer on a lower scale than if the buyer were successful, and this penalty tends to deter the fixing of too high a reserve. What the highest bidder will bid may vary from time to time and place to place even assuming the goods are identical. The presence of two or more eager potential buyers will force up the price of a lot beyond what might be regarded as its 'market' value.[19] It is also well-known that a favourable ambiance, for instance the sale of the contents of a stately house in situ, may engender an atmosphere where psychological rather than economic reasons can predominate in fixing the price of what might not necessarily be particularly meritorious lots on their own. (A historic chattels sale which attracted high prices and total proceeds of £6,389,933 was that of the Rothschild-Rosebery Estate at Mentmore in 1977.)

In terms of general economic efficiency, if a particular selling scheme maximises returns and minimises the effort expended by buyers and sellers, its utility will be the greater.[20] Whether a sale by auction will be the most appropriate way of disposing of particular goods may well depend on their type. Auctions of commodities in bulk are common throughout the world. As a means of market distribution this is obviously to be preferred in most cases over the alternative of the vendor seeking out individual buyers for small lots. The effort expended in the latter exercise would cost more than the possible difference between the aggregate prices so obtained and the price obtained at one point of time at the auction. Auctions are also a highly effective method of disposing of property for which there is no 'exchange' or readily available market. A private vendor of, let us say, antique furniture or antiquarian books or valuable paintings may approach individual dealers or retailers. However, it is difficult for him to judge whether or not he has got the best possible offer and the process can be time-consuming and expensive. The disincentive to him of the auction room is the auctioneer's commission, which varies between 10 and 20 per cent in the UK. In

---

[19] Equally 'an auction which only produces one bid is not necessarily an indication that the true market value has been achieved' (per Lord Templeman in *T Kwong Lam v Wong Chit Sen* [1983] 3 All ER 54, PC at 60). See also *Davis v Artingstall* (1880) 49 LJ Ch 609, 42 LT 507.

[20] See R. P. McAfee and John McMillan, 'Auctions and Bidding', 25 Journal of Economic Literature (1987), 699–738.

addition to this, the buyer's price may be depressed by the likelihood that under the Conditions of Sale he will also have to pay a 'premium' on top of the hammer price. Nevertheless, the auction's disadvantages may be outweighed by a surer sale. The facility is particularly useful to the private vendor or personal representatives of a deceased's estate. Some auctioneers refuse to accept lots other than from private sources.

Auctions of land provide a good barometer of the economics of this method of selling generally. Taking land as an example, in a recession there is a significant decline in the velocity of money transactions and in the amount circulating in trade. Sooner or later owners of land (whether facing insolvency or for some other reason needing to realise their asset) become desperate to sell and find that private treaty arrangements tend to fail because of diminishing demand, at least at the price asked (house owners have been particularly reluctant to believe that land, like other assets, can go down as well as up in value). In these circumstances vendors are often forced into the sale room. Here the asset will find its own level, that at which demand and supply are in reality in equilibrium. To the vendor, this may be a 'knock down' price and to the buyer a 'bargain', but it is in fact likely to be the true market price at the time and place of the auction. The auctioneer has succeeded in realising cash from a fixed asset and the economy becomes that much more fluid. The vendor's creditors are more likely to be paid and the vicious circle caused by cash flow difficulties is at least mitigated. Ultimately the market will settle down at its new, lower level, until a general economic improvement together with increased demand for assets of the relevant type produces improved prices. This effect is first likely to be noticed in the sale room, which is also a quicker barometer of market improvements than private treaty sales are likely to be. So, besides fulfilling this barometer function the auction is the only reliable means of unlocking cash in adverse market conditions which would otherwise be likely to produce severe economic dislocation. (Land auctions are analysed in detail in chapter 9.)

The auction works best when a market is as free as possible. There should, ideally, be the minimum of hidden 'extras' payable by the buyer. Ideally the buyer should know that when the hammer price is settled that is the price at which the goods may be acquired. This encourages uninhibited bidding amongst the widest possible group of buyers. If uncertainty on prices is induced by the addition of 'hidden' taxes and premiums, the transaction ceases to be a straightforward one and only the more determined, professional, buyer is likely to persevere. This reduces the number of players in the market and, in turn, ultimately distorts the market price by reducing competition amongst buyers.

In most respects, the law, as a matter of policy, does little to protect the consumer as such in the auction room (provided the goods are correctly described). The Unfair Contract Terms Act 1977 declares that in no circumstances are auction sales or sales by competitive tender to be regarded as consumer transactions. This means that the vendor is free to attempt to exclude his civil liability for quality of the lot sold which might otherwise be attached. It is only recently that the law emanating from the European Union has encroached upon this principle, both in extending the ambit of a wide variety of safety laws to goods sold at auction and not excluding such sales from review as being 'unfair' in specified circumstances.

Within the last two decades, auctions in England have been used to dispose of a wider variety of goods than formerly. Two examples may be given. Both in the USA and in the UK the growth of used-car auctions has been marked. In the USA the bulk of second-hand automobiles are sold in this way and used-car prices tend to be based on auction quotations. In England, such groups as British Car Auctions or Central Motor Auctions have streamlined the auction procedure for used cars so as to protect as far as possible the private motorist. It is estimated that in 1982 one in five of the 750,000 vehicles sold at auction in Britain was purchased by a member of the general public. 'End of the line' cars can also be auctioned by their manufacturers, as can showroom stock of dealers which has remained unsold for, say, sixty days and which is becoming a cash-flow burden.[21]

Another noticeable development in the UK recently has been the emergence of auction sales of plant and machinery. Typically, if an engineering company desires to move to new premises an auction of its machinery, machine tools, office furniture, factory equipment and motor vehicles which are surplus to requirements will be held on the site. An important Condition of Sale imposes an obligation on the buyer to remove lots from the site not later than the stipulated day, and failure to do this is penalised by heavy per diem storage charges. Plant auctions have obvious applications to firms with cash-flow difficulties who are wishing to turn their stock into cash prior to a liquidation. (The alternative of finding a purchaser for the shares, which will in part reflect an estimate of the value of the stock, can be a much less certain operation.) This type of sale, together with the Conditions of Sale applicable to it, is considered further in chapter 10.

[21] See (1983) Times, 20 May p 23.

Auctioneers: Restrictions on Trading

The profession of auctioneer is, as compared with the other professions today, relatively uncontrolled. The law does not require any minimum qualifications for practice, membership of a professional body is not obligatory, and there are no compulsory accounting rules designed to protect 'consumers'. However, there are some general restrictions on trading in connection with the form of business association utilised and as regards licence requirements.

QUALIFICATIONS

There is no requirement as to any particular qualification for practice as an auctioneer, nor is an auctioneer required to join any professional association. However, most auctioneers do in fact belong to one of the main bodies[1] and these have academic training programmes which, combined with relevant work experience, lead to professional qualifications. The absence of any minimum qualification requirement is perhaps surprising these days and, in the case of estate agent auctioneers, a change may be in the offing. The Estate Agents Act 1979[2] for the first time provides some statutory regulation of estate agents. Section 22 states (so far as is material):

(1) the Secretary of State may by regulations[3] made by statutory instrument make provision for ensuring that persons engaged in estate agency work satisfy minimum standards of competence.

(2) ... the regulations may ...

(a) prescribe professional or academic qualifications which shall also be taken to be evidence of competence;

(b) designate any body or persons as a body which may itself specify professional qualifications the holding of which is to be taken as evidence of competence.

---

[1] The main bodies are the Royal Institution of Chartered Surveyors; the Incorporated Society of Valuers and Auctioneers; the Rating and Valuation Association; and the Central Association of Agricultural Valuers.

[2] The Act provides for the Director General of Fair Trading to prohibit unfit estate agents from carrying on business. It also requires estate agents to keep separate client accounts and to maintain insurance cover against failure to account for a client's money. (For the sections dealing with accounting regulations, see Appendix 2.)

[3] At the time of writing no regulations have been made.

This provision is part of a package of controls over the activities of estate agents laid down by this Act. It may be that the consumer considerations which gave rise to this statutory intervention are less pressing in the case of auctioneers and there is at present no move to provide similar controls, which are effected ultimately through the criminal law, and negative licensing for auctioneers generally.

LICENSING

The major prerequisite for acting as an auctioneer used to be that of possession of a licence. The Auctioneers Act 1845 required, save for special excepted cases provided for in s 5, every person 'who engages or carries on the trade or business of an Auctioneer' to take out a licence, renewable annually and costing £10.[4] Failure to produce the licence could result in imprisonment for up to one month. These provisions were more of a revenue-collecting device than any attempt at regulating the profession and they were repealed finally by the Finance Act 1949. However, one important section survives, relating to display of names (dealt with later in this chapter). Whilst no *general* trading licence is now required[5], an auctioneer must have a licence or be registered in order to effect sales of certain types of goods, outlined below.

(a) Excise licences. Certain commodities including wine, spirits and tobacco can only be sold if the seller possesses an excise licence. Until recently there were concessions obviating this requirement where an auctioneer sold by sample goods for an owner who held a requisite licence in respect of premises in the same locality. Further, and more generally, the Commissioners of Customs and Excise had power to dispense with the requirement of a licence where an auctioneer sold for a private person otherwise than by way of trade. These concessions, provided by the Customs and Excise Act 1952 and consolidated in the Customs and Excise Management Act 1979 s 105(2) and (3), were removed in 1982 by the Finance Act 1981. As from 1 July 1982, auctioneers selling such goods require the appropriate excise licence.[6]

(b) Firearm registration. Problems relating to sales of firearms at auction are considered in detail in chapter 8. Registration as a firearms dealer is obviated if the auctioneer obtains a permit provided by the Chief Officer of Police in the area in which the auction is held. Whilst a certificate is normally required in order to possess a firearm or ammu-

---

[4] Auctioneers Act 1845, s 4.
[5] Save in the case of auctioneers practising in those Greater London Boroughs which have introduced licensing schemes; see (d) below.
[6] Finance Act 1981, s 11(2)(a), Sch 8 para 5.

nition, none is needed by an auctioneer possessing such in the ordinary course of his business.[7]

(c) Export licences. The obtaining of these is an obligation of the exporter of specified goods, though this has implications for auctioneers who sell them to the exporter. They are considered below in chapter 7.

(d) Local authority trading licences. Licence regimes have been instituted by Westminster City Council and The Royal Borough of Kensington and Chelsea. Both of these Greater London Borough Councils have produced conditions for auctioneers operating within their areas, pursuant to the Greater London Council (General Powers) Act 1984, s 28(3). Whilst many of the conditions concern safety and planning issues, there are also conditions relating to the conduct of sales, bidding practices and similar matters. We deal with these in chapter 6.

DISPLAY OF NAMES AND OTHER NOTICES

As mentioned above, one provision of the Auctioneers Act 1845 remains in force and is of practical importance. Section 7 states:

And be it enacted, that every Auctioneer, before beginning any Auction, shall affix or suspend, or cause to be affixed or suspended, a Ticket or Board containing his true and full Christian and Surname and Residence painted, printed or written in large letters publicly visible and legible in some conspicuous Part of the Room or Place where the Auction is held so that all Persons may easily read the same, and shall also keep such Ticket or Board so affixed or suspended during the whole Time of such Auction being held; and if any Auctioneer begins any Auction or acts as Auctioneer at any Auction, in any Room or Place where his Name and Residence is not so painted or written on a Ticket or Board so affixed or suspended, and kept affixed or suspended as aforesaid, he shall forfeit for every such Offence the Sum of Twenty Pounds.

The fine has been increased to a maximum of £500 being on level 2 on the standard scale under the Criminal Justice Act 1982, s 37(2) as amended.

In addition, notices must also be displayed containing copies of the Auctions (Bidding Agreements) Acts 1927 and 1969. The effect of these provisions are considered in chapters 8 and 9.

BUSINESS ASSOCIATION

There is no restriction as to the *type* of business association (ie sole trader, partnership or corporation) in which the auctioneer may practise. Major

---

[7] Firearms Act 1968, s 9.

firms such as Christie's and Sotheby's are companies, but it is more common to find auctioneers practising in partnerships.

With regard to partnerships, certain restrictions are laid down as to numbers. Under s 434 of the Companies Act 1948 no partnership could be formed consisting of more than 20 members. However, the position was alleviated by the Companies Act 1967 and regulations made thereunder. Since 1968 there has been no such restriction on the size of partnerships of auctioneers, provided that not less than three-quarters of the partners are members of either the Royal Institution of Chartered Surveyors, the Chartered Land Agents Society, the Chartered Auctioneers and Estate Agents' Institute, or the Incorporated Society of Valuers and Auctioneers.[8] In this way a person dealing with the larger firms of auctioneers (ie exceeding 20 partners) will be assured that a considerable degree of professional qualification exists within it.

The keynote of partnership is that its members, unlike members of a registered company, have unlimited liability. Each partner is jointly and separately responsible for the whole of the partnership debts and obligations. However, since 1907 it has been possible to create a hybrid animal whereby some partners do enjoy limited liability. Under the Limited Partnership Act 1907 a firm can be formed in which one or more of the partners are designated 'general partners' liable for all the debts of the firm whilst the remainder may have liability limited to the extent of their capital contributions. Where this form of association is employed (and it has not proved a popular mode) there is again a general ceiling as to numbers of members fixed at 20. However, a second category of dispensation is provided to auctioneers forming limited partnerships whereby the number may exceed 20 as long as two requirements are satisfied: first, not less than three-quarters of the partners must be members of either the RICS or the ISVA; and second, at least three-quarters of the partners must be general partners.[9] The Limited Partnership Act 1907 requires such firms to be registered and provides for the register to be available for public inspection.

FIRM NAME

Until recently it was necessary for every firm which carried on business under a name which did not consist of the names of the sole trader or partnership members to register the true surnames of those members in a Business Names Registry. This was required by the Registration of Business Names Act 1916. The Act was, however, much honoured in its non-

---

　　[8] See now Companies Act 1985, s 716; Partnership (Unrestricted Size) Regulations, SI 1968/1222.

　　[9] Limited Partnerships (Unrestricted Size) No 1 Regulations, SI 1971/782.

*merged with R.I.C.S

observance and over a period the registry came to contain a large element of stale information as firms ceased trading. The Government decided to cut its losses and the Act was repealed by the Companies Act 1981. With the abolition of the registry the desideratum of providing information as to the identity of partners is achieved by a self-regulating system. Now s 4 of the Business Names Act 1985 places a duty on each partner to state the name and address of every partner in the firm on all business letters, written orders, bills and the like. Where the number of partners exceeds 20, the names need not be given if the document recites the address of the firm's principal place of business and states that the names are listed and available there. A notice containing this information is required to be prominently displayed on the business premises. Finally, written notice of these particulars must be supplied on request to 'any person with whom anything is done or discussed in the course of business, who requests them'.

The new regime is enforced by a combination of criminal and civil sanctions, the former consisting of fines and the latter taking the form of a disability: the court is empowered[10] to dismiss an action brought by the firm if the defendant shows that he has suffered loss as a result of the plaintiff firm's breach of these obligations.

Despite these changes in the law, it appears that the business community is not convinced that the abolition of the register was a wise move. The London Chamber of Commerce and Industry set up its own private business names registry in 1982.

Where the firm trades as a company then the company is obliged to have its name:

(a) painted or affixed on the outside of every office or place in which the business is carried on, in a conspicuous position and in legible letters;
(b) engraved legibly on its seal; and
(c) mentioned legibly in all business letters, publications etc.[11]

If the company is limited, the name includes the word 'limited' which must therefore similarly be published.

Where a company carries on a business under a name which does not consist solely of its corporate name it must again in all business correspondence and on a prominent notice at all business outlets display its corporate name and an address at which documents may be served on it.[12]

---

[10] Business Names Act 1985, s 5.   [11] Companies Act 1985, part XI, ch 1.
[12] Business Names Act 1985, s 4.

3

Capacity and Authority

INTRODUCTORY

An auctioneer is a particular kind of agent. Pre-eminently he is employed[1] by the vendor of property to effect a sale, but frequently, an auctioneer may also act as agent of the purchaser for limited purposes. In the course of transacting his business he may additionally act in some other legal capacity, eg as bailee with a duty to care for the property in his possession.[2] The fact that an auctioneer may also act as agent for the purchaser does not, it seems, prevent him from selling his own property and thus acting as a principal; as he is not an agent of the purchaser for all purposes, no conflict of interest arises.[3] However, in this chapter we are principally concerned with an auctioneer's position as agent of the vendor. (The ambit of the auctioneer's authority as agent of the purchaser is considered in chapter 5 below.)

There are few restrictions placed upon carrying on the business of auctioneer, and no special formal qualifications are required. The only limitations are those arising from the law of contract and certain general statutory provisions relating to companies, partnerships and the like.[4] Indeed, whereas there are factors which may render a principal incapable of contracting, eg infancy, the same defect in an agent will not prevent that agent from concluding a valid contract between his principal and a third party. The explanation is that the agent is regarded as a mere conduit through which a principal acts so that the only contractual capacity that is relevant is that of the principal himself.[5] Of course, one must distinguish between an agent's capacity to be constituted an agent and his capacity to contract for a principal once so constituted.

---

[1] This word is not used here as a term of art; it has been held that he is employed not as a servant but rather as an independent contractor. *Walker v Crabb* (1917) 61 Sol Jo 219 at 220.

[2] See eg *Williams v Millington* (1788) 1 Hy Bl 81. His right of possession also gives the auctioneer a lien over the goods for his charges and commission; see ch 4.

[3] *Flint v Woodin* (1852) 9 Hare 618, 22 LJ Ch 92, though when selling as a principal he cannot sign any memorandum of sale as agent of the purchaser. However the auctioneer now probably owes a duty of disclosure by virtue of the Estate Agents Act 1979, s 21.

[4] See generally, 2 Halsbury's Laws (4th edn Reissue) paras 902–6; and see ch 2.

[5] In such a situation, however, the agent will not be liable *personally* on the contract and a third party will have to look exclusively to the principal. On the personal contractual liability of auctioneers to third parties, see ch 5.

AUTHORITY

Agency has been tentatively defined as:[6]

The relationship that exists between two persons when one, called the *agent*, is considered in law to represent the other, called the *principal*, in such a way as to be able to affect the principal's legal position in respect of strangers to the relationship by the making of contracts for the disposition of property.

Thus we are concerned with a tripartite situation, and with the rights and duties inter se of these three parties. The pivotal concept which determines these rights and duties is *authority*. Only if an agent has authority will his acts bring about the desired relationship between the principal and the third party: in the case of an auction, the contract of sale. If the auctioneer exceeds his authority, the vendor will not be bound to the purchaser but the purchaser may then be able to recover from the auctioneer for breach of warranty of authority — ie for breach of a contractually binding promise as to the extent of his authority. Sometimes an agent will act outside his *actual* authority but the law nevertheless binds the principal to the third party.[7]

In such circumstances the principal will have recourse against the agent. Writers have traditionally regarded authority as the key concept by which to explain an agent's power to bring about a contract between his principal and a third party. It may be regarded as a somewhat artificial use of the term where the principal is held bound not because he did in fact empower his agent so to act, but because circumstances merely led the third party to believe that the agent was so invested. Nevertheless it is convenient to explain and analyse the powers of an agent in terms of authority and, before examining the authority of auctioneers, we shall briefly outline the types of authority with which an agent may be clothed.

VARIETIES OF AUTHORITY

As already suggested,[8] there is a level of inconsistency in the terminology used to describe certain types of authority, an inconsistency prevalent not only in academic treatments but also in judgments given by the courts.

---

[6] Fridman *Law of Agency* (6th edn, 1990) Butterworths, p 9.

[7] In a recent article it has been observed that six different expressions are commonly used to describe this situation, viz: 'implied authority', 'usual authority', 'customary authority', 'ostensible authority', 'apparent authority', and 'agency by estoppel'. Crudely analysed the first three types describe authority which stems from the job or position, whereas the last three arise from representations made by the principal. See Richard Stone 'Usual and Ostensible Authority — One Concept or Two?' [1993] JBL 325.

[8] See n 7, above.

What follows must be regarded therefore as an attempt at providing a working classification but not, necessarily, a reconciliation of the various alternatives.

There are essentially two kinds of authority, within which may be found sub-species. Authority may be:

(a) *actual* or *real*; or it may be
(b) *apparent* or *ostensible*.

Actual authority

Actual authority of an agent is that authority which he is *expressly* given. Express authority will usually present no difficulty. If the agent is employed under a contract, as is usually the case today, the court will discover the authority by construing the contract, applying the ordinary rules of construction in order to ascertain the intention of the parties. A helpful definition of 'actual' authority is provided by Diplock LJ in *Freeman & Lockyer (a firm) v Buckhurst Park Properties (Mangal) Ltd*:[9]

An 'actual' authority is a legal relationship between principal and agent created by a consensual agreement . . . Its scope is to be ascertained by applying ordinary principles of construction of contracts, including any proper implications from the express words used, the usages of the trade, or the course of business between the parties.

From this it will be seen that in addition to that which has been expressed, the agent will be invested with such power as may be *implied*. Thus implied authority is a sub-species of express authority. Implied authority probably encompasses those things which are incidental or reasonably necessary to the carrying out of that which is expressly authorised. An aspect of this may include usual or customary authority, namely that which an agent of that type normally has. Examples would probably be the auctioneer's former power to sign the memorandum relating to a sale of land or to receive the deposit moneys. The first was probably implied in the sense of being necessary to the main purpose of effecting the sale. The second is probably better regarded as usual or customary. It must be emphasised that this authority is actual or real — the agent does in fact possess it. A difficulty arises here if a principal in fact restricts the agent's authority but fails to give notice to third parties of this fact. In such a case the principal will be bound to the third party; the law regards the agent as nevertheless possessing the authority. To regard the authority in this situation as implied and therefore actual, requires a straining of language. The alternative is to regard the

---

[9] [1964] 1 All ER 630, CA at 644.

authority as falling within the second category, namely apparent authority; the principal is bound because his omission to provide notice of the restriction of the authority that such an agent normally possesses, makes it *appear* as though the agent is so possessed.

Apparent authority

Before returning to this problem, we must outline the ambit of apparent authority. Apparent authority is the antithesis of actual authority in that the agent *in fact* has no authority but in law is regarded as being empowered to bind the principal and third party. It arises out of the conduct of the principal which amounts to a repesentation that the agent has authority. Where a third party acts upon such a representation, the principal is bound.[10] An example relating to the creation of the agency of an auctioneer was given by Lord Ellenborough CJ in the old case of *Pickering v Busk*:[11]

I cannot subscribe to the doctrine, that a broker's engagements are necessarily and in all cases limited to his actual authority . . . it is clear that he may bind his principal within the limits of the authority with which he has been apparently clothed by the principal . . . and there would be no safety in mercantile transactions if he could not . . . if one sends goods to an auction-room can it be supposed that he sent them thither merely for safe custody?

In this case Lord Ellenborough began his judgment with the conclusion that the agent had 'an implied authority to sell' but the case is, it is suggested, an example of apparent authority. Fridman[12] argues that apparent authority only arises where there is no express agency at all as mentioned above. Suppose that it is usual for an auctioneer to collect the deposit on a sale but that in fact the principal has instructed his agent not to collect the deposit, but to ensure that such be paid direct to him or, say, his solicitor. And suppose that he fails properly to notify potential buyers by for example, appropriate notice in the auction particulars. If a buyer pays the deposit to the auctioneer who then absconds, the principal will wish to deny that the payment to the auctioneer discharges such a buyer. It is clear that it does; or, to put it another way, the principal is bound. In such an instance it matters to the buyer not one jot whether the explanation is that the auctioneer had usual (implied) or apparent authority. Nor is it clear that it matters in practice vis-à-vis the principal and agent. So long as an agent acts within his actual authority, it cannot be said against him that he is in breach of contract. However, if he in fact exceeds his express instructions, the mere

---

[10] *Bowstead on Agency* (15th edn, London, 1985), Sweet & Maxwell, ch 3. And see *Freeman & Lockyer (a firm) v Buckhurst Park Properties (Mangal) Ltd*, above.
[11] (1812) 15 East 38 at 43.   [12] Fridman (n 6 above) p 60f.

application of the term 'implied' to the authority he has exercised will not prevent his acts from amounting to a breach of contract. Moreover, an agent who acts within his authority is entitled to be indemnified by his principal against all losses and liabilities properly incurred by him in the execution of his authority. It cannot be supposed that an agent acting in defiance of his express instructions could enforce such an indemnity.

It may be, therefore, that arguments about the proper classification of these varieties of authority are purely academic. Be that as it may, it is suggested that in the example of a restriction upon the usual authority of an agent, we are dealing with apparent authority. The principal is liable because he has (by omission) held out his agent as having the usual authority without restriction. Fridman[13] counters: 'But in the cases under discussion the agent is *in fact*, not by virtue of an estoppel, an agent. His authority is *actual* not apparent even though in part it may be implied and not express.' This seems (with respect) to confuse two separate points: the agent with restricted usual authority is, it is argued, an agent in fact — that is not in dispute — but that does not mean that his authority, or all of it, must needs be actual. There is no reason why an actual agent may not have both actual *and* some ostensible authority. Bowstead,[14] on the other hand, suggests that there is a strong case for treating usual authority as a third, separate form of authority, neither actual nor apparent, but concludes that the case law does not justify such a conclusion.

There are also other situations where an agency relationship may arise, and these are described below.

Agency of necessity

This arises by operation of law. It may effect either the creation or the enlargement of an agency relationship and in the latter case clearly involves the question of authority. The classic situation in which it arises is that of a carrier of perishable goods who sells them when they are uncollected. The essence is some emergency relating to the goods coupled with an impracticality for the agent to communicate with his principal.[15]

Where the necessity enlarges the authority of the agent, it might be argued that it is really a question of implied authority to act in the emergency, but this may be questioned. It seems better to regard it as a

---

[13] Fridman (n 6 above) p 65.   [14] Above, n 10.
[15] See eg *Springer v Great Western Rly Co* [1921] 1 KB 257, 89 LJKB 1010, CA. And see *Sweeting v Turner* (1871) LR 7 QB 310, 41 LJQB 58 where an auctioneer's claim to an agency of necessity re goods threatened by distress failed because although left on the vendor's premises they had become the property of the purchaser.

separate species of authority created by law in cases involving protection of property.[16]

Ratification[17]

Finally, for the sake of completeness we mention ratification by a principal of a hitherto unauthorised act. Ratification has the effect of giving ex post facto authority to the agent and is thus equivalent to antecedent authority. Some writers have doubted whether ratification can be regarded as consensual. Three conditions must be satisfied according to the classic explanation given by Wright J in *Firth v Staines*,[18] namely: (a) the agent whose act is sought to be ratified must have purported to act for the principal; (b) at the time the act was done the agent must have had a competent principal; and (c) at the time of the ratification the principal must be legally capable of doing the act himself.

THE AUTHORITY OF AUCTIONEERS

Having outlined the varieties of authority, it is proposed to detail the auctioneer's authority. Of course, as regards express authority this will depend upon his actual instructions. In this regard the courts will simply construe the agreement using the usual tools to ascertain what was intended. It is not clear whether the courts are astute to construe express authority generously or narrowly. It was suggested in one case[19] that, as a general rule, a liberal construction would be applied. However, in the Irish case of *Hawkins v Rogers*[20] it was argued by the purchaser of a race horse that the horse was sold with its engagements. The purchaser was the partner of the vendor and argued that it was understood by both of them that the horses were being sold with their engagements and that this factor was crucial. The vendor intended, however, to sell without engagements. The court held that the auctioneer is primarily an agent of the vendor and as such he sells what the vendor intends to sell and no more, in the absence of anything to the contrary. This suggests a somewhat restrictive approach. The case involved a claim by the purchaser against the vendor. Where there is a claim by the vendor as principal against his agent for exceeding his authority, the courts might take a more liberal approach where instructions

---

[16] See *China Pacific SA v Food Corpn of India, The Winson* [1982] AC 939, [1981] 3 All ER 688, HL and see the discussion in Fridman (n 6 above) p 120.
[17] See generally *Bowstead on Agency* (n 10 above) arts 13–19.   [18] [1897] 2 QB 70 at 75.
[19] *Pole v Leask* (1860) 28 Beav 562, 29 LJ Ch 888.   [20] [1951] IR 48.

are ambiguous. However, it is obviously sensible for the auctioneer to ensure that he properly understands his instructions and seeks clarification when necessary.

Subject to this kind of issue, there is little of a general nature that can be said about the content of express authority and we shall, therefore, concentrate upon consideration of various specific matters and on the meaning of certain instructions and the potential ambit of the implied and/or usual authority with which an auctioneer may be endowed.

SALE BY AUCTION

As we have seen,[21] if a person sends goods to an auctioneer, the auctioneer will have apparent authority to auction those goods. More usually of course, his authority will be express. No doubt also those instructions will usually be explicit about the nature of the sale to be undertaken. But if it is sought to give an auctioneer authority to sell otherwise than by auction, eg by private treaty, perhaps after a lot has failed to reach its reserve price at the auction, such power must be given expressly. Authority to sell otherwise than by auction will not be implied. The classic case is *Daniel v Adams*,[22] decided in the eighteenth century, where a husband and wife instructed their steward to sell certain properties by auction and fixed a reserve of £120 per property. The agent believed he had power to sell privately so long as he achieved the reserve price, and he sold in that manner to the plaintiff for £150. Mrs Adams refused to effect the sale; she had given another first refusal on the property if it was sold privately. In an action by Daniel for specific performance of the contract of sale, the court held Mrs Adams not bound, the auctioneer lacking authority to sell otherwise than by auction. Similarly in *Marsh v Jelf*,[23] which involved a claim by an auctioneer for commission when he sold privately after the property had failed to achieve its reserve at the auction, it was denied that any such sale would bind the vendor in the absence of specific instructions and it was held that there was no custom that commission was payable in such circumstances.

There are two decisions which might, at first sight, suggest that an auctioneer may have implied authority to sell otherwise than by auction. In *Else v Barnard*[24] there was a sale ordered by the court. The various lots were subject to secret reserves and the auctioneer was instructed that if they failed to achieve these prices they were to be bought in by him for the parties interested in them. The first lot did not reach its reserve and was bought in. Thereafter the successful bidder of a second lot discovered the reserve on the first. He agreed to buy it. It appears that this agreement was

---

[21] See above, pp 21–2.   [22] (1764) Amb 495. And see also *Re Loft* (1844) 2 LTOS 397.
[23] (1862) 3 F&F 234.   [24] (1860) 28 Beav 228, 29 LJ Ch 729.

struck after the auction but before the auctioneer had in fact left the rostrum. Subsequently the purchaser repudiated his purchase of the first lot and sought to resist the vendor's claim on the grounds that the auctioneer lacked authority to sell otherwise than by open bidding. The court held the sale to be good. However, it cannot be said that *Else v Barnard* is authority for the proposition that an auctioneer may, in the absence of express instructions, sell otherwise than by auction, because it is clear that the court (a) declined to decide whether this had in fact been a sale by auction, and (b) in any event held that the purchaser's actions prevented him from denying that it was. Romilly M R said:[25]

I do not go into the question whether that is a sale by auction or not, but I think it is impossible for [the buyer] to say that it is not to be treated as a sale by auction for he signs a bidding paper by which he agrees that it shall be so treated; it is impossible for him afterwards to say he is not bound by it.

The second case, *Bousfield v Hodges*,[26] decided a few years later, similarly involved an auction sanctioned by the court. This was in order to bring about an end to litigation by compromise. An auctioneer was instructed to sell at a stated reserve. However, there were no bids and the auctioneer sold by private treaty at the reserve price. Once again the purchaser resiled from the bargain and sought to invoke the auctioneer's lack of authority to sell otherwise than by auction. The court held the purchaser bound. One view[27] regards the decision in *Bousfield v Hodges* as representing a more liberal view of the auctioneer's authority, but it is submitted that such a conclusion is not justified. Romilly M R did, it is true, say that it was competent for the auctioneer to sell by private contract at the amount of the reserve bidding, but is clear that he regarded the auctioneer in this case as having been expressly authorised to do so; as he said:[28]

I do not dispute that where an agent or trustee is authorised to sell any property in a particular manner, the authority is limited to that particular mode of selling, and that he cannot exceed the scope of his authority. But that is not the case here.

The reason for this conclusion on the facts is that the whole object of the exercise was to achieve a sale at a certain figure and thereby bring about the desired compromise. Those interested in selling were unconcerned about the mode of sale employed.

It may be further observed that both of these cases involved claims by principals against third parties to enforce contracts made by agents. Provided the other requirements were satisfied, the vendors in both cases could, in any event, have simply ratified their agent's acts if no authority had

---

[25] (1860) 28 Beav 228 at 231.   [26] (1863) 33 Beav 90.
[27] Murdoch *The Law of Estate Agency and Auctions* (2nd edn, 1984) Estates Gazette, p 385. This view is not maintained in the 3rd edition (1994).
[28] *Bousfield v Hodges* (1863) 33 Beav 90.

antecedently been given. Therefore, apart from the objections already taken, it would have been unsafe to rely on these cases as authority for the proposition that a power to sell otherwise than by auction would readily be implied. Only if it were held that a vendor was bound by such a sale at the suit of the purchaser could such a proposition be advanced. The more recent case of *Garnier v Bruntlett*,[29] where vendors were held bound by a sale made by private treaty after the reserve was not reached at auction, is such a case. However here again, as in *Bousfield v Hodges*, it was held on the facts that whilst auction was the preferred mode of sale, of overriding importance was the need to achieve a minimum price, howsoever obtained, in order to discharge mortgages. If it is desired to give an auctioneer authority to sell by private treaty it must, therefore, be expressly provided.[30]

SALES IN DEFIANCE OF A RESERVE

This area gives rise to a number of related problems. The issues are complex and have not, perhaps surprisingly, all been authoritatively ruled on by the courts. It will be necessary to discuss them in some depth.

The problem of authority

What is the position where an auctioneer purports to sell property without reserve or below the reserve in defiance of his express instructions? In *Rainbow v Howkins*,[31] one Dr Dukes instructed the auctioneer Howkins to sell his pony at Rugby Cattle Market. He placed a reserve on the pony of £25. Howkins forgetfully announced the sale as being without reserve and knocked the pony down at 15 guineas. Then, realising his error, he informed the purchaser and put it up for sale again. When the bidding this time stopped at 17 guineas Howkins bought the pony in. No memorandum in writing, as was at that time required under s 4 of the Sale of Goods Act 1893, was ever signed. The purchaser, Rainbow, claimed that the sale was valid at 15 guineas or alternatively, that he was entitled to damages from the auctioneer for breach of warranty of authority.

The Divisional Court held that the sale was unenforceable by virtue of the absence of the memorandum required by s 4 but that, apart from that point, there was here a valid contract. The auctioneer *had* authority to sell

---

[29] (1974) 236 EG 867.
[30] An early example is afforded by *Green v Bartlett* (1863) 14 CBNS 681, 32 LJCP 261, the simple expedient being to instruct the auctioneer to sell 'by auction or otherwise'.
[31] [1904] 2 KB 322, 73 LJKB 641.

without reserve and thus there was nothing in the claim for breach of warranty of authority. The authority was 'an apparent authority'.[32] The conclusion that the auctioneer had apparent authority to sell without reserve seems to have been based on the assumption that it is part of the usual authority of an auctioneer to sell without reserve and that the vendor is thus at risk if he fails to give notice to potential purchasers of the restriction he has placed on that authority.

The finding that an auctioneer has usual authority to sell without reserve may seriously be questioned. That proposition, and the decision in *Rainbow v Howkins* itself, was roundly criticised by the Court of Appeal in *McManus v Fortescue* decided a few years later. Fletcher Moulton LJ said:[33]

A principal, therefore, who gives authority to an auctioneer to sell subject to a reserve price gives no power to the auctioneer, either expressly or impliedly, to accept a less price. The case of *Rainbow v Howkins* so far as it is inconsistent with this view cannot be regarded as in harmony with well established principles . . . the auctioneer . . . could not make a contract so as to bind his principal to accept less than the reserved price.

In this case an auctioneer again knocked down a lot (a corrugated iron structure resting by its own weight on dwarf walls and thus goods within the Sale of Goods Act 1893) for less than its reserve price. Here the printed auction catalogue included a condition that each lot would be offered subject to a reserve price and reserved the right on the part of the vendors to bid up to such a price. Once again, the auctioneer realising his error refused to complete the sale and the highest bidder claimed either that there was a valid contract of sale to him which the auctioneer was obliged to effect by signing the requisite memorandum, or that the auctioneer was in breach of his implied warranty of authority. Both claims were rejected.

Despite the criticism levelled at *Rainbow v Howkins*, it must be stressed that in *McManus v Fortescue* the lots were expressly offered subject to a reserve. There could, therefore, be no question of any apparent authority to the contrary nor of any estoppel against the vendor. Nor could it be said that the auctioneer in accepting a bid lower than the reserve was, in effect, warranting that he had authority to sell without reserve. As was made clear, when an auction is expressly conducted subject to a reserve, every bid is and remains only a conditional offer to buy and the acceptance of the highest bid by the auctioneer is only a conditional acceptance, the condition being that the reserved price has been reached.[34]

---

[32] [1904] 2 KB 322 at 326.   [33] [1907] 2 KB 1 at 7, CA.
[34] But see *Fay v Miller Wilkins & Co* [1941] Ch 360, 110 LJ Ch 124, CA, where the condition ceased to attach once the auctioneer signed a memorandum of sale satisfying the Law of Property Act 1925, s 40.

The vendor thus protects himself against the possibility of sales below the reserve price by the relatively simple expedient of ensuring that notification of the existence of a reserve is effected through the auction particulars.[35] He is also protected, though less assuredly, if it is made clear that the right to place a reserve on a property is provided. In these circumstances a purchaser is put on notice of the possibility that the auctioneer may in fact be limited as to his authority and thus becomes liable to enquire as to whether a reserve has in fact been fixed, or, perhaps, is saddled with constructive notice of such having been fixed if this is the case. In *Fay v Miller Wilkins & Co*,[36] the auctioneer who erroneously knocked down the property at below the reserve in these circumstances went further and signed a memorandum which satisfied the requirement of evidence in writing laid down in s 40 of the Law of Property Act 1925 relating to interests in land. Although the unwilling vendor was not forced to complete, the court allowed the claim against the auctioneer for breach of warranty of authority.[37] The warranty which is broken appears to consist of a representation that the condition implied in the subject to reserve sale is waived.[38]

Whilst the decision in *Rainbow v Howkins* has been attacked, it can be argued that neither *McManus v Fortescue* nor *Fay v Miller Wilkins & Co* directly subvert it. Indeed it may be said that indirectly they support it; for both cases where the vendor was held not bound were decided on the basis that the purchasers had *notice* of the limited nature of the auctioneer's authority to sell; actual in the former case and constructive in the latter; and notice would only be crucial if, apart from notice negativing it, an auctioneer *did* have apparent authority to sell without reserve because that was part of his usual authority. It must be pointed out, however, that what is usual may vary with particular trades or types of property sold and may change over the years.

In the New Zealand case of *Hawke's Bay Farmers' Co-operative Association Ltd v Farquharson*[39] the New Zealand Court of Appeal entertained no doubt that an auctioneer could be sued for damages by his vendor–principal for selling below a fixed reserve. Although the vendor cannot be bound by the sale, he is entitled not eg to seek return of his property or sue the buyer in conversion but may seek redress against the auctioneer.

---

[35] The vendor's instructions to the auctioneer should be express. The courts will not be astute to deduce such instructions. In Canada the courts have refused to find instructions not to sell goods below an invoice price merely from the circumstance that the goods were sent together with invoices: *Nelson v Hicks* (1899) QR 15 SC 465.

[36] Above, n 34.

[37] The argument that the auctioneer had apparent authority to sign the memorandum as a transaction separate from the sale itself was rejected because the auctioneer did not have authority to make representations as to his own authority. If an agent is to have apparent authority, the representation as to his authority must be made by his principal.

[38] See observations of Lord Greene at [1941] Ch 360, 364.   [39] [1916] NZLR 917.

SALES EXPRESSED TO BE WITHOUT RESERVE[40]

More problematic is the case where the sale is expressed to be without reserve but in effect a reserve is fixed subsequently or, what amounts to the same thing, the owner bids highest so as to buy the property in. The case which has given considerable difficulty is that of *Warlow v Harrison*[41] where a horse 'the property of a gentleman, *without reserve* Janet Pride' was advertised to be sold by auction. Harrison, a Birmingham auctioneer and dealer, put up the horse and Warlow bid 60 guineas for her. The owner, one Henderson, then bid 61 guineas and when Warlow discovered that the owner had intervened, he withdrew from the sale. The property was knocked down to the owner. Warlow thereupon claimed the horse as the highest bona fide bidder. Subsequently he brought an action against the auctioneer for breach of contract in failing to complete the sale to him. On a technicality relating to the way the claim was framed, both at first instance and on appeal, the court found for the defendant auctioneer. However, in a reserved judgment the majority of the judges hearing the appeal suggested, strictly obiter, that the plaintiff could on these facts succeed in an action against the auctioneer for breach of a collateral contract — that is one collateral to the sale — to sell without reserve. Martin B said:[42]

. . . it seems to us that the highest bona fide bidder at an auction may sue the auctioneer as upon a contract that the sale shall be without reserve. We think the auctioneer who puts up the property for sale upon such a condition pledges himself that the sale shall be without reserve; or in other words contracts that it shall be so; and that this contract is made with the highest bona fide bidder.

The difficulties stemming from this analysis are considerable and it raises fundamental questions as regards the law relating to auctions.[43] It also presents problems concerning contractual theory generally and it may, therefore, be useful at this juncture to enunciate some propositions of a basic nature before returning to examine this dictum.

Contractual analysis of auction sales

It has traditionally been said that a contract consists of a promise by one party — frequently called an offer — and acceptance of that offer plus the necessity of consideration from the promisee, that is some 'benefit' to the promisor or 'detriment' to the promisee, with which the promise is bought.

---

[40] See generally, Slade (1952) 68 LQR 238; Gower (1952) 68 LQR 457; Slade (1953) 69 LQR 21; C G Cox 'Auctions Without Reserve: A Schematic Approach' (1982) 132 NLJ 716.
[41] (1858) 1 E&E 295, 29 LJQB 14.   [42] (1858) 1 E&E 295 at 316.
[43] Scots law takes a different view. See *Fenwick v Macdonald Fraser & Co* 1904 6 F (Ct of Sess) 850, 41 Sc LR 688.

English law does not, save when the contract is by formal deed, recognise gratuitous promises. As regards sales by auction, it has long been established by the courts and has subsequently been given statutory endorsement that:

(a) the advertising of an auction sale does not amount to an offer to sell any property;[44]

(b) the bid is the contractual offer which is capable of being accepted or refused and that, as a corollary, the bid is capable of being withdrawn as is any contractual offer[45] before acceptance;[46]

(c) the contract is completed when the bid is accepted, classically by the fall of the hammer.[47]

Conceptual analysis of contracts

As suggested above, contracts can be analysed as comprising offers and acceptances cemented by consideration. Contracts can also be classified according to whether they are:

(a) *bilateral* or *synallagmatic*: these are the most common kind of contract, imposing obligations on both (or all) parties to the contract; both parties are under a contractual duty to perform.

(b) *unilateral*: here only one party is bound to perform although that performance typically only becomes due on the satisfaction of a condition by another. A classic example is the so called 'reward' situation where a promise to pay is conditioned on, say, finding stolen goods. But there is no question of the finder being under any contractual duty to act.

We can now return to the troublesome case of *Warlow v Harrison*. The statement quoted above[48] raises the following difficulties.

The nature of the bid

We have said that the bid is the contractual offer and also that it can be withdrawn at any time until it is accepted. Yet in *Warlow v Harrison*[49] it is

---

[44] *Harris v Nickerson* (1873) LR 8 QB 286, 42 LJQB 171; Sale of Goods Act 1979, s 57(2) (see Appendix 2).

[45] Except perhaps certain types of unilateral offer where the courts may imply a term that it shall not be revoked in appropriate circumstances; see eg *Daulia Ltd v Four Millbank Nominees Ltd* [1978] Ch 231, [1978] 2 All ER 557, CA.

[46] *Payne v Cave* (1789) 3 Term Rep 148; Sale of Goods Act 1979, s 57(2) (see Appendix 2).

[47] Above, n 46. See also *Dennant v Skinner & Collom* [1948] 2 KB 164, [1948] 2 All ER 29 where a provision that title to a car sold at auction would not pass to the purchaser until his cheque was cleared was ineffective because the provision was not incorporated until after the car had been knocked down.

[48] From *Warlow v Harrison* (1858) 1 E&E 295 at 316; see p 29.   [49] Above, n 48.

suggested that where a contract is made by an auctioneer with the highest bidder in a 'without reserve' sale, the highest bidder will be the buyer. This sounds perilously close to saying that the bid, or at any rate the highest bid, acts as an *acceptance* of a contractual offer. In Bateman it is said that this 'is not in accordance with well accepted and well established principles of the law of contract'.[50] However, what Martin B appears to be suggesting is that selling without reserve amounts to a quite separate offer to the class of bidders that on condition that they become the highest bidder the property will be knocked down to them; and that acceptance is by bidding. The offer is conditional on the bidder becoming the highest bidder; only by satisfying that condition does the bidder accept the offer.[51] The separate collateral contract made by the auctioneer is, therefore, a unilateral contract; the auctioneer is bound if the condition is satisfied but no one is bound to satisfy it — no one is bound to bid.[52] If this is correct then the bid by a prospective purchaser fulfils two quite separate functions: it is an offer to make a contract of sale, and it is an acceptance of a separate offer to sell to whomsoever becomes the highest bidder.

If this is the correct analysis,[53] then surprising results seem to flow. Whereas there is no breach of contract if the auctioneer simply withdraws the goods from the sale (*Harris v Nickerson*[54]), if he instead allows bidding to commence and then announces there is a reserve, he is in breach.[55]

Be that as it may, there is a further, perhaps more difficult obstacle in the way of such an analysis. It is difficult to see what consideration supports this collateral promise to sell to the highest bidder.

Consideration

The problem here is: how can it be said that the act of bidding, which amounts to acceptance, can also be the consideration for which the offer is given? Now it is perfectly possible for an act to provide both signification of acceptance and consideration; indeed it typically does in a unilateral con-

---

[50] Bateman *Law of Auctions* (11th edn, 1953) Estates Gazette, p 152.
[51] See Cox (above, n 40).
[52] Bateman (above, n 50) objects that for the auctioneer to be bound but for the bidder to be free to withdraw his bid offends against a principle of mutuality (p 158) but it is denied that any such principle obtains with a unilateral contract.
[53] The 'two contract' analysis has been applied in Ireland in a slightly different context (see *Tully v The Irish Land Commission and Ors.* (1963) 97 ILTR 174 — offer to put up a lot for sale again if there was a dispute about the last bidding), in Canada (see *Holder v Jackson* (1862) 11 UCCP 543) and in cases involving tender mechanics (see *Harvela Investments Ltd. v Royal Trust Co. of Canada (CI) Ltd. and Ors.* [1986] AC 207; [1985] 2 All ER 966.
[54] Above, n 44.
[55] Under the American Uniform Commercial Code s 2-328 (3) goods put up without reserve cannot be withdrawn.

tract,[56] but what benefit is it to the auctioneer or what detriment is it to the bidder that he bids? A number of possibilities have been canvassed,[57] including the argument that the bidder suffers detriment by bidding: he runs the risk of being bound by the contract of sale and the auctioneer benefits as the bidding is driven up. But it is difficult at first sight to see how an act which is revocable and may immediately be revoked can be of benefit to the auctioneer or be any real detriment to the bidder. This perhaps explains the not uncommon provision in auction conditions of a stipulation that bids may not be withdrawn. However, we have already suggested that, in this context, it is only with the person who becomes the highest bona fide bidder that the auctioneer ultimately contracts, and that person, ex hypothesi, will not have withdrawn his bid. It also must be admitted that there are many commercial situations where the law recognises a contract but where it is impossible without great artificiality either to analyse the relationship in terms of offer and acceptance or to find real consideration.[58]

The problems considered above are the main ones raised by the notion of a collateral contract between the auctioneer and the highest bona fide bidder, but there are others. In particular it may be difficult for the court in any given case to quantify the loss flowing from the breach by the auctioneer.[59] We have suggested that the highest bidder is the only person who contracts and therefore suffers any loss. But as Slade points out:[60]

At any time until the hammer has fallen it is always open to other persons to bid. The plaintiff at most therefore can argue that as the highest bidder pro tempore he has been deprived of the chance of obtaining the goods at the price which he actually bid. If this chance had any value at all, the court would not reject his claim to damages simply on the grounds that these were difficult to assess. The defence however will merely have to produce one witness who satisfies the court that he intended or was instructed to make a higher bid at the moment when the goods were withdrawn to make proof of damage impossible.

[56] Slade's objection (68 LQR 238 at 241) that 'the mere making of a bid is no more consideration for the promise than the effort of saying or even writing the words "I accept". . .' is not taken.

[57] See eg Gower 68 LQR 457; Treitel *Outline of the Law of Contract* (3rd edn, 1984) Butterworths, p 9.

[58] See the observations of Lord Wilberforce in *New Zealand Shipping Co Ltd v A M Satherthwaite & Co Ltd* [1975] AC 154 at 167 and the several examples given of which the first is 'Sales at auction'.

[59] In *Blackpool and Fylde Aero Club v Blackpool Borough Council* [1990] 3 All ER 25, a case involving tenders, the Court of Appeal decided that the Council were in breach of contract in failing to operate the tender machinery in accordance with their invitations to tender. Here too, difficult questions of quantification of loss would arise (although consideration of these practical consequences was deferred in that case) since there was no guarantee that, had the machinery been properly applied, the Club's tender would have been successful.

[60] Above, n 56.

One must accept, therefore, that there are a number of difficulties in the way of accepting the collateral contract idea. However, it is surely permissible to ask what would be the legal effect of advertising a sale as being without reserve if there were no collateral contract. Since the sale is not complete until the fall of the hammer, and since there would be no liability for subsequently imposing a reserve after the bidding had progressed, the statement that the sale was without reserve would be of absolutely no legal significance to the bidder. Two judges in *Warlow v Harrison*[61] suggested that the auctioneer would be in breach of an implied warranty of authority in such circumstances. However, it is difficult to understand how this could be so. The fact is, the auctioneer *was* authorised to sell without reserve; it is simply that his authority was subsequently revoked. This leads us to the final problem raised by the case. All along it has been discussed on the basis that the auctioneer in contracting to sell to the highest bidder does so, not as agent for the vendor so as to make him liable on the collateral contract, but as a principal. Indeed Martin B continued the dictum quoted above with these words:[62]

We entertain no doubt that the owner may, at any time before the contract is legally complete, interfere and revoke the auctioneer's authority: but he does so at his peril; and, if the auctioneer has contracted any liability in consequence of his employment and the subsequent revocation of conduct of the owner, he is entitled to be indemnified.

This is in accordance with well-established principles that the vendor can normally terminate the auctioneer's authority at any time before sale.[63] But if the statement 'without reserve' amounts to a collateral contractual offer, there seems little reason in theory why the principal should not be bound by it and thus unable to resile from it once it has been accepted by bidders. After all, the auctioneer states that the sale is without reserve because those are his instructions; he is *authorised* so to state. It may be said that there is no practical difference between the formulation in *Warlow v Harrison* that the auctioneer is personally liable but can look to the vendor for indemnification, and one that renders the vendor primarily liable on the contract; but if an advertisement of a sale without reserve is made on the instructions of the vendor there seems nothing in principle to prevent the court from holding that this constitutes an offer by the vendor, as principal, to sell to the highest bidder made through the auctioneer merely as agent. If however, as in this case, the identity of the principal is not disclosed, it may be that the auctioneer remains personally liable for non-delivery of the article.[64]

[61] (1858) 1 E&E 295, 29 LJQB 14.   [62] (1858) 1 E&E 295 at 316.
[63] We discuss termination of authority later in this chapter. See pp 41–4 below.
[64] On this question see ch 5.

IMPLIED AUTHORITY

Signing the contract

It used to be suggested that the classic example of implied authority as it applies to auctioneers was the authority to sign the contract of sale or the memorandum of it. This today no longer arises even in land sales (as discussed in chapter 9).

Collecting payment

Two related questions are involved here. First, is the purchaser discharged if he pays the agent? Second, is the agent liable to the principal if he fails to recover the proceeds or part of them from the purchaser? The first question turns on the extent of the agent's authority, whilst the second more properly involves the question of his duty, but it will be convenient to deal with the two questions together here.

Early cases[65] suggested that agents generally, and therefore auctioneers, had implied authority to collect the price from the purchaser, but these authorities have subsequently been refuted.[66] However the position is not entirely free from doubt. In the old case of *Williams v Millington* Lord Loughborough observed: 'In the common course of auctions there is no delivery without actual payment; if it be otherwise the auctioneer gives credit to the vendee entirely at his own risk.'[67] This dictum was cited with approval by Lord Denning in *Chelmsford Auctions Ltd v Poole*, where the then Master of the Rolls said:[68]

The vendor entrusts the auctioneer with the possession of the goods for sale by auction. The understanding is that the auctioneer should not part with the possession of them to the purchaser except against the price or, if the auctioneer should part with them without receiving payment, he is responsible to the vendor for the price.

This, said Lord Denning, was the common law position apart from any express conditions. If the auctioneer is responsible to the vendor for the price, it must be that he is authorised to collect it. It cannot be that he has

---

[65] See eg *Capel v Thornton* (1828) 3 C&P 352; *Howard v Chapman* (1831) 4 C&P 508.

[66] *Butwick v Grant* [1924] 2 KB 483 per Horridge J at 488 citing with approval a dictum of Lush J in *Drakeford v Piercy* (1866) 7 BS 515 at 522: 'that an agent authorised to sell has as a necessary legal consequence authority to receive payment is a proposition utterly untenable and contrary to authority.'

[67] (1788) 1 Hy Bl 81 at 84 and see *Woolfe v Horne* (1877) 2 QBD 355, 46 LJQB 534; *Davis v Artingstall* (1880) 49 LJ Ch 609, 42 LT 507; *Wood v Baxter* (1883) 49 LT 45; *Consolidated Co v Curtis & Son* [1892] 1 QB 495, 61 LJQB 325.

[68] [1973] QB 452, CA at 548.

a duty without a power to perform it. On the other hand, there appears to be no case directly in point. Both *Williams v Millington* and *Chelmsford Auctions Ltd v Poole* concerned actions by auctioneers against defaulting purchasers and in both cases it was held that, by virtue of the lien which possession of the goods gives the auctioneer, the auctioneer may recover the price. In the latter case the purchaser had refused to take the goods but the auctioneers had paid over the full price to the vendor. Thus the question whether the auctioneer was *authorised* to receive the price so as to discharge the purchaser vis-à-vis the vendor, did not arise. However in the more recent case of *Fordham v Christie Manson & Woods Ltd*[69] the defendants auctioned a painting and knocked it down to a bidder who refused to take it or pay for it. After the death of the vendor, his estate brought an action against the defendant auctioneers. It was held that there was no general duty at common law to get in the purchase money although here the auctioneers did have authority to receive it and account to the owner.[70] It is suggested, therefore, that the better view is that there is no implied authority to receive payment of the purchase price.

The absence of a conclusive answer to the question is probably explained by the fact that it is usual for the contract between the vendor and auctioneer expressly to provide the requisite powers. In sales of goods it is normal for the auctioneer to be authorised to complete the sale and collect the purchase price from the buyer.[71] Where land is sold it is generally provided that the auctioneer has authority to receive the deposit but not the full purchase price.

Where the auctioneer is authorised to collect the purchase money or the deposit, the question then arises as to whether there are restrictions as to the mode of payment permissible. Again, there may be express instructions but in their absence the common law has generally refused to discharge a purchaser who has paid otherwise than in cash. In *Howard v Chapman*[72] for example, a purchaser who sought to pay in kind, by giving the agent a quantity of horse hair, was held still liable to pay the price to the vendor. Moreover an agent who accounted for less than the full price where he had been persuaded to allow a set-off claimed by the purchaser against the vendor was held liable to the vendor for the balance.[73]

There are a number of old cases which are said to indicate that receipt of payment of the price by bill of exchange is inappropriate, but these may not be reliable. In *Sykes v Giles*[74] a purchaser was held liable to the vendor for the balance of the purchase price on a sale of timber when he had paid the

---

[69] (1977) 121 Sol Jo 529.
[70] See also *Hardial Singh v Hillyer* (1979) 251 EG 951 — not negligent in failing to ensure that a purchaser of land signed the memorandum *immediately* after the fall of the hammer.
[71] For an early example see *Brown v Staton* (1816) 2 Chit 353.   [72] (1831) 4 C&P 508.
[73] *Brown v Staton* (above, n 71).   [74] (1839) 5 M&W 645, 9 LJEx 106.

auctioneer by accepting a bill of exchange drawn in favour of the latter who then endorsed it for value and disappeared. But here the conditions provided that only the deposit was to be paid to the auctioneer. It is true that Parke B said that even if the auctioneer had had authority to receive the whole of the purchase money 'he had no authority to receive it in this way by means of a bill of exchange. Cash payment was intended'.[75] However the better ground for the decision is that given by Abinger CB, namely, that once the deposit moneys had been paid the authority of the auctioneer was at an end. He therefore had no authority whatsoever to accept anything from the purchaser thereafter.

Williams v Evans[76] is a stronger authority in that there were no express conditions, but here the vendor specifically instructed the purchaser not to pay the auctioneer at all, but to account directly to him. In these circumstances it is hardly surprising that the court held the purchaser, who paid the auctioneer with a bill of exchange, not discharged. However the court did expressly rely on *Sykes v Giles* as authority for the proposition that payment by bill of exchange was not valid. There is authority for saying that an auctioneer may, when authorised to collect the *deposit*, take a cheque from a purchaser[77] and that it is reasonable to do so. As Baggallay LJ pointed out,[78] 'persons cannot be expected to come to sales with large sums of money in their pocket'. A cheque is, of course, a special kind of bill of exchange. It seems hardly conceivable today that an auctioneer authorised to collect the price of goods sold at an auction would not, in the absence of express instructions to the contrary,[79] be entitled to receive a cheque. Where an auctioneer does receive the deposit there may be arguments in favour of his taking it as *agent* for the vendor and not as *stakeholder*, since receipt in the latter capacity may in certain situations jeopardise his lien.[80]

Describing the property: authority to warrant

An auctioneer will, almost inevitably, apply some sort of description to the lots as he puts them up. Later in this book we shall consider the potential liability of an auctioneer for any misdescription.[81] For the present, our concern is the question whether, in the absence of express authority from the vendor to give warranties about the property, such may be implied so as

---

[75] (1839) 5 M&W 645 at 651.   [76] (1866) LR 1 QB 352, 35 LJQB 111.
[77] *Farrer v Lacy Hartland & Co* (1885) 31 Ch D 42, 55 LJ Ch 149, CA.
[78] (1885) 31 Ch D 42 at 46.
[79] See eg *Earl of Ferrers v Robins* (1835) 2 Cr M&R 152, 4 LJ Ex 178.
[80] *Skinner v Trustee of the Property of Reed (Bankrupt)* [1967] Ch 1194, [1967] 2 All ER 1286; and see further on this, ch 5.
[81] See chs 6 and 8.

to give the purchaser rights against the vendor in the event that the warranty is proved false. A warranty, in this context, may be defined somewhat loosely as some representation of fact (which may include a opinion — see *Smith v Land and House Property Corpn*[82]) made before or at the time of the sale intended or tending to induce a party to enter into a contract.

That there is no implied authority to warrant was emphatically stated in *Payne v Lord Leconfield*[83] where a mare was sold by auction. A by-stander (presumably officious!) noted that the mare was suffering from a discharge from her nostrils. The auctioneer, in the presence of the plaintiff who subsequently bought the horse, said: 'you need not be afraid. The mare comes from Lord Leconfield; she has only got a cold upon her, and I shall sell as only having a cold.' Unfortunately, it turned out that she was suffering from chronic glanders and had to be destroyed, as had other of the purchaser's horses which were allegedly infected by her. The plaintiff's action against Lord Leconfield on the warranty failed on the ground that the auctioneer had neither express nor any implied authority to give warranties. However recent decisions have cast doubt upon whether an auctioneer has not implied authority to warrant.

In *Mendelssohn v Normand Ltd*[84] a car-park attendant employed by the defendant company insisted on being given the car keys and represented that he would look after the contents of the plaintiff's car. When a bag left in the car disappeared, the plaintiff sued the company. A written term of the contract contained in the ticket issued to the plaintiff purported to exclude any responsibility for loss. Nevertheless it was held that the company was liable; whilst the employee had no actual authority to give promises (warranties) it was within his implied authority to do so, and this overrode the written term of the contract subsequently entered into. Now this case, of course, has nothing to do with auctions. However, it was considered in the subsequent case of *Overbrooke Estates Ltd v Glencombe Properties Ltd*,[85] the facts of which were as follows.

The plaintiffs instructed auctioneers to sell certain property. Before the sale the auctioneers gave representations as to the absence of certain slum clearance or compulsory purchase plans affecting or likely to affect the property, and the purchasers bought it. Subsequently, however, they discovered that the representations were untrue and sought to resile from the contract. The vendors sued for specific performance of the contract and the purchasers resisted on the ground, inter alia, that they had been induced to enter into the contract by a material mis-representation which the auctioneers had ostensible authority to make. The auction had been conducted

---

[82] (1884) 28 Ch D 7, 51 LT 718, CA.   [83] (1882) 51 LJQB 642, 30 WR 814.
[84] [1970] 1 QB 177, [1969] 2 All ER 1215, CA.
[85] [1974] 3 All ER 511, [1974] 1 WLR 1335; approved in *Collins v Howell-Jones* (1980) 259 EG 331.

subject to printed conditions of sale which provided so far as material: 'The vendors do not make or give and neither the auctioneers nor any person in the employment of the auctioneers has any authority to make or give any representation or warranty in relation to these properties.' Brightman J granted specific performance of the contract. He distinguished *Mendelssohn v Normand Ltd* in that the printed conditions advertised the restriction on the authority of the auctioneers before the representation was made and said:[86]

It seems to me that it must be open to a principal to draw the attention of the public to the limits which he places on the authority of his agent and this must be so whether the agent is a person who has, or has not, any ostensible authority. If an agent has prima facie some ostensible authority, that authority is inevitably diminished to the extent of the publicised limits that are placed on it.[87]

'Prima facie . . . ostensible authority' is perhaps an odd expression but it is thought this refers to that implied or usual authority which is actual unless and until limited and thereafter is thus apparent or ostensible unless, as happened here, the principal takes steps to give notice of the limitations he has placed upon it. As was said earlier in another context, if the reason for the absence of implied authority is the fact of notification of an express limitation, it can be concluded that in the absence of such a limitation the auctioneer would have been clothed with authority and that authority must therefore be implied.

If a vendor makes it clear that he is inviting an auctioneer to attach particular descriptions to goods it is the auctioneer's duty so to describe them in terms, and the measure of damages for breach will be the difference between the price the goods would probably have fetched had they been sold under that description and the prices actually achieved.[88]

DELEGATING AUTHORITY

The question whether an auctioneer can delegate any of these duties or powers has tended to arise in relation to his authority to sign memoranda evidencing the sale. The general rule is *delegatus non potest delegare*: one who is himself a delegate may not delegate to another. It was well settled that an auctioneer had implied authority from both the vendor and the

---

[86] [1974] 3 All ER 511 at 516.
[87] This decision was approved by the Court of Appeal in *Collins v Howell-Jones* (1980) 259 EG 331, and applied in *Moore and Another v Khan-Ghauri* [1991] 32 EG 63.
[88] *Brown v Draper* (1975) 233 EG 99. However auction conditions not infrequently reserve to the auctioneer the right to apply his own descriptions to lots offered for sale. In such circumstances he would not be liable to the vendor. Such description must not, of course, be a false trade description — see ch 8.

purchaser to sign any memorandum required to be signed by or for either party in order that a contract of sale might be enforceable. The requirement of such written evidence of certain contracts originated in the Statute of Frauds 1677. The contracts involved were those for the sales or other dispositions of an interest in land and sales of goods for a value of £10 or above. As regards sales of goods, the relevant provision was re-enacted by s 4 of the Sale of Goods Act 1893 but was abolished by the Law Reform (Enforcement of Contracts) Act 1954. With regard to land, the requirement of written evidence to be signed by the parties to be bound re-enacted by s 40 of the Law of Property Act 1925 which was abolished in 1989 by the Law of Property (Miscellaneous Provisions) Act 1989.

Under the old law the question arose as to what extent an auctioneer had implied authority to delegate the signing of the requisite memorandum, typically, to his clerk? It is possible that one must distinguish the position vis-à-vis the vendor from that as it affects the purchaser. In the Irish case of *Dyas v Stafford* Chatterton VC said:[89]

There is, I think, a difference between the agency of the clerk in the case of a vendor from that of a purchaser. In the latter case the agency is only constituted on the moment by the bid of the purchaser who thus authorises the clerk to enter his name and bidding, and to bind him by signature. The agency for the vendor is of a more deliberate character, and arises from the employment of the auctioneer which by the usages and mode of such sales carries with it the employment of his clerk. The vendor must be presumed to have been aware of and to have adopted these usages, and thus to have given an authority to the clerk when the occasion should arise to act as his agent directly in doing those acts which it was necessary for the clerk to do.

Binding the vendor

This dictum suggests that an auctioneer has usual (a species of implied) authority to delegate his authority to sign a memorandum so as to bind his principal to an enforceable contract of sale. However there are to be found fairly categorical statements to the contrary. Bateman asserts baldly that 'there is certainly no power to delegate the signing of the memorandum under s 40 of the Law of Property Act, 1925 to a clerk',[90] but cites no authority for this. Halsbury[91] concurs with this view whilst recognising that the authorities are not particularly strong. In *Coles v Trecothick*,[92] Lord Eldon LC certainly said that there was no usage that an auctioneer's clerk was an agent of the principal, but the case is weakened by the fact that here

---

[89] (1881) 7 LR Ir 590 at 601.
[90] Bateman *Law of Auctions* (11th edn, 1953) Estates Gazette, p 23.
[91] Para 911.   [92] (1804) 9 Ves 234, I Smith KB 233.

there was an express authority, the auctioneer having warned the vendor that he would not be able to attend and the vendor having assented to the auctioneer's clerk acting, and also the fact that, in the result, the sale was concluded by private treaty. Thus the question of implied authority did not arise. Another case was *Gosbell v Archer*[93] where it was held that there was not an enforceable contract when the clerk signed the memorandum. But here it was clear that the clerk merely signed as a witness and *Coles v Trecothick* was expressly distinguished on that ground. The clearest statement that there is no implied authority was made in *Peirce v Corf*[94] in 1874. This case concerned the sale of a mare for a price in excess of £10 and Blackburn J said:[95]

> The memorandum, to be a good memorandum, must be signed in such a manner that when the auctioneer attaches his signature it authenticates the contract as to the price and conditions of sale. I have already said that the usage of sales by auction which we must take notice of is, that the auctioneer is the person who has authority to sign, and generally he does wisely if he signs upon the catalogue . . . but I take it as quite clear that the auctioneer's clerk has no authority to sign by the general custom.

The objection here, however, was that the clerk signed only a sales ledger and even assuming, which was not decided, that the clerk could be regarded as the agent of the *purchaser*, the memorandum was defective in that it made no reference to Conditions of Sale. Finally Halsbury refers to *Bell v Balls*,[96] but this case too involved the issue whether the auctioneer can delegate the signing of the memorandum so as to bind the purchaser and, if the statement by Chatterton VC in *Dyas v Stafford* is correct, different considerations may apply in such a case. With regard to that point, it might be thought unsatisfactory if the practice of an auctioneer permitting his clerk to sign were upheld or disapproved depending upon the circumstance of whether it was the vendor or the purchaser who happened to wish subsequently to resile from the sale.

Binding the purchaser

The position vis-à-vis the purchaser appears to be free from doubt. Despite the somewhat ambiguous wording used in *Dyas v Stafford* ('who *thus* authorises the clerk . . . to bind him by signature'),[97] *Bell v Balls*[98] is clear authority for the proposition that the auctioneer had no implied authority to delegate the signing of the memorandum as agent for the purchaser. That

---

[93] (1935) 2 Ad & El 500, 4 LJKB 78.   [94] (1874) LR 9 QB 210, 43 LJQB 52.
[95] (1874) LR 9 QB 210 at 214.   [96] [1897] 1 Ch 663, 66 LJ Ch 397.
[97] (1881) 7 LR Ir 590 at 601, emphasis added.   [98] Above, n 96.

case involved the auctioning of freehold land and the auctioneer invited the defendant to give him a bid. The defendant obliged and the property was knocked down to him. Thereupon the defendant maintained that he thought he was being invited to 'puff' for the auctioneer and that he had not intended bidding for the property for himself. The auctioneer's clerk subsequently signed the memorandum and the vendor sought to enforce the contract. Stirling J refused to accept that the purchaser was bound.[99] Having expressly approved *Peirce v Corf*,[100] his Lordship said that there was no ground for the contention that the auctioneer should be held entitled to delegate his authority to his clerk.

There are cases where the clerk's signature has been held to bind the purchaser, but these appear to have been decided on the basis that the particular circumstances lent themselves to the conclusion that the clerk was authorised directly by the purchaser so that no question of delegation arose. In *Bird v Boulter*[101] the purchaser of wheat at an auction was prevented from resiling from the contract of sale where the requisite memorandum was signed on his behalf by the auctioneer's clerk. After each property was knocked down, the clerk called out the name of the purchaser and, if the party assented, entered his name in a sale book. Denman CJ said: 'the clerk was not acting merely as an automaton, but as a person known to all engaged in the sale, and employed by any who told him to put down his name.'[102]

Finally, in *Wilson & Sons v Pike*[103] it was decided that when an auctioneer who is a partner in a firm employed to auction property signs the memorandum, he does so qua agent in his own right and not as a delegate of the firm.

These decisions have become, after 1989, largely of historical interest but where, for example, an auctioneer of land wishes to ensure that a written contract is created (on which see chapter 9 below) he may provide expressly that he has power to sign such a contract. In light of the present discussion, if it is desired to delegate such a power to a clerk, express authorisation must be given.

TERMINATION OF AUTHORITY

An agency will determine on the death or insanity of either party or the bankruptcy of the principal. Leaving aside those general rules, an auction-

---

[99] [1897] 1 Ch 663 at 668: the judge also said, in argument, that where the auctioneer does himself sign as agent for the purchaser this is 'not a matter to be put off'. Cf *Hardial Singh v Hillyer* (1979) 251 EG 951.

[100] Above, n 94.   [101] (1833) 4 B&Ad 443, 1 Nev & MKB 313.

[102] (1833) 4 B&Ad 443, at 497. See also *Sims v Landray* [1894] 2 Ch 318, 63 LJ Ch 535.

[103] [1949] 1 KB 176, [1948] 2 All ER 267, CA.

eer's authority may terminate in one of two ways: either (a) naturally, where the auctioneer performs all that he is authorised to do; or (b) artificially, by the principal taking positive steps to bring it to an end by revoking the authority previously given. We shall deal with each mode separately.

Natural termination

Once the auctioneer has performed the duties he is employed to perform, his authority comes to an end: he is *functus officio*. When this occurs will obviously depend upon the precise extent of his express and implied authority. Generally we can say that, unless otherwise agreed, his authority will determine after the sale has been completed. So, for example, he will not be able to deal with the terms on which title is to be made.[104] Whether he has power to rescind the contract of sale is not settled. In *Nelson v Aldridge*[105] an auctioneer at the insistence of the highest bidder, who claimed his horse was not 'fresh and active' or otherwise as described, agreed to take back the horse and return the purchase moneys. In an action against the auctioneer, the vendor recovered damages for breach of contract. Best J was emphatic: 'It was the duty of the auctioneer to sell and not to rescind, to do and not to undo.'[106]

On the other hand, in *Stevens v Legh*[107] a vendor failed in a similar action against his auctioneer who had returned the purchase price to the purchaser after the latter had discovered fraud. The answer may be that, where rescission is justified, it is circuitous not to give the auctioneer power to rescind since he would be liable directly to the purchaser and could then claim indemnification from the vendor. This is all very well when the purchaser's purported rescission is justified, but it does not follow that auctioneers have *authority* to rescind (or accept rescission of) the contract of sale and it is suggested that they should not do so. It is better that they refuse and look to their principal for indemnity, than take the risk involved in a possibly unjustified act which would leave them open to an action by the vendor. However, Conditions of Sale often make specific provision for rescission, eg if the lot is a deliberate forgery as defined and proved. In this case, the auctioneer has specific authority to rescind the contract and return the price paid to the buyer.[108]

---

[104] See *Seton v Slade* (1802) 7 Ves 265; *Strachan v Auld* (1884) 11 R (Ct of Sess) 756, 21 Sc LR 747.

[105] (1818) 2 Stark 435.

[106] (1818) 2 Stark 435 at 437. See also *Farquhar v Billman* (1901) 40 NSR 289.

[107] (1853) 2 CLR 251, 22 LTOS 84.

[108] If the 'forgery' Condition is drafted so as to give the purchaser the right to return of the money long after the auctioneer has paid the vendor, it will be too late to rescind the contract and the position is best analysed as involving a separate contract between the auctioneer as principal and the buyer — see further ch 6.

Revocation

We have already alluded to the right of the principal to revoke the auction-eer's authority in dealing with sales expressed to be without reserve.[109] The dictum of Martin B in *Warlow v Harrison*[110] that the principal can revoke his agent's authority at any time is generally correct. However there is one situation where the authority is irrevocable, namely where the agent has an agency 'plus an interest'. This arises where, for example, the auctioneer is to recoup sums advanced to the vendor out of the sale of his property; the vendor cannot revoke the authority to sell while the auctioneer's interest in the goods remains extant. An illustration is provided by *Charlesworth v Mills*.[111] There an owner of goods who was subjected to a writ of execution against him by a sheriff, agreed in writing with the plaintiff–auctioneer that if the latter paid out the sheriff he could sell the goods thus recovered and recoup himself out of the proceeds. The auctioneer did as he was asked, whereupon the vendor purported to revoke his authority to sell. The House of Lords decided in favour of the auctioneer. The authority to sell was 'irrevocable except upon terms of paying back the money'.[112] The courts are not astute to extend this idea of an agency coupled with an interest. In *Taplin v Florence*,[113] such was held not to exist in the form of a licence to enter the premises of a vendor and there to carry out the auction sale. Creswell J said that it was clear that an auctioneer who was employed to sell goods on the premises of a third party has no such interest in the goods as will make the licence to enter the premises for the purpose of selling the goods irrevocable.

For the revocation to be effective, it is not necessary that the purchaser is made aware of it. As it was put in one case where the vendor told the auctioneer that a right of way was to be reserved over land to be sold but the auction particulars previously produced were not amended:[114]

> It was said in argument that, if there were any mistake, that mistake was all on the part of the vendors, and that all that had passed was, as regards the plaintiff, res inter alios, and not binding upon him. But that argument proves too much. If admitted, it would deprive a vendor of a power to revoke an authority to sell, unless he could prove that the revocation was actually known to the party who chanced to become the purchaser. This cannot be successfully contended for. The revocation of the authority of the auctioneer is operative per se, and therefore, like a deed, is binding upon persons not parties to or conusant of it.

Thus the purchasers could not resist an action by the vendor for specific performance. In this case the auctioneer had read the altered particulars

---

[109] See above, pp 29–33.   [110] (1858) 1 E&E 295, 29 LJQB 14.
[111] [1892] AC 231, 61 LJQB 830, HL. Contrast *Chinnock v Sainsbury* (1860) 30 LJ Ch 409, 3 LT 258.
[112] [1892] AC 231 at 243.   [113] (1851) 10 CB 744, 20 LJCP 137.
[114] *Manser v Back* (1848) 6 Hare 443 at 449–50.

before commencing the sale but the purchaser's evidence that he had not heard this was accepted. The auctioneer risks being sued for breach of warranty of authority in such circumstances, and a warning given by Wigram VC that he should 'pointedly have called their attention to the fact that they had been altered and in what way'[115] is well taken.

An auctioneer's authority is revocable at any time until sale. Despite the right of the vendor to revoke his auctioneer's authority, where the auctioneer retains the goods and in fact sells them by auction, it is arguable that the bona fide purchaser without notice of the lack of authority will get a good title to the goods, leaving the vendor with a right of action against the auctioneer. This is argued on the basis that an auctioneer falls within the definition of a 'mercantile agent' under the Factors Act 1889 whereunder, by s 2(1), it is provided:

Where a mercantile agent is, with the consent of the owner, in possession of goods or the documents of title to goods, any sale pledge or other disposition of the goods made by him when acting in the ordinary course of business of a mercantile agent shall subject to the provisions of this act, be as valid as if he were expressly authorised by the owner of the goods to make the same; provided that the person taking under the disposition acts in good faith, and has not at the time of the disposition notice that the person making the disposition has not authority to make the same.

The fact that the vendor has revoked the authority of the auctioneer does not mean that he is not selling with the consent of the goods owner; see subs (2). This point does not, however, appear to have come before our courts for consideration.

Again, if the auctioneer were unable to effect a valid sale because his authority has been revoked, the disappointed buyer should be able to sue him for breach of warranty of authority.

Whereas the Factors Act 1889 may enable a bona fide purchaser to obtain title to goods notwithstanding revocation of the auctioneer's authority, it will not assist in the situation where the auctioneer simply *exceeds* his authority by selling below the reserve: if the sale is subject to reserve the purchaser cannot be one who 'has not . . . notice . . . that the [auctioneer] has not authority . . .'. See the discussion on pp 26–8.

---

[115] (1848) 6 Hare 443 at 446.

The Rights of an Auctioneer

RIGHTS AGAINST THE VENDOR

An auctioneer has a number of rights which may be exercised against the vendor, the most important being his right to be paid for his work. Also of significance is his right to be indemnified in respect of any losses or liabilities incurred in performing his mandate. An auctioneer has other subsidiary rights, such as his right to a lien over the property of his principal, which may be exercised to enforce his right to remuneration. We shall deal with these in turn.

THE RIGHT TO REMUNERATION AND EXPENSES

The right to remuneration includes both the right to agreed commission and, rarer in these days of more or less standardised forms of contract, the right to be paid a reasonable sum where the contract is silent as to the commission to be paid or where the work done is outside that provided for by the contract (a quantum meruit).

Commission

Whether the auctioneer is entitled to his commission will depend upon the terms of his contract.[1] It is necessary to determine what are the conditions upon satisfaction of which the contract provides that commission is payable, and secondly, whether they have been satisfied. The first element involves a legal question, and the second a factual one.[2]

Construction of the contract

The conditions to be satisfied before an agent, including an auctioneer, becomes entitled to his commission will depend, therefore, upon the precise

---

[1] Where the auctioneer is also an estate agent (as he frequently will be where land is sold by auction) he will be unable to recover charges as estate agent unless he has notified the vendor as to his rate of commission etc: Estate Agents Act 1979, s18.

[2] Bowen L J in *Beningfield v Kynaston* (1887) 3 TLR 279, CA, seems to suggest that the first question is also one of fact but that is doubted since construction of the contract involves legal issues.

terms of his contract. The contract must in each case be construed to ascertain the intention of the parties. There is a plethora of case law on commission contracts,[3] but as Lord Russell of Killowen pointed out in *Luxor v Cooper*:[4]

Commission contracts are subject to no particular rules or principles of their own; the law which governs them is the law which governs all contracts and all questions of agency. No general rule can be laid down by which the rights of the agent or the liability of the principal under commission contracts are to be determined. In each case these must depend upon the exact terms of the contract in question, and upon the true construction of those terms.

There is thus little to be gained from a detailed cataloguing of the cases; it is evident that a different decision may be expected when the contract as construed provides for commission to be paid:

(a) upon the introduction of a person able and willing to enter into a contract of purchase;
(b) upon the introduction of a person who enters into a binding contract of purchase;
(c) upon the introduction of a person who completes a contract of purchase.[5]

A few illustrative examples may however be given. In *Peacock v Freeman*[6] the defendant auctioneers claimed to retain commission in the following circumstances: the contract provided that commission was to be paid if the property were sold at auction but if the property 'should . . . not be sold we shall charge an auction fee of 30 guineas.' At auction the property was knocked down to a purchaser who paid a deposit to the auctioneer. Subsequently the purchaser raised certain requisitions and, as provided for in the conditions of sale, the vendors rescinded the contract of sale and repaid the deposit amount. Thereupon they demanded the deposit moneys retained by the auctioneers claiming that all that the latter were entitled to retain was the 30 guineas allowable where the property was not sold. The Court of Appeal held that on the true construction of the contract, commission was only payable upon completion when the purchaser paid or came under a liability to pay the purchase moneys. Lord Esher MR said:[7]

Land could only be said to be sold when the conveyance was complete not when there was a mere contract to sell. Therefore in this case the commission was not

---

[3] See J R Murdoch, *The Law of Estate Agency and Auctions* (3rd edn, 1994) Estates Gazette, ch 5 and Halsbury's Laws of England, Vol 1(2): Agency para 117 for a discussion of many of the cases in this area.
[4] *Luxor (Eastbourne) Ltd v Cooper* [1941] AC 108 at 124.
[5] The classification is that of Bateman *Law of Auctions* (11th edn, 1953) Estates Gazette, ch 7.
[6] (1888) 4 TLR 541, CA.   [7] (1888) 4 TLR 541 at 542.

earned under the terms of the contract itself . . . It could never be supposed that there was an implied contract with . . . the auctioneers, that the plaintiffs should not do what that contract authorised them to do.

On the other hand, in *Skinner v Andrews and Hall*[8] in substantially similar circumstances it was held that the auctioneers were entitled to their commission. Here the correspondence, which formed the contract, referred to a 'sale . . . under the hammer'. Vaughan Williams LJ emphasised that the agreement in this case involved a 'very different contract'[9] from that in *Peacock v Freeman*.

In both these cases the vendor justifiably prevented the *completion* of the contract of sale. More commonly a problem arises where the auctioneers are prevented from bringing about an auction sale by the revocation of their authority by the vendor. In such circumstances the auctioneers will wish to claim either, (a) that there is an implied term in their contract of agency precluding such revocation, and giving rise to a right to damages for its breach, or (b) that where there is a subsequent sale of the property, the terms of their contract entitle them to commission.

Implied term

The argument that there was an implied term in the agency contract, that the vendor shall not prevent the auctioneer from earning his commission by himself selling or simply revoking the authority of the auctioneer before sale or completion, was raised in *Peacock v Freeman* but was rejected because of the express term in the Conditions of Sale that in certain circumstances, one of which obtained, the vendor could rescind the contract of sale. It is axiomatic that a term cannot be implied in the face of an express term to the contrary. And it is not necessary in order to exclude the implication of a term of the kind argued for, to find an express term such as that in *Peacock v Freeman*; it seems that the express provision for commission to be paid on a certain event will be fatal both to the implication of any term to pay on any other event and to the implication of a term not to prevent that event from materialising. In *Luxor v Cooper* Lord Russell of Killowen said:[10]

I can find no safe ground on which to base the introduction of any such implied term. Implied terms, as we all know, can only be justified under the compulsion of some necessity. No such compulsion or necessity exists in the case under consideration. The agent is promised a commission if he introduces a purchaser at a specified or minimum price. The owner is desirous of selling. The chances are largely in favour of the deal going through, if a purchaser is introduced. The agent takes the risk in the hope of a substantial remuneration for comparatively small exertion.

---

[8] (1910) 26 TLR 340, CA.   [9] (1910) 26 TLR 340 at 341.   [10] [1941] AC 108 at 125.

And he continued:[11]

> My Lords in my opinion there is no necessity in these contracts for any implication; and the legal position can be stated thus: If according to the true construction of the contract the event has happened upon the happening of which the agent has acquired a vested right to the commission . . . then no act or omission by the principal or anyone else can deprive the agent of that right; but until that event has happened the agent cannot complain if the principal refuses to proceed with or carry to completion, the transaction with the agent's client.

What was said was in the context of a claim by an estate agent, but the statement of principle is arguably wide enough to apply to an auctioneer who has been prevented from earning his commission. If an auctioneer wishes to protect himself he must provide expressly in his agreement with the vendor for the circumstances in which he is to receive commission or to be paid expenses incurred in preparing for a sale which he is prevented from effecting.[12] However, one must distinguish the case where the principal has justifiably prevented the agent from bringing about the event upon the happening of which the commission is payable, of which *Peacock v Freeman* is an example, from that where the principal prevents that event from happening by breaking his contract with the purchaser. In such a case, the Court of Appeal has held, there will be a term implied on the basis of necessity that the principal will not so act.[13]

The relationship between a principal and his agent has not been, hitherto in this country, the subject of systematic regulation. However, in 1986 the Council of the European Community issued a Directive[14] with the aim of co-ordinating the laws of Member States in relation to self-employed commercial agents. These were ultimately given effect to in the UK by the Commercial Agents (Council Directive) Regulations 1993 which came into force on 1 January 1994.[15]

The regulations define a 'commercial agent' as

> a self-employed intermediary who has continuing authority to negotiate the sale or purchase of goods on behalf of another person (the 'principal'), or to negotiate and conclude the sale or purchase of goods on behalf of and in the name of that principal; but shall be understood as not including in particular:
>
> (i) a person who, in his capacity as an officer of a company or association, is empowered to enter into commitments binding on that company or association;

---

[11] [1941] AC 108 at 128–9.
[12] The position is similar in New Zealand — see *Sinclair v Stuart* (1886) 5 NZLR 85.
[13] *Alpha Trading Ltd v Dunnshaw-Patten Ltd* [1981] QB 290, [1981] 1 All ER 482.
[14] EC 86/653.
[15] SI 1993/3053 as amended by SI 1993/3173. These were made by the Secretary of State for Trade and Industry under the European Communities Act 1972, s 2(2).

(ii) a partner who is lawfully authorised to enter into commitments binding on his partners;

(iii) a person who acts as an insolvency practitioner (as that expression is defined in section 388 of the Insolvency Act 1986) or the equivalent in any other jurisdiction;

Regulation 2 goes on to provide that the regulations do not apply to commercial agents whose activities are unpaid and commercial agents when they operate on commodity exchanges or in the commodity market.

The Directive controls several aspects of the relationship between principal and agents and, in particular, for our present purposes contains a number of provisions relating to:

(1) The form and amount of renumeration in the absence of agreement.[16]
(2) Entitlement to commission on transactions concluded during the agency contract.[17]
(3) Entitlement to commission on transactions concluded after the agency contract has terminated.[18]
(4) The date when commission shall become due and be payable.[19]
(5) The extinction of the right to commission.

The main changes that are brought about in UK law as a result of these Regulations relate to compensation for agents whose agencies are terminated and, in particular provisions relating to the right of an agent to receive a proportion of commission where a transaction is completed after his agency has been terminated but where the transaction is largely attributable to his actions. These provisions might have some potential significance for auctioneers of goods but it is not at all certain that the regulations apply to auctioneers.

Whilst auctioneers are not included in the list of those expressly excepted from the Regulations it is suggested that they do not fall within the definition which refers to 'a self-employed intermediary who has *continuing authority* to negotiate the sale or purchase of goods . . .'. It may be doubted whether an auctioneer will normally be one with 'continuing authority'. There is no definition of this rather crucial expression but the main thrust of the Council Directive is aimed at harmonising the law relating to those whose activities are concerned with the interpenetration of markets. Many of the provisions of the Directive and the Regulations made under it seem designed to deal with activities of agents concerned with distributorship and allied activities.

Unless an auctioneer has a particular arrangement with a seller whereby eg he is employed to sell all the seller's goods of a class over a certain period

---

[16] Regulation 6.   [17] See Regulation 7.   [18] See Regulations 8 and 9.
[19] See Regulation 10.

of time — such as may arise in respect of unclaimed goods in the hands of the police or a transport operator — it is not thought that he would have continuing authority. Further, it is not in any event entirely clear whether it is right to regard an auctioneer as having authority '*to negotiate*' the sale or purchase of goods. (Again there is no definition of this term.)

In the absence of an authoritative ruling as to the precise ambit of the definition of commercial agent it is impossible to be categorical about the applicability or otherwise of these regulations in the case of auction sales. However, for the reasons stated, it is suggested that they do not apply and the present discussion of auctioneers' rights to renumeration etc will proceed on the assumption that the Directive has no effect on auctioneers.

Express provision where sale otherwise than by the agent

It is not uncommon, particularly with regard to estate agents' contracts, to find express provision for commission to be payable even though the sale is not effected directly by the agent but perhaps as a result of something done by him. This frequently gives rise to difficult questions as to whether the advertisements or introductions of the agent actually caused the sale. The notion of 'cause' may involve philosophical questions but the courts tend to take a more robust factual approach. A number of cases have come before the courts where it has been necessary to construe the agency contracts and decide, whether, on the facts found, the agent has effectively caused the sale. Once again, since these cases have turned on their own particular facts, they must be treated with some caution; it is not possible to deduce wide statements of principle from them. The line drawn between one decision and another has frequently been thin.

In *Bayley v Chadwick*[20] the House of Lords held auctioneers entitled to their commission when the property, a ship, was sold to one whose agent had been introduced by the auctioneers. There the contract specifically provided:

In case the ship is not sold by auction, she is forthwith to revert to the custody of the owners for private sale, but in case a subsequent sale be effected to any person or firm introduced by you or led to make such offer in consequence of your mention or publication for auction purposes, you to be entitled to the . . . commission on such sale.

This clause is quite wide, but even if there is such a clause and even if the purchaser is originally introduced to the vendor by the agents, it will not follow that a subsequent sale was by their instrumentality. In a case where a purchaser bought a lot two and a quarter years after the abortive auction,

---

[20] (1878) 39 LT 429, 4 Asp MLC 59, HL. See also *Green v Bartlett* (1863) 14 CBNS 681, 32 LJCP 261.

having attended there and bought other lots, the jury found that the sale had not been brought about as a result of the introduction of the auctioneers.[21] There is some ancient authority for the proposition that it is *customary* for the auctioneer to be paid commission if the vendor sells his property privately without the auctioneer's intervention before the auction or after an abortive auction sale. Such was found in *Rainy v Vernon*[22] where three experienced auctioneers gave evidence to that effect. But the existence of such a custom was not accepted in the more recent case of *Williams v Tucker*,[23] and the plaintiff auctioneer's reliance on *Rainy v Vernon* was unsuccessful.

Thus auctioneers have been astute to include the kind of express conditions we have been discussing. Moreover, auctioneers may not wish to make their entitlement to remuneration depend upon a finding that they effectively caused the sale or introduced the purchaser. It is simpler and safer to provide that they should be paid their commission if the property is sold before auction or within a certain time thereafter. However, even the most widely-drawn clause of this kind can prove unavailing; it is difficult to provide for every possible eventuality that can intervene and defeat the auctioneer's expectation of commission. In *John Meacock & Co v Abrahams*[24] the facts were as follows: the defendant, who was the second mortgagee of five houses, instructed the plaintiff auctioneers to sell them by auction in exercise of his remedies as an unpaid mortgagee. The contract was on the terms of the Chartered Auctioneers' and Estate Agents' Institute Conditions which provided:

Sale before auction. If a sale of the property whether arranged by the auctioneer or not, is effected between the date of acceptance of instructions and the date of the auction, commission is payable to the auctioneer on the same scale as for a sale by auction.

The auctioneers made all the necessary preparations for the sale, but at the same time the mortgagor of the properties negotiated their sale to the sitting tenants and, the day before the projected auction, succeeded in redeeming the mortgage. Thus there was nothing for the principal–second mortgagees to sell. The auctioneers claimed to recover their scale commission. At first instance they were held entitled to do so. The objection, that the clause could not be intended to cover a situation as here, where the property was sold by one other than the vendor, was not taken. The

---

[21] *Lumley v Nicholson* (1886) 34 WR 716, 2 TLR 711. The judge stressed that this was a question for the jury and that there was evidence that the sale was a separate transaction although he would have found the other way. Where more than one agent is involved in, say, sending particulars to a purchaser, the court has to determine who was the more instrumental in causing the sale: see eg *Bentleys Estate Agents Ltd v Granix Ltd* [1989] 27 EG 93.

[22] (1840) 9 CP 559.   [23] (1900) Times, March 9.

[24] [1956] 3 All ER 660, [1956] 1 WLR 1463, CA.

County Court judge thought that if it were so restricted it was open to abuse:[25]

It is argued that this does not apply because the sale that was effected was made not by the mortgagee but by the mortgagor, though in substance the mortgagee's interest was greater than the mortgagor's. There is nothing which states expressly by whom the sale must be made. Anyone can sell land taking the risk of being unable to make a title before completion. A wife could sell and get her husband to come in as vendor. A tenant could sell but he would have to get in the landlord's interest before completion. A partner could sell and attempt to do the auctioneer out of commission by getting his partner to assume the character of vendor. If 'sale' is limited to a sale by the person who instructed the auctioneer there would be a number of holes through which vendors could slip out of the network of the liability for commission ... As a matter of language the word 'sale' is wide enough to cover a sale by anyone, wide enough to cover a sale by the mortgagor. Mr Clauson, who argued attractively on behalf of a client whose conduct has not been wholly attractive, says that I should read into the clause after the word 'sale' the words 'by the vendor'. There might be cases where the purpose of the clause pointed to a restrictive interpretation. Here it is the other way about. The purpose of the clause is to prevent people doing the auctioneer out of payment for his work. The people who framed the clause were aiming at a sale by anyone. There is no reason to apply a restrictive interpretation.

The principals appealed to the Court of Appeal. The judges there were divided. The majority, Lord Justices Denning and Hodson, found against the auctioneers. They preferred a restrictive interpretation of the commission clause and held that its natural construction covered only a sale by the client;[26] they did not believe that the framers of the clause ever addressed their minds to the possibility of a sale by any person other than the client. Morris LJ dissented. He looked to the purpose of the condition and said:[27]

It seems to me ... that the purpose of the clause was to ensure that the auctioneer should not be deprived of payment for his work once he has accepted instructions from someone in a position to give those instructions ... If the property is sold before auction, it is but reasonable and fair that the auctioneer should be paid, and the language is wide enough to refer to a sale by anyone entitled to sell the freehold.

And, further, '*The purpose of the clause is to prevent people doing the auctioneer out of payment for his work.*'[28]

Whilst Morris LJ and the County Court judge were clearly more sympathetic to the auctioneer's plight, it is suggested that the decision of the majority in this case is correct. The abuse of sales by others with the

---

[25] [1956] 3 All ER 660 at 669, [1956] 1 WLR 1463 at 1475.
[26] A similar view had been suggested in the earlier case of *Murad v Hearts of Oak Society* (unreported, 4 November 1955).
[27] [1956] 3 All ER 660 at 670, [1956] 1 WLR 1463 at 1476.
[28] [1956] 3 All ER 660 at 669, [1956] 1 WLR 1463 at 1475.

connivance of the client can be dealt with by 'lifting the veil' and ascertaining that in truth the sale was by an agent of the client. If, as in this case, a mortgagor is entitled to redeem his mortgage or sell the mortgaged property at any time, it can hardly be regarded as 'doing the auctioneer out of payment for his work'; it is simply that the client has lost his right to sell the property. And if the auctioneer wishes to protect himself against such an eventuality he must provide specifically for it.

An auctioneer can, however, protect himself against the property being sold by another agent and provide for his full commission to be payable in such an event. In *Gross Fine & Krieger Chalfen v Gaynor*[29] auctioneers were appointed sole agents for the sale of a house and prepared to sell it by auction. Before the proposed sale could be effected, however, the clients sold it through another firm of estate agents by private treaty. The auctioneers were held entitled to commission at the contractually agreed rate on the price achieved in the private sale. Technically, of course, the sum was awarded as damages for breach of the contract of sole agency rather than as commission and the court also allowed a small sum as special damages to cover the costs of printing the auction sale brochure.

The amount of the commission

Assuming commission to be payable, the next question to be determined is what is the amount of the commission to which the auctioneer is entitled. In a properly drawn contract, this should pose no difficulties; but the question sometimes arises because either there is a dispute as to the terms of the contract, or the contract does not specify a sum and the courts have to imply a term into the contract.

Dispute as to the incorporation of a term

Where a contract is formed by correspondence it sometimes happens that a party to a contract argues that terms have been assented to by the other party because the latter has not objected to or varied them. As Lord Denning put it 'In some cases the battle is won by the man who fires the last shot. He is the man who puts forward the latest term and conditions: and, if they are not objected to by the other party, he may be taken to have agreed to them.'[30] This sort of problem tends to arise where both parties trade on standard forms and one then encounters a 'battle of the forms', but it is not restricted to that situation. If an agent and a client enter into negotiations in the form of a series of letters, it may fall to be determined whether a particular provision is incorporated into the final agreement.

[29] (1974) 233 EG 1015, QBD.
[30] *Butler Machine Tool Co Ltd v Ex-Cell-O Corpn (England) Ltd* [1979] 1 All ER 965, CA at 968.

In *John E Trinder & Partners v Haggis*,[31] Mr Haggis put his house in the hands of a firm of estate agents for sale. Later, his wife (with, as the County Court judge found, the authority of the husband) orally engaged the plaintiff firm, although nothing was at that time said about commission. Subsequently the plaintiffs wrote detailing their commission, but neither Mr Haggis nor his wife responded to that letter. The plaintiffs who had been engaged to introduce a person willing to sign a contract to purchase at an agreed price did so, but the clients refused to sign the contract of sale which had been drafted by their solicitors. In these circumstances the judge awarded the agents their commission at the rate specified in their letter. The Court of Appeal, by a majority, dismissed the defendants' appeal. Lord Evershed MR concluded that the defendant had by his conduct unambiguously bound himself to the terms of the letter. Denning LJ dissented; he said that silence could not make a new agreement nor could it add terms to an existing agreement. However, it seems clear that his view was in fact based on the finding that the agents had not established the existence of a binding agreement prior to the letter. It is well established that once there is a contract, a failure to respond to a letter setting out the terms will have a confirmatory effect; the dictum of Lord Denning in the *Butler Machine Tool* case is clear about that.[32]

If an auctioneer seeks to rely on a scale charges clause, or for that matter, any other clause as forming part of his contract, he must show that he has taken sufficient steps to bring it to the attention of his principal. In *Bernard Thorpe & Partners v Snook*,[33] the plaintiff auctioneers were instructed to sell the defendants' farm by auction subject to a reserve of £275,000. They sent a form to the defendants which contained their scale fees. On the reverse was a further clause which provided:

Sale After Auction. If a sale of the property, whether arranged by the auctioneers or not is effected within three months after the auction commission on the price realised shall be payable to the auctioneers on the same scale as for a sale by auction in which event any fee for non-sale shall merge in the commission then payable.

This was an adaptation of the standard clause contained in the Royal Institute of Chartered Surveyors' scale of fees booklet. At the auction the property failed to reach its reserve and the defendant, within three months, sold the property by private treaty for £285,000. The auctioneers duly claimed their commission of £5,700 and the principals claimed that they had not agreed to the condition quoted above. Whether a condition has become incorporated into a contract of agency depends upon whether the party to be bound had notice of it. Nolan J said:[34]

---

[31] [1951] WN 416.
[32] [1979] 1 All ER 965, [1979] 1 WLR 401, CA. See also *Way & Waller Ltd v Ryde* [1944] 1 All ER 9, CA.
[33] (1983) 266 EG 440.　　　[34] (1983) 266 EG 440 at 443.

The plaintiffs do not have to establish that Mr Snook actually read the critical clause. The question is whether they did all that was reasonably sufficient to give Mr Snook notice of it. The question falls into two parts: first did they adequately inform Mr Snook of the significance of the scale charges and of their reliance on it. Secondly, if so, was the supply of that document enough to convey to him the whole of its contents?

Although there was nothing on the front of the form referring to the conditions on the back, the judge found that in all the circumstances of the case the auctioneers had established that the clause had become a condition of the contract and they were entitled to their commission.

No contractual provision as to commission

If the contract is silent as to the amount of the commission payable, either because the parties have not addressed their minds to this, or because the auctioneer has failed to show that a provision as to his charges has been incorporated into the agreement, the court will readily imply a term to pay a reasonable sum. As Jessel MR observed in *Miller v Beal*:[35]

In ascertaining what amount was due . . . allowance should be made for a reasonable commission which he was entitled to charge, . . . the manifest object generally which auctioneers had in view when they entered into transactions of such a kind was to earn their commission, and it would be doing an injustice not to allow it.

What is 'reasonable' will be a matter of evidence and will normally be based upon standard charges generally operating in such a transaction. In *Newman v Richardson*,[36] an agent claimed five per cent commission on the sale of a dry dock in Swansea. The court accepted evidence from other agents that there were no special rates for the sale of such property, and said that a reasonable sum was to be ascertained on the then prevailing scales of the professional bodies.[37]

Loss of commission

Where the auctioneer has, prima facie, earned his commission, ie satisfied the condition on which it is payable, he may nevertheless lose his right to it by reason of negligence or other misconduct. There are few reported cases concerning loss of commission and those that exist are rather ancient.[38] Omission to take a step which in common usage an auctioneer would take

[35] (1879) 27 WR 403 at 404. See also *Re Page (No 3)* (1863) 32 Beav 487, 8 LT 231. The common law position has now been confirmed by statute; see the Supply of Goods and Services Act 1982, s15 (see Appendix 2).

[36] (1885) 1 TLR 348. See also *Maltby v Christie* (1795) 1 Esp 339.

[37] On the appropriate scales where sales are by order or with the authority of the courts, see ch 11. Where an auctioneer is instructed to sell by the court there is no custom or practice to allow commission when the property is not so sold but is later sold by private treaty: *Re Maitland, Pickthall v Dawes* (1903) 47 Sol Jo 709.

[38] See eg *Denew v Daverell* (1813) 3 Camp 451; *Jones v Nanney* (1824) 13 Price 76, M'Cle 25.

will amount to negligence. An example, no longer of current applicability, is a failure timeously to obtain the purchaser's signature to the memorandum of sale in respect of land.[39] In Canada, an auctioneer has been deprived of his commission when he caused loss to his principal by concealing material facts from him.[40]

Quantum meruit

We have seen that there is no room for an implied term that the principal will not prevent his agent from earning his commission save where he does so by breaking his contract with the purchaser (as in *Alpha Trading Ltd v Dunnshaw-Patten Ltd*,[41] where a contract was concluded but the principal then refused to deliver the goods to the buyer). Can the disappointed agent however claim a quantum meruit sum, ie a sum to recompense him for the work done short of performance of that upon which the commission was payable? In *Luxor (Eastbourne) Ltd v Cooper*, Lord Russell said:[42]

As to the claim on a quantum meruit, I do not see how this can be justified in the face of an express provision for remuneration which the contract contains. This must necessarily exclude such a claim unless it can (upon the facts of a particular case) be based upon a contract subsequent to the original contract, and arising from some conduct on the part of the principal.

It will be recalled that that case involved an estate agent's contract and the question arises as to whether an auctioneer's contract of agency is in *pari materia*. In some respect it may be, but there is some judicial opinion that in this situation it is not. In *Frank Swain (a firm) v Whitfield Corpn Ltd*,[43] the plaintiff auctioneer's instructions to sell properties of a company were revoked at 'the eleventh hour and fifty-ninth minute' and the judge at first instance awarded them a quantum meruit sum based upon the agreed commission calculated on the reserves that had been placed on the properties. It does not appear to have been argued that a quantum meruit claim was impermissible. However, Upjohn LJ, with whom Pearson and Ormerod LLJ agreed, did briefly advert to this question and asserted that a quantum meruit claim was available:[44]

That that is the law is not now in dispute. It is clear that an auctioneer is in a different position from an estate agent who contracts with his principal to introduce a purchaser. Until he introduces a purchaser he has no right to any commission whatso-

---

[39] See *Hardial Singh v Hillyer* (1979) 251 EG 951.
[40] *Ring v Potts* (1903) 36 N B R 42.   [41] [1981] QB 290, [1981] 1 All ER 482.
[42] [1941] AC 108 at 125. See also per Lord Wright at 141 where his Lordship gave as an additional ground the fact that the principal had not obtained any benefits.
[43] (1962) 183 EG 479.   [44] (1962) 183 EG 479 at 479.

ever; but with an auctioneer the law is different, if the properties are withdrawn from auction he is entitled to a quantum meruit for the services thrown away.

Whilst this dictum by a senior judge in the Court of Appeal must be accorded respect, it must also be treated with some caution. The opening sentence may be merely a reference to the fact that the issue was not specifically argued by the defendants in this case. It certainly would not be true to say that the legal position is not in dispute. Indeed the point had been authoritatively decided against an auctioneer by a differently constituted Court of Appeal just six years earlier in *John Meacock & Co v Abrahams*.[45] There Hodson LJ said:[46]

The alternative way in which the claim has been put — and often it is put in this class of case where there is difficulty in complying with the express terms of the contract — is upon a quantum meruit. We have had put before us, I think, every argument which could be put, supported by the correspondence showing the late date at which the defendant withdrew his instructions for the auction, and showing that, so far as he could, he confirmed the instructions and insisted, almost to the very last, that the auction should go forward ... Of course once the debt had been redeemed, they had nothing to sell. Notwithstanding the attraction of the argument that after all the plaintiffs had done their work, or a substantial part of their work, and it is hard on them that they should not be paid because the auction never took place, yet I feel that this class of case is in pari materia with estate agents cases where a professional man enters into a contract on which he is only to be paid commission, usually based on a percentage rate. If commission is to be paid on the happening of an event, there being a specific contract which goes off, he cannot claim a quantum meruit.

Faced with these two irreconcilable Court of Appeal decisions, we suggest that the decision in *John Meacock & Co v Abrahams* is more reliable. It does not appear to have been considered by the court in the later case where the point did not strictly arise for decision. In both cases the judges took judicial notice of the fact that commission rates are fixed high in recognition of the fact that auctioneers may do a lot of work on abortive sales for which they do not get paid.[47] However, there is nothing to prevent an auctioneer expressly providing for the payment of a reasonable sum for his work in such an event.

Assuming there is such an entitlement, the next question is: how much is recoverable? The question of quantification was the substantial point in issue in the *Frank Swain* case,[48] where the judge had ordered a payment to the auctioneers based on the commission rate applicable to the reserve

---

[45] [1956] 1 WLR 1463.

[46] [1956] 1 WLR 1463 at 1469. See also Denning LJ at 1466–8 and per Morris LJ at 1476.

[47] In *Luxor (Eastbourne) Ltd v Cooper* [1941] AC 108, 110 LJKB 131, the agent stood to earn £10,000 for 8 or 9 days' work. Lord Russell's observation (at 126) that this was equivalent to the then annual salary of a Lord Chancellor may explain their Lordships' reluctance in that case to award damages or any quantum meruit sum!

[48] Above, n 43.

prices. The defendants objected that those commission rates did not necessarily reflect the work done. Lord Upjohn pointed out that with a quantum meruit, one was not concerned with precise sums. There was always an element of approximation. The judge had not been in error in taking into account that the properties had been withdrawn from sale a matter of minutes before they would have come under the hammer and that there were many anxious bidders waiting in the auction rooms. The properties might well have exceeded their reserves resulting in a higher commission for the auctioneers.

The courts are likely to base their assessment of what is reasonable on evidence of usual commission rates, including any appropriate scale charges — although many scales, such as those for valuations recommended by the RICS have been abolished in recent times. Scales of remuneration may be fixed by law in various instances, see chapter 11.

Expenses

An auctioneer not infrequently provides expressly that he shall be paid his out-of-pocket expenses incurred in selling the property. If he does not, but earns his commission, he recoups himself thereout. There is however a paucity of authority on the question whether he can claim his expenses where he is prevented from earning his commission. In *Gross Fein & Krieger Chalfen v Gaynor*,[49] where the auctioneer recovered damages for breach of a sole agency provision, a separate award of special damages in respect of his expenses was made. However the contract in that case had expressly provided for expenses up to £300 to be chargeable. Where no claim for breach of contract arises, and assuming that there is no claim for a quantum meruit maintainable, it is arguable that an auctioneer may nevertheless claim reimbursement of his expenses. Bateman[50] opines otherwise, but such judicial opinion as has been expressed on the subject is in favour of such a claim. In *Chinnock v Sainsbury* Romilly M R said:[51]

Where a person agrees with auctioneers for the sale by them of property in a particular manner and he then changes his mind, the rule is — *subject to the claims of auctioneers for their expenses incurred* — this court will not enforce such an agreement.

This dictum is echoed by Lord Denning in *John Meacock & Co v Abrahams*.[52] Both dicta were obiter but there seems nothing inconsistent in

---

[49] Above, n 29.
[50] Bateman *Law of Auctions* (11th edn, 1953) Estates Gazette, p 304.
[51] (1860) 30 LJ Ch 409, but only as reported in (1860) 3 LT at 259, emphasis added.
[52] [1956] 1 WLR 1463 at 1467.

denying an auctioneer commission or a quantum meruit, ie payments in the way of *remuneration* when he is unable to satisfy the particular precondition, but allowing him to recoup his out-of-pocket expenses incurred at the behest of or on behalf of his principal. However, it is safest if an auctioneer expressly provides for this in his contract with his client. Both Sotheby's and Christie's reserve the right to charge the vendor in respect of withdrawn lots at a fee calculated by reference to a percentage of the reserve price or valuation of the property together with expenses.

INDEMNITY

An auctioneer may in the course of acting for his client incur liabilities to third parties. If he does so he will wish to recover from his principal. As we have suggested in other contexts, an auctioneer will be well advised to make express provision in his contract with his client. However, in the absence of express provision, the law may imply a promise by the principal to indemnify his agent. The circumstances in which such an implied term will be found now fall to be considered.

It can as a general proposition be stated that the existence of an agency relationship is enough for an indemnity to be implied. In *Adamson v Jarvis*, Best CJ said:[53]

... every man who employs another to do an act which the employer appears to have the right to authorise him to do undertakes to indemnify him for all such acts as would *be lawful* if the employer had the authority he pretends to have.

There is an immediate limitation on the principle as expressed by Best CJ, namely that the act must be one which would have been lawful if the principal had the authority he purported to have. If the act is known to the agent to be tortious or otherwise illegal, the auctioneer is unable to claim an indemnity in respect of losses incurred as a result of it. In such a case the agent is independently liable.[54]

The situations in which an auctioneer may seek indemnification are varied.[55] We have referred already to the right to indemnity where, for example, the principal revokes the auctioneer's authority. Disputes have, however, most commonly arisen where an auctioneer has been subjected to a claim for conversion of or trespass to goods because it has been alleged that his principal was not the true owner. *Adamson v Jarvis* itself involved

[53] (1827) 4 Bing 66 at 72.
[54] See *Dugdale v Lovering* (1875) LR 10 CP 196, 44 LJ CP 197, per Brett J, citing with approval Tindal CJ in *Toplis v Grane* (1839) 5 Bing NC 636, 9 LJ CP 180.
[55] Where an auctioneer wishes to seek an indemnity in proceedings being brought against him, he may serve a third-party notice on his principal under RSC Ord 16 (see Appendix 3). In the County Court the equivalent rule is CCR 1981, Ord 12.

a claim of this nature. In order for an auctioneer to be liable to the true owner it is necessary that he receives the property and delivers it to the purchaser with a view to passing title in it to him. The agent's ignorance of his principal's lack of title is no defence. But if the auctioneer merely acts as an intermediary in, eg, settling the price between the parties, no such liability is incurred.[56]

The principle enunciated in *Adamson v Jarvis* was wider than the decision there required. The agent was said to be entitled to an indemnity in respect of all authorised acts save those which were known by him to be unlawful. This would mean that a principal would invariably be liable to indemnify his agent where his instructions were lawful but nevertheless caused his agent to incur losses. However, it has been suggested that a principal should not have to indemnify his agent when he, the principal, has not been at fault. In *Halbronn v International Horse Agency and Exchange Ltd*,[57] the unusual facts were as follows: the plaintiff auctioneers, carrying on business in France, were instructed by the defendant to sell his mare 'Pentecost'. She was entered and described under that name in the English stud book. One Delavan, a French horse-breeder, had earlier imported a thoroughbred mare of the same name into France and claimed, and was subsequently awarded, damages from the plaintiffs on the ground that their advertising of another mare of the same name had reduced the value of his own animal. The auctioneers' claim for an indemnity against their client was dismissed on the ground that their loss was not incurred by virtue of any wrong done by the principal. Bruce J said:[58]

It was contended by Mr Vaughan Williams that the mere fact of the employment of the plaintiff as auctioneer by the defendants involved an obligation on the part of the defendants to indemnify the plaintiff against all claims arising out of the plaintiffs' conduct as auctioneer in respect of acts done by him within the scope of his authority. I am not prepared to assent to that proposition . . .

Here, since the damages recovered in the French court arose not from any act of the plaintiffs in the performance of their duty but because of a mistake as to the identity of the mare, and since that mistake was not attributable to any misdescription by the defendant, there was no right to recover an indemnity. This conclusion was tested by the learned judge by hypothesising the case where a genuine Constable was auctioned but a jury subsequently mistakenly concluded that the painting was a fake. In such circumstances, said the judge, the 'auctioneer would have no claim to recover, against the person who had entrusted him with the sale of the picture'. It is, with respect, difficult to follow the reasoning of the judge.

---

[56] See *Barker v Furlong* [1891] 2 Ch 172, 60 LJ Ch 368. The auctioneer's potential liability for conversion is discussed in ch 5.
[57] [1903] 1 KB 270, 72 LJ KB 90.   [58] [1903] 1 KB 270 at 272.

There is a dictum of the Privy Council which, in terms, says that if an agent suffers loss as a result of a court decision it matters not whether that decision is erroneous in law[59] and, in any event, it is submitted that where the loss is suffered by the auctioneer in the course of carrying out his instructions an indemnity should be implied; one is not apportioning *blame*; it is simply a question of deciding upon whom a loss should fall. And if a loss arises as a result of an authorised act, he who authorises it should bear the loss.

The observations made in the *Halbronn* case were expressly disapproved by the Court of Appeal in *Williams v Lister & Co.*[60] There Lister and Co as auctioneers had been instructed by third parties, who had let out furniture to the plaintiffs on hire purchase, to seize and to sell the furniture. This the auctioneers did and were duly sued by the plaintiffs for wrongful seizure. The auctioneers set about defending this action which was subsequently dismissed for want of prosecution after long delays by the plaintiffs. The auctioneers were held entitled to an indemnity in respect of their costs in defending the action. Since there was no successful action for wrongful seizure it cannot be said that the principals were guilty of any wrongful act in instructing them to seize and sell the furniture. Vaughan Williams LJ, who had been counsel for the unsuccessful auctioneers in the *Halbronn* case,[61] said:[62]

It is perfectly clear that this case falls within the common indemnity which arises where the agent is injured in carrying out his master's instructions, and because he has carried them out. In these circumstances the agent is entitled to be indemnified by his principal notwithstanding the observations of the learned judge in *Halbronn v International Horse Agency and Exchange Ltd*.

Buckley LJ was less restrained; he said:[63]

The defendants acted rightly as agents in defending the action, and in so doing incurred costs, and for these costs I think they are entitled to be indemnified. The case of *Halbronn v International Horse Agency and Exchange Ltd* is cited as a denial of that right. I must say that I do not understand that decision, but if it contains anything inconsistent with the present judgments, I am clearly of the opinion that it is wrong.

So long, therefore, as the auctioneer acts within his actual or implied authority, he may recover an indemnity in respect of losses incurred as a result of his performance of his duties. If, however, he goes beyond that which he is authorised to do, he will not be able to claim at common law on any implied indemnity.

[59] *Frixione v Tagliaferro & Sons* (1856) 10 Moo PCC 175 at 200.
[60] (1913) 109 LT 699, CA.   [61] Above, n 57.   [62] (1913) 109 LT 699 at 700.
[63] Above, n 62.

In *Sweeting v Turner*,[64] where the defendant auctioneer paid rent on premises owned by the vendor where goods he had auctioned were kept, in order to avoid the goods being levied for distress, it was held that no indemnity was available since his act was unauthorised. His claim that he had an agency of necessity failed because the goods had at that time ceased to be the property of the vendor-principal.

Whereas, as we have seen, an agent is entitled to defend an action, eg, in conversion,[65] arising out of the performance of his agency, he is not entitled to be indemnified as regards the costs of defending an action where the allegation against him was, substantially, that he was in *breach* of his agency. In *Tomlinson v Liquidators of Scottish Amalgamated Silk Ltd*,[66] the estate of a deceased director of a company in liquidation failed to recover on an indemnity claim either at common law or on the basis of a clause in his company's articles in respect of the expenses of (successfully) defending both criminal and civil charges of fraud brought against him in connection with his running of the affairs of the company. In answer to the estate's submission that the expenses arose by reason of acts done in the discharge of his duties as an agent of the company, Lord Tomlin in the House of Lords said:[67]

In my view the expenses incurred by reason of the allegations made against the deceased being allegations of matters which would have been a breach of his duty and which were held to be disproved or non-proven, are not expenses incurred by him by reason of an act done by him as a director in the discharge of his duties.

It has been held that where an auctioneer by virtue of his own mistake of the law incurs a liability, he will be unable to recover from his principal.[68] Similarly, where the auctioneer is negligent there will be no implied indemnity.[69] Finally, as with any implied term, there can be no implication in the face of an inconsistent express term in the contract.

LIEN

Grove J in *Hammonds v Barclay*[70] provided the classic definition of a lien arising at common law thus: 'A lien is a right in one man to retain that which is in his possession belonging to another until certain demands of him against the person in possession are satisfied.'[71]

---

[64] (1872) LR 7 QB 310, 41 LJQB 58. Above, ch 3.

[65] Unless, perhaps he defends without the consent of his principal; see *Spurrier v Elderton* (1803) 5 Esp 1, sed quaere.

[66] 1935 SC (HL) 1.   [67] 1935 SC (HL) 1 at 6.

[68] *Capp v Topham* (1805) 6 East 392, 2 Smith KB 443 where the auctioneer failed to take precautions to avoid auction duty being payable on an abortive sale under the candle. Contrast *Brittain v Lloyd* (1845) 14 M&W 762, 15 LJ Ex 43.

[69] *Jones v Nanney* (1824) 13 Price 76, M'Cle 25.   [70] (1802) 2 East 227.

[71] (1802) 2 East 227 at 235.

Property attached

An auctioneer has by virtue of the possession of his principal's property, a lien over it for his charges and remuneration. The right of retention of those goods (and documents of title in the case of land)[72] thus gives the auctioneer a security interest. This valuable right is established by custom and is independent of any right specifically provided for in his contract with his client. As long ago as 1788 it was said by the Lord Chief Justice:[73]

I entertain no doubt that an auctioneer has a possession coupled with an interest in goods which he is employed to sell, not a bare custody . . . an auctioneer also has a special property in him with a lien for the charges of the sale and the commission.

This dictum has since been endorsed in numerous cases.[74] The custom, as with most customs developed in commercial law, was established 'for the convenience of trade' and, in this area, with a view to encouraging 'factors to advance money upon goods in their possession or which must come into their hands as factors'.[75]

It is perhaps obvious that if an auctioneer is to have a lien over his principal's property, he must be entitled not only to retain it as against his principal but he must also be entitled to withhold the property from the *purchaser*. We shall see later that, independently, an auctioneer has rights against the purchaser with regard to the price and in this connection has a lien against him over the property; but, equally, in support of his rights against his vendor-principal, the auctioneer may resist a claim by the purchaser of the property in tort for wrongful interference with the goods knocked down to him.[76] The lien is a *possessory* right, however, and once the auctioneer parts with possession of the goods he loses his right.

In *Coppin v Walker*,[77] which involved an action by the auctioneer against the purchaser for the price, the court held that the auctioneer had disentitled himself from claiming the price which the purchaser sought to avoid paying, relying on a set-off against the vendor. The judges suggested that by parting with possession without giving the purchaser notice of his lien, the auctioneer lost it. However the auctioneer can, and usually will, let the purchaser take the property in return for the price since it is also well settled that he has a lien over the proceeds of sale. In *Robinson v Rutter* Lord Campbell CJ said: 'As auctioneer the plaintiff must be

---

[72] Which, it has been held in Canada, do not include plans of the property: *Blackburn v Macdonald* (1857) 6 UC CP 380, CA.

[73] *Williams v Millington* (1788) 1 Hy Bl 81 at 85 per Lord Loughborough LCJ.

[74] See eg *Lane v Tewson* (1841) 12 AD&El 116 n; *Woolfe v Horne* (1877) 2 QBD 355, 46 LJQB 534; *Benton v Campbell, Parker & Co Ltd* [1925] 2 KB 410, 94 LJQB 881; *Chelmsford Auctions Ltd v Poole* [1973] QB 542.

[75] *Houghton v Matthews* (1803) 3 Bos&P 485 at 486, 127 ER 263 at 264.

[76] *Lane v Tewson*, n 74 above.   [77] (1816) 7 Taunt 237, 2 Marsh 497.

supposed . . . to have had a lien upon the horse for the price and to have a right of lien on the price when paid for his commission and charges.'[78]

An auctioneer may also be protected if he takes merely a deposit rather than the whole price, provided that this is sufficient to cover his commission etc. However, the capacity in which he receives the deposit may be crucial. An auctioneer should perhaps take the deposit as agent of the vendor.[79] If the contract provides for him to receive it as 'stake-holder' (a provision regarded by Lord Denning MR as 'odd' and as a 'falsa demonstratio' in *Chelmsford Auctions Ltd v Poole*[80]), then in certain situations he will be unable to maintain a lien over the moneys vis-à-vis his principal. One example arose in *Skinner v Trustee of Property of Reed (Bankrupt)*,[81] where an auctioneer was instructed by a mortgagee of a farm to sell it free from the encumbrances. The property was sold to Skinner who paid the auctioneers a deposit of £3,000 as stake-holder. Before the sale was completed the vendor-mortgagees went bankrupt. Subsequently the contract of sale was completed and the auctioneers asserted a claim over the deposit monies in their hands. However the plaintiff-purchaser sought to have the money applied in or toward the discharge of the encumbrances which, contrary to the contract, had not been discharged. Cross J explained the position thus:[82]

If, as in this case, the stake-holder is an auctioneer who has a lien on the deposit for his commission and his disbursements, the question whether he can exercise his lien must, I think, depend on the trust on which in the event he holds the deposit. If the contract has gone off owing to the vendor's default, then clearly the auctioneer cannot exercise his lien for his charges because the deposit has never become the property of the vendor and is returnable in toto to the purchaser. If, on the other hand, the contract has gone off owing to the purchaser's default, it is quite obvious that the auctioneer can exercise his lien against the vendor because the deposit has become the absolute property of the vendor. But what is the position if the contract is completed . . . When the purchaser affirms the contract the vendor cannot in my judgement claim payment for the deposit in the hands of a stake-holder so long as there are outstanding encumbrances on the property sold which it is the vendor's duty to discharge . . . if a stake-holder is an auctioneer his lien will only attach to so much of the deposit as is not needed to discharge the encumbrance.

This is not a question of the auctioneer's right of lien being postponed in favour of other prior rights but rather that the deposit moneys, held as stake-holder, did not, in that character, ever become the property of the vendor so as to be capable of being affected by the lien which the auctioneer has over the vendor's property.

---

[78] (1855) 4 E&B 954 at 956, 119 ER 355 at 356; see also *Drinkwater v Goodwin* (1775) 1 Cowp 251; *Webb v Smith* (1885) 30 ChD 192, 55 LJ Ch 343, CA.

[79] Whether this is advantageous will depend on the circumstances. This matter is more fully discussed in ch 5.

[80] [1973] QB 542, [1973] 1 All ER 810, CA.   [81] [1967] 3 WLR 871.

[82] [1967] 3 WLR 871 at 874–6.

The question of priorities did arise however in *Webb v Smith*.[83] In this case the defendant auctioneers sold a brewery on behalf of a vendor who owed certain sums to the plaintiff-purchaser. The vendor by letter charged the proceeds of sale including certain deposit moneys in favour of the purchaser to the extent of this indebtedness. The auctioneers however claimed their lien in respect of their commission over the same fund. It was held that their lien took priority over the charge in favour of the purchaser. Here the charge in favour of the plaintiff was posterior to the lien. If the charge had effectively pre-dated the sale and the receipt of the deposit, it is thought that it would, on general principles, have taken priority.

Nature of the lien

A further aspect in *Webb v Smith*[84] concerned the nature of the lien possessed by an auctioneer: can it be exercised only over the specific property in respect of which the charges are incurred, or is it in the nature of a general lien attaching to a general balance in the hands of the auctioneer? The question arose because the auctioneers had also, as a distinct transaction, sold furniture belonging to the vendor and retained the balance of the proceeds of sale. Webb claimed that where a creditor held two separate funds he should pay himself out of that fund which did not prejudice the rights of another creditor. This is known as the doctrine of marshalling. The Court of Appeal held, in this case, that the doctrine was inapplicable because the auctioneers had subsequently accounted to their principal for the proceeds of sale of the furniture and thus had no lien over it. Lindley L J said:[85]

The vice of the argument for the plaintiff is that in truth there were not two funds to which the defendant could resort, that is, two funds standing upon an equal footing. The defendants had a superior right of lien as to the funds produced by the sale of the brewery.

He added however:

I think, however, that they could not have deprived the plaintiff of the benefit of his charge, if there had been two funds to which they might have resorted under equal circumstances.

This last comment begs a rather important question. If an auctioneer sells independently, under separate instructions, two items of property and their sale gives rise to separate claims for commission etc, can he exercise a lien over one item in respect of his commission earned on the sale of the other? A negative answer seems, generally, to be correct. It is true that in *Palmer*

---

[83] Above, n 78.   [84] Above, n 78.   [85] (1885) 30 ChD 192, CA at 202–3.

v Day & Sons[86] an auctioneer was held entitled to retain commission on the sale of a house out of the proceeds of sale of certain pictures, but this case turned on the application of a specific right of set-off provided by the Bankruptcy Acts.[87] The judge at first instance had held in favour of the auctioneer on the ground that there was one entire indivisible contract, but the Divisional Court found that the evidence did not support that contention. Lord Russell of Killowen LJ said:[88]

The case appears to us the ordinary one of auctioneers being instructed to sell first, the furniture and secondly the house . . . It therefore becomes necessary to consider whether his judgment can be supported on the other ground, that of mutual dealings [under] s 38 of the Bankruptcy Act 1883.

No lien will be available in respect of work done before the agency contract comes into being,[89] or for work outside the auctioneer's normal duties,[90] or where the auctioneer has waived his lien,[91] or where the auctioneer is estopped from setting it up by having previously denied the owner's title.[92] It is also possible that if an auctioneer exercising a lien accepts some other form of security instead — eg a promissory note — he will be taken to have abandoned his lien. Whether or not abandonment has occurred is a question of intention. In the case of an agent such as a solicitor, the prima facie inference is that he abandons his lien if he takes an alternative security from his client. That is because a solicitor has a special duty of disclosure vis-à-vis his client, but if the agent has no such special duty the inference will not be taken.[93] It is thought that an auctioneer is in this latter category.

Enforcement of lien

Where the lien sought to be enforced against the principal is over his goods the auctioneer may be put to the expense of keeping them properly. In the case of livestock there will be costs involved in feeding, and in the case of other goods possibly warehousing charges.[94] Since the auctioneer is a bailee

---

[86] [1895] 2 QB 618, 64 LJQB 807.
[87] Bankruptcy Act 1883, s 38. See now the Insolvency Act 1986, s 323. See also *Miller v Hutcheson and Dixon* (1881) 8 R (Ct of Sess) 489; *Houghton v Matthews* (n 75 above); *Scarfe v Morgan* (1838) 4 M&W 270, 7 LJ Ex 324.
[88] [1895] 2 QB 618 at 620–21.   [89] *Houghton v Matthews*, n 75 above.
[90] *Sanderson v Bell* (1834) 2 Cr&M 304, 3 LJ Ex 66.
[91] *Scarfe v Morgan* (n 87 above) where the court declined to hold that seeking to retain a mare for a general balance amounted to a waiver of his particular lien thereon for the charge on the particular occasion.
[92] *Dirks v Richards* (1842) 4 Man & G 574, 5 Scott NR 534.
[93] *In Re Taylor, Stileman, and Underwood, ex p Payne Collier* [1891] 1 Ch 590, 60 LJ Ch 525.
[94] In practice a lien over livestock is unlikely to arise; livestock auctioneers invariably deliver up these goods to the purchaser and, indeed, allow a week to a fortnight for payment. For livestock auctions see ch 10.

of the goods in his possession, it is his responsibility to care for them properly.[95] This duty may be onerous but, unless there is express provision in the contract of agency, the right of lien carries with it no right of sale; it is merely a passive interest giving rise only to a right to retain possession.[96] Auctioneers should, therefore, make express provision for a right of sale in such circumstances. Failing that, the court has discretion to allow a sale. In *Larner v Fawcett*[97] the Court of Appeal considered the ambit of its discretion under the precursor of the present rule: RSC Ord 29, r 4.[98] The court declined to lay down any principles but upheld the discretion of the judge at first instance who had ordered a sale of a filly in the hands of a racehorse trainer whose expenses had not been paid, there being a dispute as to ownership. However, the court did say that the mere fact that the person claiming a lien would be inconvenienced by having to retain the chattel pending determination of the issues was not, ipso facto, a reason for ordering a sale.

No problem of this sort arises where the lien is exercised against funds. An auctioneer retaining proceeds of sale as against his vendor can, and perhaps should, invest the sum and retain a proportion of the income derived therefrom. However, if pending a dispute between vendor and purchaser as to entitlement to a deposit, the auctioneer is required to pay the money into court, there is authority for the proposition that he is allowed to deduct his costs and expenses first and not wait until the determination of potentially protracted litigation.[99] The court may order the property subject to the lien to be released on the provision of security: RSC Ord 29, r 6.[100]

OTHER RIGHTS

There may be many other rights which an auctioneer may wish to reserve to himself in the contract with the vendor. For example, it is common to find in auctioneers' contracts provisions whereby the auctioneer is given: (a) complete discretion as to the description to be applied to the property to be sold; (b) reservation of the right to seek expert advice and to illustrate lots in literature at the seller's expense; (c) the exclusive right to bid on behalf

[95] See eg *Scarfe v Morgan* (n 87 above) and further ch 5.
[96] *Bartholomew v Freeman* (1877) 3 CPD 316, 38 LT 814; and see *Thames Iron Works Co v Patent Derrick Co* (1860) 1 John & H 93, 29 LJ Ch 714; *Larner v Fawcett* [1950] 2 All ER 727, CA.
[97] Above, n 96.
[98] See Appendix 3. The rule applies equally to County Court actions — see CCR 1981, Ord 13, r 7.
[99] See *Annersley v Muggridge* (1816) 1 Madd 593; *Yates v Farebrother* (1819) 4 Madd 239; *Blenkhorn v Penrose* (1880) 29 WR 237.
[100] See Appendix 3. CCR 1981, Ord 13, r 7 — see n 98 above.

of the seller when there is a reserve placed upon the property; (d) rights relating to insurance and warehousing; and (e) a right to accept rescission of the contract of sale where the lot is a deliberate forgery (as defined).

RIGHTS AGAINST THE PURCHASER

An auctioneer enjoys a number of rights against the purchaser. We have already stated that he has a lien on his principal's goods which may be enforced against the purchaser in so far as he may retain possession of them and successfully defend an action for their delivery up or for damages for their detention. Perhaps of fundamental importance, however, is an auctioneer's right to sue the purchaser for the price of goods sold.

ACTION FOR THE PRICE OF GOODS

Normally, unless an agent contracts personally, he cannot be sued or sue on the contract made by him, because the contract is that of the principal.[101] However, an auctioneer has long been held able to sue the purchaser for the price of goods.[102] The right was first enunciated in *Williams v Millington*,[103] and has subsequently been reiterated many times. However the exact principle upon which this right is based is uncertain. A number of explanations have been given: namely that it is based on his lien, or upon his special property in the goods, or on some collateral contract with the purchaser. It may be important to establish the precise basis, where for example, the lien has been lost or waived, but it is in any event clear that when the auctioneer sues the purchaser, eg for the price, he does not do so in enforcement of the contract of sale itself. In *Benton v Campbell Parker & Company Ltd*,[104] Salter J said:[105]

The auctioneer has a special property in the chattel delivered to him for sale, he has a lien on it and on the price of it. These rights . . . do not arise from the contract of sale which binds only the buyer and the principal. They arise from the contract which the auctioneer makes on his own account with the buyer . . . It is clear therefore that the auctioneer does not sue for the price by virtue of the contract of sale.

If the true explanation is that he sues on some separate personal contract, then an auctioneer's right to sue for the price of goods provides no special exception to the principle that an agent cannot sue on his principal's con-

---

[101] See eg *Bowstead on Agency* (15th edn, 1985) Sweet & Maxwell, arts 105 et seq.
[102] But not land. See below.
[103] (1788) 1 Hy Bl 81. The position is the same in Canada. See *Coate v Terry* (1875) 24 C&P 571; and in Scotland, see *Mackenzie v Cormack* 1950 SC 183, 1950 SLT 139.
[104] [1925] 2 KB 410, 94 LJKB 881.   [105] [1925] 2 KB 410 at 415–6.

tract. That this is the true explanation was expressly left open by the Court of Appeal in *Wilson & Sons v Pike*[106] where recovery by the auctioneer was on behalf of the vendor-principal whose contract the auctioneer was enforcing. In *Chelmsford Auctions Ltd v Poole*[107] Lord Denning MR emphasised that a sale by auction involved three contracts: not only those between the principal-vendor and the auctioneer and between the vendor and the purchaser, but a third[108]

between the auctioneer and the highest bidder (the purchaser). The auctioneer has possession of the goods and has a lien on them for the whole price. He is not bound to deliver the goods to the purchaser except on receiving the price ... If he does allow the purchaser to take delivery without paying the price ... the auctioneer can sue in his own name for the full price.

The reference to the 'full price' is significant. In this case the auctioneers knocked down a car to Poole for £57. Poole paid a deposit of £7 which sufficed to cover the auctioneer's charges and commission but he refused to accept or take delivery of the vehicle on the grounds that it was unroadworthy. Poole sought to meet the auctioneer's claim for the price with the defence that since their charges were covered, their interest had been satisfied, and they had suffered no loss; thus they had no cause of action. In fact, the auctioneers had accounted to their principal for the price realised. The Conditions of Sale expressly provided that the auctioneers could recover the price from a purchaser, but Lord Denning held that, apart from the express provision, the common law recognised such a right and that the right was not barred by receipt of a deposit covering the auctioneers' commission. When it is recalled that the auctioneer is generally under a duty in sales of goods to obtain the price for the vendor, the conclusion reached by the Court of Appeal in this case seems correct.

The next question which arises is whether the purchaser can successfully defend an action for the price brought by the auctioneer by showing that he has already paid the principal-vendor. Consonant with the principle that the auctioneer has a separate contract with the purchaser for the price (but not perhaps with the commercial considerations upon which it is based), the answer seems to be that payment to the vendor does not avoid the purchaser's liability to the auctioneer. Such was laid down in *Robinson v Rutter*.[109] The report of this case is not very full and it is unclear whether the plaintiff auctioneers had received their commission etc. If they had not, the decision is justifiable since the auctioneer by delivering up the goods (here a horse) to the defendant-purchaser gave up his lien therefor in exchange for the promise to be paid. However, if the auctioneer has received his commission, payment of the price to the vendor should avoid liability since

---

[106] [1949] 1 KB 176, [1948] 2 All ER 267, CA.   [107] [1973] QB 542.
[108] [1973] QB 542 at 548.   [109] (1855) 4 E&B 954, 24 LJQB 250.

the auctioneer's interests are fully satisfied and he is not at risk of a suit by the principal for the price.

This last proposition seems to be supported by two cases distinguished by Lord Denning in *Chelmsford Auctions Ltd v Poole*, viz *Holmes v Tutton*[110] and *Grice v Kenrick*.[111] In *Holmes v Tutton* the question arose whether, in an action by auctioneers for the price of goods sold and delivered, the purchaser could resist the claim by showing that he had a set-off against the vendor. Lord Campbell CJ, who had also given judgment in *Robinson v Rutter*, said:[112]

> There may be some doubt whether the auctioneer, not having the possession of the goods, and it not appearing whether he sold in his own name, and his lien for the price having been covered by the money he received, so that he might be found to have paid himself out of the proceeds received could have sued the plaintiffs for the price of the goods.[113] But if he could, we think that in an action for the price of the goods so sold it would be a good answer . . . to show for the defendant that the lien of the auctioneer was satisfied *and that he was suing merely for the principal*, and that there was a set-off as between the principal and the vendee of the goods.

The italicised words allow for a different conclusion, it is suggested, where there is such a set-off but the auctioneer is out of pocket by reason of having accounted to his principal for the price; in such a situation the auctioneer is suing on his own account and not 'merely for the principal'. In *Grice v Kenrick* the vendor had by prior arrangement agreed that the purchaser could set-off the price against debts he was owed. This was unknown to the auctioneers who, having deducted their charges, paid a sum on account to the vendor for the proceeds of sale of certain lots. The purchaser then warned the auctioneers of the arrangement he had with the vendor and told them not to pay any further sums to him. However the auctioneers failed to take heed and paid over the balance then in their hands. On these facts the court held that the purchaser could resist a claim for the price brought by the auctioneers. Hannen J said:[114]

> By the terms of the original agreement between the defendant and [the vendor] the defendant was to have the goods without payment; and it appeared that as between the plaintiff and [the vendor] the plaintiff's charges . . . had been satisfied before action. If the plaintiff were to recover the amount in the present action he would be bound to hand over the whole proceeds to his employer, who, however, by agreement between him and the defendant, was not entitled to receive anything. Any facts, therefore, which show that [the vendor] would not be entitled to recover, established a defence to an action brought by the plaintiff.

---

[110] (1855) 5 E&B 65, 24 LJQB 346.   [111] (1870) LR 5 QB 340, 39 LJQB 175.

[112] (1855) 5 E&B 65 at 81–2, emphasis added.

[113] A doubt resolved in favour of the auctioneer in *Chelmsford Auctions Ltd v Poole* [1973] QB 542, [1973] 1 All ER 810, CA.

[114] (1870) LR 5 QB 340 at 345.

A few comments need to be made in respect of this dictum. First, the apparent breadth of the last sentence is clearly limited by the context of the preceding words. Second, the bar to recovery only operated in this case on the finding that the auctioneers, having been satisfied, were effectively seeking to recover for their vendor-principal. If there had been a question of potential liability of the auctioneers to their client for the price or if they had paid the price to him, the position would, it is suggested, have been different for it could then not be said that they would be bound to disgorge the fruits of their action.[115] Similarly, if an auctioneer has been instructed to defray debts due to other creditors of the vendor out of the proceeds of sale, a set-off claimed by a purchaser will not be a good defence to an action by the auctioneer for the price save only to the extent of any balance payable to the vendor.[116]

Where a principal agrees that another may take goods at auction in satisfaction of a prior claim, the analysis may be that there is in fact no sale at auction at all. This is what occurred in the unusual case of *Bartlett v Purnell*.[117] The defendant was granted a legacy of £200 in the will of a testator whose estate was disposed of at auction. The executor of the will agreed before the sale that the defendant could take goods up to the value of her legacy in satisfaction thereof. The auction particulars provided for part payment to be paid on sale and the balance on delivery. The defendant 'bought' goods to the value of £145 and refused to pay for them. The auctioneers were held unable to sue her for the price. Coleridge J held that had she been a purchaser she would have been liable but that on the facts she did not buy at auction: 'she was to take the goods; but they were to be reckoned at the highest price bidden for them. The auctioneer wrote the name down but that was merely the necessary way of fixing such price.'[118]

We said earlier that the precise basis of the auctioneer's rights against the purchaser has been the subject of differing formulations. Whilst it is clear that an auctioneer has a lien on the goods and on the proceeds of sale for his charges and commission, it cannot be that the lien itself is the basis upon which the auctioneer may sue for the price. A lien is a *possessory* security which in itself confers no right of action. If possession of the goods were a pre-requisite to recovery of the price, no such action would lie once the auctioneer had delivered the goods to the purchaser. There are dicta which suggest that possession is necessary. In *Coppin v Walker*,[119] the plaintiff auctioneer sold goods of one Appleton in the latter's house. However he also included certain goods belonging to Appleton without disclosing this

---

[115] See also *Traynor v Larkin* (1916) 50 ILT 17 to a similar effect.
[116] *M Manley & Sons Ltd v Berkett* [1912] 2 KB 329, 81 LJKB 1232.
[117] (1836) 4 Ad&El 792.   [118] (1836) 4 Ad&El 792.
[119] (1816) 7 Taunt 237, 2 Marsh 497, above.

fact. The defendant purchased certain of these goods and took them away without paying but without demur by the auctioneer. The defendant was a creditor of Appleton and refused to pay. The court refused the auctioneer's claim for the price. Park J said:[120]

The plaintiff [sic] had a clear right of set-off against Appleton; and the auctioneer has parted with his lien, without giving the defendant notice of any claim which he had on the price, and therefore it would be gross iniquity to say that the defendant is not entitled to his set-off.

And Burrough J opined that 'it is enough for the court to decide on, that the auctioneer has parted with his lien.'[121]

The marginal note to this report states that there is no implied contract to pay on the auctioneer giving up his lien by delivery of the goods. However, in *Coppin v Craig*,[122] a subsequent case arising on the same facts, the court suggested that an action for the price did arise on such an implied promise to pay, the consideration therefor being the forgoing of the lien by delivery without payment.

In many of the cases discussed above, the auctioneer is suing for the price just because he has parted with possession without payment; it is submitted that the better view is that the right to sue does not depend upon the continuing existence of the lien itself, but rather on a implied contract arising from the delivery up of possession without payment. *Coppin v Walker* is better explained by treating the act of the auctioneer as expressly negativing such an implication, as suggested by Dallas J in that case. In other words, there will be no contract arising out of the relinquishment of the lien if, in the circumstances, the auctioneer *waives* it; but merely allowing the purchaser to take the goods will not, of itself, amount to waiver.[123]

Thus the right to sue for the price does not depend upon the continued existence of the lien but *arises out* of the lien or special property in the goods.[124] Therefore, the auctioneer must originally have possessed such an interest; and a prerequisite for this is possession of the goods. For this purpose it is settled that an auctioneer has possession when he sells goods in situ at the owner's premises. Such was expressly stated in *Williams v Millington*[125] itself and was approved in *Mackenzie v Cormack*[126] where

---

[120] (1816) 7 Taunt 237 at 241–2.   [121] Above, n 120.

[122] (1816) 7 Taunt 243, 2 Marsh 501.

[123] See eg *Jarvis v Chapple* (1815) 2 Chit 387; *Maxwell v Coyle and Wadsworth* (1889) 33 ILT 131.

[124] The special property or interest in the goods is, of course, derived from the interest of the vendor. If, therefore, the vendor has no title or right to sell the goods, the auctioneer cannot sue for the price: *Dickenson v Naul* (1833) 4 B&Ad 638, 1 Nev&M KB 721.

[125] (1788) 1 Hy Bl 81.   [126] 1950 SC 183, 1950 SLT 139.

furniture and plenishings of Keiss Castle were sold by auction at the castle. Moreover, it has been held that an auctioneer had sufficient possession to maintain an action for the price when a vendor-principal himself sold a horse at the auction rooms after buying it in at a previously abortive auction, the auctioneer's contract providing for commission to be payable in such circumstances and the auctioneer having paid the price to the vendor.[127]

In cattle auctions[128] it quite frequently occurs that private sales are effected by the owners outside the ring but on the auction premises before or after the auction sale is conducted, and the sale is then 'booked' with the auctioneer. Such sales have only relatively recently been the subject of judicial analysis. In *Murphy v Howlett* Diplock J (as he then was) described the practice thus:[129]

If the auctioneer accepts the booking he pays the seller . . . the amount of the price agreed between the seller and the intending buyer . . . As regards the cattle, the subject matter of the booked sale, the seller upon receiving his cheque or cash from the auctioneer is no longer interested in the transaction [and] the auctioneer . . . exercises all the rights of the owner . . . including the right of retaking possession if he was parted with it, and the right of re-sale.

In this type of sale the true legal analysis is that there are two concurrent sales of the cattle: a sale by the owner to the auctioneer at the agreed price less commission and one by the auctioneer to the buyer at the agreed price. Here the auctioneer suing for the price does so not on any implied contract arising from delivery but on a quite separate contract of *sale* in which he is a principal.

There is another situation in which the auctioneer sues in fact on a quite independent contract and that is where he 'advances' money to the purchaser by taking an IOU[130] or a cheque.[131] When an auctioneer takes payment in this form he may be doing so in accordance with his instructions or without the consent of the vendor-principal. *Cleave v Moore*[132] is an example of the former situation and the court held the auctioneer entitled to sue on the IOU. In such a case the obligation owed by the purchaser to the vendor to pay eg the deposit is extinguished. Where, however, the auctioneer accepts an instrument instead of cash in breach of the Conditions of Sale and without express consent, the purchaser remains liable to the vendor but this does not preclude the auctioneer from suing on the note. As Palles CB explained in *Hodgens v Keon*:[133]

---

[127] *Freeman v Farrow* (1886) 2 TLR 547.   [128] On which see ch 10.
[129] (1960) 176 EG 311 at 312.   [130] *Hodgens v Keon* (1894) 2 IR 657.
[131] *Hindle v Brown* (1908) 98 LT 791.   [132] (1857) 28 LT OS 255, 3 Jur NS 48.
[133] [1894] 2 IR 657 at 660.

The agreement by the auctioneer involved a warranty by him of authority to [accept] it; . . . By accepting it without . . . consent he plainly incurred a liability to [the vendor]. There is evidence that this acceptance was at the request of the defendant, and it therefore constituted a sufficient consideration for a promise by the defendant to the plaintiff from whom the consideration moved.[134]

Hodgens v Keon and *Cleave v Moore* both involved claims by auctioneers in respect of a deposit but there have been similar decisions in connection with claims for the price[135] and auction fees.[136]

The significance of the fact that recovery by the auctioneer is on a quite separate and independent contract lies, in the case of sales of goods, in the fact that this contract is unaffected by factors which may vitiate the contract of sale. In *Hindle v Brown*,[137] for example, the auctioneers were held entitled to sue on a cheque given them in respect of the sale of pictures notwithstanding that the sale was induced by fraudulent mis-representations made by the vendor. Here it was found by the jury that the auctioneers, who had accounted to the vendor for the price, were entirely innocent of the fraud. Had it been otherwise, their contract for the cheque would have been tainted with the fraud and voidable. It has recently been held that the auctioneer's right to sue on a cheque given for the deposit survives the vendor's justifiable rescission of the contract of sale.[138]

It is frequently the case these days that auctioneers expressly reserve to themselves a right to resell property upon the failure of the purchaser to accept it, a right not concomitant with a lien at common law. If such a right is exercised the auctioneer may no longer sue for the price but can maintain an action for damages for the difference, if any, between the auction price and the price on resale.[139] However, unless the court construes the right of sale as a duty to sell, the purchaser will be unable to resist an action for the price where the auctioneer declines to re-sell. In *Robinson, Fisher and Harding v Behar*[140] the auction particulars provided: 'All lots uncleared within [the stipulated time] shall be re-sold by public or private sale and the deficiency (if any) attending such re-sale shall be made good by the de-faulter at this sale.' The court declined to construe this provision as a mandatory order to sell (despite the use of the word 'shall') and held that the condition merely gave the auctioneers an option.

---

[134] See *Pollway Ltd v Abdullah* [1974] 2 All ER 381, [1974] 1 WLR 493 for a more recent formulation.
[135] *Hindle v Brown* (1907) 98 LT 44; affd (1908) 98 LT 791, CA; *Trapp v Prescott* (1912) 17 BCR 298, 50 SCR 263.
[136] *Gillen v Gibson* (1909) 44 ILT 17; *Montgomery v Fleming* (1905) 39 ILT 229.
[137] Above, n 135; and see *Campbell v Smith* (1887) 13 VLR 439.
[138] *Pollway Ltd v Abdullah* (n 134 above).
[139] *Lamond v Davall* (1847) 9 QB 1030, 16 LJQB 136.
[140] (1927) 1 KB 513, 96 LJKB 150. See comparable clauses in Appendix 1.

SALES OF LAND

Sales of land are in many respects not treated by the law in the same way as contracts for the sale of goods. In the context of claims by auctioneers for the price or for the deposit, the law does not permit an auctioneer in his own right to recover from a defaulting purchaser where the sale concerns land.[141] We have seen that in the case of sales of goods, in the normal case, the auctioneer sues not on the contract for sale itself but on a separate contract arising from his relinquishment of the lien or from his special property in the goods which possession gives him. In the case of land there can be no such special property. In the Irish case of *Cherry v Anderson*, Palles CB explained:[142]

upon the sale of real estate the auctioneer has no right to sue in his own name, analogous to his right in the sale of goods. In the latter case he has, or is deemed to have, a possession of the goods and a qualified property in them. On the sale of real property the right to sue depends upon the written contract alone: and unless that contract be so framed as to render the auctioneer the ostensible vendor . . . he cannot on the sale of real estate maintain in his own name an action against the purchaser.

This case concerned an action for fees in connection with the sale of lease-hold property which, under the Conditions of Sale, were payable to the auctioneer by the purchaser. The auctioneer was held unable to recover those fees. Whilst the distinction between land and goods renders an auctioneer unable to sue for the price or for the deposit in the case of land, it seems hard on the auctioneer that he cannot recover his fees from a purchaser who contracts with a vendor that he shall pay them. Moreover, it seems that in such circumstances the auctioneer will be unable to claim on a quantum meruit from his vendor principal since his contract with the vendor is inconsistent with it. An auctioneer of land will, therefore, be well advised always to insist in his contract with the vendor that the latter be responsible for his fees. This would still leave the vendor free to make whatever agreement he wishes with the purchaser in respect of them but will not affect the auctioneer's contractual rights against his principal.

If the auctioneer contracts *personally* for the sale he may, of course, sue for the price.[143] He may also recover in those circumstances where the court treats him as having advanced money to the purchaser, as for example when he accepts a promissory note or a cheque. In view of the foregoing it is

---

[141] He can however be joined as a plaintiff with the vendor in an action for specific performance of the contract of sale. For joinder of parties to an action, see RSC Ord 15, r 4 (Appendix 3). The County Court equivalent is CCR 1981, Ord 5, r 2.

[142] (1876) IR 10 CL 204 at 209. And see also *Evans v Evans* (1835) 3 Ad & El 132, 1 Hat & W 239.

[143] See eg *Fisher v Marsh* (1865) 6 B&S 411, 34 LJQB 177.

perhaps not surprising that of those cases discussed above, *Cleave v Moore, Hodgens v Keon, Pollway Ltd v Abdullah* and *Montgomery v Fleming*[144] all involved auctions of interests in land where, therefore, the only way in which the auctioneer could recover was by establishing a separate and independent contract.

RIGHTS AGAINST THIRD PARTIES

An auctioneer, although in no direct relationship with third parties, does have certain rights against them or in relation to them whereby he may protect his interest in the goods in his possession. These take the form of a positive right to bring actions against persons who unlawfully interfere with the goods in his possession, and immunities from certain otherwise lawful actions which may be taken against him. In addition, an auctioneer may avail himself of procedural remedies when adverse claims are brought by two or more persons to the goods in his possession or to the proceeds of sale.

WRONGFUL INTERFERENCE WITH GOODS

We have seen that an auctioneer's special property in or possession of the goods gives rise to certain rights against both vendor and purchaser of them. Similarly, it gives him rights against third parties who wrongfully interfere with the goods. Thus, although not the owner, the auctioneer may maintain an action in respect of the torts of trespass, conversion and detinue[145] committed against the goods in his possession. The right was expressly recognised in *Williams v Millington*,[146] where it was said that it makes no difference whether the goods are located in the auctioneer's own premises or sold on the premises of the owner. Since the auctioneer pursues these rights by virtue of possession rather than ownership (save where he sells his own goods) once the auctioneer parts with possession, the right is lost.[147]

It is perhaps obvious that the kind of interference predicated consists commonly of a wrongful damaging or taking away of the goods; and whilst trespass to land is possible, land cannot be converted or detained. Thus the

---

[144] See above, nn 130, 132, 134 and 136.

[145] Now, since 1977, abolished as a nominate tort. See Torts (Interference with Goods) Act 1977.

[146] (1788) 1 Hy Bl 81.

[147] See eg observation of Lord Campbell CJ in *Holmes v Tutton* (1855) 5 E&B 65 at 82.

auctioneer's rights here under discussion are only available with respect to goods. However, some goods may be affixed to land or buildings on it. Depending upon the degree and purpose of affixation, items may be regarded in law as either goods or land. If a third party interferes with such property, an auctioneer will be unable to sue in tort if the true legal analysis is that the property in question is land, for then he has no right of possession. Such a situation arose in *Davis v Danks*,[148] where an auctioneer was employed to sell certain machinery and other items attached to the owner's house. The defendant, to whom certain of these items had been knocked down, removed them without paying. The auctioneer sued in trespass but was held unable to recover. Park B said:[149]

[The auctioneer] cannot be considered to have such possession of the house and fixtures as would entitle him to maintain an action of trespass . . . against a party for an injury to them . . . He was only authorised at the time of his employment to sell the right of detaching and removing the fixtures, and he had no possession of them as materials and he was not in possession of the freehold.

The position would be otherwise if it was contemplated by the parties that the auctioneer was to sever the fixtures and sell them as chattels. The question of when an item will be held to be part of the land and therefore not 'goods' is beyond the scope of this book, but a few examples may indicate that no easy answer can be given (and see further, chapter 10):

(a) The following have been held to remain goods:
   (i) pictures fixed with screws into panelled walls in recesses made for them when the panelling was installed,
   (ii) a life-size statue weighing half a ton placed on a plinth forming an integral part of the elevation of a house,
   (iii) large tapestries up to 14 feet in length attached to walls and tacked onto canvas-covered wooden frames nailed to the walls.
(b) The following became land:
   (i) sculptured marble vases placed on plinths inside a house,
   (ii) a picture and tapestry attached as part of a scheme to make a room into a specimen of an Elizabethan room.

PRIVILEGE FROM DISTRESS

Distress is an ancient common law self-help remedy whereby a creditor is permitted to seize goods belonging to his debtor to be held as a pledge to compel the satisfaction of a debt or other obligation. There are certain

---

[148] (1849) 3 Exch 435, 18 LJ Ex 213.   [149] (1849) 3 Exch 435 at 437.

specific statutory rights of distress, but most commonly it was a remedy employed by landlords in respect of rent owed by a tenant.[150] In general a landlord could distrain on any goods found on the premises out of which the rent issued, whether the goods were the property of the tenant or not. However, the common law developed a number of important exceptions to this somewhat Draconian rule, the most important, for our purposes, being a general privilege relating to goods delivered to a person exercising a public trade.

In *Adams v Grane and Osborne*,[151] it was held that this immunity applied to goods sent to an auctioneer for the purpose of sale, where a landlord had sought to distrain goods which had been delivered to an auctioneer, the goods being on premises sub-let as auction rooms to the auctioneer by a tenant who was in arrears for rent. The privilege is grounded in public policy, namely: 'For the convenience and benefit of trade . . .'.[152] It appears that the quality of the auctioneer's possession of the premises in question is immaterial. In *Brown v Arundell*,[153] it was alleged that the auctioneer was trespassing on the property in which he carried out the auction. The Chief Justice found that the evidence did not support that allegation but, even if it had, it would not affect the privilege.

Thus far, we have been concerned with distraints against goods found on the auctioneer's premises pursuant to claims against the owners or occupiers of those premises. Where distress is levied against a person's goods on his *own* premises, there will be no immunity by virtue of the fact that the owner has happened to put them into the hands of an auctioneer for sale. So was held in *Lyons v Elliott*.[154] As Lush J observed:[155]

If therefore we were to hold this plate privileged, we must necessarily hold that as soon as a tenant gets into difficulties he has nothing to do but call in an auctioneer, and so oust the landlord of his remedy by distress, although he could not remove the goods for the same purpose. That, it seems to me, would be a very strange extension of the doctrine, and one by no means justified either by convenience or authority.

These old cases help to explain the policy behind the privilege but the law is now governed by the Law of Distress Amendment Act 1908. This Act simply provides, so far as is material, that a goods-owner not being a tenant or having any beneficial interest in premises in which his goods are, whose goods are being distrained upon, may serve notice of these facts upon the

---

[150] See generally 13 Halsbury's Laws (4th edn) para 201 f.

[151] (1833) 1 Cr&M 380, 2 LJ Ex 105.

[152] (1833) 1 Cr&M 380 at 387 per Bayley B. See also per Blackburn J in *Lyons v Elliott* (1876) 1 QBD 210 at 214. The immunity extends to goods kept in the yard outside the premises: *Williams v Holmes* (1853) 8 Exch 861, 22 LJ Ex 283.

[153] (1850) 10 CB 54, 20 LJCP 30.   [154] Above, n 152.

[155] (1876) 1 QBD 210 at 216. The authority of this decision is probably not weakened by the fact that the chattels in question belonged to neither the owner of the premises nor the auctioneer but to a third person who had sent them to the house for auction.

landlord and that if a landlord disregards the notice he shall be guilty of an illegal trespass. The goods-owner may, inter alia, obtain restoration of his goods and bring action against the landlord or his agent for trespass to them.

INTERPLEADER

Where an auctioneer is faced with adverse claims from two or more persons, it would be inconvenient to leave him to elect whom to satisfy. The unsatisfied claimant would presumably seek redress against him. Where the auctioneer himself claims no interest in the subject matter of the dispute, it would be more efficient for the real disputants to claim against each other. The rules of court[156] provide a simple procedure in these circumstances, known as 'interpleader', whereby the person in this position says: 'I have a fund in my possession in which I claim no personal interest, and to which you the defendants set up competing claims; pay me my costs and I will bring the fund into court, and you shall contest it between yourselves.' This was the formulation given by Lord Cottenham LG in *Hoggart v Cutts*,[157] a case which well illustrates both the kind of difficulty an auctioneer can find himself in and the fact that as an essential pre-requisite, the two or more claims must be truly adverse or competing. In this case an auctioneer was instructed to sell an estate belonging to one Thodey. The property was knocked down to the defendant Cutts who duly paid a deposit to the auctioneer. Disputes then arose between vendor and purchaser and Thodey, alleging that the contract was at an end and the deposit forfeited, instructed the auctioneer to re-sell. Subsequently the property was re-sold to Vickers, who also paid a deposit.

Cutts sought specific performance of his contract whilst Vickers sought the return of his deposit. Thodey, as vendor, claimed the deposits in respect of both sales. The Lord Chancellor, after describing interpleader proceedings in the words quoted above, held that for interpleader relief to be appropriate: 'The case must be one in which the fund is a matter of contest between the two parties, *and in which the litigation between those parties will decide all their respective rights with respect to the fund*'.[158] His Lordship held that Vickers' claim and the claims by Cutts and Thodey were not susceptible of interpleading; Vickers' claim to a return of his deposit could not possibly settle the questions between the other parties. Thus he was not a proper party to these proceedings. The proceedings were proper, however, with regard to the claims involving Cutts and Thodey.

---

[156] In the High Court by RSC Ord 17 and in the County Court by CCR Ord 33, r 6 (see Appendix 3).
[157] (1841) Cr&Ph 197 at 204.   [158] (1841) Cr&Ph 197 at 205, emphasis added.

Similarly, interpleader by an auctioneer has been disallowed when the claims made against him were one by the vendor of a horse for the price and another by the purchaser of it for damages for breach of warranty concerning the condition of the animal.[159]

The ability to interplead is most useful to an auctioneer where there is a dispute about title[160] to a lot; if, for example, he is instructed to sell by one person and then another claims to be the true owner, it may well be sensible for the auctioneer either to interplead with regard to the item itself, or, if the parties agree, sell the goods as planned and interplead in respect of their proceeds of sale.

The mode of application for interpleader relief is laid down in RSC Ord 17, r 3, for the High Court, and CCR Ord 33, r 6, for proceedings in the County Court. The court has a discretion whether to grant the relief sought. One of the matters on which the applicant must adduce evidence is that he has not 'colluded' with any of the claimants. Collusion does not necessarily connote any moral wrong-doing — it suffices if the applicant has placed himself in the position of being sued at the request and in the interests of one of the claimants.[161] Collusion, however, will only be a bar if raised by the *other* claimant. In *Thompson v Wright*,[162] auctioneers were instructed to sell goods by Wright. They advertised them for sale and were notified by Thompson that the goods were his. Wright gave the auctioneers an indemnity and instructed them to sell. This they duly did and then sought to interplead as to the rival claims to the proceeds of sale between Wright and Thompson. The vendors objected, but it was held that interpleader lay; the taking of an indemnity did not deprive the applicants of the benefits of interpleader — it did not amount to collusion — and, in any event, collusion could not be raised by the person who was a party to it.

---

[159] *Wright v Freeman* (1879) 48 LJQB 276; see also *Ingham v Walker* (1887) 3 TLR 448, CA. For a case where two firms of auctioneers were *defendants* in an interpleader action which failed, see *Greatorex & Co v Shackle* [1895] 2 QB 249, 64 LJQB 634.

[160] Problems of title to goods are dealt with in ch 6.

[161] *Belcher v Smith* (1832) 9 Bing 82, LJCP 167, and see Appendix 4.

[162] (1884) 13 QBD 632, 54 LJQB 32.

Duties and Liabilities of the Auctioneer

DUTIES TO THE VENDOR

We have seen that the authority of an auctioneer and his rights will depend ultimately upon the precise terms of the contract with his principal within the framework of the general rules of common law, in particular, the law of agency. The same is true as regards his duties and liabilities. Some specific duties will be provided for expressly in his contract but, in addition, the law lays down a number of general obligations concomitant with the agency relationship. These may conveniently be classified as:

(a) duties relating to performance;
(b) fiduciary duties;
(c) the duty to account for goods or proceeds;
(d) the duty to care for the goods.

DUTIES RELATING TO PERFORMANCE

To act in accordance with his instructions

It is axiomatic that an auctioneer, like any agent, may only perform those acts which are authorised. If he fails to obey his instructions he will be liable to his principal for any loss arising. This liability will be an additional consequence to that of failing to bring about a contract between his principal and a third party with the resultant loss of commission. Thus, as we have already seen in dealing with authority to receive payment of the price or deposit, if an auctioneer is expressly instructed to obtain cash only and he takes some other form of payment he will be liable to his vendor.[1]

Of course, if the auctioneer acts within his implied or usual authority he will incur no liability notwithstanding that he does something which has not been expressly authorised.

If the auctioneer is in doubt as to his instructions he should seek clarification. In the unusual case of *Re Bishop, ex p Langley, ex p Smith*[2] it was

[1] See above, ch 3.
[2] (1879) 13 Ch D 110, 49 LJ Bcy 1. If the auctioneer only receives notice of an injunction after the sale although before receipt of the proceeds, the court will not set aside the sale. See *Freehold Permanent Building Society v Choate* (1871) 3 Chy Chrs 440.

stated that on receipt of a telegram from solicitors advising that an injunction restraining sale had been issued by the Bankruptcy Court an auctioneer was under a duty to communicate with his principal although it was not incumbent upon him to communicate with the court. In this case the auctioneer communicated with his client, the sheriff levying execution on the goods of a judgment debtor who had subsequently filed a liquidation petition. Having received instructions to proceed with the sale, and bona fide believing the telegram to be a ruse by the debtor, he was held not liable in contempt of court when he went ahead with the sale.

To act with skill and care

An auctioneer, as a professional, is under a general duty under the common law to exercise proper skill and care in and about the sale of his principal's property. As Lord Ellenborough long ago put it in an oft-cited dictum:[3]

In the present case the plaintiff appears to have been guilty of gross negligence and the defendant has suffered an injury instead of deriving any benefit from employing him . . . I pay an auctioneer, as I do any other professional man for the exercise of skill on my behalf and I have a right to the exercise of such skill as is normally possessed by men of that profession.

That case decided that an auctioneer lost his right to commission in circumstances where he had had to return the purchaser's deposit due to the failure of the vendor of a lease to show his lessor's title. It was found that it was usual practice in such cases for the auctioneer to insert a proviso in the Conditions of Sale that the vendor was not to be called upon to show the title of the lessor and the auctioneer's negligence consisted of the failure to include such a provision. Whilst this case concerned only the auctioneer's liability to forgo his commission, he will also be liable in damages for loss occasioned to his principal by reason of his negligence. It is impossible to provide an exhaustive list of the circumstances in which such a liability may arise, but a number of instances are given below.[4]

What is the standard of care required

Lord Ellenborough referred to the exercise of 'such skill as is normally possessed by men of that profession'. In the nature of things, some pro-

---

[3] *Denew v Daverell* (1813) 3 Camp 451 at 452–3. This has more recently been made the subject of statutory provision: Supply of Goods and Services Act 1982, s 13 (see Appendix 2).
[4] Several examples are given by May J in *Fordham v Christie Manson & Woods* (1977) 244 EG 213 at 219–20. It has been decided at first instance in *Balsamo v Medici* [1984] 2 All ER 304, [1984] 1 WLR 951, that a sub-agent can be liable in negligence to an owner of goods for damage thereto (but not for misapplication of the proceeds of sale). Thus an auctioneer instructed to sell by one who is merely the agent of the owner will owe a duty of care to that owner although there is no contractual relationship between them.

fessionals are more skilled in certain aspects of their work than others. Moreover, when it comes to matters such as valuation, particularly in, say, the art world, it is recognised that some auctioneers are specialists whereas others may be more in the way of general practitioners. Recent decisions have established that the law takes account of such matters.

In *Alchemy (International) Ltd v Tattersalls Ltd*[5] the defendant auctioneers were sued by the vendor of a colt for failing to obtain an appropriate price. The main issue in the case was whether, the apparent highest bidder having disappeared, the auctioneers acted properly in delaying putting up the horse again whilst they sought (unsuccessfully) to trace and hold the successful bidder to his bargain. At the re-auction some days later, the colt achieved some 200,000 guineas less than originally.

Experts were called by both sides and gave divergent views as to what was the proper or sensible thing for the auctioneer to have done in such a dilemma. The Court applied a statement of the law adopted in a medical malpractice case: *Maynard v West Midlands Regional Health Authority*[6] in which the court endorsed an earlier dictum viz:

In the realm of diagnosis and treatment there is ample scope for genuine difference of opinion and one man clearly is not negligent merely because his conclusion differs from that of other professional men . . .

The true test for establishing negligence in diagnosis or treatment on the part of a doctor is whether he has been proved to be guilty of such failure as no doctor of ordinary skill would be guilty of if acting with ordinary care.[7]

Thus it is not enough to show that there is a body of competent professional opinion which would have acted differently if there also exists a body of professional opinion, equally competent, which regards the actions which are called in to question as reasonable in the circumstances. This approach was confirmed in the important case of *Luxmoore-May v Messenger May Baverstock*.[8] In this case, which will be discussed in some detail below, the Court of Appeal, reversing the decision of the judge at first instance, held provincial auctioneers not liable for missing a 'sleeper'. In dealing with the standard of care Slade L J said:

The defendants submitted . . . that they should be regarded as akin to general practitioners and that (1) the required standard of skill and care allows for differing views, and even a wrong view, without the practitioner holding that view (necessarily) being held in breach of his duty, (2) the standard is to be judged by reference only to what may be expected of the general practitioner, not the specialist, here provincial auctioneers, rather than one of the leading auction houses, and (3) compliance with the required standard is to be judged by reference to the actual circumstances confronting the practitioners at the material time, rather than with

[5] (1985) EG 675.   [6] [1985] 1 All ER 635.
[7] The dictum is that of Lord President (Clyde) in *Hunter v Hamley* 1955 SLT 213 at 217.
[8] [1990] 1 All ER 1067, CA.

the benefit of hindsight. The judge 'unhesitatingly' accepted these propositions, and so would I.

At first instance the judge had held the auctioneers liable on the basis that any competent valuer must inevitably have appreciated that the pictures in question had a greater potential than crossed the defendant firm's mind at least such as to put them under a duty to investigate the possibilities further than had been done in this case. It appears, therefore, that 'general practitioners' will be regarded as negligent only if it could be said that no auctioneer of ordinary skill and care would have acted or failed to act as had occurred in the case in question.

Duty to secure a binding agreement

There is a number of old cases which establish that an auctioneer is liable in negligence if he fails to ensure that a binding contract has been entered into by the purchaser. Frequently the default of the auctioneer has consisted of a failure to ensure that a contract evidenced in writing sufficient to satisfy the requirements of the Statute of Frauds 1677 and subsequent enactments based thereon, has been procured. These requirements no longer obtain with regard to either sales of land[9] or goods.[10] With regard to land sales the duty owed by an auctioneer was explained in an Irish case as follows:[11]

[An auctioneer] . . . impliedly by undertaking a work undertakes to bring reasonable care, skill and diligence to the doing of it. An important part of an auctioneer's work, when he sells real estate, on the very lowest estimate of his legal obligation to his employer is to take reasonable care to have a binding contract, under the Statute of Frauds, entered into by the person who purchases the property at the auction. It may be that he does not undertake without any qualification to make a binding contract.

The explanation of the last sentence of this dictum may be that an auctioneer would not be liable for failing to make a binding contract if the failure is caused by, eg defects in title or other similar vitiating elements for which he is not responsible. We have already seen that an auctioneer will frequently include a power to accept rescission of a contract — eg in the case of fraud, but that he probably has no authority to do so in the absence of such express provision.[12]

There are, however, other ways in which an auctioneer may fail to bring about a contract binding the purchaser: he may for example simply fail to accept a bid. In the New Zealand case of *Logie v Gillies & Hislop*[13] the

---

[9] See the discussion in ch 9, Sales of land by auction or tender.
[10] Law Reform (Enforcement of Contracts) Act 1954, s 2.
[11] *Kavanagh v Cuthbert* (1874) IR 9 CL 136 per Dowse B at 140.
[12] See above, ch 3.   [13] (1885) 4 NZLR 65.

reserve placed on an estate at Dunedin was £2,000. A bid of that amount was made, but inexplicably, the auctioneer did not accept it and the property was bought in at £2,100. After several subsequent abortive auctions at decreasing reserves, the estate was eventually sold for £1,250. It was held that the auctioneer was liable to his principal-vendor for damages, the proper measure of which was the difference between the wrongfully unaccepted bid and the true market value of the property at that time, the subsequent sale price achieved being only one means of ascertaining that value. In this case the court found the market price to have been £1,775 so that the loss was £225 plus £12 regarding the expenses of the abortive sale. It is clear then that a negligent failure to accept the bid will render an auctioneer liable in damages for any loss arising. Many auctioneers' Conditions of Sale reserve the right to refuse any bid, but it is questionable whether such a provision would protect an auctioneer in this type of situation where he does not exercise a discretion to refuse a bid but carelessly fails to accept it to the detriment of the vendor.[14]

In these days when international auctions have become more commonplace it appears that an auctioneer is at risk of a negligence suit if his, or his audience's, linguistic skills are lacking so that a mistake is made as to the price which a lot has reached, entitling a purchaser to set aside the contract. This occurred in *Friedrich v A Monnickendam Ltd*,[15] where the chairman of Christie's himself conducted a major jewellery auction in Geneva. According to the law of Geneva the auction had to be conducted in French. Many of the potential purchasers invited to the sale were from England and the United States of America. The auctioneer's French was not good and a genuine mistake occurred whereby the defendant purchaser thought that a lot had reached 190,000 Swiss francs, whereas it had in fact reached 290,000 Swiss francs, an extravagantly high price. Under Swiss law the purchaser, an English diamond-cutter, was held entitled to avoid the contract on the grounds of mistake. The case involved an action by a vendor against the purchaser but the question of negligence by the auctioneer was considered. Lord Denning said:

There was concurrent negligence on the part of the auctioneer. He should have known that the bid of 290,000 Swiss francs was not such a sum as Mr Monnickendam the expert diamond-cutter would knowingly bid. The auctioneer should therefore have assured himself by the clearest words in English that Mr Monnickendam appreciated that the figure was 290,000 Swiss francs.

Stamp LJ was of the view that the lack of care consisted not so much in the imperfection of the auctioneer's French as in a failure to give the bids in English as well, given that the auction particulars were printed in both

---

14 For a discussion of the position relating to disputed bids see ch 6.
15 (1973) 228 EG 1311.

English and French and that English-speaking people were specifically solicited to attend.[16]

Duty to describe the property accurately

Property put up for auction, whether land or goods is likely to have some description applied. This may be fairly short or there may be a fairly detailed description of any given lot. In addition to whatever may be said in the catalogue, the auctioneer may comment on the property, its condition and so forth, from the rostrum.[17]

It is probably true to say that no aspect of auctioneering is so fraught with potential hazard as the application of description to lots to be sold. Misdescriptions may give rise to criminal sanctions under the Trade Descriptions Act 1968, in the case of goods (see chapter 8) or under the Property Misdescriptions Act 1991, in the case of land (see chapter 9). Additionally, misdescribing the property may subject the auctioneer to civil liability at the suit of his client the seller and the purchaser. It is in relation to such potential civil liability, particularly in relation to the purchaser of goods that auctioneers' Conditions frequently contain exclusion clauses. The viability of these is discussed in detail in chapter 6.

In this part of this chapter we shall deal with the potential liability of the auctioneer vis-à-vis his client, the seller.

There are two aspects to this: First an auctioneer may, by misdescribing the property, render the seller liable to compensate a purchaser misled thereby and the auctioneer will be under a civil liability to the seller to indemnify him in respect of that loss. Secondly, and quite separately, an auctioneer may directly cause loss to his client as a result of a failure to describe the property to its optimum value.

(1) Exposing the vendor to liability to the purchaser

This may arise in two ways:

(a) Sale of Goods Act 1979 s 13 as amended.   Section 13 provides:

(1) where is there is a contract for the sale of goods by description, there is an implied term that the goods will correspond with the description

and subsection (3) of that section provides 'a sale of goods is not prevented from being a sale by description by reason only that, being exposed for sale or hire, they are selected by the buyer'.

---

[16] The third Lord Justice of Appeal, James L J criticised the lack of clarity in the conduct of the auction but declined to categorise the auctioneer as negligent.

[17] A misrepresentation can take the form of a misleading photograph — see *Atlantic Estates v Ezekiel* [1991] 2 EGLR 202 where a photograph depicted a thriving wine bar but the liquor licence had been revoked. See also *St. Marylebone Propeity Co Ltd v Payne* [1994] EG 156 discussed below.

As is pointed out in the more detailed discussion on s 13 in chapter 6 below, auction sales are clearly within the definition of sales by description within this statutory provision. Thus, if the purchaser can show that the goods are not as described, either in the auction particulars or orally from the rostrum, he may be entitled to reject them and claim his purchase money back. Alternatively he may claim damages being the difference between the goods he has actually bought and their value as described. To the extent that the auctioneer is responsible for applying the description to the lot in question he will be liable to indemnify his principal-seller for any loss to which he will have been exposed as against the purchaser.

A fairly early illustration of the principle involved, though the case concerned land, is *Parker v Fairebrother*[18] where an auctioneer engaged to sell certain properties described them as three-storey buildings. In fact they were only comprised of two storeys. The vendor was liable to compensate the purchaser as a result of this misdescription and the auctioneer was held bound to indemnify him.

(b) Liability under the Misrepresentation Act 1967. An additional hazard for auctioneers is the possibility that the purchaser may be able to claim rescission of the contract and, or alternatively, damages for misrepresentations which emanate either from catalogue descriptions, or, once again, from oral statements made from the rostrum. This is an alternative route for the buyer of goods at auctions and is also available in land auctions.[19]

Whilst it is clear that the auctioneer, as agent, incurs no *direct* liability to the purchaser under the Act provided his representations made on behalf of his seller client are authorised expressly or impliedly, he can expose the seller to action under the Act and, to the extent that the seller is made liable for an actionable misrepresentation, the auctioneer will be liable to indemnify him.

An action under the Misrepresentation Act 1967 will lie not only for fraudulent and negligent misrepresentations but also for those which are innocently made, that is, where the auctioneer has a reasonable belief in the truth of the statement he makes.

A detailed discussion of the remedies for misrepresentation under the Act is beyond the scope of this book[20] but a purchaser induced to enter into a contract by a material misrepresentation is normally entitled to rescind the contract or to damages in lieu of rescission. The purchaser who is a victim of an innocent misrepresentation may be denied rescission and be

---

[18] (1853) 21 LTOS 128, ICR 323.

[19] Such a right existed prior to the 1967 Act — see *Flight v Booth* (1834) 1 Bing NC 370 and see *King Brothers (Finance) Ltd v North Western British Road Services Ltd* [1986] 2 EGLR 253.

[20] See standard works on contract law such as Chitty on Contracts (26th edn, 1989), Sweet and Maxwell, London.

awarded damages instead. The right to rescind may be lost also where there is a lapse of time.[21]

Where damages are awarded it may be possible for the purchaser to recover not only reliance losses ie the difference between the price paid and the value of the asset acquired but also incidental losses which he incurs in respect of the item bought. This is illustrated by the case of *Norton v O'Callaghan*[22] where there was a claim against the vendor directly by the purchaser in misrepresentation under the Misrepresentation Act 1967. The facts were as follows:

Lot 200 in the September yearling sales at Newmarket in September 1981 was a chestnut colt named Fondu. Contained in the description of the colt was its pedigree and this included the information that his sire was Nonalco and his dam was Habanna whose sire in turn was Habitat. It was established that the Habitat line was an important factor because at that time he was beginning to establish himself with a reputation as a sire of good brood mares. The trainer acting on behalf of the plaintiffs in this action rec-ommended the horse and was eventually the successful bidder for him at 26,000 gns. (The trainer in fact 'kept a leg' ie 25% interest in the horse for himself.)

Fondu had no success whatever in his various races including a complete flop in a trainer's invitation race. In June or July 1983 it was discovered that a mistake had been made, apparently at the stud where Fondu was born, and that Fondu was not a son of Habanna at all. In fact his dam was an American horse called Moon Min, a horse whose pedigree suggested that he might well be able to perform on the dirt tracks of America but not on the turf of England.

The owners kept the horse in training until October 1983 and thereafter partly at home and with other stables in the hope that he might provide a useful point-to-point horse for the owner's son. Thus training and upkeep fees continued to be incurred until August 1984.

Subsequently a writ was issued claiming damages for breach of contract and/or misrepresentation and judgment in default was obtained; that is to say the sellers did not defend. The reason for this was that they themselves had brought in the stud owners as third parties and had obtained judgment in default from them. The case was, therefore, not concerned with liability but with damages assessment. It should be noted that the buyers did not claim a right to reject the horse and, given the delays that had occurred post-discovery of the 'defect' after 1983, such a claim would probably have been unsuccessful. Nor, it should be noted, did the buyers claim for 'loss of bargain' ie they did not claim for any loss in respect of potential resale at a

---

[21] See, for example, *Leaf v International Galleries* [1950] 2 KB 86 where a buyer of a painting wrongly described as a Constable was held disentitled to rescind the contract when he dis-covered the error five years after the sale.

[22] [1990] 3 All ER 191.

profit, stud value etc. They claimed merely for their 'reliance losses' namely the difference between the price they paid and the value of the horse actually acquired. They also claimed the cost of training fees and upkeep. These two elements need to be dealt with separately.

(i) Reliance Loss. The buyer claimed the difference between 26,000 gns and £1,500 which was the value of Fondu by the end of May/June 1983 when the defect was discovered, such value having been 'achieved' by the then known track record of Fondu.

The judge thought that this raised a difficult point because if Fondu had been correctly described as a Moon Min foal he would have had a substantial value to perhaps another purchaser and perhaps a value at least as high as the price paid ie 26,000 gns. It is also the case that the normal rule for the measure of damages in such situations is the difference between the price paid and the value at acquisition of the item. Thus subsequent falls, eg in market price are not taken into account. However, the judge held that in this case despite that normal rule, the buyers were entitled to the difference between the price paid and the value at discovery of the breach ie £1,500.

With respect, this seems right: the misdescription masked a latent defect, viz the inability of the horse to perform on turf. The fall in value after acquisition was due to that latent defect, extant at the time of sale.

(ii) Training Expenses. The defendants argued here that the training expenses, which ran to several thousand pounds were not recoverable because the buyers would have incurred such fees whatever horse they had bought: if the horse had been as described and they had bought him they would have incurred such expenses. The judge held this to be irrelevant. The fact that they might have spent such or similar sums on another animal did not preclude their recovery of the expenses which flowed from their purchasing of this animal which they would not have purchased had he been correctly described.

It should be noted that in this case the disappointed buyers sued the vendor direct but the principles would apply equally to an action against the auctioneers.

In the non-auction case of *East and Another v Mara and Another*[23] the Court of Appeal held that where a purchaser was fraudulently induced to enter into a contract to buy a business the measure of damages was to be assessed on the basis of compensating the plaintiff for all the loss he had suffered and not, as in breach of contract, on the basis of putting him in as good a position as if a statement had been true. Therefore, in addition to reliance losses, a purchaser would be able to recover loss of profits that he might have expected to make had he instead invested his money in an

---

[23] [1991] 2 All ER 733.

alternative business bought for a similar sum. This hypothetical profit element is somewhat crudely assessed.

It can, therefore, be seen that, perhaps not surprisingly, the law has traditionally been prepared to allow recovery for a greater range of losses in the case of fraud than would be the case where misrepresentations are made merely carelessly or, indeed, innocently. But where a plaintiff recovers under the Misrepresentation Act 1967 the courts have now construed the act in such a way that whatever type of misrepresentation is involved the fraud basis of recovery is appropriate.[24]

This discussion has proceeded on the basis that the auctioneer would be liable to his client if he, the auctioneer, has exposed him to liability for misdescription vis-à-vis the buyer. Of course, if the auctioneer has made statements which are expressly authorised by the seller the auctioneer will not be under any duty to indemnify him. In *Museprime Properties Limited v Adhill Properties Limited*[25] the auctioneer gave an assurance to the ultimately successful bidder about the status of rent reviews on business properties being sold. The auctioneer had directly sought confirmation of the accuracy of these statements from the vendor. When these turned out to be inaccurate and the purchaser sued, the auctioneer was held not liable.

(2) Failure to describe the property to its best advantage

Conditions of Sale frequently make express the right of the auctioneer to apply his own description to the properties offered for sale.[26] In the absence of such, an auctioneer will be liable in damages to his principal if he departs from his descriptions to the detriment of the vendor in circumstances where the vendor expressly or impliedly instructs him to sell under his descriptions. In *Brown v Draper & Co*[27] the vendor handed the auctioneer a box of items together with a list describing them. The auctioneers sold them under different descriptions and the vendor sued in negligence. He recovered damages being the difference between the prices which the goods would probably have achieved had they been sold under the vendor's descriptions, and the prices they actually fetched.

It is important, therefore, that auctioneers expressly reserve the right to sell under their own descriptions. However, if they do, it is equally important that they take care to describe the property accurately to its best advantage. Failure to do so, so that the sale fails to attract the appropriate class of bidders, or the optimum price, may render the auctioneers liable in negligence. An instructive case is *Cuckmere Brick Co Ltd v Mutual Finance Ltd*,[28] which involved a dispute between mortgagors and mortgagees of

---

[24] See *Royscot Trust v Rogerson* [1991] 3 All ER 294.   [25] [1990] EGCS 29.
[26] See eg Christie's Conditions condition B 1 (a)(ii) (see Appendix 1).
[27] (1975) 119 Sol Jo 300, 233 EG 929.
[28] [1971] Ch 949, [1971] 2 All ER 633. For observations as to valuation evidence see *Johnson v Ribbins* (1975) 235 EG 757 per Walton J at 761.

certain development land. The plaintiff mortgagors obtained finance to develop a site with 100 flats and obtained planning permission therefor. Subsequently, due to financial difficulties, they resolved instead to build 33 houses, a less lucrative, but less expensive scheme. They obtained planning permission for this revision. Subsequently they defaulted on the mortgage. The defendant bankers entered into possession and, in exercise of their power of sale under the mortgage, put the site up for auction. The auctioneers described the property as having planning permission for 33 houses but omitted to mention the permission for the more valuable flat development scheme. The main reason for this omission was that they took a pessimistic view as to the economic value of such a development and decided that it was not an attractive proposition. The sale of the site as described, realised £44,000. The judge at first instance awarded damages against the mortgagees on the basis that, properly described to include the planning consent for 100 flats, the land would have realised £65,000. Although this was not in issue in this decision it seems clear that the auctioneers would be liable to indemnify their principals in such a case. The Court of Appeal upheld the decision although there was some disagreement about the proper method of computing the true value of the property. Two of the judges considered that the conscious omission of the auctioneers amounted to negligence but one, Cross LJ, considered it to be merely an error of judgment. However, whilst the pessimistic evaluation of the property was not itself negligent, Cross LJ held them negligent in being so confident of its correctness as not to see to it that the earlier planning permission for flats was mentioned in the particulars in the hope at least of attracting some developers prepared to bid more for the property for that purpose.

Under-selling the vendor's goods

However, the real nightmare for many auctioneers will probably be that of missing a 'sleeper' and we now turn to the *Luxmoore-May case*[29] which requires detailed consideration. When the High Court judgment was handed down in 1989 it set alarm bells ringing in auctioneers' offices around the country because it seemed to suggest that a misattribution, even in so notoriously difficult a field as fine art, could easily be negligent.

Mrs Luxmoore-May instructed her late husband's firm to sell two paintings which had 'hung unadmired in a dark corner of the plaintiff's hall way' and an employee came round to look at them. She thought they might be worth about £30 but agreed to value them and gave Mrs Luxmoore-May a receipt for them on which was written 'for research' (this, it was held, gave rise to an express contractual duty to carry out research into the pictures which may or may not be a significant factor — see later).

---

[29] See n 8 above.

The employee, Mrs Z showed them to the firm's Fine Art Consultant, a dealer about whose credentials as an expert the judge was to be somewhat disparaging, but whose reputation was subsequently rescued to some extent by the Court of Appeal. He did not think much of them and valued them at between some £30–£50 the pair. Mrs Z next time she happened to be going to Christie's took them along as an after-thought and asked them at the front counter what they thought of them. Five to ten minutes later an employee of Christie's returned them without favourable comment.

Subsequently the paintings were put up for sale as lot 394 out of a total of 417 lots. The catalogue described them blandly as: 'English school. Hounds by Rocky Seashore. Panel pair. Oil on paper. 5.75 inches × 9 inches.' A reserve of £40 was placed upon them.

To everyone's delight they fetched £840 but the pleasure was relatively short lived. Five months later the paintings were sold at Sotheby's for £88,000 as a pair of Foxhounds by Stubbs. Mrs Luxmore-May was held, at first instance, entitled to recover the difference between the price obtained on her sale and the subsequent sale at Sotheby's.

Whilst the judge was at pains to point out that not every auctioneer who missed a 'sleeper' would necessarily be negligent, in this particular case the auctioneers were because

any competent valuer must inevitably have appreciated in these pictures a substantially greater potential than ever crossed [their] mind.

Thus the liability was squarely based on a failure to spot the potential and do the necessary further investigative work. It should also be noted that whilst it was clear in this case that there was a direct and specific contractual duty to research the pictures, it is thought that the judge was prepared to find that the duty existed independently as a commitment to the contract as agent for sale.

The Court of Appeal, no doubt to the relief of the auctions world, reversed the decision. A number of important issues were singled out:

(1) What was the duty of care?

The duty was found to be one to express a considered opinion as to the sale value of the Foxhound pictures and for that purpose to take further appropriate advice.

(2) What is the standard of care required?

Very importantly the Court of Appeal confirmed the finding at first instance here that a valid distinction should be made between those who may fairly be described by analogy with the medical profession as 'general practitioners' and specialists or consultants. This provincial firm of auctioneers fell squarely within the general practitioner group and the Court of Appeal held that, as in the case of the medical man in the realm of diagnosis and treatment, 'there is ample scope for genuine difference of opinion and one man clearly is not negligent merely because his conclusion differs from that of other professional men'. Thus the true test is not to see whether or not the auctioneer got his 'diagnosis' wrong but whether he has been guilty of such failure as no auctioneer of ordinary skill would be guilty of acting with ordinary care.[30]

It is clear therefore that the degree of skill and care which one is entitled to demand of a provincial auction house in such matters is rather less than one would be entitled to demand from, say, Christie's or Sotheby's. As Lord Justice Slade pointed out:[31]

Attribution . . . is not an exact science, the judgment in the very nature of things may be fallible and may turn out to be wrong. Accordingly provided that the valuer has done his job honestly and with due diligence I think that the court should be cautious before convicting him of professional negligence merely because he has failed to be the first to spot a 'sleeper'.

(3) Discharge of the Duty of Care

The Court of Appeal found that the auctioneers would have been acting in discharge of their duty if they had simply passed on the views of their consultant so the court did not have to consider whether or not they had discharged their duty by getting the advice they did from Christie's. However the judges opined that that would have sufficed.

(4) Quantum of Damages

Since no liability was found the issue of damages did not arise for consideration but the Court of Appeal was by no means satisfied that the correct measure would have been the difference between the £840 and the £88,000 obtained at the Sotheby's sale. There were a number of factors which contributed to the achievement of this price and such might not necessarily recur. It is important to note that the pictures were considerably 'restored' by Sotheby's before the sale and looked very different from the neglected articles sold by the defendant auctioneers.

Finally the Court of Appeal did venture to suggest that they were by no means convinced that the evidence produced in court demonstrated that the attribution to Stubbs was 'right'; the evidence was conflicting on this point.

The case is one of immense interest and, whilst it leaves auction houses happier than they will have been at the end of the High Court hearing, there is no doubt that auctioneers remain liable potentially for misattributions which depress the price obtained at auction and also for advice on values

---

[30] See the earlier discussion above.   [31] [1990] 1 All ER 1067 at p 1076.

and reserves which is given carelessly. Attempts to exclude liability for this in the contract with the client will again be subject to the test of reasonableness.[32]

One issue of some interest to the specialist auction houses is when consulted in the way that Christie's was (ie rather casually for an instant appraisal) what liability, if any, might they incur if they are wrong. At first instance the judge in a rather throw-away remark said that Christie's could not themselves have been liable to the provincial auctioneers however negligent they might have been. This issue was not considered by the Court of Appeal. However it is strongly arguable that unless the enquiry made of the consultant auction house is so casual as to negate any inference of reliance by the enquirer on the person possessed of the special skill, it is difficult to understand why a consultant auction house or indeed an employed consultant should not be liable for any negligent mis-statement under the *Hedley Byrne* principles.

Duty to obtain the deposit and price

We have already briefly adverted in chapter 3 to the question whether an auctioneer is liable to his principal if he fails to obtain the proceeds of sale or part of them or obtains them otherwise than in cash. In *Hibbert v Bayley*,[33] a ship was put up for sale by auction upon certain conditions including that the highest bidder should forthwith sign the contract and pay a deposit. The ship was knocked down at £2,950 and the bidder gave his name as 'Shaw & Co.' Bristol. The purchaser then excused himself from signing the contract and paying the deposit asking for half an hour to arrange matters. He disappeared and the ship was subsequently sold, after intervening lots, for £2,600. The plaintiff vendors claimed the difference, ie £350, from the defendants alleging negligence, inter alia, in failing to procure the deposit. Earle CJ directed the jury as follows:[34]

The question is, whether you think that there was a breach of duty — that is, a want of due care, in letting the purchaser go away without signing or paying, and without declaring the bidding to be void and putting the ship up again for sale *instanter*. By the conditions of sale . . . the purchaser was to pay a deposit immediately.

The jury found for the plaintiff vendor but awarded only 40 shillings nominal damages. It is not clear whether the breach of duty consisted of not obtaining the deposit or not putting the ship up for sale again immediately

---

[32] Auctioneers may regard themselves, with some justification, as being 'between a rock and a hard place': if they fail to describe a lot to its full potential, they may incur liability to the seller; if they overdescribe it, they may be liable *directly* to the purchaser: see *De Balkany v Christie Manson & Woods Ltd.* (The Independent Jan 19 1995 see further ch 6).

[33] (1860) 2 F&F 48.   [34] (1860) 2 F&F 48 at 50.

or whether the two defaults were regarded as interlinked, but it would be wrong to assume that, in the absence of express instructions to procure the deposit immediately as existed here, it would always be negligent to permit a purchaser time to pay and to leave the auction rooms without doing so. In this case evidence was given that such practice was common when the purchaser was known to the auctioneer or left an address, known to be genuine, in London.

Auction Conditions of Sale today frequently give auctioneers a discretion whether to allow the purchaser credit. In *Cyril Andrade Ltd v Sotheby & Co*,[35] a case involving some famous personnel, the auctioneers knocked down a fine suit of armour belonging originally to Count Von Trapp to a Mr Bartel who had previously acted, and they believed presently to be acting, for the American newspaper tycoon William Randolph Hearst. The sale price was £5,000 and, acting on this belief, the auctioneers allowed Mr Bartel to depart without taking a deposit from him. The conditions of sale provided that a deposit was payable 'if required'.[36] The sale was repudiated by Mr Hearst who said that Mr Bartel was not his agent and the auctioneers returned the armour to their clients. The plaintiff-vendors claimed £2,500 being the 50 per cent deposit they alleged ought to have been taken. Sotheby's gave evidence that they did not normally demand deposits unless they did not know or trust the purchaser. On these facts it was held that there was no breach of duty by the auctioneers.

The issue as to whether an auctioneer is liable to the seller if he causes loss by delaying in re-offering a lot where the purchaser disappears was considered in detail in *Alchemy (International) Limited v Tattersalls Limited*.[37] The facts, briefly, were as follows. In the September 1983 bloodstock sales at Newmarket, Tattersalls introduced an innovation: the first day, a Tuesday, was to be set aside for yearlings of exceptional pedigree vetted by the auctioneers. The sales were to be called the 'High Flyer Premier Yearling Sales' and the object was obviously to attract the big money to that opening day. In this the auctioneers were successful because they did attract, amongst others, several of the sons of the ruler of Dubai and on that day lot 117, a foal of 'Hello Gorgeous' achieved a European record price of 1.5 million guineas.

The immediately preceding lot, 116, was a 'Riverman' colt and it was with this lot that the case is concerned. This colt had a reserve of 150,000 guineas and was brought into the ring towards the end of the day at 8.00 pm. Bidding proceeded briskly and the colt was knocked down to a Mr Flood for 430,000 guineas. However Flood denied that he had made a bid of that figure claiming that he withdrew at 410,000 guineas; one Omar Assi was the

---

[35] (1931) 47 TLR 244.
[36] Contrast Sotheby's current condition 6(b) and Christie's condition 5(c) (see Appendix 1).
[37] [1985] 2 EGLR 17.

under-bidder though whether at 420,000 or only at 400,000 guineas, as he claimed, was in dispute.

The bidding was video-recorded and there seems little doubt that the colt was properly knocked down to Mr Flood at the price of 430,000 guineas. However he refused to give his name and address to the auctioneers, denied that he was the successful bidder and absented himself from the scene. He was subsequently arrested at Heathrow.

Little or no blame was attached by the sellers to Tattersalls over this, but claimed that Tattersalls were negligent in not there and then, or at the latest at the end of that first day, re-auctioning the colt or at least announcing that they would be doing so. The colt was not in fact put up again until the Thursday. The reason for this was that the auctioneer decided that it was better to try either to get Flood to honour his bid or to track down the under-bidder and secure a private treaty sale with him at the under-bid price. In the result he was unsuccessful in both these endeavours and the colt was knocked down for 200,000 guineas three days later. It is clear that by that date some of the big money had been expended.

There was no dispute about the scope of the duty owed by the auctioneers, viz to exercise reasonable care to obtain the best price for their vendor-client. Condition 4 of the Conditions of Sale of Tattersalls in terms gave the auctioneers the option, in the circumstances which arose, of putting the lot up again or selling privately either immediately or later. Experts were called on both sides and, not surprisingly, gave divergent views as to what was the proper or sensible thing for the auctioneer to have done in such a dilemma. But the interest in the case lies in the formulation of the proper approach and role of the court in such cases involving a conflict of expert evidence. As we have indicated earlier, the court applied by analogy tests which had been applied in cases involving alleged medical malpractice under which it was recognised that a specialist (which clearly Tattersalls here were) would not be liable merely because they had acted in a way which was contrary to that in which similar specialists might have done provided there was a respectable body of opinion which would have accepted their actions as proper. The judge concluded:

In my judgment the relevant expert evidence taken as a whole demonstrates . . . that [the auctioneer's] actions and decisions were fully . . . in line with a respectable body of professional opinion.

Therefore Tattersalls were not negligent.

FIDUCIARY DUTIES

Inherent in the agency relationship is the notion that it is based upon trust. An agent is in a fiduciary position vis-à-vis his principal and, as a consequence, owes him certain duties.[38] These may variously be described as duties of loyalty or duties of good faith. Essentially this means that an agent must not so place himself that his personal interests may conflict with his duty to his principal. The main instances include:

(a) taking commission from both parties,
(b) purchasing the principal's property,
(c) obtaining a secret profit.

Taking commission from both parties

The practice of auctioneers charging buyers a commission or premium on sales in addition to that payable by the vendor is commonplace today.[39] As such it is often much objected to by buyers but it may also act to the detriment of the vendor-principal. As Sargeant LJ explained in a case involving an hotel broker who sought to charge both his principal and the buyer commission:[40]

He is seeking to impose an onerous condition on the purchaser which might very well prevent the purchaser ever taking advantage of the order to view; and to impose such a condition would be in flagrant violation of his duty to the vendor which is to bring along any purchaser who can be found on the terms of the vendor paying . . . the agreed commission . . . [The] condition . . . might have the effect of stalling off a purchaser and preventing the plaintiff from securing for the vendor such a purchaser as would be acceptable to the vendor.

As regards auctions, it is clear that the imposition of a buyers' premium could have the effect of, at least, depressing the price which a buyer would be prepared to pay and this is obviously contrary to the vendor's interests.

It is not a situation, however, where the auctioneer's interests and duty conflict since it will be likewise in his and his vendor's interests to obtain the highest possible price and, therefore, taking commission from the buyer will not involve a breach of fiduciary duty provided that the auctioneer fully discloses to his vendor-principal the existence of a contractual provision entitling him so to do.[41] The position would be otherwise if the agent's interest was to obtain a low price as occurred in *Rhodes v McAlister*,[42] where a buyer had promised an agent the difference between the top price which the buyer was prepared to pay and the price at which it was sold to him. Here the agent arranged with the vendor for commission on the sale and

---

[38] For a detailed analysis of the fiduciary relationship *see Bowstead on Agency* (15th edn, 1985) Sweet & Maxwell, arts 45–55.
[39] See eg Sotheby's Conditions of Business, condition 3, and Christie's Conditions of Sale A4 and C8 (see Appendix 1).
[40] *Fullwood v Hurley* [1928] 1 KB 498 at 505, 96 LJKB 976.   [41] Above, n 40.
[42] (1923) 29 Com Cas 19, CA.

was held unable to recover from the buyer. Whether, in fact, the principal suffers any detriment is here irrelevant.[43]

Another situation where there may appear to be a potential conflict of interest is where an auctioneer, for gain or otherwise, agrees to bid on behalf of a prospective purchaser; for then he is acting as agent for two parties whose interests are antithetical. As to whether such activity is lawful is nowadays not a matter for much doubt. In *Bexwell v Christie*[44] Lord Mansfield suggested that it was, although there the question did not strictly arise for decision. However in *Fullwood v Hurley*,[45] which concerned the taking of remuneration from both sides, Lord Hamworth MR stated categorically: 'If and so long as the agent is the agent of one party he cannot engage to become the agent of another principal without leave of the first principal with whom he has originally established his agency.'[46] The crucial words are 'without leave'. It is thought that provided the auctioneer notifies the vendor and obtains his consent, actual or tacit, the practice will not involve a breach of fiduciary duty.

Sotheby's (Condition 34) provide that they will execute bids for buyers (whilst discouraging the practice somewhat by warning them that their interests are best served by personal attendance). Christie's similarly notify their willingness to accept 'commissions' (Condition A 12).[47]

Purchasing the principal's property

The purchase by an auctioneer of his principal's property is another activity giving rise to a potential conflict of interest and duty, and once again he is enjoined from so doing unless he has made the fullest disclosure of all relevant facts to his principal. As it was put by a textbook writer in the nineteenth century:[48]

If then, the seller were permitted as the agent of another, to become the purchaser, his duty to his principal and his own interest would stand in direct opposition to each other; and thus a temptation, perhaps in many cases too strong for resistance by men of flexible morals or hackneyed in the common devices of worldly business, would be held out, which would betray them into gross misconduct . . .

If an auctioneer does, without the requisite disclosure and consent, buy his client's property,[49] two consequences may flow. First, he will not be able to

---

[43] See eg per Scrutton LJ (1923) 29 Com Cas 19 at 27.
[44] (1776) 1 Cowp 395 at 397.   [45] Above, n 40.   [46] Above, n 40.
[47] The practice was commented on with approval (albeit obiter) in *Fordham v Christie Manson & Woods Ltd* (1977) 244 EG 213 at 215 per May J.
[48] *Story on Agency* p 262 para 210, cited in *Salomons v Pender* (1856) 3 H&C 639 at 643–4. And see per Coram Richards LTB in *Oliver v Court* (1820) 8 Price 127 at 160–1.
[49] By himself or in consortium with others see *Wentworth v Lloyd* (1863) 32 Beav 467; *Dunne v English* (1874) LR 18 Eq 524, 31 LT 75.

keep the property purchased but will hold it as a trustee on trust[50] for his principal at whose suit the sale will be set aside. In *Oliver v Court*[51] where an auctioneer who had also valued an estate carelessly omitting to take account of valuable timber thereon, bought it himself after an abortive auction, the principal was held entitled to set the sale aside even after a lapse of 13 years. However, whilst delay may not, of itself, preclude the setting aside of the sale, it was stressed in *Wentworth v Lloyd*[52] that where the principal delays and, as a result, evidence may have been lost, the defendant agent is 'entitled to every fair and reasonable presumption that may be drawn in favour of the direct testimony [he] adduces.'[53] This case also shows that the burden of proving that he made full disclosure and that the vendor acquiesced in his purchase lies on the agent.[54]

The second consequence of such a breach of his fiduciary duty is that the auctioneer will be disentitled to his commission and this will be so whether the principal has elected to set the sale aside or has affirmed it. As Pollock CB put it in *Salomons v Pender*:[55]

The argument has failed to convince me that a person can, in the same transaction buy in the character of a principal, and at the same time charge the seller as his agent. I cannot agree that, because the seller has chosen to abide by the sale he is therefore to be held to have acknowledged the claims of the plaintiff both as agent and purchaser.

This seems a correct result. If the auctioneer has not shown that he made full disclosure to the vendor and that the latter acquiesced in the sale to him, he has simply acted outside his authority and thus, on general principles,[56] not earned his commission; he was employed to sell to third parties and has sold instead to himself.

Given these consequences, it is obviously vital that an auctioneer ensures that he does satisfy the disclosure requirements and obtains the express consent to his purchase from his client. However, in one situation he will be free to buy, namely when his agency has terminated. In the New Zealand case of *Young v Hill Ford & Newton*[57] the facts were as follows. Young bought a property with the aid of a loan secured thereon. He then instructed Ford & Newton to prepare plans for the division of the land into small parcels for sale. Having defaulted on the mortgage, he instructed Ford & Newton to auction the properties. Thereafter the mortgagees instructed the auctioneers to sell on their behalf in enforcement of the mortgage.

---

[50] See *Lees v Nuttall* (1829) 1 Russ and M 53, affd (1834) 2 My & K 819.
[51] Above, n 48.   [52] (1863) 32 Beav 467.
[53] (1863) 32 Beav 467 per Sir John Romilly MR at 474.
[54] See also *Dunne v English* (n 49, above) where it was said that it is not enough merely for the agent to disclose that he has an interest, leaving the principal to make enquiry as to the extent thereof.
[55] (1856) 3 H&C 639 at 641.   [56] See ch 4 above.   [57] (1883) 2 NZLR 62.

Young was informed but continued to try to re-schedule his loan repayments. The auctioneers put up the properties for sale but received no bids. Fourteen days later they made an offer to the mortgagees to buy them and this was accepted. Young thereupon sought to recover the properties claiming that the auctioneers remained his agents and thus held the properties on trust for him. The Court of Appeal held that the onus of proof that the auctioneers had divested themselves of their fiduciary character lay on them and that once an agency existed subsequent purchases by an agent would be closely scrutinised. However, in the circumstances of this case, the agency had terminated and the auctioneers' purchase of the property was, vis-à-vis Young, unobjectionable. Here the auctioneers had subsequently become agents for the mortgagees from whom they had bought. As to this Williams J said:[58]

It appears that they were employed by the mortgagees to sell the property by auction; the auction proved abortive as no bid was received, and the agency of Ford and Newton so far as regards the mortgagees had therefore determined. An auctioneer is agent *pro hac vice*, and whether he succeeds in effecting the sale or not his agency is determined after the auction.

Such a categorical statement has to be treated with some caution. Much will depend upon the circumstances of the auctioneer's appointment, his conduct of the auction and so on. In *Oliver v Court*,[59] for example, it was held that the agency of the auctioneer continued after he had descended from the rostrum and that he had in any event already determined to purchase the property himself when he commenced conduct of the auction. On that basis, his agency was extant when he purchased the estate and the sale to him was set aside.

Obtaining a secret profit

It is an inexorable rule, derived from the law of trusts, that an agent must not use his position to acquire for himself any secret profit from a third party. This is so even if the principal has suffered no actual loss. There are numerous circumstances in which a 'secret profit' can arise. At one extreme the notion will include a bribe, and at the other, the relatively innocent receipt of commission from a third party for the introduction of the principal's business. The leading case as regards auctioneers is *Hippisley v Knee Bros*.[60] There the defendant auctioneers had been instructed to sell goods on terms that they were to be paid a lump sum by way of commission together with disbursements, including the costs of printing and advertising.

---

[58] (1883) 2 NZLR 62 at 88.   [59] (1820) Dan 301, 8 Price 127.
[60] [1905] 1 KB 1.

The auctioneer contracted with printers for posters and catalogues and newspaper advertisements for which they were invoiced at the normal rate. However, the auctioneers were allowed, in fact, a ten per cent discount. When accounting to their client, however, the auctioneers charged these expenses at the normal invoice price. On discovering these facts the plaintiff sued to recover the discounts and also the commission paid. As regards the discounts it was held that these were repayable to the client. The auctioneers' claim to a trade custom entitling them to such discounts did not succeed. Lord Alvestone CJ adverted to 'an extraordinary laxity in the view taken of the earning of secret profits by agents' within commercial circles.[61] Whilst the auctioneers' honest belief in their right to retain these discounts as additional profit for themselves did not affect their duty to account for them to their principal, their bona fides in this regard was relevant in the context of the claim for return of the commission. The Chief Justice said:[62]

If the court is satisfied that there has been no fraud or dishonesty upon the agent's part, I think that the receipt by him of a discount will not disentitle him to his commission unless the discount is in some way connected with the contract which the agent is employed to make or the duty which he is called upon to perform. In my opinion the neglect by the defendants to account for the discounts in the present case is not sufficiently connected with the real subject-matter of their employment. If the discount had been received from the purchasers the case would have been covered by *Andrews v R Ramsey*[63] but here it was received in respect of a purely incidental matter: it had nothing to do with the duty of selling. It cannot be suggested that the plaintiff got one penny a lower price than he would otherwise have got. Therefore I come to the conclusion that, so far as the £20 commission is concerned, the plaintiff is not entitled to succeed.

Whilst the bona fides of these auctioneers was accepted by the court, there can no longer be any doubt that agents are not entitled to retain discounts or share commissions in these situations and auctioneers must ensure that they disclose and account for such to their clients.

DUTY TO ACCOUNT

The duty to account is one of the duties owed by an agent to his principal which arises out of the fiduciary relationship which exists between them. However, it is convenient to deal with it under this separate heading. It is the duty of every agent to keep the property and money of his principal separate from his own and to preserve and keep accounts of all his dealings in the course of his agency. He must also be prepared to produce

---

[61] [1905] 1 KB 1 at 7.   [62] [1905] 1 KB 1 at 8.   [63] [1903] 2 KB 635.

all relevant books and documents relating to his principal's affairs.[64] If an agent fails to keep proper accounts or fails to pay or transfer to his principal money or property received for him the agent is liable to an action for an account,[65] normally brought in the Chancery Division of the High Court.

The significance of the fact that the duty to account arises out of the fiduciary relationship between the agent and his principal lies in the remedies available against a defaulting agent, namely that the principal can *trace* the property belonging to him in the hands of his agent in priority to that agent's ordinary creditors. Thus in *Re Cotton, ex p. Cook*,[66] the deceased was instructed in cattle sales in Bromsgrove and four other towns. It appears that he generally sold in his own name and made himself personally liable for all money received. Occasionally he gave credit to purchasers and allowed sets-off to those who were also vendors. Cook instructed him to sell certain cattle and this was duly effected but the proceeds were not immediately collected. Thereafter the auctioneer committed suicide but his son obtained outstanding payments due and paid the money into a separate bank account. The auctioneer's estate being insolvent, the question arose whether a sum of £40 17s 6d in respect of the proceeds of sale of Cook's cattle was recoverable by the latter or whether it was properly kept by the trustee in bankruptcy as part of the general assets of the estate into which Cook could prove his debt together with the other creditors. The Divisional Court held that the auctioneer had established a course of dealing in which he became a principal, buying and selling on his own account and that Cook merely looked to him as a debtor. The Court of Appeal, however, found such a course of dealing negatived by the express conditions of business of the auctioneer and held that the question was whether Cook was entitled to say: 'These cattle of mine were entrusted to you for a particular purpose, as commission agent to sell for me. That is a fiduciary position and the fiduciary relation applies to the money received from the sale of the cattle entrusted to you for sale'.[67] This question was, on the facts, answered in the affirmative; the proceeds belonged to the principal and he could trace into the insolvent auctioneer's estate ahead of the general creditors by virtue of the fiduciary relationship existing between them. If, however, the facts had been as the Divisional Court had found them — that the auctioneer in fact sold as principal on his own account, having bought them from his client — no fiduciary relationship would have existed nor attached to the proceeds and the seller would merely have been an unpaid creditor. This kind of

---

[64] See generally *Bowstead on Agency* (15th edn, 1985) Sweet & Maxwell, art 52.

[65] See Supreme Court Act 1981, s 61(1) and Sch 1. The relevant rules are to be found in RSC Ord 43 (Appendix 3).

[66] (1913) 108 LT 310.   [67] (1913) 108 LT 310 at 311 per Cozens-Hardy MR.

arrangement is not uncommon in cattle auctions where sales are effected outside the ring and booked with the auctioneer.[68]

The right to trace property exists both at law and in equity. The latter remedy is more efficacious when money is involved because at common law the right to trace is lost when the true owner's property is no longer identifiable. Equity however is prepared to unscramble bank accounts containing moneys belonging to several persons. It is beyond the scope of this book to examine the remedy in any detail, but the right to trace would be lost if the property were taken by another without notice of the rights of the true owner, having given value for it. So, in *Marten v Rocke Eyton & Co*,[69] unpaid vendors were held unable to trace into the bank account of the defaulting auctioneer when the bankers had taken the balance therein in satisfaction of an overdraft, without notice that the balance comprised moneys due to the vendors.

The fact that the auctioneer holds his principal's property in a fiduciary character and is not merely a debtor may have serious consequences in other contexts. In *Crowther v Elgood*[70] an auctioneer found himself committed to prison having failed to account for proceeds of sale of farming stock sold on behalf of a deceased. Whilst imprisonment for debt has largely been abolished by the Debtors Act 1869, there remain some cases of debt where imprisonment is still possible. By s 4 of the Act committal is available in the case of 'default by a trustee or a person acting in a fiduciary capacity and ordered to pay by a Court of Equity any sum in his possession or under his control'. Cotton LJ was in no doubt that a defaulting auctioneer was caught by this provision:[71]

In the first place, was the appellant acting in a fiduciary capacity in the transaction? In my opinion he was. He was an auctioneer, and as such he held the goods in trust to sell them for the benefit of the person who entrusted them to him; and if any deposit was paid at the time of the sale, he held it in trust for the vendor . . . and when he has received the money produced by the sale he holds that as the money of his principal.

It is clear therefore that an auctioneer is at risk if he fails properly to account and he will in the absence of express authority to the contrary only escape liability if he does so direct to the principal himself. There is no implied authority to pay proceeds or a deposit to his client's solicitors.[72] The

---

[68] See eg *Murphy v Howlett (a firm)* (1960) 176 EG 311, and ch 10 below.

[69] (1885) 53 LT 946, 34 WR 253.   [70] (1887) 34 Ch D 691, CA.

[71] (1887) 36 Ch D 691 at 696.

[72] See *Brown v Farebrother* (1888) 58 LJ Ch 3 at 4 per Kekewich J, although in that case auctioneers instructed to sell by the plaintiff acting under a court order and under a duty to pay proceeds into court were held discharged when they paid the proceeds over to solicitors for the vendor for that purpose. It seems that in this case the auctioneers *did* have actual authority so to do.

auctioneer must remain willing and able to account to his principal. In *Lowe v Gallimore*[73] it was held that a principal could enforce this duty after having revoked an earlier instruction to pay proceeds of sale into a bank account pending resolution of a dispute surrounding them. Further, in *Crosskey v Mills*[74] the defendant auctioneer was instructed to sell goods by one W Crosskey the brother of a deceased who had given the plaintiff a bill of sale. The deceased's widow instructed the auctioneer to hold the proceeds to satisfy all the creditors of the deceased. It is unclear whether the plaintiff concurred in such an arrangement,[75] but in any event he subsequently instructed the auctioneer to account to him. It was held that the auctioneer was bound to do so: 'the plaintiff was the person who originally employed the defendant to sell. Therefore prima facie, the defendant was bound to account to the plaintiff.'[76]

The problem in these cases can be regarded as stemming from conflicting instructions from the principal. However, the major area of difficulty for an auctioneer exists where a third party lays claim to the goods or their proceeds. As we shall see later, if the third party's claim is justified, the auctioneer is exposed to an action in tort for conversion of the true owner's property. The auctioneer may, therefore, be caught on the horns of a dilemma but in certain circumstances may be able to escape liability for failing to account to his principal where he invokes the right and title of a third party: the 'jus tertii' defence.

The jus tertii defence

In *Crosskey v Mills*[77] it was expressly held that there no third party had shown any title to the money but that if such had been shown the auctioneer might have had a defence to an action by the principal. The precise circumstances where this defence will be available now fall to be considered. The common law position has been affected by the Torts (Interference with Goods) Act 1977. The Act does not represent a masterpiece of clear draftsmanship and it may well be that its provisions do not apply at all to cases where a principal sues an agent for failure to account to him for the proceeds of sale. We shall therefore first outline the position at common law, and then consider the impact of the statute.

---

[73] (1851) 18 LTOS 63, 241.   [74] (1834) 1 Cr M&R 298, 3 LJ Ex 297.
[75] The marginal note to the law report, (1834) 1 Cr M&R 298, suggests that he did. Parke B at 302 says that the evidence does not bear this arrangement out but then says that the plaintiff may have been a trustee for the general creditors. Whilst the auction catalogue was headed 'For the benefit of creditors' it does not appear that this was ever submitted to the plaintiff for approval. On the other hand, it is suggested in the report that a sale for the creditors generally did at one time represent the plaintiff's intentions.
[76] (1834) 1 Cr M&R 298 at 301–2 per Parke B.   [77] Above, n 74.

Common law

In *Hardman v Willcock*[78] an auctioneer was instructed by the plaintiff to sell certain goods he possessed. Before the sale the auctioneer was given notice by assignees of an insolvent that the goods belonged to them and that the plaintiff had obtained them from the insolvent under a fraudulent arrangement devised to defeat their claim. Having subsequently sold the goods, the auctioneer refused to account to the plaintiff for their proceeds. The plaintiff duly brought an action for money had and received to his use and the auctioneer pleaded the defence of jus tertii, that is, the right of the assignees as third parties entitled to the property. The court accepted the general proposition that an agent is under a duty to account to his principal, but held the defence good on the ground that the principal had taken the goods as part of a fraudulent scheme to defeat the rights of the true owners. A defence based on a notion of fraud by the client is somewhat narrow and the principle was explained and extended a few years later in *Biddle v Bond*[79] where an auctioneer refused to account to his principal, a landlord selling a tenant's goods under distraint for rent. Here again, the auctioneer received notice just before the sale from the tenant claiming that the distress was void. The court held that the defence of jus tertii was available against the principal. Blackburn J explained the rationale thus:[80]

We do not question the general rule that one who has received property from another as his bailee or agent or servant must restore or account for that property to him from whom he received it . . . But the bailee has no better title than the bailor and consequently if a person entitled as against the bailor to the property claims it, the bailee has no defence against him.

Whereas normally, an agent is estopped from denying the title of his principal, the estoppel ceases when the possession on which it is founded is determined by the agent being 'evicted' by someone with a better title. There must be something in the nature of an eviction or dispossession (although this need not be physical); mere *notice* of another's claim does not suffice. The agent can set up the jus tertii only if he defends by virtue of the title and on the authority of the true owner.[81] And the defence is not restricted to cases where the principal has been guilty of fraud on the true owner. Blackburn J pointed out that the position is precisely the same whether the bailor was honestly mistaken as to the rights of the third person or fraudulently acting in derogation of those rights.[82]

   An auctioneer then, in order to have a valid defence to an action brought by his principal for failure in his duty to account must prove two things: first,

[78] (1831) 9 Bing 382 n.   [79] (1865) 122 ER 1179, 6 B&S 225.
[80] (1865) 122 ER 1179 at 1181.
[81] See *Rogers Sons & Co v Lambert & Co* [1891] 1 QB 318, 60 LJQB 187, CA.
[82] (1865) 122 ER 1179 at 1181.

he must prove the title of the adverse claimant by whose authority he is defending the claim and, second, he must show that he has not by his conduct estopped himself from setting up that adverse claim. Where an auctioneer knows of an adverse claim but disregards it and sells for his principal he cannot then deny his principal's title by invoking that of the third party whose claim he has disregarded. This was the difficulty into which the auctioneer placed himself in *Re Sadler, ex p Davies.*[83] Here the auctioneer with due notice of two claims effectively took sides. He was held to be estopped from denying the title of one of two persons who had concurrently instructed him to sell. This case is distinguishable from *Biddle v Bond,*[84] where the notice of the conflicting claim came only a short time before the sale was due to be commenced so that it could not properly be said that the auctioneer made an election. The obvious course for an auctioneer who has notice of rival claims to property is to interplead.[85]

Statutory modifications

The Law Reform Committee considered the law relating to the jus tertii defence to be unduly complex and restrictive. The Committee favoured relaxation of the rules in order to avoid multiplicity of actions. They recommended that whenever a wrongful interference with goods was alleged the defendant should have power to apply to join any third parties claiming competing rights. The Committee's proposals were largely enacted in 1977 by the Torts (Interference with Goods) Act. Section 8 provides:

(1) The defendant in an action for wrongful interference shall be entitled to show, in accordance with rules of court, that a third party has a better right than the plaintiff as respects all or any part of the interest claimed by the plaintiff, or in right of which he sues, and any rule of law (sometimes called jus tertii) to the contrary is abolished.
(2) Rules of court relating to proceedings for wrongful interference may —
    (a) require the plaintiff to give particulars of his title;
    (b) require the plaintiff to identify any person who, to his knowledge, has or claims any interest in the goods;
    (c) authorise the defendant to apply for directions as to whether any person should be joined with a view to establishing whether he has a better right than the plaintiff, or has a claim as a result of which the defendant might be doubly liable;
    (d) where a party fails to appear on an application within paragraph (c), or to comply with any direction given by the court on such an application, authorise the court to deprive him of any right of action against the defendant for the wrong either unconditionally, or subject to such terms or conditions as may be specified.

---

[83] (1881) 19 Ch D 86, 45 LT 632, CA.   [84] Above, n 79.
[85] On interpleader see above, ch 4.

(3) Subsection (2) is without prejudice to any other power of making rules of court.

There is an immediate difficulty over the parenthesis in subs (1). It is not the defence based on the invocation of the jus tertii that is abolished, but the *limitations* on that defence outlined above. Thus, if the 1977 Act applied in the situations under consideration, the basic rule laid down by the common law – that generally a bailee cannot deny the title of his bailor – is abrogated. *Rogers Sons & Co v Lambert*[86] is therefore no longer good law and an auctioneer defendant would always be able to invoke the defence of jus tertii.

But does the Torts (Interference with Goods) Act 1977 apply where the auctioneer fails to account for proceeds of sale to his principal? Section 8 refers to the rights of a defendant 'in an action for wrongful interference'. Section 1 defines such as:

(a) conversion of goods (also called trover),
(b) trespass to goods,
(c) negligence so far as it results in damage to goods or to an interest in goods,
(d) subject to section 2, any other tort so far as it results in damage to goods or an interest in goods.

The problems with this definition are two-fold. First, it is doubtful whether a fund representing proceeds of sale of goods would be regarded as 'goods' within the definition.[87] Second, and more difficult to surmount, is the fact that a vendor seeking such proceeds could invariably bring an action for breach of *contract*. A right to the proceeds of sale is usually expressly provided and if it is not, such will be implied. Thus the action would not be one for conversion, trespass, negligence or any other tort.

One is driven to the conclusion that the 1977 Act simply does not apply to a retention by the auctioneer of the proceeds of sale.[88] This is rather unfortunate; the consequence is that an auctioneer who before sale learns of a rival claim to goods may freely invoke the jus tertii and enjoin the rival in any action against him for their return. Whereas if he sells the goods and seeks to set up the jus tertii as a defence to an action in respect of the proceeds, framed in contract, he can only invoke the jus tertii subject to the strict common law rules outlined above.

It is thought that despite the very general wording of s 8(1) of the Torts (Interference with Goods) Act 1977, even where the Act does apply, a specific estoppel such as that which was found in *Re Sadler*[89] could still

---

[86] Above, n 81.
[87] Money is specifically excluded: Torts (Interference with Goods) Act 1977, s 14(1).
[88] Murdoch *The Law of Estate Agency and Auctions* (3rd edn, 1994) Estates Gazette, p 304 is of a similar view.
[89] Above, n 83.

operate to prevent the auctioneer setting up the defence. The 1977 Act seeks to ameliorate the position of a defendant who finds himself subject to two or more rival claims. If he has chosen to throw in his lot with one of the rivals he should account to him and face the legal wrath of the other.

Where the provisions of the Act are available to the defendant he is permitted to name any interested rival, and apply for his being joined. The rules of court referred to in s 8(2) are to be found in RSC Ord 15, 10A(2) for the High Court, and CCR 1981, Ord 15, 4(1) for the County Court.

An auctioneer will also have a defence to an action for money had and received where his receipt of the proceeds of sale or deposit is only conditional so that the purchaser's claim to its return is valid. In *Hardingham v Allen*[90] for example, a horse was sold at auction under the contractual condition that if it was warranted quiet in harness it could be returned within a prescribed period if it did not correspond with that description. The horse was then to be tried and examined by an impartial person whose decision would be final. A purchaser returned a horse under this condition and the auctioneer duly paid back the purchase money. The vendor-plaintiff's claim for the purchase price as money had and received failed. Coltman J held: 'With regard to the money received by the defendant as the price of the horse [it] was received conditionally only and never in fact became money had and received to the use of the plaintiff.'[91]

The decision in *Murray v Mann*[92] where the purchaser justifiably rescinded the contract for fraud is to similar effect. However, we have already noted[93] that the question whether an auctioneer is entitled, in the absence of express authority, vis-à-vis his principal to accept rescission of a contract is not entirely free from doubt. If he unjustifiably does so he will be liable to account for the money he ought to have received and retained.[94]

Interest

We have already seen that, by virtue of his fiduciary relationship with his principal, an auctioneer may not make any profit out of his agency. It is perhaps obvious therefore that where an auctioneer holds money which belongs to his principal, any interest which it earns must be accounted for to him.[95] The question arises whether an agent holding money for his principal is under a *duty* to invest it so that it yields interest and is liable for such

---

[90] (1848) 5 CB 793.   [91] (1848) 5 CB 793 at 797–8.
[92] (1848) 2 Exch 538, 17 LJ Ex 256.   [93] See above, ch 3.
[94] See *Nelson v Aldridge* (1818) 2 Stark 435 and contrast *Stevens v Legh* (1853) 2 CLR 251, 22 LTOS 84.
[95] The general principles are discussed in *Bowstead on Agency* (15th edn, 1985) Sweet & Maxwell, art 54.

interest as could have been earned if he fails to do so. At common law the position was as follows:

(a) If an agent not expressly under a duty to invest his principal's money merely allows it to remain dead in his hands he is not liable to account for any interest it could have earned.[96]
(b) If, however, the agent mixes his principal's money with his own or makes any use of it he is liable to pay interest.[97]
(c) Similarly if an agent wilfully withholds accounts or money or is guilty of any fraudulent dealing with his principal's money he will be liable for interest.[98]

The common law has now been rendered somewhat obsolete by the Law Reform (Miscellaneous Provisions) Act 1934 which gives the court a wide general discretion to award interest on any debt or damages between the date when the cause of action arose and the judgment.[99]

DUTY TO CARE FOR THE GOODS

The main legal relationship between a vendor and an auctioneer is that of agency, but in addition there exists in connection with goods a relationship of bailment. Bailment is a legal institution of some antiquity and complexity and it is possible within the scope of this book to discuss its impact in the field of auctions only in rather brief and general terms.[100] As a leading author has noted, 'bailment stands at the point at which contract, property and tort converge.'[101]

The salient feature of bailment involves the delivery of goods by the bailor into the custody of another, the bailee. Bailment is usually but not invariably for reward. Although an auctioneer will generally be a bailee for reward there are situations where the bailment may be gratuitous — as where he is in possession of a prospective vendor's goods for valuation purposes if he does not charge for such or, vis-à-vis the purchaser, after a sale but before collection by him.[102] Originally it was thought that bailment presupposed redelivery by the bailee but this is not longer so. A bailment

---

[96] *Rogers v Boehm* (1798) 2 Esp 701.
[97] Above, n 96.   [98] *Turner v Burkinshaw* (1867) 2 Ch App 488, 17 LT 83.
[99] Questions relating to interest earned on deposits received by auctioneers are dealt with separately below.
[100] The major modern work of reference is N E Palmer *Bailment* (1979) Law Book Company. See also 2 Halsbury's Laws (4th edn) para 1501 f.
[101] Palmer (above, n 100) p 1.
[102] The classic classification of the various sorts of bailment is to be found in *Coggs v Bernard* (1703) 2 Ld Raym 909, 1 Com 133 per Holt CJ, viz: (a) custody of goods without reward, (b) loan of goods, (c) hire of goods, (d) pawn or pledge of goods, (e) carriage of goods or other performance of service for reward, and (f) the same, without reward.

can clearly exist where it is envisaged, as is the case with auctions, that the bailee will deliver the goods to a third party — the purchaser after the sale. But if the sale is abortive, the auctioneer will again be holding the goods as a bailee for the vendor with the concomitant rights and duties created by the relationship. A failure to return such goods without lawful excuse such as in exercise of his lien, or pleading the jus tertii, will render the auctioneer liable in conversion.

In the case of auctions the bailment will usually be contractual and its terms will depend upon the precise terms of that contract. Subject to such provisions, the duty of the auctioneer at common law will be to take reasonable care of the goods in his custody. In the old case of *Maltby v Christie*[103] an auctioneer was instructed to sell a quantity of plate glass. A dispute arose as to whether the auctioneer was entitled to deduct commission at the rate of $7\frac{1}{2}$ per cent. No commission had been agreed between the parties but the defendant claimed there to be a trade custom that such an amount was usual in view of the extraordinary risks attending the sale of such goods. Lord Kenyon in denying the auctioneer's claim said that he was of the opinion that the auctioneer as bailee was only bound to take such care of the goods as he would exercise in respect of his own, and that for a loss arising from misfortune or unavoidable accident he was not liable.

Such a general statement as to the duty and standard of care must be treated with some caution. Some bailments involve benefit to both bailor and bailee, some create benefits only to the bailor, and some create benefits only to the bailee. According to Halsbury, 'an ordinary degree of care and skill is usually required where both benefit from the transaction; slighter diligence, perhaps, where the benefit is wholly that of the bailor . . . and greater diligence where the benefit accrues only to the bailee.'[104] However, in *Houghland v R R Low (Luxury Coaches) Ltd*,[105] the Court of Appeal preferred simply to say that the standard of care depended upon the circumstances of the particular case, it being artificial frequently to try to fit a particular case into the various rigid categories.[106] Moreover it has been held that where the bailment is contractual, as with auctions it usually is, if the bailee deals with the property entrusted to him in an unauthorised manner, he takes upon himself the risks of so doing. Thus if, for example, an auctioneer were to warehouse his principal's goods with a third person, in breach of contract whereupon the goods become destroyed by fire, the auctioneer will be liable.[107] This raises the question whether in the absence of express provision, a bailee may sub-contract out his duties. The answer

---

[103] (1795) 1 Esp 340.   [104] 2 Halsbury's Laws (4th edn Reissue) para 1803.
[105] [1962] 1 QB 694, [1962] 2 All ER 159, CA.
[106] For a detailed consideration of this question see Palmer (above, n 100) pp 288–302.
[107] See eg *Lilley v Doubleday* (1881) 7 QBD 510, 51 LJQB 310; *McMahon v Field* (1881) 7 QBD 591, 50 LJQB 552, CA.

turns on whether the contract involved is one, the essence of which is the personal skill and care of the bailee employed. As Denning LJ put it in *Edwards v Newland & Co*:[108]

There are many bailments in which the bailee is entitled to make a sub-bailment: the repairer of a motor-car, for instance, can often quite reasonably send away a part of it to another firm for repairs; a carrier of goods may need to entrust them to another carrier for part of the journey; a hirer may himself often, quite lawfully, sub-hire the goods. It all depends upon the circumstances of the particular case. The contract here is a contract for the storage of furniture. In such a case, in my opinion, the personal skill and care of the contractor is of the essence of the contract. Much skill and care is necessary in appointing the men who are to handle the goods, in selecting the place where they are to be stored, in seeing that it is reasonably fireproof and burglarproof and in choosing the caretakers. The owner of the goods is entitled in these respects to the personal skill and care of the contractor. If the contractor employs a sub-contractor, he does it at his own risk.

Liability for negligence

The most obvious situations in which the auctioneer will be liable to his vendor-principal will be where he fails to take reasonable care of the latter's goods either prior to the sale or whilst they remain in the auctioneer's custody and control after the sale pending delivery to the buyer or redelivery to the seller where there is an abortive sale.

An instructive case is *Spriggs v Sotheby Parke Bernet and Co*.[109] In that case the plaintiff decided to sell a diamond valued at some £22,000 and deposited it with Sotheby's for inclusion in their next important diamond sale. It was envisaged that the auctioneers would make the stone available for viewing before the sale. The contract between Spriggs and Sotheby's provided, inter alia, by clause 2

I accept that whilst you take all reasonable care in handling the property on behalf of clients, you are not responsible for loss or damage of any kind whether caused by negligence or otherwise, the property being accepted at owner's risk.

Whilst being viewed the gem was stolen. The viewing arrangements were that the stones were displayed in special cases in a viewing gallery. When a viewer wished to see a particular stone it would be handed to him by a porter. The porter might then be called to another part of the viewing gallery to deal with another request to see a different item. Thus several lots could be handled by different persons at different positions in the room at the same time. To guard against the obvious risk of theft in this situation, four security guards were posted around the room. Nevertheless, Mr

---

[108] [1950] 2 KB 534, CA at 542.   [109] [1986] 1 Lloyd's Rep. 487.

Sprigg's diamond, lot 290, was stolen by a viewer while the porter's attention had been diverted by another customer.

At first instance the judge held that Sotheby's had not been negligent: they had employed a retired Detective Chief Inspector as Head of Security; security guards were posted in the room; if gems were to be sold reasonable facilities had to be provided for their viewing; even if it could be said that the porter should not have allowed his attention to have been distracted by another viewer, it was impossible to impose a duty to maintain such vigilance as to prevent a theft which might occur in seconds.

On appeal, however, it was held that the duty of Sotheby's as bailees for reward was to take reasonable care of the goods entrusted to them and that such a bailee had to show, and the onus was on him, that the loss or damage occurred without his neglect or any neglect of his servant to whom the duty was delegated. The court held that the duty involved two aspects: the provision of a safe system of security and, secondly, the diligent operation of it; in this case it was held that there was not in operation a safe system. It was defective in so far as it allowed extremely small but valuable items to be handled by persons who were strangers to Sotheby's in circumstances where the porter would have to turn his back on them; moreover the security guards could not be certain of having an uninterrupted view of proceedings.

We deal with exemption clauses generally in chapter 6 but it may be convenient here to look briefly at the impact of the exempting provision referred to earlier. The clause appeared on the reverse of the form which the customer signed. However, immediately above the place where he signed was printed a notice referring to the Conditions of Sale. The exclusion clause provided for insurance by Sotheby's at an extra cost at seller's option although in fact this was excluded in this case as Mr Spriggs had insured the diamond himself.

There was much arcane argument as to the construction of the clause particularly as to the effect of the opening words: 'I accept that whilst you take all reasonable care . . .' but the court was satisfied that the words 'whether caused by negligence or otherwise' were clear and adequate to exclude any liability for any act of negligence by Sotheby's or any person for whom they would be responsible. Thus, and ultimately quite simply, the auctioneers escaped liability because they had incorporated a suitably worded exclusion clause in their contract with their customer. It is important to note, however, that this contract was entered into in 1977, just before the coming into force of the Unfair Contract Terms Act. Thus the exclusion clause in this particular case did not have to satisfy the statutory test of 'reasonableness' as would now be the case. It might be instructive to consider how the courts would have approached the case had it been governed by the Act.

The requirement of reasonableness

The test of reasonableness is substantially undefined in relation to exclusion of negligence generally, this not being a case involving sale. Thus one would be left merely with the bland words of section 11 of the Act which provides:

In relation to a contract term, the requirement of reasonableness . . . is that the term shall have been a fair and reasonable one to be included.

Nevertheless, the courts are likely to be influenced by the considerations which do apply specifically to cases of sale and, in particular to the importance of the relative bargaining strengths of the parties and the extent to which the incorporation of the clause is something which is negotiable. Here Mr Spriggs was described as 'a business man . . . well used to contracts and no doubt to contracts containing exclusions clauses'. Clearly, it would normally be more reasonable to proffer a contract containing such an exclusion clause to a hard-bitten business man than, say, to a little old lady in straightened circumstances seeking to sell her engagement ring.

The extent of the exclusion

The clause here provided a total exclusion and not merely a financial limitation of liability. As a general proposition, it seems that the wider the ambit of the exclusion clause the less likely it is that it will be regarded as reasonable.

The availability of insurance cover

The relevance of insurance is problematic. As regards the clause in this case, whilst the plaintiff did not take up the offer of insurance, it is clear that the insurance provision was a relevant consideration in the construction of the clause. Moreover, the fact that insurance cover was available at modest extra cost might be thought to make even a total exclusion of liability for loss fair and reasonable.

Very much on balance, it is suggested that had the *Spriggs* case fallen to be decided under the provisions of the Unfair Contract Terms Act 1977 the exclusion would have been effective.

As a post-script to the discussion it is interesting to note that Sotheby's now have a very detailed condition in respect of the risk of loss or damage to their vendor-principal's goods whereunder, unless specifically instructed otherwise, Sotheby's will assume risk of loss and the expense of that assumption of risk will be for the vendor (see condition 20: appendix 1).

If Sotheby's is to assume such risk, this will be at the expense of the seller or consignor and Sotheby's liability for loss or damage to any property will not exceed the amount estimated by Sotheby's to be from time to time the current value of the property at auction, less Sotheby's commission and expenses nor in any event will it exceed:

(a) the 'hammer price' less Sotheby's commission and expenses if the property has been sold;
(b) the reserve, less Sotheby's commission and expenses if the property has not been sold after being offered for sale and the reserve has been determined;
(c) the mid saleroom estimate, less Sotheby's commission and expenses in any other case.

A final problem in relation to the duty of care concerns the question whether a bailee is responsible for the loss of the bailor's goods due to their theft or other depredations by an employee. There are two possible bases for such a liability: first, the bailee may be liable personally in so far as his selection of the employee may have been negligent.[110] Auctioneers frequently deal with very valuable merchandise and it is incumbent upon them to select and supervise their staff with care. In the absence of negligent selection, will he be liable, secondly, for the depredations of his employee — ie *vicariously*? Broadly speaking, an employer will be vicariously liable for the torts of his servant acting within the course of employment. Thus a bailee will be liable for the theft or conversion of his bailor's goods committed by an employee where such is employed in some part to perform tasks involving care of the goods. He may not however be liable if, say, the goods are stolen by a tea-lady.[111]

As we have said, these duties are subject to express contractual variations. Auctioneers' contracts frequently make some provision for their potential liability[112] and their efficacy now depends upon the ordinary rules of common law and the provisions of the Unfair Contract Terms Act 1977 discussed more particularly elsewhere.[113]

DUTISES AND LIABILITIES OWED TO THE PURCHASER

An auctioneer may be liable to the purchaser of lots in a variety of ways. To a limited extent he has been regarded as the purchaser's agent. More

---

[110] See *Jobson v Palmer* [1893] 1 Ch 71, 62 LJ Ch 180.

[111] There may be some doubt whether the employer's duty is here properly categorised as vicarious; it may be that it is better regarded as personal liability, he being answerable for the way in which his employee carries out a duty of care which the employer has delegated to him. See the alternative formulations in *Morris v C W Martin & Sons Ltd* [1966] 1 QB 716, [1965] 2 All ER 725, CA.

[112] See Christie's B5; Sotheby's Conditions of Business 20 (see Appendix 1).

[113] See ch 6.

significantly, he will in certain circumstances be personally liable in contract. Finally, the general law imposes certain duties on auctioneers in and about the conduct of their business.

THE AUCTIONEER AS AGENT OF THE PURCHASER

We have mentioned in passing that the auctioneer, whilst primarily of course the agent of the vendor, was also, to a limited extent, the agent of the purchaser. It seems to have been well settled by the early nineteenth century[114] that the auctioneer was the agent of the purchaser for the purpose of signing the memorandum then required to make enforceable certain contracts of sale. Both contracts for the sale etc of land and those for the sale of goods, where the value exceeded £10, were required to be evidenced in writing but today only contracts for the sale of land concluded prior to 27 September 1989 are significant in this context. The position is discussed in detail in chapter 9.

The agency of the auctioneer vis-à-vis the purchaser has been described as follows:[115]

Where there is a sale by public auction and the property is knocked down by the auctioneer to the highest bidder, the auctioneer is not only the agent of the vendor, but he is also the agent of the purchaser, the highest bidder; and ... he is the purchaser's agent clearly to this extent, that he is entitled to sign in the name and on behalf of the purchaser, a memorandum sufficient to satisfy the provisions of the Statute of Frauds ...

Most of the cases where this agency has been invoked have involved claims by vendors or auctioneers against defendant purchasers seeking to resile from their bargains. The question arose, however, to what extent if at all, this agency involved obligations on the part of the auctioneer to the purchaser. In other words did this agency involve *duties* to sign the memorandum on the part of the purchaser so that he could insist that he became a party to the contract, and, if so, does it follow that he could further insist that the auctioneer sign on behalf of the vendor so that the contract became enforceable? It is clear from the cases cited earlier that the authority to sign on behalf of the purchaser is irrevocable after the property is knocked down to him[116] and it would be surprising, not to say commercially unfortunate, if

---

[114] See *Emmerson v Heelis* (1809) 2 Taunt 38; *White v Proctor* (1811) 4 Taunt 209; *Farebrother v Simmons* (1822) 5 B & Ald 333; *Eden v Blake* (1845) 13 M&W 614, 14 LJ Ex 194.

[115] *Sims v Landray* [1894] 2 Ch 318 per Romer J at 310. Cf *Chaney v Maclow* [1929] 1 Ch 461, 98 LJ Ch 345, CA; *Bell v Balls* [1897] 1 Ch 663, 66 LJ Ch 397; *Van Praagh v Everidge* [1902] 2 Ch 266, 71 LJ Ch 598 (revsd [1903] 1 Ch 434, 72 LJ Ch 260, CA, on the ground that there was no sufficient memorandum).

[116] *Chaney v Maclow*, n 115 above. And see (1929) 45 LQR 289.

an irretrievably bound purchaser could not be certain that the vendor too would be bound or that if he was not, a remedy would lie against him or through his agent, the auctioneer.

It must be accepted that despite their (recently diminished) importance there is no conclusive authority on these questions. Since the abolition of formalities in auction sales of land is comparatively recent, it remains relevant to consider the authorities. In *Johnston v Boyes*[117] a freehold inn, the White Hart at South Mimms, was put under the hammer. The Conditions of Sale provided that the highest bidder would be the purchaser and pay immediately a deposit of ten per cent and sign the requisite memorandum. The plaintiff deputed her husband to bid for her but did not trust him to the extent of furnishing him with cash. When the property was knocked down to him he sought to sign the memorandum and, having no cash for the deposit, offered his own cheque. Unfortunately, by coincidence, the solicitor to the vendor, who sat as registrar of the local county court recognised the husband as one who, the previous week, had sworn to be penniless. He therefore instructed the auctioneer not to permit the husband to sign in any capacity. The would-be purchaser was denied an injunction restraining the sale of the property to any other persons. The court was prepared to accept that a vendor could be liable in damages in such circumstances, not on the contract of sale itself which remained unenforceable but on an agreement that a contract of sale would be effected with the highest bidder. However in the event, the action failed because, since the pre-condition of payment of a deposit of ten per cent in cash had not been fulfilled, there was no breach of the agreement contained in the Conditions of Sale. A similar case is *McManus v Fortescue*[118] where the purchaser claimed against the auctioneer for his refusal to sign the memorandum of sale relating to personal property then required by s 4 of the Sale of Goods Act 1893. Here the auctioneer, having knocked down the property to him, refused to complete the memorandum because he had erroneously knocked it down below a reserve to which the item had been expressly subject. The Court of Appeal in affirming the decision at first instance, held the auctioneer not liable on the grounds that, in such circumstances, all bids and all acceptances thereof are subject to the condition that the reserve has been reached. Thus the fall of the hammer did not produce a sale at all. This analysis is, it is submitted correct, but it leaves unanswered the contention that an auctioneer is liable for failing to sign a memorandum where the sale *is* completed unconditionally by the fall of the hammer either where the sale is without reserve or the fixed reserve is reached.

[117] [1899] 2 Ch 73, 68 LJ Ch 425; injunction proceedings are reported at 14 TLR 475.
[118] [1907] 2 KB 1, 76 LJ KB 393, CA.

The judgments in these two cases are, it is argued, consistent with the proposition that an action will lie when a purchaser is prevented from signing the memorandum or the auctioneer declines to do so as his agent in circumstances where the purchaser has fulfilled all the required conditions. However, as was recognised in *McManus v Fortescue*,[119] the existence of a right to sign is not enough to protect the purchaser: he must also be able to insist that the auctioneer completes the memorandum as agent of the vendor or that the vendor himself signs. Without such a reciprocal duty on the part of the auctioneer, the purchaser will only be able to bind himself, leaving the vendor to decide whether he wishes to be bound. Yet in the relatively modern case of *Richards v Phillips*,[120] Pennycuick J, responding to the contention that the auctioneer was bound to sign on behalf of the vendor rendering the contract enforceable at the suit of the highest bidder, said:[121]

The . . . contention raises a question of law which has been the subject of one or two inconclusive dicta, but . . . not of any actual decision . . . An auctioneer is primarily the agent of the vendor . . . there is no doubt that he becomes also the implied agent of a purchaser to sign the memorandum on behalf of the purchaser. But it is not at all clear to me how this implied agency on behalf of the purchaser can make it part of his duty to the purchaser to sign the memorandum on behalf of the vendor.

In this case again the question did not in the result arise for decision because it was held that there had been a genuine dispute about rival bids justifying the withdrawal of the lot and its re-offer for sale. On this aspect of the case, the decision was upheld on appeal.

The duty, it is suggested, can be regarded as arising in this way: the purchaser, as highest bidder, impliedly or expressly authorises the auctioneer to effect an enforceable contract by adding his signature to the requisite memorandum. As part of this agency relationship, and impliedly imported into it to give it business efficacy, is a corresponding duty to ensure that the contract is mutually enforceable; that the purchaser effectively is the purchaser by obtaining or supplying the vendor's signature. And it is submitted that cases such as *Johnston v Boyes*[122] and *McManus v Fortescue*[123] are entirely consistent with such an analysis. The auctioneer has power to sign on behalf of and to bind both parties. This authority is, as regards each party, irrevocable after the property is knocked down. It is difficult to see why a purchaser should be left without a remedy if the vendor is not bound (as we have seen, a vendor can recover from the auctioneer if he fails to secure an agreement binding the purchaser).[124] Were it otherwise, the agency between auctioneer and purchaser would

---

[119] Above, n 118.   [120] [1969] 1 Ch 39.   [121] [1969] 1 Ch 39 at 52.
[122] Above, n 117.   [123] Above, n 118.
[124] See the discussion in the first section of this chapter, 'Duties to the vendor'.

largely be, as it has been called, a spurious agency enuring exclusively to the benefit of the vendor.

PERSONAL CONTRACTUAL LIABILITY TO THE PURCHASER

An auctioneer may be personally liable to the purchaser in contract[125] in three distinct ways, and we shall consider each in turn.

Breach of warranty of authority

If an agent, including an auctioneer, sells property without or in excess of his authority he will be liable to the purchaser in damages for breach of the implied warranty that he does, in fact, possess the authority exercised. The simplest situation is where the agent has no authority to sell at all. In *Anderson v John Croall & Sons Ltd*[126] auctioneers sold a mare after a selling race, the trainer's lad having failed to remove her from the paddock after the weighing up so that the auctioneers were misled into believing that she was being offered for sale. The owners refused to deliver her and the purchaser claimed against the auctioneer for 35 guineas being the difference in price between that at which she had been knocked down to him and the price which she had fetched six months later. The Court of Sessions in Scotland allowed such a claim being damages for breach of the warranty that they were authorised to sell, 10 guineas being deducted in respect of costs of upkeep.

More problematic is the position where the auctioneer has some authority to sell but exceeds it. The obvious case where this may arise is where the auctioneer is instructed to sell subject to a reserve and sells below it. We have already discussed this problem in chapter 3 from the point of view of the auctioneers' ability to bind his principal. If, as we have suggested, the seller is not bound on the contract of sale because the bids and any acceptance remain conditional, the question arises whether the auctioneer is liable to the purchaser for breach of warranty of authority. If the fact that a reserve is or may be fixed is notified to purchasers, as it usually is through the auction particulars, the auctioneer will not normally be liable for breach of warranty because the purchaser has notice of the restriction on that

---

[125] Liability for breach of warranty of authority may alternatively lie in tort where it is negligent or fraudulent: *Bowstead on Agency* (15th edn, 1985) Sweet & Maxwell, art 120 et seq.
[126] 1903 6 F (Ct of Sess) 153, 41 Sc LR 95.

authority, or notice of the possibility that it may be restricted and he is put on enquiry as to whether it has been. That was decided in *McManus v Fortescue*.[127] However in *Fay v Miller Wilkins & Co*[128] auctioneers were held liable to the purchaser because they went further than merely knocking the property down; they proceeded to sign the then requisite memorandum on his behalf. This was held to amount to a waiver of the condition that the property was sold subject to the reserve. Until the abolition of s 40 of the Law of Property Act 1925 in 1989 the position was, therefore, (after the abolition of similar evidentiary requirements in relation to certain goods in 1954) that an auctioneer could only be liable for breach of warranty of authority for selling below the reserve in the case of land. The distinction thus drawn in the treatment of sales was difficult to justify. The difficulty for the purchaser is that even if he knows that there is or may be a reserve placed on the property, he will not know whether it has in fact been reached. Should he not be entitled to assume that it has if the auctioneer knocks the property down to him, or, at any rate, should he not have redress against the auctioneer in such circumstances? The liability would not attach for falsely representing that he had authority to sell without reserve but for representing that the reserve had been reached. In *Fay v Miller Wilkins & Co* the auction Conditions empowered the vendor to fix a reserve. Clauson LJ, after reiterating that in such circumstances the purchaser took the risk that in selling at the knock-down price the auctioneer might be exceeding his authority, went on to say that the purchaser relies: '. . . in practice on the care and honesty of the auctioneer as a professional man, and in law on his . . . right to sue the auctioneer on the warranty of authority implied in the fact of his selling on the principal's behalf at the figure named in the note.'[129] Whilst this dictum is not entirely free from ambiguity it lends some judicial support to the proposition that an auctioneer, in concluding the formalities required for the sale of the property which is or may be subject to a reserve, represents that the property has reached or exceeded the reserve price and that, if it has not, whilst he cannot enforce the sale against the vendor, the purchaser can sue the auctioneer on that representation. Since now, both in respect of land and chattels, the contract is both valid and enforceable on the fall of the hammer without more, it is suggested that no action will now lie for breach of warranty of authority in these circumstances.[130]

---

[127] Above, n 118.   [128] [1941] Ch 360, CA.   [129] [1941] Ch 360 at 367.

[130] The position would, it is argued, be different in land sales if the conditions stipulate that the purchaser enter into a written contract and the auctioneer is empowered to sign such on behalf of the purchaser and purports to do so notwithstanding the failure to reach the reserve. Where the auctioneer thus takes these further steps he can be regarded as representing that he has authority to waive the condition inherent in a subject to reserve sale.

Liability on the contract of sale

Whilst the general rule is that an agent is not liable on the contract which he makes on behalf of his principal, there is a number of exceptions. Liability may attach because of particular strict rules relating to certain kinds of contract. Thus an agent will be liable where he makes a contract by deed and himself executes it. He is liable even though he is described as acting for and on behalf of his principal.[131] Additionally an agent will be liable if his principal is undisclosed. This is axiomatic in that, in such circumstances, the *fact* of his agency is not revealed to the purchaser at all. Here the purchaser may also sue the principal once he discovers his existence. It might have been arguable that an auctioneer could never sell for an undisclosed principal in that, qua auctioneer, he inevitably sells only the property of another. Indeed there have been judicial suggestions to this effect.[132] Unfortunately, however, this is not the case. It has been settled, at least since the case of *Flint v Woodin*[133] in 1852 that there is no objection to an auctioneer selling his own property to the purchaser. In such a case, clearly, the auctioneer sells as principal.

More uncertain, however, is the question whether an auctioneer may be liable personally in contract if the fact of his agency is disclosed but the *identity* of his principal is not. It is very important here to distinguish between the case where the principal is undisclosed, where the agent will always be liable, and the case where the existence of the principal is disclosed but his identity is not.[134] In such circumstances it is not possible to be dogmatic as to whether the agent incurs personal liability on the contract. In some cases the identity of the vendor may be important to the purchaser so that a purchaser who contracts with an agent who declines to name his principal may be taken to do so only on the basis that the agent undertakes some concurrent liability. In other circumstances the identity of the seller may be of no interest. In *Teheran-Europe Co Ltd v S T Belton (Tractors) Ltd* Diplock LJ said:[135]

---

[131] See *Bowstead on Agency* (above, n 135) art 109, and see also art 110 re liability on bills of exchange etc.

[132] See eg per Blackburn J in *Mainprice v Westley* (1865) 6 B&S 420 at 429 reporting the opinions of Cockburn C J and Shee J: 'In the employment of an auctioneer the character of an agent is necessarily implied and the party bidding at auction knowingly deals with him as such . . .' See also in similar vein at first instance in *Anderson v John Croall & Sons Ltd* 1904 6 F (Ct of Sess) 153, 41 Sc LR 95.

[133] (1852) 9 Hare 618, 22 LJ Ch 92.

[134] Regrettably, the judges have not always made such distinctions with care: 'the case [is] one of disclosed agency and undisclosed principal', *Benton v Campbell Parker & Co* [1925] 2 KB 410 per Salter J at 414; and per Blackburn J in *Mainprice v Westley* (above, n 132) at 429 where, speaking of the sale in *Warlow v Harrison* (1859) 1 E&E 309, 27 LJQB 14 (involving the sale of a horse sold as 'the property of a gentleman') his Lordship said 'the principal was not disclosed . . . he was a concealed principal'.

[135] [1968] 2 QB 545, CA at 555.

A person may enter into a contract through an agent whom he has actually authorised to enter into the contract on his behalf or whom he has led the other party to believe he has so authorised but we are concerned here only with actual authority. Where an agent has such actual authority and enters into a contract with another party intending to do so on behalf of his principal it matters not whether he discloses to the other party the identity of the principal or even that he is contracting on behalf of a principal at all, if the other party is willing or leads the agent to believe that he is willing to treat as a party to the contract anyone on whose behalf the agent may have been authorised to contract. In the case of an ordinary commercial contract such willingness of the other party may be assumed by the agent unless either the other party manifests his unwillingness or there are other circumstances which should leave the agent to realise that the other party was not so willing.

However, there are several cases involving auctions which suggest that where the name of the principal-vendor is not given, the auctioneer invariably incurs contractual liability to the purchaser. As long ago as 1792,[136] Lord Kenyon held an auctioneer liable where a bond was not assigned to the purchaser within the contractual period. Although it is not clear from the brief report of this case, it appears[137] that the fact of agency was disclosed but the name of the principal was not. The purchaser was said to be entitled to look to the auctioneer 'personally for the completion of the contract'. In *Franklyn v Lamond*[138] it was held that the auctioneer was liable for the non-transfer of certain company shares sold at auction. Here the judge, Wilde C J, opined that the auctioneer had contracted personally. The auctioneers were described as such in the catalogue and they argued unsuccessfully that this sufficed as an indication of agency absolving them from personal liability. The case is not particularly strong on the question of personal liability where the fact of agency is disclosed because the Chief Justice observed that 'their character as agents was no [sic] otherwise intimated to the purchaser' and that 'this is the simple case of parties who have sold as principals, turning round and saying that they are merely agents.' However, more modern cases have reiterated the principle that: 'Where an agent purports to make a contract for a principal, disclosing the fact that he is acting as an agent, but not naming his principal the rule is that, unless a contrary intention appears, he makes himself personally liable on the authorised contract.'[139]

The nature and scope of this personal liability falls to be considered. In *Wood v Baxter*[140] the purchaser of wheat and straw sold by a tenant sued the auctioneers when the landlord refused to allow him to remove the straw, invoking a custom that such was to remain on the land. It was held that the

---

136 *Hanson v Roberdeau* (1792) Peake 120.
137 Per Salter J in *Benton v Campbell Parker & Co* [1925] 2 KB 410 at 417.
138 (1847) 4 CB 637, 16 LJCP 221.
139 *Benton v Campbell Parker & Co* [1925] 2 KB 410 per Salter J at 414.
140 (1883) 49 LT 45.

claim failed because the auctioneer had done all he could to effect delivery and was not responsible for the vendor's lack of title (if such there was) to sell. Williams J said:[141]

What is the character and extent of the contract entered into by the auctioneer when he sells without disclosing the name of his principal? The answer to this is, that it depends upon the conditions of sale, upon what is said by the auctioneer at the time, upon the surrounding circumstances, and upon the nature of the subject matter of the sale. In the first place, it would certainly be going too far to say that an auctioneer, selling without disclosing the name of his principal, makes himself a contracting party in the same way and to the same extent that another agent acting for an undisclosed principal does. The auctioneer sells, not as an owner having a right to sell by virtue of his own right of property, but as an auctioneer empowered and entrusted by his employer to sell. If he is selling livestock or implements in the market place or furniture in a room, the extent of his contract would ordinarily be to deliver the goods to the buyer; if he was selling shares in a joint stock company, it would be to procure a transfer to the purchaser; if he was selling timber stacked in a yard or loaded on board ship or growing crops on a farm, it would be in each case to give such constructive delivery as according to the nature of the subject matter was practicable and usual. Upon making such delivery, his obligation would ordinarily be fulfilled.

Thus it appears that the liability of an auctioneer in these circumstances is essentially only for non-delivery. Despite that Williams J says that 'his contract is very nearly that of an ordinary vendor',[142] it is clear from the decision in that case, and also from *Benton v Campbell, Parker & Co*[143] that no liability attaches to the auctioneer for any want of title (logically, because as an expressed agent he does not claim to have any). The earlier cases of *Hanson v Roberdeau*[144] and *Franklyn v Lamond*[145] are consistent with a limited liability to deliver, since failure to deliver was in each case the complaint, but the question arises whether such a limitation is consonant with principle. If the rationale of fixing the auctioneer with personal liability is that given by Salter J in *Benton*'s case,[146] namely that 'a purchaser is willing to contract with an unknown man . . . but only if the agent will make himself personally liable if called upon to perform the contract',[147] there seems little justification or commercial logic in limiting the duty of performance to delivery only. Should not the purchaser have recourse against the auctioneer if the goods are defective or unfit for their purpose too?

It is suggested, however, that the reason for rendering the auctioneer liable is not because of any assumption that the identity of the vendor is crucial, but simply because the duty to deliver is the reverse of the coin that

---

[141] (1883) 49 LT 45 at 46. See also *Payne v Elsden* (1900) 17 TLR 161.
[142] Above, n 140.   [143] [1925] 2 KB 410.
[144] Above, n 136.   [145] Above, n 138.
[146] [1925] 2 KB 410.   [147] [1925] 2 KB 410 at 414.

an auctioneer may sue for the price.[148] We concluded in chapter 4 that the auctioneer's right to sue for the price is based upon his implied contract arising out of the delivery up of possession of the goods sold, and that this contract is quite separate from the contract of sale. Although Williams J suggested in *Wood v Baxter*[149] that the auctioneer could be sued upon the contract of sale, the better view is that expressed in *Benton v Campbell, Parker & Co* that:[150]

These rights and liabilities do not arise from the contract of sale which binds only the buyer and the principal. They arise from the contract which the auctioneer makes upon his own account with the buyer . . . The duty to deliver and the right to receive the price are usually expressed in the conditions of sale. But whatever its terms may be, the contract is entirely independent of the contract of sale.

If it is right that the duty to deliver is the correlative of the right to sue for the price, then it is obvious that liability should not extend beyond a duty to deliver. Normally delivery causes no problem in practice since chattels sold are in the sale room and available for removal by the buyer. But occasionally large chattels such as a grand piano are sold 'off site' and it is in this sort of situation that non-delivery could arise. It is, however, difficult to see why such a duty is then only imposed, in the absence of express provisions,[151] where the principal is unnamed or unidentified.[152] Moreover, there is a difficulty concerning sales of land. In such cases unless the auctioneer contracts as vendor, we have argued that he has no right to sue for the price and, therefore it would follow, that there could be no correlative personal liability to deliver. The absence of such liability would strengthen the argument in favour of rendering the auctioneer liable as agent of the purchaser to complete the necessary memorandum binding the vendor, advocated in the earlier part of this section.

Finally, it could be argued that the best reason for making the auctioneer personally liable where he declines to name the vendor is that if the auctioneer fails to identify him, the purchaser will be unable to bring actions against the vendor. However, we suggest that this practical obstacle can be overcome by an action for discovery. Normally, discovery will not be avail-

---

[148] See eg per Field J in *Woolfe v Horne* (1877) 2 QBD 355 at 360, and per Rowlatt J in *Page v Sully* (1918) 63 Sol Jo 55.

[149] Above, n 141.   [150] [1925] 2 KB 410 at 415–16.

[151] An example of a case where the duty to deliver was expressed in the Conditions of Sale is *Woolfe v Horne* (above, n 148) where the relevant provision read 'if any deficiency shall arise, or from any cause the auctioneers shall be unable to deliver any lot or portion of a lot, then in such a case the purchaser shall accept compensation for the same . . .' On the other hand in *Page v Sully* (above, n 148) McCardie J suggested that the liability could be excluded by appropriate provisions.

[152] A principal remains unnamed where the property is described as 'the property of a gentleman' as in *Warlow v Harrison* (1859) 1 E&E 309, 29 LJQB 14, and also it seems where the sale is expressed to be 'By order of Mr J Spurling and Others' (even if it later transpired that the named person was the seller of the particular lot) as in *Page v Sully* (above, n 148).

able save against a party to an action. There, of course, lies the problem because if the auctioneer is not personally liable — where the action is for something other than non-delivery — he cannot be made a party to the action. However, there has been developed, or perhaps revived, a right to bring an action for discovery against a non-party. In *Norwich Pharmacal v Customs and Excise Comrs*[153] a plaintiff who owned a patent for a chemical compound was held entitled to seek discovery from the defendants as to the names and addresses of importers who had infringed their patent. The defendants to this action — an action for discovery only — were of course in no way implicated in the infringement. Lord Reid said that if through no fault of his own a person gets mixed up in the tortious acts of others so as to facilitate their wrong-doing he may incur no personal liability but he comes under a duty to assist the person who has been wronged by giving him full information and disclosing the identity of the wrongdoers. If an innocent party is so enjoined then a fortiori an auctioneer unreasonably refusing to disclose the identity of his principal should be. The only difficulty with this principle is that Lord Reid refers expressly to tortious acts of others, whereas in our situation the claim will normally be in contract. Other judges, eg Lord Morris,[154] refer simply to persons who have information about 'wrongdoers'. It seems to us that the *Norwich Pharmacal* case lays down a principle of fairly general application and that it would be unreasonable to assume that it was restricted to cases involving torts. We say this because of the rationale behind this recently revived action: it was thought that discovery would never lie save against a party to proceedings because of the so-called 'mere witness' rule, namely that you cannot obtain information by discovery from the person who will in due course be compellable to give that information as a witness. But as was pointed out in the *Norwich Pharmacal* case, if the information in the possession of the commissioners was not to be made available by discovery, no action could ever be begun because the identity of the wrongdoers would remain unrevealed. Similarly, discovery against the auctioneer would be justified simply because without it the purchaser would be unable to bring an action against the wrongdoer, eg a seller in breach of implied terms under the Sale of Goods Act 1979. In these circumstances no hardship is involved in limiting the auctioneer's liability to non-delivery.

It may be that, as a matter of specific contractual agreement, the auctioneer will owe duties to the buyer. So, as was held in the recent decision in *De Balkany v Christie Manson & Woods*[155], where the auctioneers expressly promised on their own account to 'repurchase' a deliberate forgery, that amounted to an independent contractual liability to the buyer. This is

---

[153] [1974] AC 133, [1973] 2 All ER 943, HL.   [154] Above, n 153.
[155] 1995 (The Independent Jan. 19 1995).

significant in that the ability of the buyer to pursue relevant remedies under the contract of *sale* against the seller may have been less extensive.

The foregoing discussion has proceeded on the assumption that the auctioneer has sold goods. Hitherto, an auctioneer would not sign a contract of sale concerning land in such a way as to render himself liable personally. Now, under the Law of Property (Miscellaneous Provisions) Act 1989 the contract itself — and not merely the evidentiary memorandum — may be signed by an agent. If the auction particulars stipulate both that the purchaser enter into a written agreement[156] and that the auctioneer may sign such on behalf of the vendor he may, in appropriate circumstances — eg where the vendor is unnamed — attract personal liability.

OTHER LIABILITY

Under the general law an auctioneer may incur liability to the purchaser in a variety of circumstances. Generally speaking, the liability will arise from a failure to take proper care either of the purchaser's goods, or his person, or for mis-statements in and about the sale of the property.

Duty with regard to the goods purchased

When specific goods are sold to a purchaser ownership of them will, unless a contrary intention appears, pass to the purchaser when the contract is made,[157] ie on the fall of the hammer. Thereafter they are the purchaser's goods. If the auctioneer retains possession of them, he will become the bailee of the purchaser. As such he will be under a duty to take reasonable care of them, apart from any express exclusion of liability provision which will be subject to the test of reasonableness under the Unfair Contract Terms Act 1977.[158] In practice, however, it is rare to find that title to property passes to the purchaser on the sale. Both Sotheby's and Christie's conditions provide that ownership shall not pass until payment and that credit may be given. Sotheby's give the buyer five days in which to remove the goods purchased where they have been paid for or where credit has been given, and provide further that after collection or the five-day period the buyer will be responsible for any loss. This leaves open the potential liability of the auctioneers during the collection period. Christie's Conditions are now of similar effect. Those in use at the time of the 1st edition

---

[156] See below ch 9.   [157] Sale of Goods Act 1979, s 18, r 1.
[158] See generally ch 6 and see the discussion above relating to the liability of the auctioneer as bailee of the seller; the principles apply, *mutatis mutandis*, as between auctioneer and purchaser.

of this book provided that the risk passed to the buyer from the fall of the hammer.[159] The effect of such a clause requires consideration. Where the ownership passes to the buyer and the auctioneer retains possession during a period when the purchaser may collect, the auctioneer is the bailee of the purchaser and, as such, owes him a duty to take reasonable care of his goods. Where the property does not pass to the purchaser pending payment, the analysis is different. Neither ownership nor possession passes to the buyer and, therefore, he cannot be a bailor although he has an interest in the preservation of the goods. The law is clear that such a person cannot, in the absence of a contract with the person in whose custody they were — eg carrier or warehouseman — sue in negligence for any failure to take care of them. This is because in order to maintain such an action a party has to be their owner; if he is not then none of *his* property is damaged or lost and his loss is purely economic and not recoverable.[160] However, in the case of auctions, there is a separate contract with the buyer on the terms of the Conditions of Sale. Whether such a contract would include an implied term, in the absence of the exclusions commonly found, to care for the goods of a purchaser who has not become their owner, is, however, doubtful.

Liability for physical injury

An auctioneer may be liable in negligence if those attending the auction are damaged by goods, eg by a frisky horse, or by the state of the auctioneer's premises. The duties of care are owed not only to one who becomes a purchaser but to all those who are lawfully present at the auction, and we shall consider the ambit of this liability briefly in the following section of this chapter, 'Duties and liabilities to third parties'.

Liability for misrepresentations

In dealing with the duty owed to the vendor to describe the property accurately we make the point that whereas the vendor may be liable for misrepresentations, including those made quite innocently, under the Misrepresentation Act 1967, no direct liability thereunder attaches to the auctioneer acting within his authority.[161] However, an auctioneer may still render himself civilly liable to the purchaser for mis-statements made in the

---

[159] Christie's Conditions of Sale A9; Cf Sotheby's Conditions of Business 9, 10 and 12. (See Appendix 1.)

[160] See *Leigh and Sillivan Ltd. v Aliakmon Shipping Co Ltd.* [1986] 2 WLR 902.

[161] There is no need to render the auctioneer as agent directly liable under the 1967 Act because his principal will be in such circumstances; there is also separate liability in common law — see below.

auction particulars or orally from the rostrum, under the common law. What follows is necessarily a truncated account. Readers are referred to the standard works on contract and tort for detailed consideration. There are three separate possible bases of liability, and these are given below.

In deceit

A person who causes loss to another by means of fraud will be liable to an action in tort for deceit. Fraud is a serious charge to be levelled at anyone but especially at a professional person and, in order for it to be made out, fairly stringent tests have to be satisfied. The House of Lords has held that it cannot be proved unless it can be said of a person that: 'he knowingly made a false statement or one which he did not believe to be true, or was careless whether what he stated be true or false'.[162] A prerequisite to a successful action against an auctioneer under this tort is, therefore, that it be shown that he did not honestly believe what he said was true. If he did have that honest belief, however foolish, credulous or negligent he might have been, he will not be liable to the purchaser for deceit.

In negligence

For 70 years after the decision in *Derry v Peek*[163] it was thought that no liability could attach for mis-statements if they were made merely negligently. In 1963 however, the House of Lords delivered a judgment of exceptional importance for professional men in *Hedley Byrne & Co Ltd v Heller & Partners Ltd*.[164] That case concerned a banker's reference on which another party relied but the decision is of very wide scope. The House of Lords said that a person could owe a duty of care to another in giving information or advice and that such a duty would exist where there was some 'special relationship' between the parties. The precise circumstances when such a special relationship will be held to exist have not been exhaustively stated, but in general it can be said to arise whenever someone possessed of special skill undertakes to apply it for the assistance of another person who relies upon it.[165] There appears to be no reported instance of an auctioneer being held liable under the *Hedley Byrne v Heller* doctrine, probably because purchasers will normally prefer to take recourse against

---

[162] *Derry v Peek* (1889) 14 App Cas 337, 58 LJ Ch 864, HL.   [163] Above, n 162.
[164] [1964] AC 465, [1963] 2 All ER 575, HL.
[165] The more restrictive test suggested by the majority in Privy Council in *Mutual Life and Citizens' Assurance Co Ltd v Evatt* [1971] AC 793, [1971] 1 All ER 150, PC, that the advisor should be in business as the supplier of information or advice or expressly have claimed to possess special skill, has not been regarded as conclusively limiting the English authority. However, even on the basis of such a narrow interpretation, an auctioneer would normally be, prima facie, regarded as owing a duty of care.

the vendor in cases of negligent mis-statement made by the auctioneer as his agent. The reason for this is that the vendor's liability under s 2(1) of the Misrepresentation Act 1967 is somewhat easier to establish, because under the Act it is for the vendor positively to disprove negligence, whereas at common law the onus would be on the purchaser to prove it. However, there can be little doubt that an auctioneer is in a special relationship vis-à-vis a purchaser.[166]

A difficulty arises as to exclusion of liability. We discuss elsewhere the impact of the Unfair Contract Terms Act 1977,[167] and it is clear that a vendor seeking to rely on the exclusion of liability clauses commonly found in auctioneers' conditions would have to show that such reliance was reasonable. As regards the auctioneer seeking to avoid liability for negligent mis-statements, the position is the same. In *Hedley Byrne v Heller* the bank were, in the result, held not liable because they had expressly disclaimed liability by heading their advice 'without responsibility'. Normally a person cannot avoid liability for negligence simply by broadcasting that he does not incur it, but the basis of the duty in this area is that the defendant has expressly or impliedly *undertaken* that he will give his advice or information with care. Obviously if he says in advance that he undertakes no such thing, no duty will arise. This kind of disclaimer differs from exclusion clauses as traditionally construed in that it does not seek to avoid the loss arising from a breach of duty but, rather, prevents the duty arising in the first place: 'a man cannot be said voluntarily to be undertaking a responsibility if at the very moment that he is said to be accepting it he declares that he is not.'[168] The Unfair Contract Terms Act 1977, s 2(2), subjects to a test of reasonableness a term or notice excluding or restricting 'liability for negligence' and it was once thought that this does not cover a term which negates the existence of the duty. However, the House of Lords has now clarified the position and held that the Act applies equally to disclaimers of this sort. They, too, must, therefore, satisfy the test of reasonableness.[169]

On a collateral warranty

As stated, whilst tort imposes liability on auctioneers for deceit or negligence, there is no liability for purely innocent mis-statements. However,

---

[166] An estate agent has been held to be potentially liable to the buyer for negligently misdescribing the acreage of property in *McCullagh v Lane Fox and Partners* (1994 EGC 5) although in the result the claim failed because the purchaser could establish no loss. Whilst in *Gran Gelato Ltd v Richcliff (Group) Ltd* [1992] 1 All ER 873 the court suggested that there was no need for separate personal liability to attach to an agent acting within his authority, this may depend upon whether, as for example in the *McCullagh* case, the principal has excluded his liability vis-à-vis the purchaser. See now *De Balkany v Christie Manson & Woods* [1995] The Independent, Jan. 19 1995 discussed fully in ch 6.

[167] See ch 6.   [168] Per Lord Devlin in *Hedley Byrne v Heller* [1964] AC 465 at 533.

[169] See *Smith v Eric S Bush* [1989] 2 All ER 514.

such liability may be imposed contractually on the basis that the auctioneer has made a collateral warranty.[170] Essentially the collateral contract is construed on this basis: the auctioneer effectively says to the successful purchaser 'if you will make the contract of sale with the vendor I promise that (eg) the horse is sound etc.' Thus the promise by the auctioneer is said to be part of a contract collateral to the main contract of sale which contains a representation which induces the formation of that contract, though it may not become incorporated in it. In such a way an auctioneer can be made liable for a representation, including one made innocently, which induces the formation of the main contract. Since the representation amounts, independently, to a term of a separate, collateral contract, the auctioneer will be liable for breach of it unless he can point to an exclusion clause which is apt to protect him. Once again, therefore, he will have to show that such a clause is reasonable.

DUTIES RELATING TO THE DEPOSIT

Invariably, in the case of sales of land by auction, and sometimes in chattel auctions, the Conditions of Sale require the purchaser to pay a deposit to the auctioneer. In such cases the auctioneer incurs certain liabilities with regard to the sums so paid. The requiring of a deposit has a two-fold purpose: first, to provide a part-payment of the purchase price — provided that the sale goes ahead to completion — but secondly and primarily, it is to 'guarantee that the purchaser means business' or to provide 'a security for the performance of the contract'.[171]

When such a deposit is paid to an auctioneer, the duties and liabilities which ensue depend largely upon whether he receives it as agent for one of the parties (usually the vendor) or as a stakeholder. The capacity in which the auctioneer holds the deposit is usually made clear by the contract;[172] but, if it is not, the law presumes that an auctioneer receiving a deposit does so as stakeholder whereas an estate agent and eg a solicitor do so as agent for the vendor.[173] The significance of the distinction was explained by Bowen LJ in *Ellis v Goulton* as follows:[174]

[170] See eg *Webster v Higgin* [1948] 2 All ER 127; *Andrews v Hopkinson* [1957] 1 QB 229, [1956] 3 All ER 422.
[171] *Soper v Arnold* (1889) 14 App Cas 429, HL, per Lord MacNaghten at 435, and Lord Herschell at 433.
[172] See eg National Conditions of Sale which provides for the deposit to be paid to the auctioneer as stakeholder. See also Standard Conditions of Sale, 2nd edn, which incorporate the Law Society's Conditions of Sale 1992 and are to similar effect.
[173] Conceded in *Furtado v Lumley* (1890) 54 JP 407, 6 TLR 168, but if the receipt for the deposit is signed by the auctioneer as agent for the vendor, he will hold it as such: *Bamford v Shuttleworth* (1840) 11 Ad&El 926; *Ellis v Goulton* [1893] 1 QB 350.
[174] [1893] 1 QB 350 at 352–3.

When a deposit is paid by a purchaser under a contract for the sale of land, the person who makes the payment may enter an agreement with the vendor that the money shall be held by the recipient as agent for both vendor and the purchaser. If this is done, the person who receives it becomes a stakeholder, liable in certain events to return the money to the person who paid it. In the absence of such agreement the money is paid to a person who has not the character of stakeholder; and it follows that, when the money reaches his hands it is the same thing so far as the person who pays it is concerned as if it had reached the hands of the principal. If so, it is impossible to treat money paid under these circumstances and remaining in the hands of the agent as there under any condition or subject to any trust in relation to the payer.

Thus as a stakeholder the duty of the auctioneer is to hold the deposit money as agent for both parties and not to part with it until the event upon which it becomes payable to one party or the other takes place. If he pays the money over to the vendor before completion or while a dispute is continuing relating to the contract of sale, he will be liable for it as money had and received to the purchaser's use;[175] whereas if he received it as *agent* it is the vendor who will be accountable to the purchaser in the event that the sale falls through, since payment to the agent is virtually payment to the principal.[176]

An auctioneer holding as stakeholder should, therefore, not pay over any deposit to his vendor until he has satisfied himself that the sale has been satisfactorily completed. Most of the old cases cited so far concerned protracted disputes about title. If, however, his vendor is importunate for payment to him of what is, after all, part payment of the price, the auctioneer may pay it over but he should ensure that he obtains an indemnity from him.[177] The basic duty of the auctioneer as described above is well settled. Two important questions remain, however, as to which a certain degree of doubt may be entertained. The first relates to liability to pay interest on the deposit, and the second concerns responsibility where the deposit is lost.

Interest on the deposit

This subdivides into two separate concerns: whether the auctioneer is liable to invest the deposit money so that it yields interest and, in default, is liable for sums which could have been earned to the party ultimately entitled; and secondly, even where the answer to that question is no, whether if the

---

[175] *Edwards v Holding* (1854) 5 Taunt 815, 1 Marsh 377; *Burrough v Skinner* (1770) 5 Burr 2639, 98 ER 387.

[176] *Bamford v Shuttleworth* (above, n 173).

[177] An appropriate form may be found in 3 Encyclopaedia of Forms and Precedents (5th Edn), Form 14.

auctioneer does in fact invest the deposit, he is entitled to keep the interest yielded.

Liability for non-investment

The first question has frequently arisen for decision, and it is clear that no interest is payable on deposit moneys whilst properly in the auctioneer's hands as stakeholder. In *Lee v Munn*[178] a purchaser claimed back his deposit with interest from the auctioneer when the vendor was unable to make the title. The court held that no interest could be recovered by him since negotiations for the sale had been continuing throughout but it was suggested, obiter, that the auctioneer could be liable for interest if the contract was rescinded and the auctioneer wrongly retained the deposit after demand had been duly made.[179] In *Gaby v Driver*[180] the purchaser's contention that interest would automatically run from the contractual completion date when the vendor failed to meet it was rejected, but again it was suggested that a claim for interest could be maintained after a valid demand and refusal. The purchaser's remedy, where the vendor is in breach of contract, is to sue the vendor and claim loss of income on the deposit moneys as special damages.[181]

Liability for interest earned

Less certain is the position where the auctioneer does, in fact, invest the deposit moneys. Here there is some division of opinion amongst the judges. Since deposits on sales of land are usually at least ten per cent of the purchase price, the sums earned by a busy land auctioneer may not be insignificant. The earliest case in which the question seems to have received detailed consideration is *Harington v Hoggart*[182] in 1830. Here the auctioneer was requested by the vendor's solicitors to invest the deposit in certain government securities and the vendor offered an indemnity in case such investment caused loss. The auctioneers, who held the deposit as stakeholders, said they would do as asked but only if the purchaser concurred. He did not, and the fund was not invested. In the result the sale was only completed some eight years after the deposit had been paid, due to protracted title disputes. The purchaser claimed interest on the deposit. Lord Tenterden the Chief Justice was clear that the auctioneers as stakeholders dealt correctly with the request of the vendors to invest the money. However he went on to consider what the position would have been

---

[178] (1817) 8 Taunt 45.
[179] (1817) 8 Taunt 45 per Dallas J at 54 and per Burrough J at 55.
[180] (1828) 2 Y&J 549.
[181] See *Curling v Shuttleworth* (1829) 6 Bing 121, 3 Moo & P 368.
[182] (1830) 1 B&Ad 577.

had the sum yielded interest, and concluded that if a stakeholder chose to invest the funds he would be liable for any loss accruing, and 'if he is to answer for the loss it seems to me he has a right to any intermediate advantage which may arise.'[183] Moreover, whilst it was in the stakeholder's possession, the deposit fund belonged to neither vendor nor purchaser so that any interest yielded belonged to the stakeholder. This last point is not thought to be compelling: there is no reason why a stakeholder should not hold the interest as an accretion to the principal sum for whomsoever of the parties ultimately becomes entitled to it. Moreover, the notion that the right to any profit is the corollary of his potential loss is also objectionable. There are many situations where an agent may be liable to disgorge profits made even though he would be also liable to make good losses. The real question is whether the stakeholder should be distinguished from one who holds a fund as an agent. Such a distinction has been carefully maintained with regard to basic duties relating to the deposit. On the other hand it might be argued that the stakeholder is, as has frequently been stressed, the agent of *both* vendor and purchaser and that as such he should never be able to keep profits yielded by a fund which belongs to one of them. However a rationale for such a distinction was suggested in the modern case of *Potters (a firm) v Loppert*, viz:[184]

The interest represents not merely a reward for the agent's trouble but also as a recompense for the sterilisation of the property vis-à-vis the estate agent during the period between payment of the deposit and the conclusion of the contract or its breakdown with the consequences that the agent has no prospect of earning a commission on its sale to any other party so long as the property remains sterilised.[185]

As will be obvious, all this was said in connection with an estate agent's position but it is arguable that similar reasoning can be applied to that of an auctioneer engaged to sell property; a vendor's solicitor, eg instructed to receive a deposit as agent, is in an entirely different position. But the simplest rationale is that given by Harman J in *Smith v Hamilton*, namely that 'the stakeholder is not bound to pay interest. He retains the benefit of it: that is his reward for holding the stake.'[186]

In the course of his judgment in *Potters v Loppert*,[187] the Vice-Chancellor expressly approved *Harington v Hoggart*[188] and stressed that a stakeholder was not in a position of a fiduciary agent under a duty to account to his principal for profits made. Contrary views have been expressed, most no-

---

[183] (1830) 1 B& Ad 577 at 586–7.
[184] [1973] Ch 399, [1973] 1 All ER 658. This case concerned a pre-contract deposit paid to an estate agent but much of the discussion concerned the liability of an auctioneer-stakeholder of a contract deposit.
[185] [1973] 1 All ER 658 at 669 per Pennycuick V-C.   [186] [1951] Ch 174 at 184.
[187] Above, n 184.   [188] Above, n 182.

tably by Sachs LJ in *Burt v Claude Cousins & Co Ltd*[189] to the effect that a stakeholder is a trustee for whomsoever becomes entitled to the fund, but the better view is that the stakeholder's liability sounds in contract or quasi contract for money had and received, and that whilst he retains it he does not do so as trustee for either party so as to disentitle him from profits earned by it. It is here that the significance of receiving the deposit as stakeholder rather than merely as agent of the vendor is most potently marked.[190] In this connection we should point out that where the auctioneer is an estate agent his duties as to the holding of clients' money are now governed by the Estate Agents Act 1979. It is clear that where he holds a deposit as agent for one party, he is liable to pay and account for interest, but that where he holds as stakeholder he is not.[191]

Loss of the deposit

The argument in favour of permitting the auctioneer when stakeholder to retain profits made out of the deposit moneys is based, at the end of the day, on the maintenance of a distinction between the capacity of the stakeholder and that of one who is merely an agent. A final question arises as to upon whom the liability should fall in the event that the auctioneer, through infraction or otherwise, causes the deposit to be lost, usually by reason of his insolvency. If he is the agent of one party one would expect that the risk of loss would fall on that party and, indeed, that is the position. Conversely, if the auctioneer is a stakeholder and as such is liable 'to hold it in medio pending the outcome of a future event',[192] one might have expected the risk of loss to fall equally on either party, vendor or purchaser, who subsequently becomes entitled to it; he is equally the agent of both. However, it appears[193] to be the law that the vendor will bear the risk of loss so that he

---

[189] [1971] 2 QB 426, [1971] 2 All ER 611, CA. See also per Cross J in *Skinner v Trustee of Property of Reed (Bankrupt)* [1967] Ch 1194, [1971] 2 All ER 1286. The decision of the House of Lords in *Brown v I R C* [1965] AC 244, [1964] 3 All ER 119, HL, that a professional adviser is in a fiduciary relationship and as such cannot make a profit out of his client's money when entrusted with it, is not doubted but only begs the question when that person is a stakeholder.

[190] Whilst in that situation it is advantageous for the auctioneer to be a stakeholder, it is necessary to bear in mind that in one situation he is in a stronger position if he acts as agent in receiving the deposit moneys — namely where he is seeking to exercise his lien against a vendor who has become bankrupt. The auctioneer can only exercise his lien against the vendor's property and the deposit will only have that character when the auctioneer holds it as his agent. See ch 4.

[191] See Estate Agents Act 1979, ss 14–15 (see Appendix 2), and Estates Agents (Accounts) Regulations 1981, r 7. On the Act generally see Murdoch *The Law of Estate Agency and Auctions* (3rd edn. 1994) Estates Gazette, ch 6.

[192] Per Denning M R in *Burt v Claude Cousins & Co Ltd* [1971] 2 QB 426.

[193] Murdoch (above, n 191) p 317, but the authorities are not entirely convincing and are of some age.

will be liable to recompense a purchaser who becomes entitled to its return and must give credit for it as part payment once it has been paid to the auctioneer. So was stated in *Fenton v Browne*,[194] but this case concerned a private sale where the deposit was paid to an estate agent who absconded and went bankrupt. The decision that the vendor was liable for the loss of the deposit is explicable in that the money had been paid to the estate agent qua agent of the vendor. As such, as we observed earlier, the fund is treated as having been paid to the vendor himself. What was said about auctioneers was necessarily obiter therefore. An unusual case is *Smith v Jackson & Lloyd*,[195] where a purchaser who was allowed into possession pending completion sought an order that the rent to be assessed by the court have deducted from it interest on the deposit he had paid. This was allowed by the court which rested on *Fenton v Browne* on the grounds that it was reasonable that the vendor be treated as having had the benefit of the stake because it amounted to part payment of the purchase price and because he could require the auctioneer to invest the money for his benefit. Neither of these reasons is, it is submitted, convincing. The part payment is only conditional pending completion which there had not taken place; and the notion that the vendor could require investment of the sum for his benefit is denied by *Harington v Hoggart*.[196] Finally there is the decision in *Rowe v May*,[197] where a mortgagee refused to complete until the purchaser of his interest paid him the balance of a deposit which the purchaser had already paid to a defaulting auctioneer. The court held that the mortgagee must take the risk of its loss. Romilly MR said:[198]

Where a purchaser pays a deposit on his purchase-money to the auctioneer and it is lost, on whom does the loss fall? If the matter goes off, because the vendor cannot make a good title it is the vendor's duty to repay the deposit and the loss occasioned by the non-completion; and in case an action were brought against him for breach of the contract, the amount of deposit not repaid would be part of his loss, and the purchaser would be entitled to add it to the damages; so if the contract be completed and the deposit cannot be recovered from the auctioneer, *who for this purpose is the agent of the vendor*, it will be the vendor's loss, and not that of the purchaser.[199]

The italicised words are crucial. It appears that the Master of the Rolls was treating the auctioneer as agent rather than stakeholder. If the auctioneer

---

[194] (1807) 14 Ves 144.   [195] (1816) 1 Madd 618.

[196] (1830) 1 B&Ad 577. *Smith v Jackson & Lloyd* (n 195 above) was followed the same year in a case where it was held that a vendor was entitled to have the money paid into court and not repaid to a purchaser dissatisfied with the vendor's title, pending settlement of that dispute: *Annesley v Muggridge* (1816) 1 Madd 593.

[197] (1854) 18 Beav 613.

[198] (1854) 18 Beav 613 at 616–17, emphasis added.

[199] In the case of an estate agent auctioneer the remedies available to his client are greatly enhanced by the Estate Agents Act 1979. Section 13 provides that a client's money is held in trust thus taking it out of the bankruptcy pool and rendering available the rules relating to tracing etc.

were the vendor's agent, the result would be unremarkable. If however the courts are assimilating the position of stakeholder and agent, it is contrary to principle. There is however one explanation for this line of cases which can, we suggest, be supported: in the first of this quartet of cases, *Fenton v Browne*, Sir William Grant MR rationalised the decision thus: 'Upon a sale by auction the vendor determines who is to receive the deposit. The auctioneer is not a stakeholder of the purchaser: at least not of his choice ... Under these circumstances it would be to hard to throw [the] loss upon this purchaser.'[200]

Where the parties are put at risk as to the honesty or financial stability of the auctioneer-stakeholder it is justifiable to render the vendor liable for any loss, since it is the vendor who selects the stakeholder — the purchaser has no choice but to entrust the auctioneer with the stake. The antiquity of the cases in this area may be a happy sign that today these risks are minimal.

DUTIES AND LIABILITIES TO THIRD PARTIES

CONVERSION AND ACTS AMOUNTING TO CONVERSION

An auctioneer may owe a number of general duties — for example under the law relating to negligence (which we consider briefly below) — and he may also incur liabilities to a third party who is not either a seller or buyer concerned with the sale. The prime example of the latter is the liability which attaches when an auctioneer wrongly converts the property of another. This will arise if the auctioneer *sells* the property on behalf of a principal who is not entitled to sell, or where he wrongfully *delivers* property to one who is not entitled to receive it with notice of that fact, or where he *retains* property to which a third party is entitled. A conversion may be defined as an unlawful act of interference with goods inconsistent with the right of a third party whereby the latter is deprived of their use and possession. It is a tort for which the remedy is primarily damages; but where goods are detained by a person being sued, the court may order their return. Where such a remedy is available, the court may give the defendant the option of retaining them and paying damages instead.[201] Damages will be assessed by reference to the value of the goods, which in the case of a sale by auction will not necessarily be the price realised.[202] In addition, damages may be awarded for any consequential loss arising out of the conversion.

---

[200] (1807) 14 Ves 144 at 148. Approved in *Burt v Claude Cousins & Co Ltd* [1971] 2 QB 426 at 450 per Sachs LJ.

[201] Torts (Interference with Goods) Act 1977, s 3.

[202] *Davis v Artingstall* (1880) 49 LJ Ch 609, 42 LT 507: 'the plaintiff is entitled to the real value of the goods sold, and not merely to what they fetched at auction, which cannot be assumed to be the real value of the goods' (per Fry J at 610).

Sale without the authority of the true owner

The principal may simply have stolen them, or he may have a right of possession but not yet become their owner. Old cases frequently involved sales on behalf of vendors who had transferred the goods previously under a bill of sale in order to give security for a loan. A more modern manifestation concerns goods, typically cars, 'sold' under a hire-purchase agreement. Where a car is sold in this way, the 'buyer' in fact is given possession and the intention is that the property will become his. However, the legal analysis is that unless and until the hirer exercises an option to purchase, on paying the final instalment, he remains simply a hirer. As such he is entitled only to possession. The finance company which finances the deal is the true owner of the vehicle. If the hirer during the currency of the agreement 'sells' the car, the finance company will be able to maintain an action in conversion against him and if he sells through an auctioneer, the latter too will be liable if the purchaser gets title or if the auctioneer delivers the car to the purchaser with the intention of transferring title.[203]

It must be emphasised here that the liability of the auctioneer does not depend upon any deliberate or negligent wrongdoing: he is liable in conversion to the true owner even if he is totally innocent and acts in complete good faith. In *Union Transport Finance Ltd v British Car Auctions Ltd*[204] as recently as 1978 it was argued that auctioneers acting in good faith were incapable in law of converting goods when merely selling for a principal who, it transpired, had no title. However the Court of Appeal in that case were clear that the point had been established by the House of Lords in *Hollins v Fowler*[205] and it cannot now be seriously questioned. In 1971 the Law Reform Committee considered whether the 'innocent handler' (as opposed to the innocent acquirer, ie the purchaser) should be protected but concluded, on balance, that he should not. It was felt that auctioneers and others in a similar position carry on a business in which this risk is incidental and for which insurance is available.

There may remain, however, an argument open to the auctioneer that in certain circumstances he did not in fact effect the sale at all but merely acted in a lesser capacity to bring the seller and buyer together. In *Cochrane v Rymill*[206] one Peggs borrowed money from Cochrane and the loan was

---

[203] Although conversion is essentially a wrong against possession, the finance company by law has a right to possession if, prior to the wrongful sale, it exercises the right to terminate the hiring, for eg non-payment of an instalment, normally contained in the contract. It also seems that he can establish a sufficient right to possession as a result of the hirer's delivery up of the vehicle to the auctioneer for sale since this is anathematic to the bailment. See *Union Transport Finance Ltd v British Car Auctions Ltd* [1978] 2 All ER 385, CA; *North Central (or General) Wagon & Finance Co Ltd v Graham* [1950] 2 KB 7, [1950] 1 All ER 780, CA.

[204] See n 203 above.   [205] (1875) LR 7 HL 757, 44 LJQB 169.

[206] (1879) 40 LT 744, 43 JP 572, CA.

secured on a number of cabs and carriage horses, the borrower effecting a bill of sale in favour of Cochrane. Subsequently Peggs instructed the defendant auctioneer to sell the charged goods. The auctioneer gave the seller an advance on the proceeds of sale, sold the goods and, after deduction of the advance, paid the proceeds to Peggs. The holder of the bill of sale sued the auctioneer in conversion. Notwithstanding that Cochrane had been at fault in failing to register the bill of sale, the auctioneers were held liable. Bramwell LJ held that here there had been a clear dealing with the property and an exercise of dominion over it coupled with its delivery to another. However, he distinguished such a dealing by auctioneers from one where the auctioneer would not be liable in conversion thus:[207]

Supposing a man were to come into an auctioneer's yard holding a horse . . . and say 'I want to sell my horse; if you will find a purchaser I will pay commission' and the auctioneer says: 'Here is a man who wants to sell a horse; will anyone buy him?' If he then and there finds him a purchaser and the seller himself hands over the horse there could be no act on the part of the auctioneer which could render him liable for conversion.

This dictum has given rise to no little difficulty. The fact that in this case the auctioneer, having made the vendor an advance, had a lien on the goods sold, clearly, of itself, took the case out of the 'mere conduit' example given, but it would not be correct to conclude that where the auctioneer does not have such an interest in the sale, he will automatically be within its scope. In a subsequent case against the same auctioneer a couple of years later,[208] the court held the defendant not liable in conversion. There the horses were sold by private contract before the auction and the auctioneer took his commission and gave a delivery order to the purchaser. The Court of Appeal found the auctioneer to have not converted the goods as against the rights of the holder of a bill of sale relating to the horses. The auctioneer was held to be a mere conduit. *Cochrane v Rymill*[209] was distinguished on the ground that here there was no question of the auctioneer selling for his own benefit but the salient distinction must be simply that the auctioneer did not effect the sale at all.[210] The case of *Turner v Hockey*[211] does, at first sight, suggest that whenever the auctioneer sells without having a personal interest in the sale, he does so merely as a conduit pipe but that decision has been doubted and explained on the basis that there all the auctioneer did was to communicate an offer, the sale being concluded privately by the vendor with the purchaser. Whether, in such circum-

---

[207] (1879) 40 LT 744 at 746.

[208] *National Mercantile Bank v Rymill* (1881) 44 LT 767, CA.

[209] Above, n 206.

[210] See observations of Collins J in *Consolidated Co v Curtis & Son* [1892] 1 QB 495 at 501–2.

[211] (1887) 56 LJQB 301.

stances, the auctioneer generally escapes liability must again be doubted however.

This situation arose in somewhat special circumstances in *R H Willis & Son (a firm) v British Car Auctions Ltd*,[212] the facts of which require some elaboration. Here a hire-purchase buyer in breach of his agreement placed the car in the hands of the defendant auctioneer for sale subject to a reserve. The property did not reach its reserve and the auctioneers, in pursuance of the usual practice, invited the purchaser and vendor to join them at their 'provisional bid office', where the vendor agreed to accept the bid. It was argued that here the auctioneers had done something less than effect the sale; no sale at auction had been concluded because since the goods had not reached their reserve the bids and acceptance remained conditional nor, it was argued, had they sold the property themselves by private treaty; they had merely introduced a prospective purchaser to the vendor. However, the Court of Appeal rejected that argument. The judges looked to the business purpose behind the fairly elaborate provisional bid procedure, namely that it was to bring about a sale, and to the fact that in such cases, as also in those where a sale is effected through the fall of the hammer, the buyer is required to pay an indemnity fee[213] and he concludes a contract on the terms of the Conditions of Sale. In all these circumstances the court held the auctioneer liable for conversion of the car since they had effectively sold it. The court doubted the correctness of both *National Mercantile Bank v Rymill*[214] and *Turner v Hockey*.[215]

We can conclude, therefore, that where the auctioneer effects the sale (whether at auction or by private treaty) of property which his principal is not entitled to sell, he will be guilty of conversion. Now it is a general principle of commercial law that where the seller is not the true owner, the purchaser from him will not get title: nemo dat quod non habet.[216] However, the desirability of protecting commercial transactions is also a crucial concern of the law. Thus the law permits certain exceptions to this general principle. If the auctioneer knocks down goods to a bidder he will be liable in conversion if he couples that act with a dealing, with intent to pass the title whether or not the purchaser does in fact get title to them. If the purchaser *does* get a good title so that the true owner is divested of his goods, then a fortiori the auctioneer will incur liability in conversion. But in such a case the purchaser will not also be liable — he gets title and cannot be sued by the former owner. Where he does not get title both he and the

---

[212] [1978] 2 All ER 392, [1978] 1 WLR 432, CA. See the discussion of this case in ch 10, below.

[213] The insurance point pressed heavily on Lord Denning in particular, as did the fact that the auctioneers took their commission (albeit at a reduced rate).

[214] Above, n 208.

[215] Above, n 211.

[216] The rule is partially set out in the Sale of Goods Act 1979, s 21(1).

auctioneer will be potentially liable. And it may be in the interests of the auctioneer to show that the purchaser does not become the owner of the goods, because if the true owner elects to sue the purchaser rather than the auctioneer, the latter may escape. A purchaser liable in conversion to the true owner may seek to sue the auctioneer in turn. However, the appropriate cause of action here would be for breach of warranty of authority. But an auctioneer will only be liable for such a breach if he has *expressly* warranted the vendor's title, for we have already seen that no such warranty will be implied: *Benton v Campbell Parker & Co.*[217] (Failing a remedy against the auctioneer, a purchaser who finds himself answerable to the true owner in conversion will be left with a right of action against the vendor himself on the contract of sale. In every contract for the sale of goods there is an implied condition that the seller has title or the right to sell them by virtue of s 12 of the Sale of Goods Act 1979 and that term cannot be excluded in any contract whether the sale is a consumer or non-consumer sale.)

Thus it is important to be aware of those circumstances where the purchaser will get a good title, leaving the auctioneer alone[218] liable to the former owner of the goods. Both the common law and statute have provided exceptions to the basic principle that the rights of the true owner should remain inviolable, and these will now briefly be noted.[219]

Estoppel

Section 21(1) of the Sale of Goods Act 1979 provides that a purchaser shall obtain on a sale no better title than the seller had, 'unless the owner of the goods is by his conduct precluded from denying the seller's authority to sell.' The quoted words indicate that a fairly general exception arises by way of estoppel when the true owner's conduct has led the purchaser to believe that the seller is entitled to sell. Many of the other specific statutory exceptions appear to be based on this notion too. It is a question of fact whether an owner of goods has sufficiently invested the seller with the indicia of property as opposed merely to possession.[220]

---

[217] [1925] 2 KB 410, 94 LJKB 881 (above). Even if the purchaser has no contractual claim against the auctioneer he has a right to *contribution* (Civil Liability (Contribution) Act 1978, s 1), but the amount of such is entirely at the discretion of the court.

[218] His client the non-owner seller will also be liable and the auctioneer will be entitled to join him as co-defendant or claim an indemnity but, in many of these cases, recovery against the vendor will, in practice, prove difficult.

[219] For a detailed account, readers are directed to Benjamin *Sale of Goods* (4th edn, 1992), Sweet & Maxwell.

[220] Estoppel was successfully pleaded in *Eastern Distributors Ltd v Goldring* [1957] 2 QB 600, [1957] 2 All ER 525, CA, a case involving a complicated hire-purchase swindle.

Sale in market overt

Another general common law exception, formerly enshrined in the Sale of Goods Act 1979[221] is where property has been sold in market overt. Market overt is 'an open, public and legally constituted market.'[222] Such a market could be set up by statute or under a charter. It is also established by custom that every shop within the city of London is market overt. There is nothing in the character of auction sales that made them, ipso facto, sales in market overt and relatively few were.[223] The sale must have taken place between the hours of sunrise and sunset. Market overt is more usually a pertinent factor when the *vendor*, against whom it is alleged that he is not the owner, claims he became such because he bought the goods previously in market overt. For sales after 2 January 1995 the doctrine is abrogated.

Sale under a voidable title

Where the seller has a voidable title, eg where he has obtained the property in the goods by fraud, the owner may take steps to avoid the title of the seller but until he does so the seller may pass a good title to a *bona fide* purchaser. However if the seller has obtained title by inducing a material mistake, the sale to him is absolutely void and he will have no title to pass to such a purchaser.

Sale by a mercantile agent

Section 2(1) of the Factors Act 1889 provides:

Where a mercantile agent is, with the consent of the owner, in possession of goods, or of the documents of title to goods, any sale, pledge or other disposition of the goods made by him when acting in the ordinary course of business of a mercantile agent shall, subject to the provisions of this Act be as valid as if he were expressly authorised by the owner of the goods to make the same; and provided that the person taking under the disposition acts in good faith and has not at the time of the disposition notice that the person making the disposition has not authority to make the same.

An auctioneer is such a mercantile agent but in this context the provision is of no avail to a purchaser of stolen goods, for the auctioneer is not in possession of them or their documents of title 'with the consent of the owner'. However, where an auctioneer is in possession of goods with the consent of the true owner he may pass a valid title to a purchaser of them

---

[221] Section 22 repealed by the Sale of Goods (Amendment) Act 1994, s 1 as from 3 January 1995.

[222] Per Jervis CJ in *Lee v Bayes & Robinson* (1856) 18 CB 599, 25 LJCP 249.

[223] For a case where it was argued, unsuccessfully, that in accordance with the custom of the market, the sale *had* to be by auction, see *Bishopsgate Motor Finance Corpn Ltd v Transport Brakes Ltd* [1949] 1 KB 322.

under this section even if the possession was given to him for a purpose other than sale. As Denning LJ explained in *Pearson v Rose & Young Ltd*:[224]

the owner must consent to the agent having them for a purpose which is in some way or other connected with his business as a mercantile agent. It may be for display or to get offers, or merely to put in his showroom; but there must be a consent to something of that kind before the owner can be deprived of his goods.

This section may be relevant where an auctioneer receives goods for sale *from* a mercantile agent, and we consider this briefly below.

Sale by seller remaining in possession

Where a seller sells goods to a purchaser but retains possession of them or their documents of title, a second sale to another purchaser will effectively pass title to the latter if he acts in good faith and without notice of the prior sale. This exception was provided by s 8 of the Factors Act 1889 and substantially reproduced by s 24 of the Sale of Goods Act 1979. It is immaterial in what capacity the seller has been left in possession. So for example, it suffices if the original buyer leaves the goods with the seller merely as bailee to care for them.

Sale by buyer in possession

Somewhat more complicated is the position where a buyer is given possession of the goods although the title in the property is not passed to him until some later date. This is covered now by s 25(1) of the Sale of Goods Act 1979 which provides that a sale by such a buyer shall 'have the same effect as if the person making the delivery or transfer were a mercantile agent in possession of the goods or documents of title with the consent of the owner'. A sale by a mercantile agent in such circumstances will, as we have seen, pass a good title to the purchaser under s 2(1) of the Factors Act 1889 provided the purchaser acts in good faith and without notice of any restriction on the agent's authority to sell. A sale under a hire-purchase agreement does not fall within s 25(1) of the Sale of Goods Act 1979, and special provisions are made for sales by hirers under certain such contracts. Also excluded is a 'conditional sale' where the price is payable by instalments with title to the property remaining in the seller until payment of the last instalment.

Where, however, the original sale to the buyer is merely conditional upon eg the price being paid but the buyer is given possession of the goods, a subsequent sale by that buyer is within the exception. Section 25 of the Sale

---

[224] [1951] 1 KB 275, CA, at 288.

of Goods Act 1979 does not provide that the effect of the sale is as if the buyer had the authority of the owner, as it does under s 24, but rather that the effect is the same 'as if' the original buyer was selling as a mercantile agent. This rather odd provision has been construed to mean that the subsequent purchaser only gets a good title and is thus immune from an action for conversion if the original buyer in possession sold to him *in the manner* in which a mercantile agent would have sold in the ordinary course of his business. Thus if an original buyer sells a car without releasing the log-book, the subsequent purchaser from him will not get a good title vis-à-vis his seller because a mercantile agent would, selling in the ordinary course of business, have delivered up the log-book.[225]

Sales of motor vehicles subject to hire-purchase agreements

Sales of motor vehicles under hire-purchase agreements are dealt with separately because they became especially prevalent in the 1950s and 1960s. It is relatively easy for hirers to pass themselves off as owners and sell the cars to unsuspecting purchasers. Section 27 of the Hire-Purchase Act 1964 as reenacted by the Consumer Credit Act 1974 provides that where the purchaser of the car from the hire-purchase 'buyer' is a 'private purchaser' as defined, acting in good faith and without notice of the hire-purchase (or conditional sale) agreement, that purchaser will get a good title to the vehicle.

It must be reiterated that the effect of all these exceptions is to protect the purchaser who thereby gets a good title. They do nothing to prevent the auctioneer from being liable in conversion for selling the particular goods. Indeed they place it beyond doubt that he is liable since the sale and delivery not only has the intention of passing the property to the purchaser but is actually effective to do so. The only way in which an auctioneer could protect himself from suit would be if he could show that the delivery to him of the goods in question amounted to a disposition under those exceptions whereby he, the auctioneer, got title; a subsequent sale or retention would then be of the auctioneer's own property and not that of another. Such an argument was advanced on the basis of the Factors Act 1889 in *Shenstone v Hilton*[226] where the buyer under a conditional sale agreement, before he acquired title, sent the goods, a piano, to the defendant auctioneers for sale. The auctioneers duly sold and the true owner — the seller under the conditional sale agreement — sued them in conversion. The auctioneers claimed to be protected by s 9 of the Factors Act, the precursor of s 25(1) of the Sale of Goods Act 1979, in that they had received the goods from a buyer in possession. Bruce J construed the section as including a delivery to the auctioneers for sale. He said: 'I should be prepared to hold that a

---

[225] See *Newtons of Wembley Ltd v Williams* [1965] 1 QB 560, [1964] 3 All ER 532, CA; *Lambert v G & C Finance Corpn Ltd* (1963) 107 Sol Jo 666.

[226] [1894] 2 QB 452.

delivery of goods on the terms that they should be sold by the person to whom they were delivered for the benefit of the person delivering them was a "disposition" ... [within the section].'[227]

It is difficult to see how such a mere transfer of possession could be regarded as a disposition so as to protect the auctioneer from a conversion action in these circumstances. The 'disposition' (if indeed such it would be) in any event, on the terms of the section, only has 'the same effect as if the person making the delivery or transfer were a mercantile agent'. The effect of a delivery by a mercantile agent would be to give the auctioneers at most a right to possession but it would not, it is submitted, give them any *title*, so that any subsequent sale by them would still interfere with the title of another; the true owners would have an immediate right to possession against the conditional sale buyer on his delivering the goods to the auctioneers for sale, by parity of reasoning with the hire-purchase cases discussed earlier.

In *Waddington & Sons v Neale & Sons*[228] an owner entrusted goods, again a piano, to a dealer to sell for cash or to hire out. The dealer, a mercantile agent, took it to the defendant auctioneers for sale and when this was duly effected the owners sued them in conversion. The auctioneers relied on s 2(1) of the Factors Act 1889 contending that the delivery to them for sale by the dealer was a sale or pledge within the subsection. In fact, since the auctioneers advanced a sum to the dealer in contemplation of selling it, this might have been a rather stronger case than that of *Shenstone & Co v Hilton*.[229] However, the court held that the Act did not protect them. Phillimore J was clear that this was neither a sale nor a disposition, and it seems that the main argument was that it was a pledge. However this too failed, the true analysis being that it was merely a deposit of goods incidental to a transaction that was not authorised.[230] It is submitted that this is the correct approach.

Whilst it may seem hard on the auctioneer that he is exposed to liability by the wrongful act of others even where he is totally innocent,[231] we repeat that insurance is available to cover such business risks. Moreover in one of the more notorious areas, sales of motor vehicles subject to hire-purchase agreements, the auctioneers can usually ascertain whether the vehicle is let on hire-purchase by checking with the body known as HPI (Hire-Purchase Information) with which finance companies normally register vehicles whose purchase they finance.[232]

[227] [1894] 2 QB 452 at 456.   [228] (1907) 96 LT 786, 2 BTLR 464.
[229] Above, n 226.
[230] See also *Kendrick v Sotheby & Co* (1967) 111 Sol Jo 470: auctioneers held not entitled to retain goods which were sent to them for sale and on which they had made an advance, by a person merely instructed to keep them in order to obtain photographs.
[231] He is of course, a fortiori, liable if he has notice of the seller's want of title: *Hardacre v Stewart* (1804) 5 Esp 103.
[232] There is no legal duty on finance companies to do so and failure will not amount to an estoppel: *Moorgate Mercantile Co Ltd v Twitchings* [1977] AC 890, [1976] 2 All ER 641, HL.

Refusal to deliver up to the owner

It is well settled that conversion can be committed by a wrongful refusal to deliver up possession of goods to the person entitled to them upon his demand. An auctioneer may obviously be in some difficulty if goods are being claimed by both his principal and a third party. In appropriate cases the auctioneer should interplead.[233] However, short of such action, an auctioneer is entitled to make reasonable enquiries to ascertain the true ownership of the goods. In *Lee v Bayes & Robinson* Jervis CJ said:[234]

> As between master and servant, or perhaps as between Principal and Agent, where the servant or agent receives from his master or Principal goods which belong to a third person, on their being demanded of him by such a third person he is entitled to say 'I received them from my . . . Principal and I require a reasonable time to ascertain whether the party making the demand is the real owner'; and such qualified refusal would not be evidence of a conversion . . . But if, as in this case, and in most other cases cited, the man who holds the goods chooses to set up the title of his bailor, and to rely on it, he is doing an act which is foreign to . . . his duty. He asserts a title adverse to the title of the real owner and is guilty of conversion.

Thus a refusal pending the obtaining of instructions from the vendor-principal would be a justifiable qualified refusal,[235] but a refusal to release goods until expenses incurred had been paid, would not.[236]

Other acts short of a sale[237]

For the sake of completeness we mention that conversion can be committed by the transfer of possession without sale. A re-delivery to the vendor after notice of a third party's title would probably amount to such. Additionally, although it is difficult to conceive of many situations in which such depredations might occur in the context of auctions, a deliberate destruction of goods is also conversion, but if loss is caused simply negligently, it is not. However in such a case, the ordinary law of negligence would provide a remedy against the careless auctioneer.

All the foregoing discussion assumes that the sale by auction has been on the instructions of one who has not the right to sell them. If he has, no

---

[233] We have discussed interpleader in ch 4, above.
[234] (1856) 18 CB 599 at 607. See also *Turner v Ford* (1846) 15 NW 212.
[235] *Alexander v Southey* (1821) 5 B&Ald 247.
[236] *Loeschman v Machin* (1818) 2 Stark 311.
[237] Although not a conversion as such it is convenient to mention here that if an auctioneer accepts instructions to deal with goods of a deceased, which do not emanate from the properly-appointed personal representatives, he may find himself liable for any losses suffered by the estate as an 'executor de son tort': *Nulty v Fagan* (1888) 22 LR Ir 604.

question of conversion can arise. So, even if the goods had previously been stolen, if the principal had obtained them in circumstances rendering him the true owner, for instance where he bought them in market overt, the auctioneer will be able to sell them with impunity. Usually of course the question whether the vendor had, or had acquired, the right to sell will be determined by the English law principles discussed above but occasionally foreign law is involved.

In the recent case of *Winkworth v Christie Manson & Woods Ltd*[238] the rather unusual facts were as follows. Winkworth had owned certain works of art in England and these were stolen. They found their way to Italy where they were bought by an Italian. Subsequently this buyer sent them to Christie's for auction and some were sold. Winkworth, having obtained an undertaking from Christie's that they would not part with the remaining articles or the proceeds of sale, sued the Italian vendor in conversion. A preliminary question of law arose before the High Court in England, namely whether English or Italian law should be applied to the issue whether the Italian defendant had title to the goods and the proceeds of sale. The court decided that, using English principles of private international law, on these facts the appropriate law to be applied was Italian.

Thus the rights of a true owner of English goods, situated in England, can be defeated by a transaction in another country in accordance with the law of that country, even though the owner had never consented to their going there.

The implications of the *Winkworth* case in the context of the seller's right to sell are discussed in chapter 6.

OTHER DUTIES TO THIRD PARTIES

Negligence

As mentioned above, an auctioneer may be liable under the tort of negligence for carelessly damaging a person's goods or for injuring him. There is little to be gained from an attempt at listing the variety of instances in which such a liability might be incurred, but there is one area worthy of special — albeit brief — mention, namely the liability attaching to the occupier of premises.

Although all persons are under a general duty to take reasonable care not to injure those who would with reasonable forseeability be harmed if care were not taken, statute has provided specially for the liability of those who occupy or control premises. The Occupier's Liability Act 1957, as amended,

---

[238] [1980] Ch 496, [1980] 1 All ER 1121.

provides that the 'occupier' owes to all his visitors (which include those permitted to enter under a licence) a common duty of care. This duty of care is defined by s 2(2) of the Act as: 'a duty to take such care as in all the circumstances of the case is reasonable to see that the visitor is reasonably safe in using the premises for the purpose for which he is invited or permitted to be there.' The duty relates both to the state of the premises themselves and also to activities carried on there. So an auctioneer might, not too fancifully, be liable if improperly penned cattle injured persons attending the auction or if a bidder were injured falling as a result of a defective step in the auction rooms.

Whilst the 1957 Act applies not only to those who actually occupy premises but also to those in control of them, it is thought that an auctioneer would not be regarded as having sufficient control of eg the principal-vendor's house or place of business in which he is conducting the auction.[239] In *Walker v Crabb*,[240] however, where a mare which was being auctioned on the vendor's premises injured the plaintiff, the vendor himself was held not liable in negligence on the ground that the control of the entire sale and responsibility for the chattels lay on the auctioneer.

It is open to an occupier to satisfy the duty imposed on him by strategically placed warning notices where such a warning given is in fact sufficient to render the visitor safe. However, *exclusion* of a liability is a different matter. The Occupier's Liability Act 1957 permitted an occupier to modify the common duty of care 'so far as he is free to'. This has now been greatly affected by the Unfair Contract Terms Act 1977 which makes any purported exclusion of liability for negligence causing death or personal injury wholly ineffective,[241] and, as we have seen, renders any other type of exclusion subject to a test of reasonableness. On the other hand a warning notice is still useful since, even if it does not render the duty of care satisfied, it may make it easier to point to some contributory negligence by the visitor with the result that any compensatory damages will be apportioned under the Law Reform (Contributory Negligence) Act 1945.

Nuisance

A nuisance is the user of land so that the use and enjoyment of neighbouring land by another is diminished. Clearly, the business of auctioneering may constitute a nuisance to others and may be actionable. In the nineteenth century the owner of a coffee-house near Covent Garden succeeded

---

[239] Pre-Act this was the position laid down in Scotland: *Nelson v Scott, Croall & Sons* 1892 19 R (Ct of Sess) 425, 29 Sc LR 354.
[240] [1916] WN 433, 33 TLR 119.   [241] Section 2.

in an action against a defendant auctioneer when the latter's vans obstructed the door and the stench from the horses rendered the coffee-shop 'incommodious and uncomfortable'.[242] This lone reported case may be somewhat outmoded on its facts, but doubtless in appropriate circumstances an action would lie today.

[242] *Benjamin v Storr* (1874) LR 9 CP 400, 43 LJCP 162.

6

Conditions of Sale Affecting Buyers and Bidders

INTRODUCTION

The importance of Conditions of Sale in the conduct of an auction cannot be overestimated. Conditions of Sale form the flesh on the bones of the law of auctions. Their primary purpose, traditionally, has been to govern the relationship between the seller (and his agent, the auctioneer)[1] on the one hand and the successful buyer on the other. It is this relationship, imposed primarily by the law of contract and of sale of goods (in cases other than land) between the seller and the buyer that needs particularly careful exploration. Modern Conditions of Sale very often include conditions particularly appropriate to the relationship between the auctioneer and the *seller* as well. The contractual effect of these is reached by a different route. They form part of an ordinary business contract, between the seller and the auctioneer as his agent, made well before the auction. The contractual stipulations, if binding, will confirm or modify the position of the seller as it would have been according to ordinary principles of the law of agency and contract explored earlier in this book. Whilst conditions affecting sellers must dovetail with those affecting buyers, the two sets of rules must be kept separate to avoid confusion. One vital difference is that those affecting sellers must be imposed at the latest when the seller consigns the goods for sale as part and parcel of the contract for the auctioneer's services. Those affecting bidders and buyers are normally imposed at a much later stage by incorporation in the catalogue.

We shall now focus on the Conditions of Sale affecting *buyers* and examine their effect in typical sales of chattels. We then go on to discuss conditions affecting bidders and others present at the auction. Chattel sales of a less usual nature and which can pose special problems will be dealt with separately.

---

[1] The problems involved in a buyer suing a seller whose identity is not disclosed, are explored above, in ch 5.

THE CONTRACTUAL FRAMEWORK

The Sale of Goods Act 1979, reproducing a similar provision in the 1893 Act, provides the basic contractual framework of the auction sale by stating as follows:

57(1) Where goods are put up for sale by auction in lots, each lot is prima facie deemed to be the subject of a separate contract of sale.

(2) A sale by auction is complete when the auctioneer announces its completion by the fall of the hammer, or in other customary manner; and until the announcement is made any bidder may retract his bid.

(3) A sale by auction may be notified to be subject to a reserve or upset price, and a right to bid may also be reserved expressly by or on behalf of the seller.

(4) Where a sale by auction is not notified to be subject to a right to bid by or on behalf of the seller, it is not lawful for the seller to bid himself or to employ any person to bid at the sale, or for the auctioneer knowingly to take any bid from the seller or any such person.

(5) A sale contravening subsection (4) above may be treated as fraudulent by the buyer.

(6) Where, in respect of a sale by auction, a right to bid is expressly reserved (but not otherwise) the seller or any one person on his behalf may bid at the auction.

The effects of s 57(4) and (5) are: (a) to prohibit the seller or his agent to bid and the auctioneer to take any such bid unless the right to bid is so reserved, in practice in the relevant Conditions of Sale; and (b) to allow the buyer to treat any sale contravening s 57(4) as fraudulent. He may thus rescind the sale at his option and would also seem to be entitled to damages in respect of the fraud. The general position is discussed in more detail below.

In essence, the function of the Conditions of Sale is to regulate the position of the buyer once he has made a successful bid which is accepted 'by the fall of the hammer'. A collateral purpose, which may give rise to much more difficulty when analysing enforceability of the appropriate conditions, is to regulate conduct of persons present at the auction generally even where they are *not* successful buyers. But before considering questions of the validity of Conditions of Sale, it is first essential to establish that the potential defendant who is alleged to be in breach of a particular condition has in fact been bound by that condition.

INCORPORATION INTO THE CONTRACT OF CONDITIONS

It is a basic and well known principle of contract law that a clause can be incorporated into a contract by *notice* or by *course of dealing*.

With regard to whether the potential defendant, typically the buyer, has notice of the contractual terms, a great deal of authority exists on this problem in the context of exemption clauses. These cases are of limited value when considering the typical auction situation where buyers will normally have acquired a catalogue and where the catalogue reproduces the relevant Conditions of Sale or draws attention to where they are on display. It is, of course, essential that notice of the relevant conditions is given before or at the time of contracting. They cannot be successfully incorporated into a contract after the contract has been made.[2] Where there is any doubt as to whether sufficient notice has been given, the court will take into account such factors as whether the conditions in question are of a standard nature. It is then probable that annexation of the conditions to catalogues issued to buyers would be held sufficient. If, on the other hand, the condition is an unusual one, the court would require far more effort to bring the condition in question to the buyer's notice. In *Thornton v Shoe Lane Parking Ltd*, Lord Denning said: 'Some clauses I have seen would need to be printed in red ink on the face of the document with a red hand pointing to it before the notice could be held to be sufficient'.[3]

In the case of auctions, it was held as long ago as 1801 that where the Conditions of Sale are printed and posted up under the auctioneer's box, and the auctioneer declares that the conditions are as usual, there is sufficient notice to purchasers of the conditions.[4] In the Scottish case of *Laing & Sons v Hain*,[5] it was held that at sale by auction where the Conditions of Sale empowered the vendor to resell in certain circumstances, it was not necessary to show that the conditions were read or exhibited at the sale.

Where there is a possibility that the purchaser might be able to argue that he has no notice of the relevant conditions, an alternative way in which he could still be bound is by reference to a course of dealing. This simply means that a clause may be incorporated in the contract, despite a lack of specific notice, where previous dealings between the parties can be proved to have taken place and it can be inferred from these dealings that similar clauses

---

[2] See eg *Olley v Marlborough Court Ltd* [1949] 1 KB 532, [1949] 1 All ER 127, CA. At least one recent unreported County Court case has gone against the auctioneer-plaintiffs on the buyer arguing that he was ignorant of the existence of any Conditions of Sale. A way round this disastrous conclusion is suggested in the text.

[3] [1971] 2 QB 163 at 170 (a case concerning an exemption clause referred to in a parking ticket). See also *Spriggs v Sotheby Parke Bernet & Co Ltd* [1986] BTLC 422 (CA) where it was held that auctioneers were in breach of their duty as bailees for reward of the plaintiff's property (a diamond) but that the contractual exemption clause was effective to exclude liability for negligence. See further discussion of this case in ch 5.

[4] *Mesnard v Aldridge* (1801) 3 Esp 271.

[5] 1853 15 Dunl (Ct of Sess) 667, 25 Sc Jur 405.

would apply in each case.[6] The relevance of this to auctions is obvious, though it may seldom be necessary to resort to this principle. However in essence the auctioneer would argue that although a buyer might not have specific notice of a relevant condition because, for instance, he did not purchase a catalogue with the Conditions of Sale annexed, nevertheless because he had attended previous auction sales he must be taken to be aware of the fact that Conditions of Sale exist and of their nature.

In practice, many auctions now proceed on the basis that all potential bidders are first required to fill in a form with detail of name and address and in return are given a number, or paddle, by reference to which they record a successful bid. It is good practice also to include on this form an acknowledgment that by signing it the bidder agrees to participate in the auction on the basis of the Condition of Sale (which should be in the catalogue and on display).

VULNERABILITY OF CONDITIONS OF SALE

Assuming that it has been established that en bloc the Conditions of Sale in question are binding contractually on the potential defendant and cover the problem that has arisen, it is then necessary to consider whether any particular condition is open to attack as being 'unreasonable'. Prior to 1973, any person arguing that a contractual stipulation which excluded or limited the liability of the other party was not binding on him had to argue that there was a fundamental breach of contract, or that the stipulation was not incorporated in the contract and therefore not binding on him. The courts struggled with this problem for many years and although the case law thus generated is now far from irrelevant it is realistic to assume, in the light of recent dicta, that the courts will look primarily for guidance at the statutory provisions now incorporated in the Unfair Contract Terms Act 1977,[7] and, from 1995, the new Regulations referred to below, though it must always be remembered that such clauses are construed contra proferentem and any

---

[6] See eg *Hardwick Game Farm v Suffolk Agricultural and Poultry Producers' Association Ltd* [1969] 2 AC 31, [1968] 2 All ER 444, HL.

[7] See Lord Denning's graphic review of these developments in *George Mitchell (Chesterhall) Ltd v Finney Lock Seeds Ltd* [1983] 1 All ER 108, CA, at 111, in which he described such developments as the Unfair Contract Terms Act 1977 as heralding 'a revolution in our approach to exemption clauses'. In *Spriggs v Sotheby Parke Bernet & Co Ltd* (see n 3 above) the judgments proceeded on the basis that there had been no fundamental breach such as to negate the exemption clause, following *Photo Production v Securicor Ltd* [1980] AC 827, [1980] 1 All ER 556, HL. The events occurred in 1977, whereas the Unfair Contract Terms Act 1977 did not come into force until February 1978. Section 2 thereof, relating to purported exclusion of negligence liability, was not reproduced from previous leglislation and on negligence being established, might otherwise have been relevant.

inadequacies in wording may resolve the problem in the buyer's favour without further ado.

The main object of the complex Act of 1977 is to make void or make subject to 'the reasonableness test' relevant exemption clauses. The main provisions, ss 2–7, apply only to 'business liability' as defined. A number of contracts, such as contracts of insurance, are exempted from the scope of the Act altogether. Only two aspects of the Act will be dealt with here, these being those aspects most relevant to Conditions of Sale in auctions.[8] The new Regulations stemming from the EC directive on Unfair Terms in Consumer Contracts (93/13/EEC) will then be discussed separately.

CONDITIONS RELATING TO THE TITLE TO, COMPLIANCE WITH DESCRIPTION OF, AND QUALITY OF THE GOODS SOLD

It is necessary to start with the implied conditions dealing with the above matters in the Sale of Goods Act 1979. Sections 12–15 as amended by the Sale and Supply of Goods Act 1994, contain the following implied terms, of which this is a summary:

(a) that the seller has the right to sell the goods (s 12);
(b) that where there is a contract for the sale of goods by description, the goods will correspond with the description (s 13);
(c) that where the seller sells goods in the course of a business, that the goods supplied under the contract are of satisfactory (formerly 'merchantable') quality, except as regards defects specifically drawn to the buyer's attention before the contract is made; or if the buyer examines the goods before the contract is made, as regards defects which that examination ought to reveal (s 14(2));
(d) where the seller sells goods in the course of a business and the buyer, expressly or by implication, makes known to the seller any particular purpose for which the goods are being bought, that the goods are reasonably fit for that purpose except when the buyer does not rely, or it is unreasonable for him to rely, on the skill or judgment of the seller (s 14(3));
(e) where the sale is by sample, inter alia, that the bulk shall comply with the sample (s 15).

With regard to the implied terms of quality and fitness for purpose (above), it is the implied condition of quality which is likely to be of importance in

---

[8] The relevant sections of this Act, of the Sale of Goods Act 1979, as amended, and of the Misrepresentation Act 1967 are to be found in Appendix 2.

the auction situation. This is because it is unlikely that in an auction sale the buyer would either expressly or by implication make known to the seller the purpose for which the goods are being bought, or place any reliance on the seller's skill or judgment.[9]

It will also be noted in the context of the two terms of quality and fitness that they apply only to sellers selling goods '*in the course of a business*'. Section 14(5) states:

The preceding provisions of this section apply to a sale by a person who in the course of a business is acting as agent for another as they apply to a sale by a principal in the course of a business, except where that other is not selling in the course of a business and either the buyer knows that fact or reasonable steps are taken to bring it to the notice of the buyer before the contract is made.

The significance of this sub-section (introduced in 1973) is often overlooked. It means that where an auctioneer is selling goods on behalf of a private vendor *and due notice is given to bidders of that fact*, s 14 will not apply at all since the sale will not be 'in the course of a business'. Experience suggests that few auctioneers do this,[10] although some do specifically restrict themselves to selling goods entered by private sellers only. If this fact is known to bidders it would probably be sufficient to make s 14 inapplicable in the first place. Those auctioneers who accept goods from all sources and fail to discriminate in the catalogue or otherwise between those entered by private and those entered by business vendors will be deemed to sell goods 'in the course of a business' and s 14 will apply except insofar as it can validly be negated or modified.[11]

The question now arises as to how far the Conditions of Sale may seek to negate or limit these important implied terms in sales of goods. The position is dealt with by s 6 of the Unfair Contract Terms Act 1977 as amended, which runs as follows:

(1) Liability for breach of the obligations arising from —
    (a) section 12 of the Sale of Goods Act 1979 (seller's implied undertakings as to title, etc);
    (b) section 8 of Supply of Goods (Implied Terms) Act 1973 (the corresponding thing in relation to hire-purchase),
    cannot be excluded or restricted by reference to any contract term.

---

[9] Conditions of Sale often stipulate that buyers 'should exercise and rely on their own judgment' (see eg Sotheby's Condition 16 in Appendix 1). It would thus presumably be 'unreasonable' within s 14(3) above, to rely on the seller's skill or judgment.

[10] Specific lots may be described eg as 'The Property of a Lady'. This statement with its aura of gentility would probably imply that the seller was a private one; the antithesis of a 'trader'. If, as in *Friedrich v A Monnickendam Ltd* (1973) 228 EG 1311, the lot is falsely stated to be 'sold by order of Executors' and this description is regarded as false to a material degree (since there is evidence that such descriptions encourage bids), there is likely to be an offence contrary to s 1 of the Trade Descriptions Act 1968 See also p. 85.

[11] This policy was suggested by the Law Commission Report No 24, First Report on Exemption Clauses (1969) paras 53–5.

(2) As against a person dealing as a consumer, liability for breach of the obligations arising from —
 (a) section 13, 14 or 15 of the 1979 Act (seller's implied undertakings as to conformity of goods with description or sample, or as to their quality or fitness for a particular purpose);
 (b) section 9, 10 or 11 of the 1973 Act (the corresponding things in relation to hire-purchase),
 cannot be excluded or restricted by reference to any contract term.
(3) As against a person dealing otherwise than as consumer, the liability specified in subsection (2) above can be excluded or restricted by reference to a contract term, but only in so far as the term satisfies the requirement of reasonableness.
(4) The liabilities referred to in this section are not only the business liabilities defined by section 1(3), but include those arising under any contract of sale of goods or hire-purchase agreement.

As will be seen from the above, much depends on whether a bidder at an auction can be described as 'a person dealing as a consumer' or as 'a person dealing otherwise than as a consumer'. The answer to this is made clear by s 12(2) of the Unfair Contract Terms Act 1977, which states, 'But on a sale by auction or by competitive tender the buyer is not in any circumstances to be regarded as dealing as a consumer.' This policy decision[12] to exclude auction sales from being categorized as consumer sales, despite the fact that many individual buyers will in fact be, in the economic sense, consumers rather than intermediaries intent upon re-sale, makes it clear that the Sale of Goods Act obligations in ss 13, 14 and 15 of the 1979 Act *can* be excluded or restricted by reference to a contract term, 'but only in so far as the term satisfies the requirement of reasonableness'.

If Conditions of Sale therefore purport to exclude the seller's liability for, for example, goods which prove to be of unsatisfactory quality, by what criteria is the reasonableness of the exemption clause in question to be judged? The answer to this question lies in s 11 and Sch 2 of the Unfair Contract Terms Act 1977. Section 11 stipulates that the requirement of reasonableness is 'that the term shall have been a fair and reasonable one to be included having regard to the circumstances which were, or ought reasonably to have been, known to or in the contemplation of the parties when the contract was made'. Section 11(2) goes on specifically to state that for the purposes of s 6, discussed above, whether a contract term satisfies the requirement of reasonableness shall be determined by having regard to the matters specified in Sch 2. Schedule 2 stipulates the following matters:

---

[12] The policy was the one recommended by the Final Report of the Molony Committee (Cmnd 1781, 1962) para. 445; and Law Commission Report No 24 (1969), paras 110, 114–19.

(a) the strength of the bargaining positions of the parties relative to each other, taking into account (among other things) alternative means by which the customer's requirements could have been met;

(b) whether the customer received an inducement to agree to the term, or in accepting it had an opportunity of entering into a similar contract with other persons, but without having to accept a similar term;

(c) whether the customer knew or ought reasonably to have known of the existence and extent of the term (having regard, among other things, to any custom of the trade and any previous course of dealing between the parties);

(d) where the term excludes or restricts any relevant liability if some condition is not complied with, whether it was reasonable at the time of the contract to expect that compliance with that condition would be practicable;

(e) whether the goods were manufactured, processed or adapted to the special order of the customer.

To summarise, s 6 of the Unfair Contract Terms Act 1977 provides:

(a) that the implied term that the seller has the right to sell may not be excluded at all;

(b) that the implied terms relating to description, quality and (where appropriate) fitness and compliance with sample (ss 13, 14 and 15 respectively) may be excluded or restricted only insofar as the contract term in question complies with the reasonableness test. However, in each case it must be considered whether the sale is 'in the course of a business'. If the vendor is a private seller and this is known to or notified to buyers, no terms as to quality and fitness are implied in the first place. (It should be added that s 15 of the 1979 Act, which is subject to similar restrictions on exemption clauses, is not generally appropriate to *chattel* auctions since it deals with sales by sample.)

There is a further section of the Unfair Contract Terms Act 1977 which may, in some circumstances, need consideration. Section 3 runs as follows:

(1) This section applies as between contracting parties where one of them deals as consumer or on the other's written standard terms of business.

(2) As against that party, the other cannot by reference to any contract term —
   (a) when himself in breach of contract, exclude or restrict any liability of his in respect of the breach; or
   (b) claim to be entitled —
      (i) to render a contractual performance substantially different from that which was reasonably expected of him, or
      (ii) in respect of the whole or of any part of his contractual obligation, to render no performance at all,
   except in so far as (in any of the cases mentioned above in this subsection) the contract term satisfies the requirement of reasonableness.

It is conceivable that a buyer alleging a breach of contract other than a breach of one of the implied terms already described and dealt with by s 6 of the Unfair Contract Terms Act 1977, might argue that though he does not deal 'as a consumer', he does contract on the seller's 'standard terms of business'. Accordingly any Condition of Sale excluding or restricting any liability for breach of contract by the seller or affecting the performance of the seller's obligations as described in s 3(2)(b) must be subject to the requirement of reasonableness, the test for which is explained under 'Misrepresentations' below. In fact it is doubtful if s 3 could be applied to the auction situation. Although the auctioneer's Conditions of Sale are his 'standard terms of business' within the meaning of this section, and although he is the seller's agent, a court (it is submitted) would be unlikely to hold that these conditions are the *seller's* 'written standard terms of business', since the seller may have to rely on them on a single occasion only and, even if a trader, may well have distinct standard term contracts for sales taking place in the ordinary course of his business rather than through the auction house. It is these which would be his 'written standard terms of business', not the auctioneer's Conditions of Sale.

MISREPRESENTATIONS

Conditions of Sale may attempt to disclaim liability for misrepresentations made by the vendor or his agent, the auctioneer, and this problem is extensively discussed in the context of sales of land.[13] Similar principles apply to auctions of chattels. Any attempt to exclude the buyer's rights to rescind the contract or claim damages for material misrepresentations is, by s 8 of the Unfair Contract Terms Act 1977 (replacing s 3 of the Misrepresentation Act 1967) made subject to the requirement of reasonableness. It will be for the vendor to show that the term in question satisfies this requirement, namely that the term 'shall have been a fair and reasonable one to be included having regard to the circumstances which were, or ought reasonably to have been, known to or in the contemplation of the parties when the contract was made' (s 11(1)).[14]

IMPLEMENTATION OF THE EC DIRECTIVE ON UNFAIR TERMS AND CONSUMER CONTRACTS (93/13/EEC)

This Directive was adopted by the Council of Ministers on 5 April 1993 and introduced for the first time into the UK law of contract a general concept of 'fairness'. It means, as is the case with liability for dangerous products,

---

[13] See ch 9.

[14] A misrepresentation may also amount to a *contractual* miscrepresentation. Where there is no effective exclusion clause and the catalogue misdescribes the goods — eg table napkins 'the authentic property of Charles I' worth £105 instead of the £787 bid — the buyer may either annul the contract or claim damages under s 13 of the Sale of Goods Act 1979 as in *Nicholson and Venn v Smith-Marriott* (1947) 177 LT 189.

that there are two layers of legislation to be considered — that covered by the Unfair Contract Terms Act 1977 (considered so far as relevant to auctions above) and that covered by the new regulations implementing the Directive. The coverage of the two measures is not the same. The 1977 Act deals mainly with exclusion clauses in consumer contracts but extends also to business contracts, negotiated contracts and the areas outside contract law affected by exclusion notices. By contrast, the Directive is concerned only with terms in consumer contracts which have not been individually negotiated, but is not confined to exclusion clauses. Nevertheless, the effect of the Directive is to create a separate regime alongside that and in some cases overlapping the 1977 Act. Some commentators tried to persuade the government to repeal the 1977 Act and reduce the law to a single code. The government, however, refused to do this and the 1977 Act stays as it was. The basic reason given was that the test of fairness in the Directive has similarities to the test of reasonableness to which a majority of the terms within the scope of that Act are subject. 'The existence of the similarity should reduce any problems arising from overlap between the two measures.'[15]

In its application to auctions, the Directive and the consequential regulations make no attempt to deal specifically with contracts arising as a result of public auction, whereas the 1977 Act makes the position clear from the start by stating that a buyer on a sale by auction or by competitive tender is not under any circumstances to be regarded as dealing as a consumer (s 12(2)).

The Directive was implemented in the UK from 1 July 1995 by the Unfair Terms in Consumer Contracts Regulations, SI 1994/3159.

The scene is set by Article 1(1) and Regulation 3 which state that the regulations apply to any term in a contract concluded between a seller or supplier and a consumer where the term has not been individually negotiated. Certain contracts not relevant here, such as those relating to employment or succession rights, are excluded. Article 2 and Regulation 2 define a 'consumer' as meaning a natural person who is acting for purposes which are outside his business. A 'seller' means the person who, acting for purposes related to his business, sells goods, and 'supplier' means the person who, acting for purposes related to his business, supplies goods or services. Clearly, then, an auctioneer falls within the definition of 'supplier'.

The core of the Directive is contained in Article 6(1) and Regulation 5(1). The latter states that 'an unfair term in a contract concluded with a consumer by a seller or supplier shall not be binding on the consumer.' This, of course, raises the question as to what is meant by 'unfair'. For this we refer to Article 3(1) and Regulation 4(1) which states that an 'unfair term'

---

[15] See DTI Consulation Document, October 1993.

means any term which contrary to the requirement of good faith causes a significant imbalance in the parties' rights and obligations under the contract to the detriment of the consumer, taking into account the nature of the goods or services for which the contract was concluded and referring to all circumstances attending the conclusion of the contract and all relevant terms.

It will be seen that the above Regulation refers to 'the requirement of good faith'. Outside contracts of insurance and other specialised cases, the concept of 'good faith' as such is not one familiar to English lawyers in the contractual context. A test of 'reasonableness' would have been more familiar in the UK. However, 'unfairness' is the concept around which the Directive centres and the only guidance provided by the Regulations (see Regulation 4(3)) is that in determining whether a term satisfies the requirement of good faith, regard must be had in particular to the matters specified in Schedule 2 of the Regulations. Schedule 2 reproduced in Appendix 2, includes the following:

(1) the strength of the bargaining positions of the parties; and
(2) whether the consumer had an inducement to agree to the term; and
(3) whether the goods or services were sold or supplied to the special order of the consumer, and
(4) the extent to which the seller or supplier has dealt fairly and equitably with the consumer.

Applying these stipulations to the auction scene, it seems clear that the auctioneer is a supplier and that the Conditions of Sale are not individually negotiated and therefore prima facie fall within the scope of the Regulations. Of course, it would have to be shown in any particular case that the buyer was actually a 'consumer' as defined, since the Regulations have no effect outside the consumer-supplier nexus. But since the auctioneer will probably not know whether the buyer is a consumer or not, and clearly Conditions of Sale must be drafted so as to effect all bidders, whatever their status, it needs to be ascertained whether in any particular case a Condition of Sale normally found in auctions is in fact likely to be struck down. In this connection some help is provided by Article 3(3) and Regulation 4(4) which refer to an Annexe (contained in Schedule 3 to the Regulations) giving an 'indicative and non-exhaustive list of the terms which may be regarded as unfair'.

Of the list of terms in the Annexe, almost of all them are not terms which would normally be found in standard Conditions of Sale at an auction. (A complete list, for reference, will be found set out in Appendix 2, should this view appear too sanguine.) There is, however, one, listed as 1(b), which could conceivably be relevant. This is a term which has the object or effect of 'inappropriately excluding or limiting the legal rights of the consumer vis-à-vis the seller or supplier or another party in the event of total or partial non-performance or inadequate performance by the seller or supplier of any of the contractual obligations . . .'. Now, it could be argued that a condition attempting to absolve the seller and auctioneer from the consequences of misdescription of the goods is an attempt to exclude the legal rights of the consumer as against the seller or supplier for total, partial or inadequate performance by the seller or supplier — because the goods are not of the contractual description. Similarly it could be argued that the sale of defective goods, in the sense that they are 'unmerchantable' (or unsatisfactory), also falls within this rubric because liability is invariably excluded in this situation.

Of the two examples, that of Conditions of Sale attempting to eliminate liability for misdescription is probably the more serious. Section 13 of the Sale of Goods Act 1979 imposes this obligation on all sellers, whether or not the seller is selling in the course of the business. Yet a typical Condition of Sale will exclude liability, both as regards the auctioneer and the principal, in respect of errors of description or for the genuineness or authenticity of any lot (see, for example, Sotheby's Condition 16). This condition is often mitigated by a 'deliberate forgery' provision, but if the description applies to a lot which is not a deliberate forgery, under English law before the Directive the only way this condition could be attacked is by applying the test of reasonableness under the Unfair Contract Terms Act 1977. After the implementation of the Directive the court would need to consider whether the inclusion of this term amounted to 'inappropriately excluding or limiting the legal rights of the consumer . . .'. This is, of course, assuming that the court would, under Article 3(1) and Regulation 4(1) hold the term to be essentially an 'unfair term' not satisfying the requirement of good faith as exemplified in Schedule 2 and explained above. On the face of it, a condition of sale excluding liability for misdescription looks vulnerable. The consequences of this are outlined below.

Where the issue is whether the Conditions of Sale at the auction inappropriately excludes an implied term (under the Sale of Goods Act 1979) for fitness or quality, the position is more complicated. For a start, the 1979 Act implies no such term unless the seller is selling 'in the course of a business'. The consumer will have no idea of the status of the seller at the auction, in most cases. Should the seller be a private person, the consumer cannot expect any guarantees relating to condition or performance. In addition, there are other circumstances, discussed below, where s 14 will not apply even without an exclusion clause. There is a stronger case, therefore, for arguing that the usual blanket exclusion of any warranties or guarantees relating to the *condition* of the goods is not 'inappropriate' since all goods are likely to be 'second-hand' and in many cases the law will imply no terms as to quality in any case. If the catalogue does so expressly, eg by stating that the goods are 'in good condition', this is a different matter and it will fall under the discussion of 'misdescription' above.

If a Condition of Sale in a contract concluded with a consumer by the auctioneer is found to be 'unfair' applying the above tests, Regulation 5(1) (and Article 6(1)) make it clear that the condition is not binding on the consumer. (The rest of the contract is not affected — see Reg 5(2)). It is thought, though, that auctioneers will prefer to avoid making radical alterations to standard Conditions of Sale until the position is established by litigation. There are, however, two factors which should be taken into account in all cases, in addition to those outlined above.

The first is that Article 5 and Regulation 6 imposes an obligation on sellers or suppliers to ensure that any written term of a contract is expressed in plain, intelligible language, and if there is doubt about the meaning of a written term, the interpretation most favourable to the consumer is to prevail. This should be a further encouragement to auctioneers to have a good look at their existing Conditions of Sale and assess how far they are in 'plain, intelligible language'. Presumably the 'doubt' must be in the mind of an educated judge rather than a lay consumer, and if this is so a condition expressed in traditional terms but which is not ambiguous will presumably yield no possibility of being 'interpreted' in favour of the consumer. The Government suggests, however, that there is nothing to prevent the courts taking into account the way in which terms are drafted when considering whether they satisfy the requirement of good faith. The principle seems similar to the contra proferentem rule familiar to UK lawyers.

Secondly, once the term is established, whether or not as a result of litigation, as being 'unfair' in standard form contracts, Article 7(1) and Regulation 8 make provision for preventing the continued use of this type of term. In the UK the Director General of Fair Trading is charged with the duty of considering any complaint that a contract term drawn up for general use is unfair, and if he considers that it is he has power to bring proceedings for an injunction against the person relying on the term. (A similar regime applies in the UK, also pursuant to a EEC Directive, as regards misleading advertising — see the Control of Misleading Advertisements Regulations, SI 1988/915). The adequacy of this is being challenged.

COMMON PROBLEMS CONCERNING BUYERS, DEALT WITH BY CONDITIONS OF SALE

Throughout the ensuing discussion, reference will be made to the Conditions of Business of Sotheby's and of Christie, Manson & Woods Ltd.[16]

---

[16] The conditions in question and the other material reproduced in Appendix 1 are the copyright of the auction houses to whose sales they refer, and have been reproduced in this book by kind permission.

THE SELLER'S TITLE

It has already been pointed out that s 12 of the Sale of Goods Act 1979 lays down, for the purposes of auction sales, an unequivocal condition that the seller has the right to sell the goods in question. Furthermore, the Unfair Contract Terms Act 1977 precludes the exclusion or restriction of this implied condition in any circumstances (s 6(1)). It cannot be over-emphasized that a sale by auction does not confer legitimacy on the title to goods where the seller has none. If the goods are stolen or otherwise belong to someone different from the seller, the buyer at auction will get no better title than the seller had — ie usually none at all. Since nothing can be done by way of a contract term to modify this position, both Sotheby's and Christie's content themselves by imposing a condition upon the seller that he is entitled to sell.[17] Should it transpire that the seller has not title to sell, the buyer is entitled to rescind the sale and recover the price paid.[18]

The above paragraph is subject to caveats. Firstly, in *Benton v Campbell Parker & Co*[19] it was stated that the position was that whilst not warranting the title of the seller the auctioneer, in a sale of specific goods, impliedly does warrant that he knows of no defect therein.

Secondly, in deciding whether or not the seller has title to sell, careful account must be taken of the legal system which must decide such matters. The point is important where goods are auctioned which were sold previously abroad. This occurred in the *Winkworth v Christie, Manson & Woods Ltd.*[20] Here the goods in question were stolen in England from W. They were subsequently taken to Italy and sold and delivered by a third party to the present vendor. The contract in question was made in Italy and the contractual rights of the parties were governed by Italian law, the goods being at the time of such sale and delivery physically situated in Italy. The vendor had subsequently delivered them to Christie's in England for sale by auction on his behalf. When W discovered these goods not already sold, in the possession of Christie's, Christie's gave an undertaking not further to part with possession of the unsold goods pending determination of the ownership as between W and the vendor. The crucial issue was, therefore, whether the sale in Italy had the effect of conferring on the vendor a title to the goods valid even against W, from whom they had been stolen. In *Cammell v Sewell*,[21] Pollock CJ had held that if, as here, property was disposed of in a manner binding according to the law of the country where

---

[17] See Sotheby's Condition 17; Christie's Condition B 2.
[18] See *Rowland v Divall* [1923] 2 KB 500; *Butterworths v Kingsway Motors Ltd* [1954] 2 All ER 694, [1954] 1 WLR 1286. (The *auctioneer's* potential liability for conversion is discussed in ch 5.)
[19] [1925] 2 KB 410.
[20] [1980] Ch 496, [1980] 1 All ER 1121, also discussed above, see ch 5.
[21] (1858) 3 H&N 617 at 638, Pollock CJ.

it was, that disposition was binding everywhere. The view of Pollock CJ was subsequently affirmed by the Court of Exchequer Chamber and had subsequently been accepted as a principle of private international law. Accordingly, Italian law applied to govern the situation and it was irrelevant that the goods had been brought back for sale in England or that the former owner was a British subject. The moral of this case is that since under many continental systems of law bona fide purchasers of chattels will get a good title even to stolen goods, it should not be assumed that English domestic law can exclusively be relied upon to answer vital questions of title.

There are many other circumstances where the seller's title may be in issue in that for one reason or another someone else has a prima facie claim to ownership of the goods.[22] But the auctioneer cannot investigate consignors' titles routinely and can only guard against the consequences of being sued, however innocent he may be, for conversion by taking a complete indemnity from the consignor. (The flowchart reproduced in Appendix 4 indicates how the courts are likely to resolve problems of title to stolen goods, particularly in the light of the complex effect of the Limitation Act 1980, section 4.)

NON-COMPLIANCE WITH DESCRIPTION

Auction sales are clear examples of sales by description within s 13 of the Sale of Goods Act 1979. Section 13(3) reinforces this point by stating that 'a sale of goods is not prevented from being a sale by description by reason only that, being exposed for sale or hire, they are selected by the buyer'.[23] Where the buyer finds that the goods he has bought at auction do not comply with the catalogue description, his first line of attack will be to sue the seller for breach of the implied condition of compliance with description.[24] This is a situation which most standard Conditions of Sale seek to guard against by an appropriate disclaimer. Condition 16(a) of Sotheby's is typical, and runs:

Goods auctioned are usually of some age. All goods are sold with all faults and imperfections and errors of description. Illustrations in catalogues are for identification only. Buyers should satisfy themselves prior to sale as to the condition of each lot and should exercise and rely on their own judgment as to whether the lot accords

---

[22] Some of these situation are analysed in the context of valuable artefacts in B W Harvey, *Violin Fraud* (1992), OUP ch 7. See the discussion of title problems in ch 5 above.

[23] There are a number of decided cases holding that sales in shops or by reference to advertised descriptions are sales by description. See *Godley v Perry* [1960] 1 All ER 36, 1 [1960] 1 WLR 9, and *Beale v Taylor* [1967] 3 All ER 253, [1967] 1 WLR 1193, CA.

[24] See *Nicholson and Venn v Smith-Marriott* (1947) 177 LT 189, mentioned above.

with its description. Subject to the obligations accepted by Sotheby's under this Condition, none of the seller, Sotheby's, its servants or agents is responsible for errors of description or for the genuineness or authenticity of any lot, no warranty whatever is given by Sotheby's, its servants or agents, or any seller to any buyer in respect of any lot and any express or implied conditions or warranties are hereby excluded.[25]

Even ignoring the possible effect of the EEC Directive on Unfair Contract Terms considered above, the effect of a Condition of Sale purporting to preclude reliance on a catalogue description is not easy to assess. It could be argued that the description must be read in the light of the appropriate condition and as part of it. This, in turn, would make the description so qualified as to make it difficult for a buyer to argue that the property had actually been misdescribed. On the other hand, the courts are more likely to see this type of condition as an exclusion or restriction falling within the Unfair Contract Terms Act 1977. As has been explained above, the courts are then obliged to consider whether the condition complies with the test of 'reasonableness'. The analogous position where a Condition of Sale purports to disclaim liability for misrepresentations is fully considered in chapter 9. If such decisions as *South Western General Property Co Ltd v Marton*[26] are any guide, there is a marked tendency in modern decisions to lean against the effectiveness of these disclaimers. On the other hand, broad disclaimers as to descriptions in the context of auctions are widespread. A disclaimer of a fundamental misdescription that would, for instance, give rise to prima facie criminal liability under s 1 of the Trade Descriptions Act 1968 (see chapter 8) would probably fall victim to the reasonableness test. The condition containing the disclaimer might also be held to be 'unfair' within the meaning of the Regulations implementing the EC Directive on Unfair Contract Terms discussed above. Both these possibilities remain to be tested in the auction context, but the practical advice to the auctioneer is to exercise extreme caution over descriptions applied, particularly where questions of attribution are involved.

'Deliberate Forgeries'

Both Sotheby's and Christie's make specific provision for any lot which proves to be a 'deliberate forgery'. This phrase is usually only apt to de-

---

[25] See also Christie's Condition of Sale A 11.

[26] (1982) 263 EG 1090, discussed in ch 9. For a recent example of the Court of Appeal holding an exclusion clause in a computer firm's standard terms and conditions unreasonable and unenforceable, see *St Albans City and District Council v International Computer Ltd* Times, Nov 11 1994.

scribe fake works of art, postage stamps, musical instruments and their labels, and similar items. The phrase is defined in Sotheby's Condition 40(e) as follows: ' "Deliberate forgery" means an imitation made with the intention of deceiving as to authorship, origin, date, age, period, culture or source which is not shown to be such in the description in the catalogue and which at the date of the sale had a value materially less than it would have had if it had been in accordance with that description.' References in the Conditions of Sale to a 'deliberate forgery' must be read in this context.[27] In the case of Sotheby's, where Condition 16(b) is included, the buyer is given the right to return the forged lot within a stipulated period of the date of the auction in the same condition in which it was at time of the auction, accompanied by a statement of defects and other details. If Sotheby's is then satisfied that the item is a 'deliberate forgery' as defined, and that the buyer has and is able to transfer a good and marketable title to the lot free from any third-party claims, the sale will be set aside and any amount paid in respect of the lot will be refunded. The period during which the buyer has this right varies from five years in the case of fine art to 21 days in the case of a postage stamp. Christie's Condition A 11(b) stipulates a similar right to return the purported 'forgery' within five years of the date of the sale. The condition can only be construed as a direct, subsidiary, contract between auctioneer and buyer, not necessarily involving the seller at all. The consideration may be the buyer's premium or the advantage to the auction house of the buyer's attendance and bidding.

This type of condition is by no means unique to the large London auction rooms. Its virtue is that it provides an opportunity to the buyer of goods at auction where the type of goods is peculiarly subject to the problem of forgery, to rescind the sale. From a business point of view it therefore removes a major potential disincentive to the less expert or more nervous bidder. On the other hand, the potential cost of implementing this policy by the auction houses, particularly where the time limit is lengthy, can be high.

Sotheby's Condition 22 authorises rescission of the sale and refund to the buyer who prays in aid Condition 16 (above). The seller is obliged to return the proceeds of sale, though if the mistake is committed solely by the auction house, a seller might resist this provision, even though the seller then becomes entitled to return of the forgery. Christie's Condition B6 limits the right of rescission to the time before the proceeds of sale have been remitted of the seller. If the forgery is discovered after this but within the time allowed, presumably the auctioneers bear the loss mitigated by the proceeds of any resale of the now correctly described article.

It must nevertheless be borne in mind that where the buyer has the right to sue in respect of a breach of the condition of compliance with description

---

[27] The word 'deliberate' seems otiose. A forgery could hardly be other than deliberate. Christie's in their A 11 omit 'deliberate'.

(assuming that it has not been effectively disclaimed) at common law and under the Sale of Goods Act 1979, he would have the right to reject the goods before acceptance takes place and thereafter to sue for damages. When does acceptance take place? Section 35(4) of the Sale of Goods Act 1979 (as amended) provides that this occurs 'when after the lapse of a reasonable time he retains the goods without intimating to the seller that he has rejected them.' There is little authority on the meaning of 'a reasonable time' in this particular context, but it may be that the only effect of 'the deliberate forgery' condition discussed above is to give the buyer much longer than he would normally have to rescind the sale. His rights otherwise would take the form of a claim to damages which would be assessed by reference to the difference between the lot as it was described and the lot as it actually is, as measured by reference to the time when the buyer, acting with reasonable diligence, could have discovered the position.[28] This course of action is extinguished after the expiration of six years from the date on which the cause of action arose, ie normally the date of the sale, by virtue of the Limitation Act 1980, s 5.

In order to guard against the possibility of forgery, the major auction-houses adopt a policy of caution when attributing valuable artefacts to particular artists or makers. The catalogue description must be read by reference to the definitions in the Conditions of Sale of such phrases as 'attributed to . . .' 'with signature . . .' and the like. It should also be noted that the right to reject a 'deliberate forgery' is modified by: (a) a 'state of the art' defence of accuracy by the standards of the time of the description, and (b) a restriction of the right to reject to the actual purchaser and not his assignee. But an unreasonable failure by the auctioneer to comply with the requirements of such a condition, perhaps by a denial that an object is a deliberate forgery in the teeth of supporting expert evidence, would lay the auctioneer open both to an action for damages and possible criminal liability under the Trade Descriptions Act 1968, s 14 (false statements as to services).

At a late stage in the preparation of this new edition an interesting and important decision in the High Court was described in the press[29] which involved a close analysis of Christie's 'forgery' Condition. At Christie's auction in 1987 a painting described in the catalogue as 'Egon Schiele and signed with initials . . . painted in 1908' was bought by the plaintiff for £500,000 excluding buyer's premium. The provenance of the painting had a long and involved history which included its exhibition in a Zurich museum as a painting by Schiele. It became owned by Dr Schlag, a retired psychol-

---

[28] See eg *East Ham Borough Council v Bernard Sunley & Sons Ltd* [1966] AC 406, [1965] 3 All ER 619, HL; *Johnson v Agnew* [1980] AC 367, HL at 401.

[29] *De Balkany v Christie Manson & Woods Ltd* (The Independent Jan. 19, 1995, transcript) 1993 D No. 1089. See *Antiques Trade Gazette* (1995) 21 January, p 1 and (1995) 4 February, p 4.

ogist in Switzerland, who agreed to sell it through Christie's. Some three years after the sale an eminent art critic published a catalogue of Schiele's paintings which cast considerable doubt on the genuineness of the painting in question. The initials were placed in an untypical position for the painter and there were other suspicious features. The plaintiff complained to Christie's in 1991 within the five years from the date of purchase given by their Condition to return a forged painting and rescind the contract. Another expert was asked for an opinion who noticed 'ill-matched over-painting' and suggested it be subjected to chemical and spectrographic tests. As a result of this evidence given at a seven day hearing in December 1994 the learned judge, Morison J, found that an unnamed person had extensively over-painted what had previously been on the canvas. The extent of the over-painting was 94% of the surface area and had been done some time after the artist's death. The initials of the artist were part of the over-painting and therefore had been added later. On the balance of probabilities, and with considerable hesitation, the judge found that the painting underneath was by Schiele but what had been bought was a painting which was almost wholly made by an unknown person. The judge concluded that the over-painting must have been intended to deceive the viewer into believing that the initials were painted by Schiele. This was possible to disguise the extent of the over-painting which had covered the original monogram. The over-painter therefore intended to deceive as to authorship and the date and age of what was visible on the painting. It was only with the aid of an ultra-violet lamp that this state of affairs was discovered.

The case involved a fascinating discussion of whether a painting which was originally by the stated artist could cease to be so if so over-painted. Christie's argued that the problem related purely to the condition of the painting and did not change its essential identity. But, on the wording of Christie's Condition, the judge did not accept this argument. The addition of the initials was fatal. The 'forgery' Condition was also dependent upon (a) the buyer acting promptly and (b) a 'state of the art' (including the consensus of expert opinion) exception if the catalogue description was reasonable at the time of the sale. The judge held that the plaintiff had acted without delay on becoming aware, by virtue of the 1990 scholarly publication, that there might be a problem. The state of the art exception did not apply because Christie's were unable to prove not only that they relied upon the opinion of scholars in making the description but, by implication, that they were reasonably entitled to do so. Here, any competent art dealer or auctioneer would have been able to tell that the picture had been substantially over-painted and the initials put on subsequently if a careful inspection had been made. Two expert witnesses gave evidence to this effect and one stated that virtually all that was visible was the restorer's work and he would have dismissed the painting out of hand. Christie's were acquitted of fraud (which was not alleged in any event) but not of acting unreasonably, and the plaintiff had therefore proved that the painting was a forgery within the meaning of Christie's Conditions and no exception thereunder was available to relieve Christie's of liability.

There was another allegation against Christie's which, because of the above reasoning, it became unnecessary for the judge formally to decide. That was whether Christie's had any liability to the plaintiff in tort. Here the judgment (which was at this point obiter) becomes difficult to follow. The first question in the reader's mind might be why it was necessary to argue this point at all. As stated above, the obvious course of action in these circumstances would be against the *vendor* in respect of the inaccurate description of the goods given by the vendor's agent, the auctioneer. However, in this case the vendor was not sued, perhaps because of jurisdictional difficulties. That left the auctioneers themselves the only target. The forgery Condition was (exceptionally) a contractual one between the auctioneer and the buyer. If it applied and the auctioneers repudiated it, there was a straightforward breach of contract. The remedy did not depend on a sophisticated analysis of whether there was a duty of care where only economic loss results, which is part of the law of tort. However, as stated above, the judge felt obliged to say something on this topic even though it was not necessary for the decision.

Briefly, he held that on the authorities and because Christie's took responsibility for the catalogue description which is an important feature from the buyer's point of view, and because the buyer paid a premium, he was inclined to the view that there was an assumption of responsibility such that Christie's became prima facie liable to a buyer for negligent misstatement in the catalogue entry. However, referring to the numerous Conditions which excluded Christie's responsibility for 'the correctness' of any statement of description, his conclusion was that they had effectively disclaimed any responsibility which they would otherwise have. He did not regard this conclusion as satisfactory because it meant that a buyer had got nothing of substance for his premium. The oddity about this part of the judgment is that there is no discussion of whether any such disclaimer should first be assessed for reasonableness under the terms of the Unfair Contract Terms Act 1977. This Act does not simply apply to the contractual situation. Section 2(2) of the Act states that a person cannot 'exclude or restrict his liability for negligence except in so far as the term or notice satisfies the requirement of reasonableness.' 'Negligence' is defined as the breach of any common law duty to take reasonable care or exercise reasonable skill (s1(1)). The requirement of reasonableness is that the notice (not being a notice having contractual effect) should be fair and reasonable having regard to all the circumstances obtaining when the liability arose or (but for the notice) would have arisen (s11(2)). In a number of cases, but particularly the House of Lords decision in *Smith v Eric S Bush*,[30] a case involving a negligent surveyor's report on which a third party relied, it was made clear that the Act does catch disclaimers of this sort and the court should consider such matters as whether the parties are of equal bargaining power, how difficult it was for advice to be obtained elsewhere, how difficult the task was for which liability was being excluded, and what would be the practical consequences of, for example, insurance, on the court's decision on the question of reasonableness.[31] It is submitted, therefore, that should the question of the auctioneer's duty of care towards the buyer in terms of accuracy of descriptions again be in issue, careful reconsideration will need to be given not only to the question of whether the duty exists but as to whether any disclaimers, which in practice invariably exist, are subject to the Act's reasonableness test and whether they are so reasonable. The imbalance of power and knowledge between the auctioneer and most buyers suggests strongly that auctioneers' disclaimers may be vulnerable.

In summary, the implications of this case are twofold. Firstly, where property is patently misdescribed and falls within the definition of a forgery in the auctioneer's own Conditions, the auctioneer may expect the purchaser to bring an action to enforce that Condition under the ordinary law of contract. It is then a question of construing the Condition, which may be differently worded from that of Christie's, to see whether it actually covers the event. Secondly, instead of suing the vendor the disaffected purchaser may sue the auctioneer if it can be established that there is a breach of a duty of care to the purchaser in the making of the catalogue description. (Although the judge placed reliance on the fact that there was a buyer's premium paid here, this does not occur in by any means every auction and in an action in tort rather than contract should not be regarded, it is submitted, as in any event an essential feature.) Given that a duty of care does arise, there would then be a battle as to whether the disclaimers in the Conditions were effective to absolve the auctioneer from such liability. This matter awaits an authoritative decision, but in a number of recent cases such disclaimers have been struck down as unreasonable. The auguries are poor for the auctioneer.

UNSATISFACTORY GOODS

It is almost universal for Conditions of Sale to attempt to exclude faults and imperfections in goods sold. As has already been explained, the implied

---

[30] [1990] 1 AC 829.
[31] See the discussion in *Tort Law*, Markesinis and Deakin (1993), OUP, pp 94, 665–6.

term of 'satisfactory', formerly 'merchantable', quality is likely otherwise to apply, subject to certain qualifications. These qualifications are best explained by examining the position of a successful buyer wishing to bring an action against the seller for subsequently discovered defects in the goods sold. He must first overcome the following hurdles which are imposed by section 14 of the Sale of Goods Act 1979 as amended by the Sale and Supply of Goods Act 1994 (respectively the 1979 Act and the 1994 Act):

(a) If the seller is a private seller, the buyer must show that he did not know this and that no reasonable steps were taken to bring this fact to his notice before the contract was made (s 14(5)).

(b) Since the implied term of quality only applies where the defects in question were not specifically drawn to the buyer's attention before the contract was made, he must show that this did not occur.

(c) If, as normally happens, he examined the goods before bidding, he must show that the defects in question were not such as that examination ought to have revealed.[32]

(d) Finally, the buyer must show that the defects do render the goods not satisfactory. The 1994 Act amends section 14 of the 1979 Act and the new section 14 (2A) states that goods are of satisfactory quality if they meet the standard that a reasonable person would regard as satisfactory, taking account of any description of the goods, the price (if relevant) and all other relevant circumstances. Aspects of the quality of goods are fitness for the purposes for which goods of the kind in question are commonly supplied, appearance and finish, freedom from defects, safety and durability (s 14 (2B)). The psychology of the above is directed primarily to new goods. There are no separate tests for second-hand goods but the fact that items in auctions are usually not new in undoubtedly to be considered when applying the expression 'all other relevant circumstances'. Some assistance can probably be gained from judicial construction of the former concept of 'merchantability' in the context of used goods. As Lord Denning stated, merchantability 'means, that on the sale of a second-hand car, it is merchantable if it is in usable condition, even though not perfect . . . A buyer should realise that when he buys a second-hand car, defects may appear sooner or later; and in the absence of express warranty, he has no redress.'[33] Should the buyer actually succeed in showing that the goods are not of satisfactory quality and that there has been a

---

[32] See *Thornett and Fehr v Beers & Sons* [1919] 1 KB 486, 88 LJKB 684 (inspection of outside only of glue barrels held to impute notice of their internal condition). Despite that decision, it is now thought that 'that examination' is the examination actually made by the buyer, however superficial.

[33] *Bartlett v Sidney Marcus Ltd* [1965] 2 All ER 753, CA, at 755.

breach of the implied term, the seller will then have to rely on the disclaimer of liability in the Conditions of Sale. This is subject to the reasonableness test under the Unfair Contract Terms Act 1977, as explained above.[34] However auction sales are not consumer sales and so long as such disclaimers are subject to the test of reasonableness they are likely to continue to figure prominently in standard Conditions of Sale until it is unequivocally established that in *all* circumstances this is unreasonable, or that the clause is unfair within the 1994 Regulations (above).

Similar remarks apply pari passu to the implied term of fitness for purpose in the unlikely case of its being implied in these circumstances.

THE BUYER'S PREMIUM

In 1975 both Sotheby's and Christie's introduced the buyer's premium. Sotheby's Condition 3 runs, accordingly, thus:

The buyer shall pay to Sotheby's a premium at the 'stated rates' on the 'hammer price' together with Value Added Tax at the standard rate on the premium, and agrees that Sotheby's, when acting as agent for the seller, may also receive commission from the seller in accordance with Condition 19.

In November 1992 Sotheby's increased the buyer's premium from 10% to 15% on lots up to the value of £30,000 and 10% thereafter subject to an overall maximum figure of £1,500. The 'stated rates' are those published by Sotheby's from time to time. Most, but not all, other auction houses followed suit. Following the VAT changes described in chapter 12 the wording concerning VAT will need to be adjusted.

The right to extract the additional 15% on the hammer price from the buyer is thus imposed by a contractual condition. Some aspects of the auctioneer's position vis-à-vis the seller in this respect, are examined elsewhere.[35] The practice of imposing a buyer's premium is now widespread throughout the UK, though its introduction was not unattended by controversy, it being alleged that the introduction of the buyer's premium was as a result of collusion between Sotheby's and Christie's and consequently this agreement was registrable as a restrictive practice under the Restrictive Trade Practices Act 1976. It is understood that this allegation, made by a

---

[34] See above. Such a clause is both void and criminally illegal in a *consumer* sale — see Consumer Transactions (Restrictions on Statements) Order, SI 1976/1813.

[35] See ch 5. Attention is also drawn to the provisions of the Consumer Protection Act 1987, s 21(1)(a) which makes it an offence to convey an indication that 'the price is less than in fact it is'. Avoidance of this offence will depend upon the buyer's knowledge of any buyer's premium which is to be charged to him.

group of dealers was rejected by the Office of Fair Trading on the ground that there was insufficient evidence of actual collusion.[36]

The VAT dimension in discussed specifically in chapter 12.

PAYMENT BY THE BUYER

Auction sales continue to depend to a large degree on trust between auctioneer and buyer. Nevertheless standard Conditions of Sale will seek to secure as far as possible that the buyer identifies himself and pays for the goods as soon as possible. This effect is usually achieved by stipulations, broadly as follows:

(a) The buyer on making a successful bid must forthwith supply his name and address and, if so required, his bank or other suitable references; or a system involving the registration of name and address (and perhaps other information) in exchange for a numbered 'paddle' without which bids may not be accepted.

(b) The buyer may be required to pay forthwith the whole or part of the purchase price, and if he fails to do so the lot or lots may at the auctioneer's absolute discretion be put up again and resold. In other words, failure to pay would be regarded as a fundamental breach of contract.

(c) Various reserve rights may also be secured against the purchaser. These might include later resale of the goods with liability by the buyer to meet any deficiency; the right to store the lots at the expense of the buyer until collection; the right to charge interest at a stipulated rate on the purchase price to the extent that it remains unpaid for more than (say) 7 days from the date of the sale.[37]

COLLECTION OF PURCHASES AND PASSING OF THE PROPERTY

Property in goods passes according to the rules contained in s 18 of the Sale of Goods Act 1979 unless otherwise agreed. In the absence of such agreement the property will pass to the buyer when the contract is made, that is, on the fall of the hammer.[38] Most Conditions of Sale contract out of this general position by stating that the ownership of any lot purchased shall not pass to the buyer until he has made payment in full to the auctioneers. Furthermore, the buyer is put under a liability to take away the lot at his

---

[36] In 1983 Andrew Faulds MP unsuccessfully introduced a Private Member's Bill (the Buyer's Premium (Abolition) Bill) to abolish the premium.

[37] See Sotheby's Conditions 6 and 15, and Christie's Conditions of Sale, 7 and 10.

[38] See s 18, r 1, Sale of Goods Act 1979.

own expense within a stipulated period (often 5 or 7 working days after the auction).[39]

BUYER'S RESPONSIBILITIES FOR LOTS PURCHASED

In practice the safekeeping of goods bought by buyers during the auction, and the prevention of damage thereto, can give rise to problems. In a crowded auction-room accidents can all too easily happen or goods purchased may be stolen. Under the Sale of Goods Act 1979 the risk remains with the seller until the property in the goods has transferred to the buyer. Where a dispute arises as to this, the first step is therefore to assess whether the property has passed to the buyer or not (which may depend on whether the buyer has paid for the goods) and then prima facie responsibility for loss or damage lies with whoever at the time is the owner. This rule, laid down by s 20 of the Sale of Goods Act 1979, is specifically subject to variation of the position: (a) where delivery has been delayed through the fault of the seller, and (b) where the law of bailment affects the position by imposing duties of care on the bailee (in this case the auctioneer). This latter point has been discussed elsewhere in detail.[40] Its significance here is that should the Conditions of Sale of the auctioneer attempt to contract out of an existing duty of care, once again the clause is likely to be regarded as an exclusion clause whose validity will be judged by reference to the Unfair Contract Terms Act 1977 and its requirement of reasonableness.

Sotheby's Condition 12 states:

The buyer will be responsible for loss or damage to lots purchased from the time of collection or the expiry of 5 working days after the day of the auction, whichever is the sooner, and neither Sotheby's nor its servants or agents shall thereafter be responsible for any loss or damage of any kind, whether caused by negligence or otherwise, while any lot is in its custody or under its control.[41]

Christie's Condition 9 states that: 'The property in a lot shall not pass to the Buyer until he has paid the Purchase Price in full.' Christie's Condition 9 goes on to state that the purchased lot(s) shall be at the buyer's risk in all respects from the time of collection or the expiry of seven days from the date of sale, whichever is the sooner.

---

[39] See Sotheby's Condition 10, and Christie's Conditions of Sale 7 and 8.

[40] See ch. 5 p 125.

[41] Facilities exist for insurance of the goods at the seller's expense and at his option per Sotheby's Condition 20. However cover is expressed to cease at 'the earlier of the ownership of the property passing from the seller or the seller or consignor becoming bound to collect the property'. Presumably such insurance would cover uncollected goods for those five working days where the property has not passed to the buyer because he has not paid for the goods (see Sotheby's Conditions 9 and 10).

CONDITIONS GOVERNING THE CONDUCT OF THE AUCTION

ARE BIDDERS OTHER THAN THE BUYER BOUND?

This question most often arises in the context of discussion of the problem of 'without reserve' sales. Here, typically, the auctioneer either refuses to accept the bid of the highest bidder or, as in *Warlow v Harrison*,[42] accepts a bogus bid from the seller himself. We have already fully discussed the implications of *Warlow v Harrison*,[43] and it must be re-emphasised that there are two possible views. One is that there can be no contract with the highest bidder since he merely makes an offer which is not accepted by fall of the hammer. Just as a bidder may withdraw his bid before the fall of the hammer, it follows that the seller is equally entitled to withdraw the goods before this point of time.[44] The alternative view is that an advertisement that a sale should be without a reserve is a conditional offer to the whole world capable of acceptance by anyone who, relying on the advertisement, attends the auction and bids. The consideration for the contract is said to be found in the rule that 'an act done at the request of another, express or implied, is sufficient consideration to support a promise'.[45] The difficulties in accepting this view of a 'collateral contract' with buyers generally, are explored above.[46]

However, it is of interest that the Full Court of the Natal Provincial Division of the S African Supreme Court was prepared to accept the idea in principle that such collateral contracts are capable of arising, though it will be noted that the analysis which follows does not deal with the difficult question of consideration. In *Shandel v Jacobs*,[47] an auction sale was held under conditions which included the following:

(1) Each bid will be an offer to purchase and the party making the highest accepted bid will be the purchaser, the sale to become complete on acceptance of the bid by the auctioneer as indicated by the fall of the hammer or otherwise. The advance in the bidding will be regulated by the auctioneer who will have the sole right of deciding who was the last bidder. In the event of a dispute between two or more bidders the lot in dispute may be put up and resold at the discretion of the auctioneer.

(2) The auctioneer may, at his discretion and without assigning any reason therefor, refuse a bid or withdraw an article either before or after it has been put up for auction.

---

[42] (1859) 1 E & E 309, 29 LJQB 14.   [43] See above, p 249 f.
[44] This was the view taken in *Fenwick v MacDonald, Fraser & Co Ltd* 1904 6 F (Ct of Sess) 850, 41 Sc LR 638.
[45] See LCB Gower (1952) 68 LQR 458.   [46] See above, pp 29–33.
[47] 1949 (1) SA 320, cited in George (1949) 65 LQR 310.

The plaintiff made the highest bids for various articles but his bids were refused by the auctioneer, apparently out of malice. The articles were in fact knocked down to other persons attending the sale. The disappointed plaintiff therefore sued the auctioneer for damages. Carlisle J stated:[48]

The action, as I understand it, is founded upon a breach of an implied term of the contract between the plaintiff and the auctioneers, the contract itself being embodied in the Conditions of Sale . . .

The questions that arise are, I think, twofold:

(a) Do the Conditions of Sale constitute a contract between the auctioneer and a bona fide bidder for any article which is put up?

(b) If so, is it implied in such Conditions that the auctioneer shall carry them out without mala fides?

It seems to me that the first question must be answered in the affirmative. In the case of *Estate Francis v Land Sales (Property) Ltd*, Broome J said:[49]

'An auction is a form of competitive bargaining with the object of a contract of sale resulting carried out in accordance with certain rules. These rules are the Conditions of Sale. They are framed by the seller to represent the terms upon which he is prepared to submit his property to competition. They are, so to speak, the rules of the game and they bind all the players . . .'

'The question then arises, who are the players who are so bound? The Conditions of Sale are agreed upon in the first instance between the seller and the auctioneer and between these two they rest upon a contractual basis. When goods are offered for sale pursuant to them, they form the basis of the bargaining carried on between the auctioneer and the bidders. That the bidders are, as Broome J put it, the players, I have no doubt and, since an auctioneer usually acts for an undisclosed principal, the rules as between him and the bidder may bind the auctioneer personally. In *Warlow v Harrison*,[50] Martin B pointed out that in a sale by auction there were three parties, namely: the owner, the auctioneer, and the portion of the public who intended to bid. He further pointed out that, in most cases of sale by auction, the owner's name is not disclosed and he remains a concealed principal. The name of the auctioneer only is published and where the sale is announced by them to be without reserve, that, according to all the cases of law and equity, meant that the property should be sold to the highest bidder whether the sum bid be equivalent to the real value or not. This judgment goes on to say that 'the highest bona fide bidder at an auction may sue the auctioneer as upon a contract that the sale shall be without reserve'.[51]

Carlisle J concluded that all the Conditions of Sale form a contractual relationship between the auctioneer and the bidding public,[52] and held that it was an implied term that the auctioneer should carry out the conditions without mala fides.

[48] 1949 (1) SA 320 at 325.   [49] [1940] NPD 441 at 457.
[50] (1859) 1 E&E 309, 29 LJQB 14, [1843–60] All ER Rep 620.
[51] (1859) 1 E&E 309, 29 LJQB 14, [1843–60] All ER Rep 620 at 622.
[52] *Shandel v Jacobs* 1949 (1) SA 320 at 326.

The significance of this is that it shows a willingness by the courts to give validity to stipulations, in this case in Conditions of Sale, outside the strict contractual nexus between seller, auctioneer and buyer. There are a number of conditions besides a possible one relating to sales 'without reserve', which fall into this category. For instance it may be stipulated that the auctioneer shall have the right to refuse any bid which does not exceed the previous bid by a specified percentage and, by the same token, there may be a condition stipulating that no bidder shall withdraw his bid. In the absence of modern and conclusive authority we can only reiterate that the willingness of a court to imply a collateral contract in these circumstances remains to be verified, at least in the UK.

Nevertheless, as indicated above, if bidders in practice sign a form as a preliminary confirming that they accept that they are bound by the Conditions of Sale, including those affecting the conduct of the auction, it would be surprising if any court were to hold other than that this was contractually binding. Consideration for such a collateral contract would be the advantage of the licence given to those present to attend the auction and be eligible to bid and buy.

DEFINITION OF BUYER

For the auction room contract to fall into place, 'the buyer' must obviously be defined. To put the matter beyond doubt, Conditions of Sale normally define 'the buyer'. In the case of Sotheby's Condition 1, the buyer is defined as follows:

The highest bidder shall be the buyer at the 'hammer price', and any dispute shall be settled at the auctioneer's absolute discretion. Any bidder acting for any person who is not bidding shall be jointly and severally liable with that person for satisfaction of all obligations and liabilities hereunder.

The second sentence of this Condition is a revision of the former provision whereunder it was possible to state to the auctioneers, and then to get their written acknowledgment, that the bidder acted on behalf of a named principal. Christie's in their Condition A 2(b) have retained this facility. Their Condition A 2(a) defines the Buyer as the highest bidder acceptable to Christie's.[53] This condition goes on to state that if

during or immediately after the sale of the lot, the auctioneer considers that a dispute has arisen or that there is any other reason for so doing, he may at his absolute discretion immediately put up the lot again for sale.

---

[53] The auctioneer will exercise his discretion where eg the highest bid in the salesroom matches the highest bid left in advance of the sale by an absent potential buyer.

In practice, identifying the bid of experienced bidders can take a great deal of skill on the auctioneer's part. The *Auction Companion*[54] relates that a dealer wishing to bid for a Rembrandt at Christie's in 1965 made the following arrangement:

When Mr S is sitting down he is bidding. If he bids openly he is bidding. When he stands up he has stopped bidding. If he sits down again he is not bidding until he raises his finger. Having raised his finger, he is bidding until he stands up again.

Not surprisingly, the Rembrandt was knocked down to another bidder, at which Mr S loudly complained and the picture was again put up for sale when Mr S was successful by openly bidding 760,000 guineas.

It will be seen from this saga that there is a need for a condition which attempts to allow the auctioneer to settle disputes as to the highest bidder and these are considered in detail below. Nevertheless, the gentlemanly practice which occurs in some circles where an auctioneer has closed the bidding by fall of the hammer and is then confronted with a further purported bidder whom he has not previously identified, at which he proceeds — with the successful bidder's permission — to reoffer the lot, is open to grave objection. The contract is completed at the fall of the hammer, and there is no consideration (although there may be moral pressure) for the hitherto successful bidder to abandon his contractual rights as buyer. In this situation (certainly in law, and, it is strongly suggested, in ethics), the auctioneer ought to accept the position and not attempt to reopen the bidding where there is no genuine dispute.

A slightly different problem arises when the undisputed highest bidder has second thoughts, or realises that he has made a mistake. An operative mistake in law cannot generally arise where the parties agree in the same terms on the same subject matter. But a 'mutual' mistake, annulling their contract, may occur where eg a bidder bids for what he believes to be bales of tow whereas the auctioneer is in fact offering bales of hemp, though his catalogue description is not clear. This occurred in *Scriven Bros v Hindley & Co*,[55] where it was held that there was no genuine agreement between the parties and no binding contract. Mistaken judgment or motive is irrelevant. In *Friedrich v A Monnickendam Ltd*,[56] the Court of Appeal considered the auctioneer's duty where questionable bids are made. The case concerned a jewellery sale held by Christie's in Geneva. The facts arose out of confusion by the English highest bidder as to whether the auctioneer had called 290,000 Swiss francs for some diamond pendants, or, as he thought, 190,000.

[54] Daniel and Katherine Leab *The Auction Companion* (1981) Macmillan.

[55] [1913] 3KB 564 See *Bell v Lever Bros Ltd* [1932] AC 161, HL, at 224, per Lord Atkin, and, in equity. Also *Tamplin v James* (1879) 15 Ch D 215, CA, at 217 per Baggally LJ.

[56] (1973) 228 EG 1311. See also p. 85.

'The auctioneer should therefore have assured himself by the clearest words in English that Mr Monnickendam appreciated that the figure was 290,000 Swiss francs' (per Lord Denning). The Court of Appeal held the contract to be vitiated by mistake (among other factors).

DISPUTED BIDS

An unresolved case in course of litigation is known to the authors which illustrates many of the pertinent points and where the approximate facts are as follows. A bidder bid for a valuable item in an auction the proceedings of which were tape-recorded. The bidding followed a regular course until the sum of, say, £40,000 was reached when the auctioneer brought down the hammer and announced the bidder in question to be the buyer. There was then a long pause, some muffled conversation with another person sitting at the front of the sale room, and then a re-opening of the proceedings by the auctioneer despite audible protests by the original bidder. The auctioneer nevertheless proceeded and the original bidder again made an unmatched bid, this time at, say, £150,000. When the time came to settle for the lot the buyer insisted on paying the original price, £40,000, only. The auctioneers argued that they were entitled to re-offer the lot on the basis of standard Conditions which stated that the auctioneers had 'absolute discretion without giving any reason . . . in case of a dispute to put up any Lot for auction again.'

In this context, 'any dispute' can legitimately be assumed to be a dispute about a *bid*, and some standard Conditions specifically refer to 'disputes respecting a bid' (see, for example, below). Was there such a dispute?

Some guidance is obtainable from the decision in *Richards v Phillips*.[57] The case concerned the sale by auction of the Lyric Theatre, Hammersmith. A Condition referred to circumstances where 'if any dispute arises respecting a bid' a property could at the vendor's option either be put up again at the last undisputed bid or be withdrawn. The reserve price was £25,800. The bidding opened at £10,000. The plaintiff bid £15,000 orally and the auctioneer bid £20,000 on behalf of the vendor. At about the same time as the auctioneer's bid of £20,000, another bidder, D, made a motion to bid £20,000. The plaintiff and the auctioneer, on behalf of the vendor, made alternate bids culminating in a bid of £26,000 by the plaintiff. D also signalled the bid at £26,000 at about the same time, but the auctioneer did not see this. D heard none of the plaintiff's bids, but the auctioneer heard all the plaintiff's bids and was throughout unaware of D's bid. When D realised that the accepted bid was not his, he protested. The auctioneer's clerk

---

[57] [1969] 1 Ch 39, CA.

corroborated D's bids. The property was put up for sale again and the plaintiff eventually succeeded at £37,500. The plaintiff issued a writ claiming damages of £11,500 against the auctioneers, being the difference between £37,500 and £26,000. The same issue as described above arose, therefore, namely whether the auctioneer was entitled to re-offer the lot in the circumstances.

The Court of Appeal considered the circumstances of the auction which, to say the least, were peculiar. The auction was held in a room opening on to a street where there was a certain amount of noise. D (a professional auctioneer himself) appeared to be an extremely lethargic bidder given to making vague motions with his sales card. The auctioneer never saw these. People sitting immediately in front of D did see the relevant gesture and assumed that he had made a bid. The auctioneer had only heard the plaintiff, but, on the other hand, D had heard nothing of what the plaintiff said. Harman, LJ described it as 'a thorough comedy of errors'.

In these circumstances the Court of Appeal considered the argument on behalf of the plaintiff that there never was any bid except that of the plaintiff. D's motions, being unobserved by the auctioneer, were ineffective as bids. However, probably because D's material bid was in fact seen by the auctioneer's clerk, the court held that this was a 'dispute concerning a bid' within the meaning of that phrase and the auctioneer was acting properly in putting up the property again for sale. However, at first instance Pennycuick, J commented:

It is competent for a bidder to make his bids by signals but he can only make an effective bid by communicating it to the auctioneer, and if his signal fails to register through no fault of the auctioneer he has, I think, simply failed to make a bid in any relevant sense.'[58]

This is an important statement, and though strictly obiter in the sense that it was not required for the decision, the whole of Pennycuick J's judgment seems to have been adopted without qualification by the Court of Appeal. On the facts of *Richards v Phillips* D's bid was communicated, via the auctioneer's clerk. But if, in the case first referred to above, it was found on the facts that the alternative alleged bidder was not 'bidding' until *after* the hammer fell, then the two decisions could be distinguished. The alternative bidder had failed in his duty to communicate his bid before the hammer fell. There was at that stage no 'dispute respecting a bid'.

Another problem with regard to re-offering disputed lots is to decide at what stage it is too late for the auctioneer to take advantage of this facility. For instance, if there is a genuine dispute about a bid that the auctioneer himself is not aware of at the time, can the auctioneer re-open the bidding on the disputed lot after the elapse of a significant period and, perhaps, after

---

[58] See [1967] 3 All ER, 876 at 881.

the sale of a good many intermediate lots? The standard conditions themselves do not normally specify at what stage the re-offering can take place.
Professional opinion seems to favour the theory that any re-offering must
occur before proceeding to the next lot in the catalogue. There is much to
be said for that viewpoint. The whole import of the Condition is to vary
s 57(2) of the Sale of Goods Act 1979 ('a sale by auction is complete when
the auctioneer announces its completion by the fall of a hammer . . .') by
imposing a condition subsequent. It is surely undesirable that commercial
certainly should be abrogated in this manner except for the shortest possible time. A somewhat similar position arises where several consecutive lots,
forming a set, are first offered individually on a conditional basis and then,
finally, immediately re-offered as a 'set' subject to the aggregate of the
individual prices being at least equalled. The first 'sale' is therefore subject
to a condition precedent. (For an example of this, see Sotheby's Musical
Instrument Sale of 1 November 1994, lots 228–31, being a quartet of instruments by an Italian maker.)

MINIMUM INCREMENT

Problems can arise in practice where bidders attempt to control incremental
increases from the floor. Some Conditions of Sale will forbid this practice
altogether by making the right to bid conditional on acceptance of the
increments suggested by the auctioneer. This is however somewhat inflex-
ible, and Sotheby's Condition 2 states: 'The auctioneer shall have the right
to refuse any bid which does not exceed the previous bid by at least 5 per
cent or by such other proportion as the auctioneer shall in his absolute
discretion direct.' Problems can in practice arise as to what increment has
been offered by a particular bidder, especially where two or more bidders
are bidding simultaneously. Again, much depends on the skill of the auctioneer who should make it clear to each bidder at what price he is bidding.
The practice at some fine art sales, or sales of commodities with much above
average value, can be to allocate to a particular bidder who is indicating
interest a suggested price representing a conventional incremental or percentage increase. In other words, the auctioneer calls out the increments
after he has 'registered' a bid. An analysis of this situation would cause
considerable difficulties in the law of contract since offers must be made at
an ascertainable price. The best that can be suggested is that the bidder, in
making a bid for a lot at an unidentified increment, is making a conditional
offer which he must be allowed to withdraw should the increment then
prove unacceptable to him (unless, of course, it can be shown that an
experienced bidder knew by convention the price of the invitation being
made by the auctioneer).

ADMISSION TO PREMISES

Bidders are licensees on the premises of the auctioneers. There is no reason in law why such licence should not be withdrawn unilaterally since it is not obviously granted for any consideration. Sotheby's Condition 35 accordingly states that the company 'shall have the right, at its discretion, to refuse admission to its premises or attendance at its auctions by any person.'

REFUSAL TO ACCEPT BIDS ETC

Similarly, auctioneers may have good reason to refuse to accept a bid from a bidder whose integrity is in doubt. Sotheby's Condition 36 states that the company 'has absolute discretion without giving any reason to refuse any bid, to divide any lot, to combine any two or more lots, to withdraw any lot from the auction and in case of dispute put up any lot for auction again.'

'PHANTOM' AND UNHINGED BIDDERS

Auctioneers occasionally experience problems in practice with bidders who succeed and then simply disappear, unidentified, or who are identified but plead that they were not in their right mind when bidding. The conduct clearly involves a breach of contract by the bidder-buyer.

The 'phantom' is best dealt with by having a system of 'paddle' bidding so that each bidder is identified by a predetermined number carrying details of name and address in the auctioneer's books.

The second type of buyer, who argues, in effect, temporary insanity, apparently did emerge in a well publicised case in the London salerooms involving his paying an exaggerated price for the lot in question. In these circumstances attention is drawn to the rule in the law of contract that although a contract is vitiated by the mental incapacity of one party, this is only so if (a) the mental derangement can be medically established and (b) the mental incapacity was known, or ought reasonably to have been known, to (in our case) the auctioneer. The burden of proving this lies on the plaintiff.[59] Normally the auctioneer will not suspect a bidder of being mentally deranged and the defence can therefore hardly arise. But it is theoretically possible for the bidding to become so widely exaggerated that it might be said that no sane person would be bidding at this level. The difficulty with that argument is that there must, by definition, be an under-bidder

---

[59] *See Molton v Camroux* (1848) 2 Exch 487; affd (1849) 4 Exch 17; *Imperial Loan Co v Stone* [1892] 1 QB 599.

(unless a very rash auctioneer is taking bids 'off the wall'). In a truly competitive situation, who is the auctioneer to say that the bidding is wildly extravagant? Nevertheless, if the auctioneer suspects that an overenthusiastic bidder is likely to purport to revoke, he should bear in mind the power given under most conditions of sale to refuse a bid in his sole discretion (see eg Sotheby's Condition 36).

BIDDING PRACTICES

The conditions considered above are those which are commonly included in order to ensure, perfectly properly, that the auctioneer remains in control of the conduct of the auction. The auctioneer may, additionally, wish to provide conditions relating to bidding practices and the setting of reserves. A typical provision is that found in Sotheby's Conditions. Condition 18 under the heading 'Reserves' provides:

The seller shall be entitled to place prior to the auction a reserve on any lot, being the minimum 'hammer price' at which that lot may be treated as sold. A reserve once placed by the seller shall not be changed without the consent of Sotheby's. Sotheby's may at their option sell at a hammer price below the reserve but in any such case the sale proceeds to which the seller is entitled shall be the same as if the lot had sold on the reserve. No seller may bid, nor may any third party bid, on the seller's behalf. Where a reserve is being placed, Sotheby's may, on behalf of the seller, bid up to that reserve.

This provision removes the right of the vendor to bid save through the agency of the auctioneer. A number of linked enquiries need to be undertaken here.

(1) What is the exact scope of the right to bid by or on behalf of the vendor?
(2) What is the effect of any misuse of such a right?
(3) What controls, if any, might be introduced.

Scope of the right to bid

Auctioneers frequently see the power to bid on behalf of the vendor as indispensable, if they are to achieve a proper price or a sale at all.

Auctioneers tend to be justly proud of their rostrum-craft and in their ability to wring the highest possible prices on behalf of their principals out of a possible passive, if not recalcitrant, audience. Exciting an atmosphere of competition is at the heart of this craft and doubtless an audience frequently will need to be prodded into activity. It is useful in such a situation for the auctioneer to have the power to start the ball rolling. If the seller has a right to bid himself, either directly or through someone acting for him this may assist the auctioneer in his task. It is even more helpful if the auctioneer is nominated as the seller's agent for this purpose since he has full control of the timing and extent of such bidding.

On the other hand, an unrestricted right so to bid, or at any rate an unrestricted exercise of that right, is likely to work to the severe disadvantage of uninitiated buyers who may end up paying more than they would otherwise have done, or perhaps worse, buying when they would not have bought at all had the truth been known. (Whilst in some cases the 'puffing' may have only prompted the making of bids by genuine bidders, in others the buyer may have been the sole genuine bidder, his competitor being merely a phantom at the back of the room.) There is a tension then, not surprisingly, between the interests of the seller and those of the buyer.

In considering the legal position, it is necessary, initially, to distinguish the position as it obtained at common law and in equity, and subsequently under statute. There is considerable confusion as to the law in this area due no doubt in part to the co-existence of differing rules at law and in equity and the separate and slightly different statutory modifications in the case of land on the one hand and goods on the other.

Common law

It may at first sight seem odd to speak about the seller making bids: it is trite learning that a bid at auction amounts to a contractual offer to buy the lot put up for sale.[60] How then can it be that one who is already the owner can make an offer to buy? The answer may simply be that the bid by the seller is, when accepted by the auctioneer, effectively merely a rejection of the previous bidder's offer; and, of course, it is generally open to an offeree to decline to accept an offer unless he has divested himself of that power.[61] Be that as it may, it has for several centuries been accepted that a seller can bid and that no fraud is perpetrated against the subsequently successful buyer provided that the auction is notified to be subject to such a power. In *Bexell v Christie*[62] a horse was sent for sale at an auction, the conditions providing that 'goods should be sold to the best bidder'. It was alleged that the seller's instructions to the auctioneer were that he should not let the horse go for less than £15. The horse was knocked down to the highest bidder for £6. 16s. 6d. In rejecting the seller's claim against the auctioneer, Lord Mansfield said:

---

[60] *Payne v Cave* (1789) 3 Term Rep 148.

[61] A 'without reserve' sale is an instance of an offeror divesting himself of his power to decline to accept.

[62] (1776) 1 Cowp 395; 98 ER 1150.

The question is, whether a bidding by the owner of the goods at a sale under these conditions . . . is a bidding within the meaning of the conditions of sale . . . An owner of goods set up to sale at an auction would never bid in the room himself. If such a practice were allowed, no one would bid. It is a fraud upon the sale and upon the public. Disallowing it is no hardship upon the owner. For if he is unwilling his goods should go at an under price, he may order them to be set up at his own price, and not lower: such a direction would be fair: or he might (have) it inserted in the conditions of sale, that he himself might bid once in the course of the sale . . .[63]

Lord Mansfield clearly grounded himself on the notion that un-notified 'puffing' amounted to a lack of good faith and fraud. As he observed:

The basis of all dealings ought to be good faith; so more especially in these trans-actions where the public are brought together upon a confidence that the articles . . . will be disposed of to the highest real bidder: that could never be the case if the owner might secretly and privately inhance the price, by a person employed for that purpose; yet tricks and practices of this kind daily increase, and grow so frequent that good men give into the ways of the bad and the dishonest in their own defence.[64]

Thus we must consider two separate scenarios: the one where the sale is expressly 'without reserve' or to that effect and the other where the sale is not so expressed, when the vendor may set a reserve or bid (or employ a 'puffer').

(1) 'Without reserve' sales

If property is sold 'without reserve' no bidding by or on behalf of the seller is permissible. This was emphatically stated in *Meadows v Tanner* where the Vice-Chancellor, Sir John Leach, said that if there is a sale expressed to be 'without reserve' the employment of a puffer disentitles the vendor re-course to a court to enforce the contract of sale.[65] It is clear that a sale may be 'without reserve' even though that precise linguistic formulation is not employed. Thus if the Conditions of Sale make it plain that the highest (bona fide) bidder is to be the purchaser then any contrivance by which open and genuine competition is prevented will render a sale void.[66]

---

[63] Ibid 396–7. The analysis and the moral foundations underpinning it were approved by Lord Kenyon in *Howard v Castle* (1796) 6 TR 642.

[64] See above.

[65] (1820) 5 Madd 34. See also *Warlow v Harrison* (1858) 1 E&E 295, 28 LJQB 18. Affd (1859) 1 E&E 309. For a discussion of the auctioneer's liability for failing to knock the property down to the highest bona fide bidder in a 'without reserve' sale see above pp 29–33.

[66] See *Robinson v Wall* (1847) 2 PH 372; *Green and Anor v Baverstock* (1863) 32 CP (NS) 181 per Byles J at p 182:

Whenever there is a sale by auction, whether or no it is advertised to be without reserve, and it appears, either from special notice or from the nature of the transaction, that the goods are to be sold to the highest bidder, then the presence of one puffer is some indication of fraud. This is a rule which is much older than the oldest law of England. It is a rule of general morality.

(2) Non-without reserve sales

If the seller wishes to prevent his property being sold below a certain price he is permitted to stipulate a reserve price on his goods and sell subject to it or himself to bid *provided he notifies the public of his intention*.[67] Otherwise, it is said, the sale will be regarded as fraudulent and voidable by the buyer.

It will be noticed that Lord Mansfield states the two options of setting a reserve and reserving a right to bid as alternatives.

Equity

It may appear surprising, given the grounding of the Common law's approach in notions of fraud on the purchaser and good faith, that equity took a less strict view of un-notified bidding or employment of a puffer by the seller: it was not a fraud on the buyer, in a non-without reserve sale, if the bidding was made

merely to prevent a sale at an under-value and they stated previously what they conceive to be the true value below which the lot ought not to be sold.[68]

Under this formulation it appears that the fixing of a figure over which the puffer is not authorised to bid is a precondition to the entitlement of bidding. It is clear from the judgment of Sir William Grant in this case that an important distinction is drawn between the employment of a puffer to bid up to what is, in effect, a reserve price and using another (and a fortiori and by definition, other*s*) to boost the price. Thus equity appears to have taken the view that the employment of a puffer was not a fraud on the purchaser where it was equivalent to the setting of a reserve price.

It will be recalled that Lord Mansfield had formulated the common law position in terms of allowing a vendor either to set a reserve or bid in exercise of an express power. If these are alternatives and the bidding is seen as fulfilling the same function as the setting of a reserve, there is something to be said for equity's non-insistence of notification of a puffer or right to bid; after all, the fact of a set reserve price does not have to be notified: it suffices if the conditions provide for the power to set one: *Fay v Miller Wilkins & Co*.[69]

What is less certain, both as regards Common law and equity, is whether puffing is fraudulent only when it induces a sale *immediately*, that is when there is no genuine bidder or when the purchaser's ultimately successful bid is directly preceded by a bid by or on behalf of the seller. There are suggestions that equity would not regard it as fraudulent if the puffed bid

[67] Confirmed in *Howard v Castle* (1796) 6 TR 642; 101 ER 748.
[68] *Smith v Clark* (1806) 12 Ves. 477 at p 479 per Sir William Grant.
[69] [1941] Ch 360.

merely excited subsequent genuine competition.[70] Lord Mansfield's formulation is very broad and does not make such distinctions but it must be pointed out that *Bexell v Christie* involved a without reserve sale so that observations as to the effect of un-notified bidding in other sales are obiter. Moreover, *Howard v Castle*, in which Lord Mansfield's dictum was expressly approved by Lord Kenyon, the Chief Justice, was a case where the only bidders, other than the purchaser, were puffers employed by the vendor.

However, no such distinctions have been the *ratio* of any case and the sole distinction between the position in equity and at common law remained that in the former but not the latter an un-notified 'reserved bidding', as it was called in *Thornett v Haines*[71], was permissible and did not vitiate the sale.

Statute

(1) Land

The conflict between the approaches of the Common law and equity was regarded as requiring resolution. In 1867 Parliament enacted the Sale of Land by Auction Act which expressly recited the desideratum of putting an end to 'such conflicting and unsettled opinions' and provided that the Common law position should prevail. Section 5 provides:

The particulars or conditions of sale by auction of any land shall state whether such land will be sold without reserve, or subject to a reserved price, or whether a right to bid is reserved; if it is stated that such land will be sold without reserve or to that effect, then it shall not be lawful for the seller to employ any person to bid at such sale, or for the auctioneer to take knowingly any bidding from any such person.

Just two years after the passing of the Act the first case arose in which s 5 fell for consideration. In *Gilliat v Gilliat*[72] realty was put up for sale by auction. The conditions of sale included a provision that 'the sale is subject to a reserved bidding which has been fixed by the Judge to whose Court this cause is attached'.

The property was knocked down to a purchaser at £29,000 which was the reserve price but the purchaser sought to resile from the contract on the ground that a puffer had made several bids, including one for £28,900 immediately preceding the purchaser's successful bid.

Lord Romilly, MR in a judgment comprising just three sentences held that the sale should be set aside on the ground that the provisions of s 5 had not been complied with. He said:

---

[70] *Smith v Clarke* n 68. above.   [71] (1846) 15 M&W 367, per Pollock CB at p 371.
[72] (1869) LR 9 Eq 60.

I think the Act makes a distinction between a reserved bidding and a reserved right to bid. It says that you must state whether there is a reserved price or not, and further, if you state that there is a reserved price, you must also state that a right to bid is reserved in order that you may employ a person to bid on your behalf. Therefore this sale must be set aside, and the purchaser must have his costs of this application.

A number of observations may be made about this case. First it appears from the report that the purchaser's counsel was stopped by the court without arguing the case. Second, the defendants relied on *Mortimer v Bell*[73] to the effect that where a sale was expressly subject to a reserve there arose by implication a right to employ a puffer so that the Act could not require both that it be stated in the Conditions of Sale that a lot is subject to a reserved price and that a right to bid is reserved. Lord Romilly, however, clearly held that it was not sufficient to state that there was a reserved price but that if it was desired to have the right to employ a person to bid on behalf of the vendor this also had to be stated.

Given the expressly stated aim of the legislation this decision is unsurprising. As s 4 states:

whereas there is at present a conflict between Her Majesty's Courts of Law and Equity in respect of the validity of sales by auction of land where a puffer has bid, although no right of bidding on behalf of the owner was reserved, the Courts of Law holding that all such sales are absolutely illegal, and the Courts of Equity under some circumstances giving effect to them, but even in Courts of Equity the rule is unsettled: And whereas it is expedient that an end should be put to such conflicting and unsettled opinions: Be it therefore enacted, That from and after the passing of this Act whenever a sale by auction of land would be invalid at law by reason of the employment of a puffer, the same shall be deemed invalid in equity as well as at law.

It is only if, at law, the placing of a reserve price *implied* a right also to bid that the construction placed upon the Act by Lord Romilly would be wrong. However, as we have seen, Lord Mansfield in *Bexell v Christie* suggested that the right to place a reserve on a lot and the right for the vendor to bid were alternative methods of protection which a vendor might properly employ; this formulation does not, it is suggested, allow the construction that the one method implies the other.

Gilliat v Gilliat was followed, chronologically, by two cases. In *Parfitt and others v Jepson* in 1877[74] leasehold premises were put up for sale by auction and amongst the Conditions it was provided that:

The highest bidder shall be the purchaser, and if any dispute arise between bidders the lot in dispute shall be put up again and resold.

The vendor shall have the right by himself or his agent of bidding once for the property.

---

[73] (1847) 2 Ph 372.   [74] (1877) 46 LJCP 529.

Once again the defendant purchaser sought to resile from the contract which he signed on the ground that the vendor had employed secret puffers. What had in fact happened in this case was that the auctioneer on behalf of the vendor made three bids until the property reached £320. Thereupon the auctioneer applied to the vendor to know what his reserve was and it was announced that it was £350. The defendant purchaser then bid £351 and was declared the purchaser at that price.

The court was clear that the sale could not be enforced against the purchaser. Grove J held that the statement of the reserve by the vendor at the auction did not render the previous biddings by the auctioneer inoperative. As he pointed out:

One of the objects of puffing at a sale is to induce the outsiders to suppose that a competition for the purchase is going on, and to increase the price which may be obtained for the property by the excitement of such supposed competition. What actually took place on this occasion might have had an effect upon the sale, and certainly if an auctioneer and another person were to run up the property until it came near the reserve without their doing so being considered biddings, so that the naming of the reserved price should be considered the first bidding, it would be allowing a reprehensible practice and to my mind it would make the sale voidable at the option of the purchaser, both at Common Law and under the statute.

Thus there had been several biddings by or on behalf of the vendor.

It is clear that this case does not in any way assist with the construction of s 5 in so far as the requirements as to statements in the Conditions is concerned. It was decided against the vendor on the basis that his notified right was to bid once whereas in fact several bids were made by or on behalf of the vendor.

The third case in the trilogy is *Hills and Grant Ltd v Hodson*[75] in which the issue was whether, in order to satisfy s 5 and state that a sale was subject to a reserve, particular express words needed to be used. Luxmoore J held that incorporation of a Condition entitling a vendor to buy-in property was tantamount to a statement that the property was being sold with a reserve and that the provisions of the Act were complied with 'so long as it is made plain, by whatever words may be chosen, that the sale is subject to a reserve.' In fact the purchaser in this case had failed to rely on s 5 in his pleadings and the judge held that it was improper to allow an amendment so that reliance on that section could be made.

It is interesting to note that in neither of the cases following *Gilliat v Gilliat* was that case cited in the judgments. In the light of that it remains authoritative as to the major point which it decides, namely, that under the Act the statements which must be contained in the Conditions of Sale are not three separate 'alternatives', inclusion of any one of which amounts to compliance with the statute.

[75] [1934] Ch 53.

It is clear that if the sale is stated to be 'without reserve or to that effect' then nothing more need or can, indeed, be said. A right to bid is inimical to a 'without reserve' sale and the exercise of any such right would render the auctioneer[76] (and via a duty to indemnify the auctioneer in respect of his authorised acts, the vendor) liable to the purchaser. If the statement is accompanied by any purported attempt to allow the vendor to bid then the sale simply is not a 'without reserve' sale. If the sale is expressly stated to be subject to a reserve (or there are words to that effect) then, on the clear authority of *Gilliat v Gilliat*, if it is desired to enable the vendor to bid such a right to bid must additionally and separately be provided for in the Conditions. Bateman[77] submits otherwise arguing that the Act merely required that one of three things be stated; either that the sale is without reserve, or that it is subject to a reserve price, or that a right to bid is reserved. The Act does not read (Bateman submits) that the Conditions shall state whether such land shall be sold without reserve or subject to a reserved price *and* whether a right to bid is reserved. Each requirement is divided by the word 'or'.

As a matter of construction in vacuo this argument has some attractions but given that the sole purpose of the Act was to clarify the position relating to the use of un-notified puffers and given that at Common law any such use rendered the sale void the Act would not be achieving its stated objectives if one was allowed to infer a right to bid by or on behalf of the vendor by the mere indication that the sale was not a 'without reserve' sale. It is therefore suggested that the true position is as stated in *Gilliat v Gilliat*, namely that unless a right to bid is expressly notified in the conditions the exercise of bidding by or on behalf of the vendor renders a sale void and that is no less the case where the sale is expressly subject to a reserve or to that effect.

One final point must be made about the dictum of Lord Romilly in that case. He held that the Act requires that it be stated 'whether there is a reserved price *or not*' (emphasis added). It is submitted that there is, in fact, no warrant for the proposition that there must be a clear statement in the conditions either that the sale is 'without reserve' or that it is 'subject to reserve'. If the Conditions are silent on the subject then, it is submitted, the sale is subject to reserve since only if it is expressly stated to be 'without reserve' or to that effect, will it be a 'without reserve' sale.

The following propositions are therefore advanced:

(a) In a 'without reserve' sale there can be no bidding by or on behalf of the vendor; the property cannot be bought in and the auctioneer will be

---

[76] See *Warlow v Harrison* above n 65.
[77] Law of Auctions (11th edn, 1953) Estates Gazette.

liable to the highest bona fide bidder if he fails to knock the property down to him.

(b) If the sale is expressly 'subject to a reserve' then the auctioneer is only bound to knock the property down to the highest bidder once the bids have reached the reserve price. However, the mere setting of a reserve or the creation of a right to set a reserve does not, by itself, imply or create a right to bid on the part of the vendor or those acting as his agent therefor.

(c) The express notification of a right to bid will suffice in the case of a sale of land under the Sale of Land by Auction Act 1867 to enable bids to be made on behalf of the vendor. It is not necessary, in that situation, also to indicate that the sale is subject to a reserve because the express creation of a right to bid by or on behalf of the vendor prevents the sale being a 'without reserve' sale.

(d) Thus, whilst an expressed right to bid makes the sale subject to reserve, a subject to reserve sale does not, ipso facto, create a right to bid.

(2) Goods

Thus far we have only considered the situation with regard to sales of land. The position concerning goods is now regulated by s 57 of the Sale of Goods Act 1979. Subsection 3 provides:

A sale by auction may be notified to be subject to a reserve or upset price, and a right to bid may also be reserved expressly by or on behalf of the seller.

And subsection 4 provides:

Where a sale by auction is not notified to be subject to a right to bid by or on behalf of the seller it is not lawful for the seller to bid himself or to employ any person to bid at the sale, or for the auctioneer to knowingly take any bid from the seller or any such person.

Subsection 5 provides that a sale contravening subsection 4 may be treated as fraudulent by the buyer.

Section 57 is, broadly speaking, similar in effect to that of ss 4, 5 and 6 of the Sale of Land by Auctions Act 1867 as those sections should, it has been submitted, be construed. Section 57 does not, in terms, say that there is no right to bid in a 'without reserve' sale but, it is submitted, in view of the unambiguous prohibition of such both at Common law and in equity, such remains the position after this codifying statute.

Thus it is beyond argument that in the case of goods, an express and specific right to bid must be notified (though not necessarily *in the Conditions* — ie an oral statement from the rostrum would do) if the vendor or his agent is to bid.

One further argument that might be advanced in favour of the construction of s 5 of the Sale of Land by Auctions Act 1867 in the way that it has been argued for above is that it equates that position in respect of land with that of goods. There have, hitherto, been some important differences between sales of land and sales of other property at auction, not least in relation to the necessity for a memorandum evidencing the sale in the case of land in order for the contract to be enforceable[78] but today no formalities are required in order to create valid and enforceable contracts for the sale of either land or other property at auction.[79]

It would be difficult to justify on any rational principle the existence of differences in the abilities of vendors or auctioneers to bid for lots depending upon the particular species of property concerned. The conclusion is, therefore, that both on principle and authority, any right to bid by or on behalf of the vendor must always be expressly notified, whether or not the sale is also subject to reserve.

Misuse of the right to bid

Vendor bidding contrary to Sale of Land by Auctions Act 1867 or Sale of Goods Act 1979

Here, as we have seen from the old cases, the contract is voidable at the option of the purchaser. That is to say the purchaser may have the contract set aside, refuse to pay the purchase price and, or alternatively, obtain the refund of any deposit or payment made. The contract is regarded as voidable for fraud at the purchaser's option. Section 57(5) of the Sale of Goods Act 1979 expressly so provides but the Sale of Land By Auctions Act 1867 is less precise, speaking only of the sale being 'invalid'.

Auctioneer taking bids contrary to the Sale of Land by Auctions Act 1867 or Sale of Goods Act 1979

If the auctioneer knowingly accepts bids which are made contrary to these statutory provisions then once again the contract of sale will be voidable for fraud. If the purchaser wishes none the less to keep the property but, as a result of the wrongful bidding, he has paid more for the item than he would, he may be able to recover damages either against the vendor or the auctioneer in the tort of deceit. The auctioneer's liability in deceit has been considered in chapter 5 above. Usually the deceit lies in some false statement knowingly made with regard to the subject matter of the transaction, for

---

[78] There was a requirement in relation to sales of certain goods that contracts be in writing until 1954. See Sale of Goods Act 1893, s 4 as amended by Law Reform (Enforcement of Contracts) Act 1954.

[79] See the abolition of evidentiary requirements in relation to auction sales effected by the Law of Property (Miscellaneous Provisions) Act 1989.

example a false representation in the description. However, it seems that an action in deceit would also lie for the fraudulent conduct involved in taking improperly made bids.

It is well settled that representations may be implied from a party's conduct. As it has been put in a standard text:

If one conducts himself in a particular way with the object of fraudulently inducing another to believe in the existence of a certain state of things contrary to the fact and to act upon the basis of its existence and damage results therefrom to the party misled, he who misled him will be just as much liable as if he had misrepresented the facts in express terms.[80]

Where the bid that is wrongly taken has merely taken the price up to the reserve it may be argued that no loss is caused to the ultimately successful purchaser since the taking of the wrongful bid has enabled the purchaser to acquire the property where without it he would have been unsuccessful. However, it is countered that a purchaser could validly argue that he would not have bid at the price he did or indeed acted to acquire the property at all had he known of the true position; that true position might be that there were no genuine bids at all, ie that there was no competition for the lot. Alternatively, it might be that there was some genuine bidding but the level was boosted by wrongfully taken bids. If either can be shown, and it is a matter of evidence, then the deliberate fostering of a false appearance of genuine competition is, it is submitted, a false representation such as vitiates the contract.

Inventing bids

If the auctioneer actually invents bids, ie takes them 'off the wall' or chandelier, the position is the same as that stated above. Where the auctioneer has the authority to bid on behalf of the vendor it may be very difficult to distinguish the bona fide exercise of that right from the pure invention of bids. However, where there is no such right to bid on behalf of the vendor or where the vendor's rights have already been exercised and further bids are taken, it is suggested that this is the invention of bids. Where this is accompanied by conduct which is designed to give the impression that actual bids are being taken from the room then the level of deception is greater.

In these circumstances it may be that the auctioneer is additionally guilty of a criminal offence. The offence is the dishonest obtaining of property by deception contrary to section 15 Theft Act 1968.

---

[80] See Clerk and Lindsell on Torts (16th edn, 1989), Sweet & Maxwell, London, paragraphs 18–13.

The criminal offence

Section 15 provides as follows:

(1) A person who by any deception dishonestly obtains property belonging to another with the intention of permanently depriving the other of it shall on conviction on indictment be liable to imprisonment for a term not exceeding 10 years.
(2) For purposes of this section a person is to be treated as obtaining property if he obtains ownership, possession or control of it and 'obtain' includes obtaining for another or enabling another to obtain or to retain.
(3) Section 6[81] shall apply for purposes of this section with the necessary adaptation of the reference to appropriating, as it applies for the purposes of section 1.
(4) For the purposes of this section 'deception' means any deception (whether deliberate or reckless) by words or conduct as to fact or as to law including a deception as to the present intentions of the person using the deception or any other person.

In this section the word 'property' is treated as including money.[82]

Some of the elements of this offence would not be difficult to establish, although others may cause some difficulty. It would appear that the auctioneer who invents bids in the sense described above, ie bids where no right to bid on behalf of the vendor exists or where that right has been exhausted, makes a 'deception' within the meaning of s 15(4) since he has deliberately made a false representation as to fact by his words and conduct, namely that there have been bids genuinely made with a view to purchase when this is not the case. Since money will be paid over by a successful bidder, there is an obtaining of property belonging to another and there is an intention of permanently depriving the other of it.

More difficult, however, will be the questions as to whether the deception is a *cause* of the obtaining and whether there is *dishonesty*.

(1) Causation

For the deception to be a cause of the obtaining, it must have operated on the victim's mind and have influenced him in parting with his property. Where an auctioneer has taken bids 'off the wall', it will have to be shown that the successful bidder entered the bidding in consequence of those bids. If a single bidder successfully enters a bid after the auctioneer has taken a bid or several bids 'off the wall' and those bids operated to trigger the successful bid at the higher price, it can be said that the deception is a cause of the obtaining. Less clear, however, is the position where bids are taken 'off the wall' and are followed by one or more genuine bids from other persons before the successful bidder enters his bid. In this case, it might be

---

[81] Section 6 makes provision for a person to be treated, in certain instances, as having the intention of permanently depriving another of property.

[82] See Theft Act 1968, s 4 which applies not only to the offence of theft in s 1 but has general application under the Act: s 34(1).

said that the intervention of other persons with genuine bids breaks the chain of causation.

Further, if it can be shown that the successful bidder would in any event have made his bid, and at the price he made it, the deception cannot be said to be the cause of the auctioneer obtaining property when money is paid over. In such circumstances no offence of deception under s 15 would be committed. This would be the case whether or not there were any intervening genuine bids.

However, under these circumstances, an auctioneer might be guilty of attempting to obtain by deception.[83]

(2) Dishonesty

Whether an auctioneer will be acting dishonestly will be a question of fact for the jury to decide. In order to be dishonest the conduct must be both such that ordinary and reasonable people would regard it as dishonest and, secondly, the defendant must appreciate that his conduct is so regarded. If the jury were to find that reasonable auction participants regard the inventing of bids as a perfectly honest way of proceeding, then the auctioneer will not be dishonestly obtaining property by deception. If, however, such behaviour is regarded as dishonest then, if the other elements in the offence have been satisfied, the auctioneer will be guilty unless the auctioneer can show that he did not appreciate that his conduct at the auction would be regarded as dishonest.

This is, naturally enough, a somewhat sensitive area for auctioneers and many regard the ability to invent bids as necessary in the interests of their vendor-client and perhaps even in the interests of purchasers who would otherwise be unsuccessful in their bids to acquire property subject to a reserve. Their views are no doubt fortified by official support for this practice expressed in a press release given by the Director General of Fair Trading in 1980:[84]

Another man spends more on a car than he intended because of brisk bidding only to discover later that he has been the only genuine bidder because the auctioneer has included the right to bid on behalf of the vendor in his Conditions of Auction and has been — quite legally — inventing other bids to push up the prices.

Despite this view, it is our opinion that an auctioneer inventing bids remains potentially liable criminally under s 15.[85] But the practical difficulties of

---

[83] Under the Criminal Attempts Act 1981.

[84] OFT, 29 October 1980.

[85] The Theft Act 1968, s 2(1)(a) states that appropriation of another's property is not to be regarded as dishonest if the defendant appropriates the property in the belief that he has a claim of right in law to deprive the other of it. This refers to a belief in a claim of right under the civil law, not a mistake as to the effect of the criminal law. If the auctioneer genuinely believes that taking bids 'off the wall' constitutes an appropriate manner of bidding for his vendor, such a belief, whilst going to dishonesty, would not amount to a belief in a claim of right under this section.

establishing safe grounds for prosecution are formidable not least in showing that the relevant bid was an 'invented' bid rather than a genuine and
legitimate one on behalf of the vendor.

If there is no successful bidder because, despite the 'puffing', the reserve
is never reached it may be that, once again, the auctioneer could be convicted of an attempt to obtain property by deception: it would seem that the
auctioneer, with intent to commit the offence, does an act which is more
than merely preparatory to its commission. This would suffice to establish
liability under the Criminal Attempts Act 1981.

Subject to what is said about dishonesty above, it would seem that where
the sale is 'without reserve' a s 15 offence is clearly committed if the auctioneer invents bids since, in such circumstances, there would be no question of the auctioneer being able to protest that he was merely bidding on
behalf of the vendor: as we have seen, such bidding would not, in a 'without
reserve' sale, be permissible. In other circumstances the lesson from all this
is that it is likely to be illegal and is certainly in our view unethical to take
successive bids 'off the wall' even below reserve.

Controlling the right to bid

As is clear from the preceding discussion, the right to bid on behalf of a
vendor was seen by the Common law as being a protective device to prevent
a sale at an undervalue. Thus, originally at least, it afforded a protection
similar to that of setting a reserve. Whilst equity took a less clear view, the
Sale of Land by Auctions Act 1867 ensured that the divergent paths con-
verged in the case of land sales after 1867. It may, therefore, be questioned
whether the vendor should be entitled both to set a reserve and to bid. Most
would agree, in any event, that there should be no right to bid, even where
such is reserved, above any set reserved price although there is nothing in
the express words of either the Sale of Land by Auctions Act 1867 or the
Sale of Goods Act 1979 which expressly precludes this. Auctioneers' Conditions of Sale, where they provide that the auctioneer is to bid on behalf of
the vendor, invariably limit the exercise of the right up to the reserve price
and not beyond it. Nevertheless, it may be thought desirable that this
should be made explicit.

Licensing

Two London Boroughs exercising powers under the Greater London
Council (General Powers) Act 1984 have introduced licence conditions and
codes of practice relating to auctions conducted within their jurisdictions.

The Westminster City Council Conditions provide, inter alia, by Condition 12:

The registrant or any other person having the conduct or management of the premises or stall shall ensure that no bids are to be entered on the seller's behalf after the Reserve Price has been reached.

The preceding condition provides a general requirement that any relevant sale 'is conducted in good faith'.

One also finds detailed regulation in the United States of America. The City of New York Department of Consumer Affairs has regulated auctions in that city since the 1930s. Regulation 13 currently provides:

After bidding has reached the reserve price of a lot:

(a) the auctioneer may not bid on behalf of the consignor or the auction house;
(b) the auctioneer may only accept bids from persons other than the consignor or the auction house.

It is suggested that these regulations reflect the generally accepted notion that bidding above the reserve by or on behalf of the vendor is wrongful but, perhaps also, that the law needs to be explicit on this. It is surely not sufficient that this be controlled through localised licensing regimes and statutory modification seems to be the sensible answer.

If it is the case that there is to be no bidding by or on behalf of the vendor beyond the reserve, and there is a set reserve, the question remains — what is the purpose of bidding by the vendor and should this be permitted? Puffing by the vendor, where there is already a set reserve, cannot be designed to prevent a sale at an undervalue. It must be designed in order to enable the vendor or, today more commonly, his agent the auctioneer, to stimulate a dormant audience. It may well be argued that this is a necessary power if auction sales are to be successful and, as indicated earlier, some in the profession argue that this is also in the interests of a buyer since if bidding does not reach the reserve he will be disappointed. On the other hand, it is obvious that the exercise of a right to bid on behalf of the vendor can (and some would argue is designed to) give an impression of competition for a lot which is wholly false. That is, it is suggested, no less deceptive than, say, an estate agent telling a prospective purchaser that he already has an offer and obtaining thereby a higher offer when in fact no offer had been received. This is specifically an offence under the Estate Agents (Undesirable Practices) No 2 Order, 51 1991/1032 Sch 3 para 1 and, as such, triggers the enforcement powers of the Director General of Fair Trading under the Estate Agents Act 1979.

The argument that it is also in the purchaser's interests is somewhat disingenuous; whilst it is true that he will not get the property at auction if the lot does not reach the reserve, it is perfectly possible to give the auctioneer a level of discretion in effecting a sale below the reserve or, indeed, to provide the sort of provisional bid arrangements which are commonplace in vehicle auctions.[86]

In 1986 the Director General of Fair Trading commissioned a report on auctions regulation.[87] The report recommended that consideration should be given to the introduction of provisions (either by means of changes in the law or through a code of practice) along the lines of regulations 12 and 13 of the New York Code but the OFT has not implemented this and there are no current plans to do so.

The exercise of rights to bid by or on behalf of the vendor presents fairly prickly problems. Whilst cogent arguments can be advanced for the proposition that the vendor does not require the right to puff in order satisfactorily to protect his interests and that the exercise of such bidding rights can unfairly disadvantage the buyer at auction, these rights have for long been an established part of the auctions scene and, in contrast with the profession of estate agents, there does not appear to have been, recently, a ground swell in favour of control and reform amongst the consumer protection lobby.

Pretending that an item has been sold

There is one further practice which is commonplace at auctions which may be regarded as undesirable. That is where an auctioneer purports to knock down a lot to a purchaser when in fact it has not been sold.

There are several objections to this practice: it clearly deceives vendors into believing that the auction process is invariably or almost invariably successful and yet we know that it is not uncommon for perhaps a third of lots put up for sale not in fact to be sold at all. But the real objection to the practice is, once again, that it suggests a market, and indeed a market price, for particular kinds of goods which does not in truth exist. This problem is particularly acute when a number of similar lots are sold in quick succession. As these lots are apparently knocked down at certain prices bidders for subsequent lots may be deceived into believing that supply and demand have interacted to produce an appropriate price. The codes of practice of Westminster City Council and the Royal Borough of Kensington and Chelsea have sought to deal with this by proscribing the inclusion of unsold items in post-sale advertising. Whilst this addresses the problem of distortion of success from the viewpoint of prospective vendor-clients, it does not deal with the problem of distortion as it affect buyers. The New York regulations in this regard are more potent. Condition 12 provides:

If the reserve price is not bid, the auctioneer may withdraw a lot from sale. At the time of such withdrawal and before bidding on another lot begins, the auctioneer

---

[86] See chapter 10 below.
[87] The author of the report is John Houghton, a barrister.

shall announce that the withdrawn lot has been 'passed' 'withdrawn' 'returned to owner' or 'bought-in'.

Doubtless auctioneers would object that an immediate announcement that the lot has not reached its reserve would depress the market and be detrimental to the interests of sellers of other lots still to be put up for sale. However, it is surely fair to assume that at any auction there are likely to be a number of genuinely interested potential buyers and if a lot has failed to reach its reserve that failure is likely to be attributable to the fact that the reserves have been set unrealistically high. If this practice were outlawed it might encourage the setting of more realistic reserves. The Houghton report expressly recommends the adoption of a provision along the lines of Condition 12 of the New York Code but, as stated, that report has not yet been acted upon. It is however, now the practice of many UK auctioneers clearly to indicate 'not sold' or 'passed' where this occurs.

GENERAL COMMENT ON CONDITIONS OF SALE

It can be seen from the selective analysis in this chapter that Conditions of Sale attempt to deal with a wide variety of problems concerning actual and potential buyers. In some cases these conditions, if binding contractually, will — either by modifying the Sale of Goods Act 1979 (as amended) or by filling a gap in the law — govern the contractual situation without further ado. Other Conditions will be in the nature of exemption or exclusion clauses and their validity is likely to be tested, sooner or later, under the general requirement of reasonableness or fairness imposed by the Unfair Contract Terms Act 1977 or the EC Directive. The standard conditions used by Sotheby's and Christie's are appropriate for large London auction-rooms but may seem unnecessarily elaborate to country auctioneers or estate agents whose business includes occasional auctions.

In drawing up a simpler but adequately comprehensive code, a delicate balancing act is needed between the object of protecting the auctioneer from unwanted liabilities and the seller from guarantees of quality (and the like) on the one hand and the danger of both presenting a disproportionately lengthy and complex body of 'small print' and having a material condition condemned by a court as 'unreasonable' within the Unfair Contract Terms Act 1977 or 'unfair' under the EC Directive discussed above. Each firm of any tradition and standing has its own ethos and auctions policy — for example on whether or not to charge for buying goods in. Their General Conditions will probably need 'bespoke tailoring' and also, incidentally, now rewrite to be drafted in 'plain, intelligible language' under the said Directive. The professional bodies have not so far published 'model' terms for chattel auctioneers, no doubt for similar reasons.

Export Licensing

OUTLINE OF THE SYSTEM

The Department of National Heritage has general powers to regulate the export of goods, these powers being derived from the Import, Export and Customs Powers (Defence) Act 1939. Although this draconian Act was originally designed primarily to regulate trading with the enemy at the beginning of the second world war, it continues to provide the authority for Orders made by Parliament regulating amongst other things, the export of antiques, collectors' items and the like. It is odd that this Act continues to apply to the export of goods in such different circumstances to those originally envisaged and that the power given to declare by Order that the relevant emergency has ended, under section 9(3), has not been exercised.

The fundamental sanction supplied by the 1939 Act is that if goods are exported in contravention of an Order made under the Act, those goods are deemed to be prohibited goods and are liable to forfeiture; furthermore the exporter of the goods or his agent, or the shipper of the goods, is liable, in addition to any other penalty under the enactments relating to customs, to a further penalty on Level 5 of the standard scale laid down by the Criminal Justice Act 1982.

A large number of Orders have been made successively under this Act both to control exports to particular States and to provide a general prohibition on exportation without an export licence.[1]

Superimposed upon the UK's long-standing export control system is the European Union's (EC's) own régime for the control of 'cultural' goods exported out of the European Community. Thus, a UK licence issued by the Department of National Heritage ('DNH') is required for *inter-Community trade* in relevant cultural goods valued at or above the relevant UK licence limits, and (2) for export out of the European Community (for example, to the USA), of those goods valued at or above the UK licence limit but below the EC licence limit. Discussion initially will be of the UK's 'domestic' system of control, then of the EC's régime, and then a summary of the totality of control together with practical guidance on dealing with the

---

[1] See the Export of Goods (Control) Order, SI 1992/3092 as amended by SI 1992/3305. Currently restricted destinations are Iraq, Libya, Serbia and Montenegro.

situation from the exporter's point of view. The importance of these provisions is partly that under s3 of the 1939 Act criminal liability for breach of the export rules rests not only on the exporter but also on his agent or shipper, and partly that the existence of these controls may inform the bidding by foreign buyers who could expect advice from the auctioneer.

It should be carefully noted that if an EC licence is also required then that must always be obtained whether or not the goods fall within the UK's domestic exclusions — in other words, the Department of National Heritage's licence is not in itself sufficient when an EC licence is required to export outside the EC. But as stated below, once an EC licence is obtained there is no need also to obtain a UK licence.

UK DOMESTIC CONTROL

The law at present in force in the UK and in the Isle of Man provides that a licence is needed to export from the UK and from the Isle of Man to any destination those goods listed in the chart set out in Appendix 4 unless *either* the chart indicates specifically that no UK licence is required *or* the exporter holds an Open Individual Export Licence ('OIEL') (suitable for regular exporters) or the goods fall within the Open General Export Licence. It should be particularly noted that OIELs do not apply to objects controlled under the EC Regulations, but where a licence has been obtained under the EC Regulations the Open General Export Licence removes the need for a UK licence as well.

The general principle is to impose control over antique items more than 50 years old if of the minimum value of (currently) £39,600. Where goods consist of a matching set or a pair of articles, the value is of the set or pair. The minimum value is radically reduced (currently to £6,000) if the item is a photograph or negative more than 50 years old or a non-photographic portrait of a British historical personage more than 50 years old. This expression is defined in the Open General Export Licence (Antiques) of September 1993 as meaning any living or dead person carrying an entry in the Dictionary of National Biography, 'Who's Who' or 'Who was Who'. The figure is reduced to zero if the item is a manuscript, archive or architectural, scientific or engineering drawing produced by hand, in each case more than 50 years old.

The Open General Export Licence (Antiques) referred to above gives certain further exceptions or imposes conditions not expressed in the said chart. For instance, musical instruments may be exported for a period of less than three months if for use by a professional musician or may be exported permanently if imported for less than three months in the course of work by a professional musician, provided in each case the exportation or importation is under cover of an approved carnet arrangement. This is clearly intended to cover the departing or arriving professional musician such as violinists carrying a Stradivari violin or other similarly valuable instruments. The Licence also allows relevant portraits of British historic personages to be exported if at least of the value of £6,000 but less than £119,000 if the exporter obtains the certificate from either the Director of the National Portrait Gallery or the Keeper of the Scottish National Portrait Gallery that in his opinion the article is not a work of national importance. Rather similar principles apply to the export of clothing or footwear (from £6,000 to £39,600) where the certificate is from the Director of the Victoria and Albert Museum.

In addition to this, there are also export restrictions in the UK on items such as those incorporating animal material from endangered species. Thus, items containing eg ivory, whalebone, or tortoiseshell need export licences granted by the Department of the Environment. These restrictions stem from the Endangered Species (Import and Export) Act 1976. Firearms are subject to specific controls mentioned below.

FIREARMS

Firearms between 50 and 100 years old require both a 'strategic licence' from the Department of Trade and Industry and a DNH Licence for cultural goods if of the value of £39,600 or above. If under 50 years old a DTI strategic licence is required. Firearms over 100 years old and worth more than £20,000 or £39,600 require either a UK or an EC licence respectively. Overseas buyers collecting firearms and shotguns must be in possession of the relevant UK firearm or shotgun certificate.

CRIMINAL LIABILITY

It is irrelevant that the exporter intends to bring the goods back, but *R v Berner, Levine and Levine*[2] seems to show that the accused must know of the prohibition in question, though this is not obvious from the wording of s 3.

Substantial criminal penalties are imposed on knowingly or recklessly making false statements in order to obtain any licence or permission (art 5) and Customs and Excise officers have powers of search where a person is about to leave the UK.

[2] (1953) 37 Cr App R 113.

EC CONTROL

The EC position is controlled by Council Regulation (EEC) No. 3911/92 (OJ No. L395/1) on export of cultural goods. One of the recitals states that it 'seems necessary to take measures in particular to ensure that exports of cultural goods are subject to uniform controls at the Community's external borders.'

The Regulation applies certain financial thresholds in Ecus to each category of item and these are to be converted into national currencies as on 1 January 1993. They are indicated in the chart in Appendix 4.

The Regulation also contains the controversial and as yet unimplemented provisions in Art 2 for the return of cultural objects unlawfully removed from a Member State. When an object is of limited archaeological or scientific interest there is an existing discretion allowing Member States to dispense with the requirement of an EC licence, as to which the DNH will advise. Where a licence is being applied for under the EC Regulation, but the object is valued below the relevant UK monetary limit (eg a drawing valued at or above £11,900 (EC limit) but below £39,600 (UK limit)), the object is not considered to be a potential 'national treasure'; and a licence will be granted, subject to satisfaction that the object has not been illegally exported from another EC Member State on or after 1 January 1993. Similarly, an object that has been imported within the last 50 years is not normally considered to be a potential 'national treasure'.

PROCEDURE

Both UK and EC licences are obtained by filling in the appropriate form issued by the Department of National Heritage. By way of example, a completed Application Form for the export of cultural goods outside the EC is included in Appendix 4, together with its Annexe (The 'Commodity Code' is that given against the item in the text of the EC Regulation). A somewhat similar form (ELU Form C) needs to be completed to obtain a UK licence. The UK application form requires a full description of the object in question. For instance, in the case of a work of art, antique or collector's item, the description should state the style or class to which the object belongs (eg by Raphael, style of Adam, Chelsea cloisonné, mezzotint, Sheffield Plate etc), the nature of the material, the general colour, period, country or origin and exact measurements. In the case of a painting, the full title by which it is usually known should be given and an indication as to whether it is signed and, if dated, the date. Gold and silver articles require details of the hallmark and photographic positives or negatives, the name of the photographer and the particulars of the subject.

This form also requires the application to be accompanied by a non-returnable monochrome photograph of all relevant items (the only exceptions being photographs and manuscripts unless specifically asked for) of at least 16.5 cm × 21.6 cm in size. Articles imported within the last 50 years are required to carry all known provenance.

Leading auctioneers often make administrative arrangements to apply for export licences for successful bidders along with other arrangements for consignments for the goods abroad.

CASES REFERRED TO THE REVIEWING COMMITTEE

On the application for an export licence being made it is referred by the Department to an appropriate expert adviser who may either

(a) raise no objection to the export, or
(b) recommend that an export licence be refused for the object because of its national importance.

Cases under (b) are referred by the Department to the Reviewing Committee on the Export of Works of Art. The Committee considers such case as is stated in writing by the applicant along with a written statement from the Department of National Heritage's expert adviser. These statements are exchanged before the meeting and both parties are invited to attend or be represented at the Committee's meeting to make further representations and answer questions from the Committee. The object in question is required to be brought to the meeting or to be made available for it to be seen by the Committee.

THE COMMITTEE'S DECISION

The criteria which the Committee adopt to decide whether the object is of national importance are known as the Waverley criteria, indicated by the following questions:

(a) Is the object so closely connected with our history and national life that its departure would be a misfortune?
(b) Is it of outstanding aesthetic importance?
(c) Is it of outstanding significance for the study of some particular branch of art, learning or history?

The final decision is notified to the applicant without reasons. If the Committee concludes that the object satisfies one or more of the Waverley criteria it will recommend to the Secretary of State for National Heritage that a decision on the export licence application be deferred for a specified period (normally between two and six months) to enable an offer to purchase at or above the recommended fair market price to be made. If the Secretary of State accepts the recommendation and if a valid offer to purchase is received (which the owner is not obliged to accept) during the deferral period, from a public institution or a private source, an export licence will normally be refused. Similarly, where owners make known their intention to refuse a valid offer, the Secretary of State will normally refuse an export licence at that time. If such an offer is not received, an export licence will normally be granted. The price recommended is that which the Reviewing Committee considers reasonable, after taking advice if necessary. The Committee takes account of exemptions from tax and capital gains tax which may apply if the object is sold to one of the bodies listed. These bodies include national, university or local authority museums and galleries.

COMMENTS

The export licensing system has come into particular prominence because of the huge buying power, in particular, of American museums and collectors, and a tendency for works of art to be bought at auction by such buyers.[3]

The history of the matter was that in 1950 the then Chancellor of the Exchequer appointed a committee under the chairmanship of Lord Waverley 'To consider and advise on the policy to be adopted by His Majesty's Government in controlling the exporting of works of art, books and manuscripts, armour and antiques and to recommend what arrangements should be made for the practical operation of policy.' In 1952, this committee recommended that there should be an age limit for articles requiring special scrutiny (and also objects should generally not be subject to special scrutiny on grounds of national importance if they were worth less than a stated figure). The criteria for the granting or refusal of a licence as explained above were devised by the Waverley Committee in 1952. Between 30 and 50 cases are considered by the Committee each year, and the application of the criteria combined with a temporary refusal of an export licence has in fact achieved the effect of keeping most of the items considered important within the UK. However in 1983, for example, when some 50 cases were considered, the 5 most expensive items reviewed left the country since funds were not available to keep them.[4]

In 1994 the long saga of Canova's sculpture representing the Three

---

[3] See Geraldine Norman 'Put Art in a New Framework' (1984) Times, 14 April; and Leslie Geddis-Brown 'Must Treasures Go to the Highest Bidder?' (1984) Sunday Times, 15 July.

[4] See Geraldine Norman (n 3, above). See also 'The Getty Factor' (1984) Sunday Times, 7 October.

Graces, formerly resting in Woburn Abbey, was resolved, the John Paul Getty Museum in California having initially made an offer to buy it for £7.6 million in 1989. Export licences were successively deferred by the responsible Minister until in 1994, in some understandable exasperation, the Getty Museum authorities applied first to the High Court and then the Court of Appeal (unsuccessfully) for the Government's decision to be judicially reviewed. However, by this time, the necessary funds to keep the statue in the UK had been raised.

This rather obscure field of law and administration also poses economic and ethical problems. On the face of it an owner of a valuable object should not be prohibited from selling to the highest buyer for external considerations without, at least, compensation. On the other hand it is clearly important to keep objects of national importance within the UK and this is a policy adopted by most States. France, Italy and Germany are understood to have systems which permit a total ban on the export of a work, whether or not a local institution has the money to buy it. This, however, does amount to confiscation of a proportion of the wealth of the owner. The policy is nevertheless presumably compatible with Article 1 of the First Protocol (1952) to the European Convention of Human Rights (1950) which provides that 'No-one shall be deprived of his possessions except in the public interest.'[5]

THE LEGAL INFRASTRUCTURE

The delay over the refusal to grant an export licence in respect of the Three Graces caused considerable publicity and adverse press comment — the point validly being made that the long delay involved before a decision could be made brought the UK art market into considerable disrepute. However, from the legal point of view, the position appears to be as follows. Firstly, in a few rare cases, if a leading auction house thinks it appropriate a specific arrangement may be made that a sale is subject to the obtaining of an export licence. The vendor is then obliged to make appropriate arrangements. In other cases, the failure of a foreign buyer to obtain an export licence does not affect the validity of the contract, partly because it seems to be established in practice that no warranty is given on an auction sale that any particular item is capable of being exported and partly because the

[5] The Labour Party's shadow Minister for the Arts was reported in 1984 to be in favour of a total ban on specified works, coupled with power to delay export for up to two years in other cases. Opponents of this policy, which could severely affect London's central position for art-dealing in pre-Impressionist works, argued that a better answer is to modify VAT, so as to equate sales to museums with export sales, increase inheritance tax incentives for donors to public bodies and introduce American-style income tax deductions for monetary donations to museums, thus increasing museums' ability to compete in the market.

actual sale to the foreign buyer is not affected. He always has the option of keeping the relevant item in the UK if necessary.

It is understood that it has been held in an unreported decision that where an auctioneer knows that a buyer intends to export relevant goods without obtaining an export licence, as required, he is justified in refusing to release the relevant item to the buyer on the grounds that otherwise he would be implicated in the commission of a criminal offence.

In private treaty sales, foreign buyers would, of course, be well advised to make it a condition of the contract that an export licence is granted and for full reimbursement of the cost to take place if it is not within a reasonable time. This, by its nature, cannot be an arrangement applicable to an auction where the identity of the buyer is not established until the hammer falls.

CULTURAL PROPERTY

As regards cultural property, the General Assembly of the United Nations on 2 November 1993, in the context of the return of 'irreplaceable cultural heritage to those who created it,' made a further resolution to encourage the restitution of cultural property to the countries of origin concerned. An Inter-governmental Committee is established for the promotion of the return of cultural property to the country of origin. A number of countries belong to the Convention on the Means of Prohibiting and Preventing the Illicit Import, Export and Transfer of Ownership of Cultural Property adopted on 14 November 1970 by the General Conference of the UN Education, Scientific and Cultural Organisation. The policy behind these resolutions remains highly controversial and difficult to implement in practice. It will be noted, however, that the EC Regulation discussed earlier does make the grant of a licence subject to the object not having been illegally exported from another EC state on or after 1 January 1993. So although the object may be in the 'wrong' member state, at least it may not be further exported out of the EC altogether.

Although not of direct importance to auction sales, legislation now exists regulating (a) the export of cultural goods from the EU to third countries, and (b) within the EU, the return of cultural objects removed from one member state to another (see Council Regulation 3911/92 (9 Dec. 92) and The Return of Cultural Objects Regulations 1994 (S1 1994/501).

Criminal Practices at Auctions and their Consequences

MOCK AUCTIONS

Mock auctions have little to do with the activities of genuine auctioneers. A hall is hired, a carnival atmosphere created, and as Kenneth Jones J stated in *R v Ingram*:[1]

The average holiday-maker going into one of these premises with his eyes open would realise that these proceedings were as much to do with a true auction as visiting a shooting gallery further down the street is to do with participation in the rifle championships at Bisley.

In a short but useful article, A. T. H. Smith[2] describes the history of mock auctions and the reasons for a protective legislation. Drawing on the debates which have taken place from time to time on this matter, he describes a typical mock auction as follows:

A man working outside a booth (the 'pitchgetter') would encourage passers-by to enter. When a large enough crowd had gathered inside, another man (the 'top man') would sell (either genuinely, or to an accomplice) a comparatively valuable article at a give-away price. The audience were showered with gifts and then invited to show their willingness to participate in an auction by buying an unopened packet (a 'nailer') — those unwilling to do so were then sent away. A considerable amount of junk was then sold, sometimes by the use of the suggestion that the seller would return some of the purchase price — the suggestion being implanted by one or two samples in which money was then returned. This was known as 'gazoomping the Sarkers'.

Apparently problems caused by mock auctions are of long-standing. In 1924 it was estimated that there were some 1,500 mock auctions in operation and that over £8m was being spent at them. The activities involved were thought to be beyond the reach of the criminal law at the time. The Mock Auctions Act 1961 was introduced as a Private Member's Bill specifically designed to prevent fraudulent practices at auctions of this sort. On reading the Act it is not entirely clear against which mischief in particular the Act is aimed and its provisions have been sufficiently ambiguous to give

[1] (1976) 64 Cr App Rep 119.   [2] (1981) NLJ 49.

rise to a number of reported cases. A summary of the Act and the main cases thereon now follows.

It is an offence, punishable by sentences of a fine of the statutory maximum and/or imprisonment of three months on summary conviction (unlimited fine or two years on conviction on indictment), to promote or conduct or assist in the conduct of a mock auction.

A sale of goods by way of competitive bidding is a mock auction if during the course of sale: (a) a lot is sold to a person bidding for it at a price lower than the amount of his higher bid for that lot, or part of the price is repaid or credited to him or stated to be so (unless the goods are found to be defective); or (b) the right to bid is or is stated to be restricted to persons who have bought or agreed to buy one or more articles; or (c) any articles are given away or offered as gifts (Mock Auctions Act 1961, s 1).

'Competitive bidding' is defined in the Mock Auctions Act 1961, s 3(1), as including:

any mode of sale whereby prospective purchasers may be enabled to compete for the purchase of articles whether by way of increasing bids or by the offer of articles to be bid for at successively decreasing prices or otherwise.

In *Lomas v Rydeheard*,[3] it was held by the Divisional Court (on appeal from the Crown Court) that where the defendant offered articles for sale to customers assembled in his salerooms, calling out a series of progressively decreasing prices, but not asking for bids until his final price when he offered the item to an individual in the crowd who bought it without bargaining, this was still 'competitive bidding' since it could be inferred that prices would have been reduced further if people had been unwilling to buy. The Mock Auctions Act 1961 applies to lots comprising plate, linen, china, glass, books, pictures, prints, furniture, jewellery, articles of household or personal use or ornament or any musical or scientific instruments or apparatus (s 3).

In *Clements v Rydeheard*,[4] the defendant held sales at which he offered, at a fixed price, a number of boxes with undisclosed contents and selected the purchasers from those who put up their hands. Purchasers of later lots were similarly selected but only from those who had purchased boxes. The Divisional Court held that this was a sale by competitive bidding.

Competitive bidding includes any mode of sale whereby persons can compete for the purchase of articles in any way, whether or not by reference to price. In *Allen v Simmons*,[5] the audience was asked by the respondent who would pay him 30 p for a set of glasses. Hands were raised. There was only one set of glasses. The successful 'bidder' was sold the glasses for 1 p

---

[3] (1975) 119 Sol Jo 233, 237 EG 801. [4] [1978] 3 All ER 658, 143 JP 25.
[5] [1978] 3 All ER 662, [1978] 1 WLR 879.

and a similar performance took place relating to an offer for sale of an undisclosed item for 50 p.

In the view of Melford Stevenson J[6] it was difficult to form a precise view of the meaning of the word 'otherwise' in s 3(1) of the Mock Auctions Act 1961, but the subsection did contemplate bidding in what was or appeared to be competition with other bidders. The mere fact that the effect of the bid depended on the whim of the person conducting the so-called auction did not matter. Following *Clements v Rydeheard*,[7] the court in effect construed s 3(1) (set out above) as stopping at the words 'may be enabled to compete for the purchase of articles', and the offence had accordingly been committed. As has been pointed out[8] there seems to be no point, and indeed no justification in law, in construing s 3(1) in this curtailed way. Either decision could be justified by simply relying on the words 'or otherwise'.[9]

In addition to prosecutions, normally brought by trading-standards departments of local authorities, the Office of Fair Trading has also taken action and given warnings in a number of cases. In 1979 the Office of Fair Trading wrote to all chief trading-standards officers suggesting local Codes of Practice to protect consumers in this area. The assumption is that all hirers-out of public halls in a particular area can guard against abuses by incorporating appropriate conditions in the letting contract.

In April 1982 publicity was given to the fact that written assurances had been given by a mock auctioneer to the Director General of Fair Trading under Part III of the Fair Trading Act 1973. Breach of such assurances can lead to court orders, which if not complied with, could lay the offender open to a fine or imprisonment for contempt of court. The assurances in question were in respect of nine offences under the Bargain Offers Orders and for conducting mock auctions contrary to the Mock Auctions Act 1961 in respect of which the trader was convicted in various magistrates' courts during the preceding year.

In December 1982 a press release was issued by the Director General of Fair Trading to the following effect:[10]

The busy pre-Christmas shopping period is a time of year when hundreds of one-day sales are being held. Many such sales turn out to be mock auctions, which are not only against the law, but can only be described — in today's slang — as a rip off. Be on your guard.

---

[6] *Allen v Simmons* [1978] 3 All ER 662 at 667, [1978] 1 WLR 879.

[7] Above, n 4.   [8] [1978] Crim LR at 363.

[9] It was confirmed by the Court of Appeal (Criminal Division) in *R v Pollard* (1983) 148 JP 679, CA (sales of goods from a lorry in Petticoat Lane, goods being thrown into the crowd and sold at reducing prices etc) that the words 'or otherwise' should not be construed ejusdem generis with the preceding words involving bidding on an increasing or reducing basis. The element of competition can be eg by reference to the first buyer to raise a hand.

[10] OFT, London EC4A 1PR.

'Once enticed by the prospect of a bargain, people can only too easily be caught up in an atmosphere with is skilfully created and manipulated by the salesman. And they are highly likely to be persuaded to part with large sums of money for items of little value,' said Sir Gordon [Borrie].

'I have evidence of people handing over £50 for a sealed, plain cardboard box. They had seen others in the audience getting bargains and expected the same. But what they hadn't realised was . . . those other people were working hand-in-glove with the salesman! Once the victims left the sale and opened their boxes, they realised they had spent £50 on a cheap watch or radio they could have bought elsewhere for £5.'

Sir Gordon advised, 'Don't be tricked into parting with good money for inferior goods. If you go to a one-day sale, keep your wits about you and watch for the danger signals. If the salesman sells goods to someone who is not the highest bidder, if you can only bid for certain goods after you have agreed to buy other articles, or if the salesman is giving goods away or offering gifts, you may be at a mock auction — the salesman is breaking the law, and almost certainly intends you no good, so beat a hasty retreat.

'Of course not all one day sales are swindles — at some you can find a bargain. And you can look after your interests by examining the goods before you buy them and by making sure you have a note of the seller's address. But beware of the offer that is too good to be true — "mock auctioneers" are looking for victims, not customers!'

AUCTION RINGS

The activity of auction rings gives more concern to auctioneers, private buyers and apprehensive sellers than any other phenomenon encountered in the ordinary auction-room.[11]

As to the prevalence of the practice, in one[12] of only two known success-ful prosecutions under the Auctions (Bidding Agreements) Act 1927,[13] Lewis-Bowen J at the Swansea Crown Court in passing sentence against ten antique dealers stated that rings were 'part and parcel of the antiques world'. Counsel appearing for five of the dealers had argued that the Act was applied so rarely that it must be a matter of public policy not to use it. He stated that his clients were doing something that had become a pattern of life in the trade.

A typical ring works in the following way. A group of buyers who are generally in trade as dealers agree to buy articles at auctions at less than the

---

[11] For an excellent general survey of the position see A. T. H. Smith 'Auction Rings' [1981] Crim LR 86, to which article the authors are much indebted.

[12] See the account of this case in (1983) Sunday Times, 4 September. The other case is *R v Jordan* [1981] CLY 131, Swansea Crown Ct.

[13] *R v Barnett* [1951] 2 KB 425, CCA, concerned an unsuccessful charge of conspiracy to contravene the Act.

value such articles would otherwise probably fetch, by not competing against each other. When one of the 'ring' has successfully bid for the article, there follows afterwards a 'knock-out' which normally takes the form of a second auction held privately by the members of the ring. The article is then sold to the highest bidder within the ring, and the difference between the price actually paid to the auctioneer and that paid by the highest member of the ring at the second auction is distributed between all members according to an agreed formula.

There are several aspects to this practice which require comment. Firstly, its economic effect is to deprive the seller, as the consumer of the auctioneer's services, of the true value of his goods. One of the points in favour of an auction as a market for selling goods is that where the market value for such goods is unascertained, a free auction should normally supply that market value. Many a seller has been pleasantly surprised by the high value realised for an article, the value of which he had not appreciated. Equally, if a survey were done, there would probably be many sellers who obtain substantially less than the true value of their goods as compared with the price realised at the 'knock-out'. In other words, an auction is a forum in which free competition should reign. The existence of an auction ring prevents true competition and is associated with parallel objectionable practices, such as members of the ring 'discouraging' private buyers by bidding such a private buyer up beyond the limit on one article in order to inhibit him from bidding for others, or even sometimes by various veiled threats and bad behaviour securing the non-participation of private buyers.

A further aspect of auction rings which requires comment is that, by their nature, they are difficult to detect and to prove. Both the successful prosecutions brought to date have been the work of one particular Welsh detective who specialises in this type of operation. He is quoted as commenting:[14]

Dealers who refuse to join the ring can find the others ganging up on them so they are unable to buy anything . . . The crooked auction is flawed. Sometimes the auctioneer can be in on the ring himself and gets a cut from the knock-out. It can be a difficult racket to break. You have to have the co-operation of the auctioneer. Some of them don't like offending dealers because it interferes with sales.

In the second Swansea case,[15] proof was only possible by virtue of the fact that the knock-out was spotted by the detective in question as taking place on a remote Welsh beach where the proceedings were recorded by a police photographer.

Having regard to the nature of the auction-ring operation it is scarcely

[14] See above, n 12.   [15] See above, n 12.

useful to point out that technically an auction ring is a restrictive practice and should be registered as such under the Restrictive Trade Practices Act 1956. In addition, s 3(2) of the Auction (Bidding Agreements) Act 1969 gives the seller the right to avoid a contract where one of the purchasers is a dealer in a ring. He has an alternative right to bring an action for damages. The problem of a private seller proving the existence of a ring is even more acute than that facing the police authorities because of the comparatively weak position of the seller in probative terms compared to the powers of the police in forensic investigation.

AUCTIONS (BIDDING AGREEMENTS) ACTS 1927 AND 1969[16]

The sale which apparently prompted Lord Darling to introduce the Bill leading to the 1927 Act, which was designed to eliminate rings, was a spectacular one which occurred in 1919 when the war-wounded 7th Baron Foley of Kidderminster came of age and put his house, Ruxley Lodge, and its contents, which included a superb library of more than 13,000 volumes collected over many generations, up for sale. The library was a dealers' dream. It included illustrated books from the 17th and 18th centuries, early books on vellum, natural history, botany and ornithological books with hand-coloured plates and four Shakespeare folios. Unfortunately the auctioneers, Castiglione and Scott, were experts on auctions of land and buildings but not books. The scene was dominated by some 81 booksellers who participated in the 'post-sales settlement', ironically held in the nearby Ethical Hall. Each received a net dividend of £125, a considerable sum at the time. Some 24 London dealers then advanced to the second round, 15 to the third and 8 (including such prestigious firms as Quaritch, Maggs, Pickering and Chatto, and Percy Dobell whose annotated catalogue provided the evidence for all this) participated in the final round. Each finalist pocketed a dividend of £470. Obviously, books at the actual sale had gone at a knock-down price. For instance, a Shakespeare 1st folio was bought by Quaritch for £100 when it was known from the results of other sales that its actual value should have been between £1,500 and £2,000. It was calculated that Quaritch's total outlay on 34 lots was £6,135 of which the vendor and the auctioneer shared only £188. Some 97% went to members of the ring. The saleroom total was £3,714 but this was advanced in the first 'settlement' to £10,292; and by the fourth round the total advancement was £19,696.[17]

The key criminal sections of these Acts (as amended) run as follows.

[16] See Appendix 2 for full text.
[17] See Editorial, *Bookdealer*, No. 986 31 January, 1991 3–4 reviewing A. & J. I. Freeman *Anatomy of an Auction: Rare books at Ruxley Lodge 1919*, London, 1991.

Auctions (Bidding Agreements) Act 1927

1. *Certain bidding agreements to be illegal*
(1) If any dealer agrees to give, or gives, or offers any gift or consideration to any
   other person as an inducement or reward for abstaining, or for having abstained, from bidding at a sale by auction either generally or for any particular
   lot, or if any person agrees to accept, or accepts, or attempts to obtain from any
   dealer any such gift or consideration as aforesaid, he shall be guilty of an offence
   under this Act, and shall be liable on summary conviction to a fine not exceeding
   [the statutory maximum], or to a term of imprisonment for any period not
   exceeding six months, or to both such fine and imprisonment:
   Provided that, where it is proved that a dealer has previously to an auction
   entered into an agreement in writing with one or more persons to purchase
   goods at the auction bona fide on a joint account and has before the goods were
   purchased at the auction deposited a copy of the agreement with the auctioneer,
   such an agreement shall not be treated as an agreement made in contravention
   of this section.

. . .

3. *Copy of Act to be exhibited at sale*
   The particulars which, under s 7 of the Auctioneers Act 1845, are required to be
   affixed or suspended in some conspicuous part of the room or place where the
   auction is held shall include a copy of this Act, and that section shall have effect
   accordingly.

Auctions (Bidding Agreements) Act 1969

1. *Offences under Auctions (Bidding Agreements) Act 1927 to be indictable as well
as triable summarily, and extension of time for bringing summary proceedings*
(1) Offences under section 1 of the Auctions (Bidding Agreements) Act 1927
   (which, as amended by the Criminal Justice Act 1967, renders a dealer who
   agrees to give, or gives, or offers a gift or consideration to another as an
   inducement or reward for abstaining, or for having abstained, from bidding at a
   sale by auction punishable on summary conviction with a fine not exceeding the
   statutory maximum or imprisonment for a term not exceeding six months, or
   both, and renders similarly punishable a person who agrees to accept, or accepts, or attempts to obtain from a dealer any such gift or consideration as
   aforesaid) shall be triable on indictment as well as summarily; and the penalty
   that may be imposed on a person on conviction on indictment of an offence
   under that section shall be imprisonment for a term not exceeding two years or
   a fine or both.

. . .

(5) This section applies only to offences committed after the commencement of this
   Act.

2. *Persons convicted not to attend or participate in auctions*
(1) On any such summary conviction or conviction on indictment as is mentioned in
   s 1 above, the court may order that the person so convicted or that the person

and any representative of him shall not (without leave of the court) for a period from the date of such conviction—

(a) in the case of a summary conviction, of not more than one year, or

(b) in the case of a conviction on indictment, of not more than three years, enter upon any premises where goods intended for sale by auction are on display or to attend or participate in any way in any sale by auction.

(2) In the event of a contravention of an order under this section, the person who contravenes it (and, if he is the representative of another, that other also) shall be guilty of an offence and liable—

(a) on summary conviction, to a fine not exceeding [the statutory maximum];

(b) on conviction on indictment, to imprisonment for a term not exceeding two years or to a fine or to both.

(3) In any proceedings against a person in respect of a contravention of an order under this section consisting in the entry upon premises where goods intended for sale by auction were on display, it shall be a defence for him to prove that he did not know, and had no reason to suspect, that goods so intended were on display on the premises, and in any proceedings against a person in respect of a contravention of such an order consisting in his having done something as the representative of another, it shall be a defence for him to prove that he did not know, and had no reason to suspect, that that other was the subject of such an order.

(4) Any person shall not be guilty of an offence under this section by reason only of his selling property by auction or causing it to be so sold.

(5) This section applies only to offences committed after the commencement of this Act.

Explanatory notes on these provisions

(a) In England and Wales, a prosecution for an offence under s 1 of the Auctions (Bidding Agreements) Act 1927 cannot be instituted without the consent of the Attorney-General or the Solicitor-General (s 1(3)).

(b) Section 2 of the 1927 Act enabled vendors to treat sales the subject matter of a conviction under s 1 as induced by fraud. As from the commencement of the 1969 Act, s 3 thereof substitutes the simpler remedy of allowing affected purchasers to avoid the contract without the necessity for a conviction. This is discussed in detail below.

(c) By s 1(1) of the Auctions (Bidding Agreements) Act 1969, offences under the 1927 Act are also triable on indictment and the penalty on conviction on indictment is imprisonment not exceeding two years or a fine or both.

(d) The reference in s 3 of the 1927 Act to s 7 of the Auctioneers Act 1845 is to the requirement which states that, 'if any auctioneer . . . begins any auction or acts as auctioneer at any auction at any room or place where his name and residence is not painted, printed or written on a ticket or board affixed or suspended as required by this section, an offence is committed.' The penalty is not exceeding level 2 on the standard scale

(Auctioneers Act 1845, s 7, as amended by the Criminal Law Act 1977, s 31, and Criminal Justice Act 1982, s 46, discussed further in chapter 2).

(e) Section 4 of the Auctions (Bidding Agreements) Act 1969 requires a copy of that Act also to be displayed.

(f) The subject matter of s 1 of the 1927 Act is 'any dealer'. A 'dealer' is a person who in the normal course of his business attends sale by auction for the purposes of purchasing goods with a view to reselling them (s 1(2)).

(g) The 'statutory maximum' fine is in 1994 £5,000, but this sum may be altered from time to time by virtue of the Magistrates' Courts Act 1980, s 32, and the Criminal Justice Act 1982, s 74.

Interpretation of these statutory provisions

Section 1 of the Auctions (Bidding Agreements) Act 1927 poses a number of difficulties. Section 1(1) clearly proscribes the giving of consideration of some kind by one person to another as an inducement to the latter for abstaining, or having abstained, from bidding. Presumably most auction-ring agreements or arrangements involve: (a) an understanding as to which member should bid, (b) an understanding that the other members should not bid, and (c) an understanding as to the maximum bid that should be offered. It is probable that this mutual exchange of implied promises constitutes consideration within the group. It has been pointed out that on the analogy of criminal conspiracy, there need be proof of no more than a 'tacit understanding between conspirators as to what should be done'.[18]

The second difficulty is the interpretation of the proviso as to the registration of partnership agreements. Clearly if there is a genuine partnership it would be nonsensical to treat this partnership as an illegal ring. On the other hand the Act implicitly distinguishes the genuine partnership from the ad hoc arrangement between rival dealers which may be arrived at to form a ring at an individual auction. The economic consequences of the ring are essentially the same as those which would accrue to a genuine partnership — ie the partners have a share in the accretion of value. On the other hand, in a genuine partnership, this accretion of value would only be arrived at on the eventual resale of the item from a partnership to an outsider. In a ring, the accretion occurs at an intermediate stage, and it is this accretion which, it can be argued, really belongs to the seller at the auction. The proviso to s 1 adopts the fairly blunt weapon of excluding from the provisions of s 1 the case where a dealer has previously to an auction entered into

---

[18] A. T. H. Smith 'Auction Rings' [1981] Crim LR 86 at 88. But proving 'inducement' may be a problem.

an agreement in writing with one or more persons to purchase goods at the auction bona fide on a joint account. Before the goods are purchased he is required to deposit a copy of the agreement with the auctioneer. Presumably only where such an agreement is in *writing* can it be exempted from its prima facie illegality if the further condition relating to its deposit is fulfilled. This could, however, result in the rather ludicrous situation of two longstanding 'partners' attending the same auction without thinking of entering into any written agreement relating to their activity at that particular auction, not bidding against each other, and subsequently apparently committing a criminal offence since the consideration for the passive partner's non-participation is the prospect of a share in the resultant profit on sale of the item.

Possible reform

The fact that two successful prosecutions have been known to have been brought demonstrates that the offence is not 'only ever honoured in its breach'.[19] However, there remain formidable difficulties in the way of the prosecutor, and the event of two successful prosecutions since 1927 hardly inspires confidence that the Auction (Bidding Agreements) Acts 1927 and 1969 are effective in protecting the public from auction rings, if it is desired to do so.

There is an argument of policy that auction rings should be recognised as legal. Provided the seller fixes a realistic reserve, this is his primary insurance in not parting with his goods at a gross undervalue. Furthermore, the fact that a ring is operating does not necessarily mean that a satisfactory price was not obtained. It must be a matter of fortune as to whether there is a rival ring, an individual dealer or a private collector who is prepared to bid the goods up. Furthermore, dealers must be allowed to exploit their expertise and recognition of a valuable piece lying undiscovered by other experts is all part of the trade.

On the other hand, it can be argued, the existence of auction rings threatens to bring the auction process into considerable disrepute when private sellers subsequently find their goods resold at a hugely inflated price. Also, new entrants to a particular saleroom may be permanently discouraged by the predatory behaviour of existing rings. It is patently in the auctioneer's own interests that this practice is at least regulated. One suggestion for reforming the law is to abolish the offence created by the 1927 Act and, instead, simply direct that collective bidding is permitted, but

---

[19] See A. T. H. Smith 'Auction Rings' [1981] Crim LR 86 at 91.

the agreement to do so must be in writing and notified to the auctioneer. Similarly the auctioneer who has a financial stake in the article for sale should disclose this fact to those bidding. The alternative would be to abolish the offence altogether but also to enforce the registration of 'ring' partnerships as restrictive practices and for this registration to be well publicised. The public dislike of rings might well discourage their ready formation if the necessity to register were better enforced.

SETTING SALES ASIDE

The natural consequence of conducting a sale induced by fraud is to allow the vendor to exercise his civil right to set the sale aside. Section 2 of the 1927 Act so decreed, provided that there had been a relevant prosecution and conviction. As from 1969 this was replaced with a wider provision not requiring a conviction if an offending agreement can be proved. Section 3 of the 1969 Act runs as follows:

3. *Rights of seller of goods by auction where agreement subsists that some person shall abstain from bidding for the goods*
(1) Where goods are purchased at an auction by a person who has entered into an agreement with another or others that the other or the others (or some of them) shall abstain from bidding for the goods (not being an agreement to purchase the goods bona fide on a joint account) and he or the other party, or one of the other parties, to the agreement is a dealer, the seller may avoid the contract under which the goods are purchased.
(2) Where a contract is avoided by virtue of the foregoing subsection, then, if the purchaser has obtained possession of the goods and restitution thereof is not made, the persons who were parties to the agreement that one or some of them should abstain from bidding for the goods the subject of the contract shall be jointly and severally liable to make good to the seller the loss (if any) he sustained by reason of the operation of the agreement.
(3) Subsection (1) above applies to a contract made after the commencement of this Act whether the agreement as to the abstention of a person or persons from bidding for the goods the subject of the contract was made before or after that commencement.
(4) Section 2 of the Auctions (Bidding Agreements) Act 1927 (right of vendors to treat certain sales as fraudulent) shall not apply to a sale the contract for which is made after the commencement of this Act.
(5) In this section, 'dealer' has the meaning assigned to it by section 1(2) of the Auctions (Bidding Agreements) Act 1927.

One rather spectacular case relevant to s 3 is known to the authors which was eventually settled on strictly confidential terms and can only be alluded to, therefore, in the abstract. However, senior counsel were involved in an analysis of the legal position under the section and it makes a revealing case study of the effect of this section on the seller's right to avoid the contract.

A body of trustees ('O') owned certain chattels, one of which was consigned to a provincial auction house in circumstances where no one recognised the chattel as being of any real value. It was then sold for a much greater sum than had been anticipated but, as it turned out, a fraction of its real value. Some months later the chattel was re-sold by one of the major auction houses in London for over 300 times its sale price at the provincial saleroom — a classic example of a 'sleeper' initially getting through the net. Prior to the London sale research had revealed the chattel to be of great historical importance. When 'O' was told about the second (London) sale by an outsider it was also revealed that a successful bidder at the provincial auction sale ('B1') had had an attack of conscience and had revealed to a museum officer (an unsuccessful bidder at the later sale) that the previous provincial sale had been 'ringed'. He made a statement explaining that several dealers had recognised the chattel as being 'interesting' (but had not specifically identified it) and those dealers agreed not to bid against each other at the sale and that after B1's successful bid there was a subsequent 'knock-out' in a nearby cafe. B2 had been the successful buyer at the 'knock-out'. None of the others allegedly involved was prepared to corroborate this story, though it appeared plausible.

Turning now to the application of s 3(2) of the 1969 Act, it states that where a contract is avoided because of the sale of the lot having been 'ringed', then, if the purchaser has obtained the goods and restitution thereof is not made, those participating in the ring are jointly and severally liable to make good to the seller the loss (if any) sustained by reason of the operation of bidding agreement.

The first problem was that *if* the purchaser at the second, London, auction ('B3') had obtained a good title to the chattel (because notice to avoid the provincial sale might have occurred too late, for reasons that will be explained, to stop title passing), the former owner's rights are limited to damages to 'make good the loss'. What was the loss? Counsel advised that the measure of damages would be limited to the difference between the price at which the chattel was sold at the first sale and the price that the chattel would have fetched if the sale had not been ringed but *before* the chattel had been identified for what it truly was. In other words, it is necessary simply to assume that the provincial sale was not 'ringed' and that no one in the auction room knew what the chattel was. On this test the damages would be likely to be so low that an action would not be worth pursuing.

The alternative course, therefore, was to claim restitution of the chattel or, since it had been 'resold' spectacularly well, to make a proprietary claim to the proceeds of sale instead. The issue of the timing of the sequence of events then becomes important (see diagram below). Here the former owners, O, had given B1 (the buyer at the first auction who had informed about the ring) a notice purporting to avoid the sale, but by that time the chattel had been resold twice, once to B2 and then in London to B3. Without this complication the position would have been much simpler. If B1's title was voidable then B2, who took from him with notice of the ring at the knockout, also inherited a voidable title. The chattel would have been eminently recoverable at that stage.

Where a resale to an innocent party, such as B3, occurs, s 23 of the Sale of Goods Act 1979 states that where the seller of goods has a voidable title to them (ie B2) but his title has not been avoided at the time of sale, the buyer (ie B3) acquires a good title to the goods, provided he buys them in good faith and without notice of the seller's defect of title. Had B1's title (and therefore B2's title also) been avoided 'at the time of sale'? A 'sale' takes place, by s 2(4) of the 1979 Act, when *property* in the goods is transferred from the seller to the buyer. At this point a crucial piece of information was revealed. B3, the buyer at the London sale, had asked to defer full payment. Accordingly, since the London auctioneers used a standard condition stopping the passing of property in a lot until full payment is made therefor, the notice to B1 appeared to be in time to prevent the ownership of the chattel passing from B1 to B2 and on to B3. B3 might have attempted to rely, alternatively, on s 25 of the Sale of Goods Act 1979 or s 9 of the Factors Act 1889 (sales by buyers in possession with consent of the seller to have the same effect as if authorised by the owner). However, since in *National Employers' Mutual General Insurance Association Ltd v Jones*[20] the House of Lords construed 'the owner' as being 'the seller', ie B1, and both B1 and B2 had voidable titles, O's title was preserved.

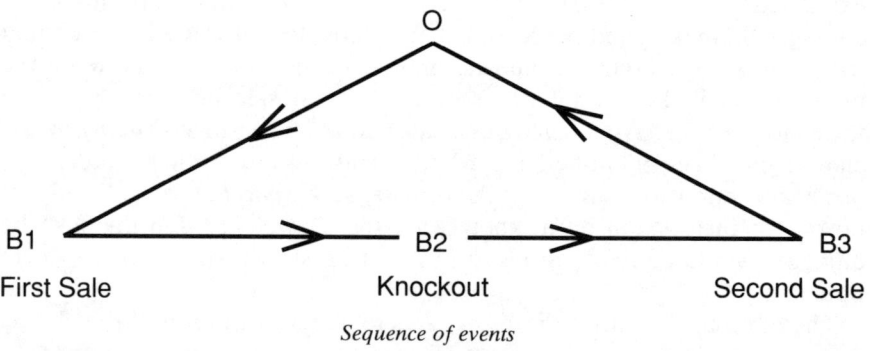

Sequence of events

---

[20] [1988] 2 WLR 952.

OTHER DISHONEST PRACTICES AT AUCTIONS

It goes without saying that fraud by the auctioneer or his staff which adversely affects his principal, the seller, involves a breach of the civil fiduciary duty owed by agent to principal (fully discussed in chapter 5). The question arising here is whether any fraudulent practices that might occur constitute *criminal* offences.

We will not spend much space here discussing the more obvious case of theft by someone if the principal's (or purchaser's) property is stolen from the auction premises. A person is guilty of theft if he dishonestly appropriates property belonging to another with the intention of permanently depriving the other of it.[21] 'Belonging' is widely defined in s 5(1) of the Theft Act 1968 as including 'belonging to any person having possession or control of it or having in it any proprietary right or interest'. Section 5(3) specifically states that where a bailee is under an obligation to deal with goods in a particular way, the property is regarded (as against him) as belonging to the bailor, but for technical reasons the auctioneer-bailee who steals his principal-bailor's goods is regarded as being within s 5(1) above, since the principal is still the proprietary owner. In the auction-room, however, if a *third party* steals a particular lot before the auction takes place, the theft is the loss of the vendor. If the theft takes place after the sale, the loss is likely to fall upon the purchaser. The owner who is unable to recover his property will be advised to scrutinise the Conditions of Sale carefully. A typical one reads: 'Until sold, each lot shall be at the Vendor's risk and it shall be his duty to preserve the same. After the fall of the hammer such risk and duty shall devolve upon the Purchaser'.[22] Assuming the validity of this type of condition, whether the owner recovers his loss may depend upon whether he has effected insurance cover. This can sometimes be the case under an ordinary domestic chattels policy; in other cases the auction-house will effect cover for the vendor, charging him with the premium. It is usual for such insurance to cover against the risks of fire, burglary and water damage but not accidental damage or breakage. It is not the usual practice to insure the property in favour of a *purchaser* during such time as the goods are at his risk.

On a more sophisticated level, the trust inherent in the auction situation can easily be abused. For example, before cataloguing, a member of the auctioneer's staff may spot an item in a deceased's estate which his expertise teaches him is of some value. If the chattel sale contains numerous

---

[21] Theft Act 1968, s 1.

[22] Where the theft is facilitated by the auctioneer's negligence, this type of condition is subject to the requirement of reasonableness (and is thus open to challenge on this ground) by virtue of the Unfair Contract Terms Act 1977, s 2. See also Sale of Goods Act 1979, ss 17, 18 and 20.

miscellaneous lots, the item in question may be secreted along with other items being sold as a single lot in a container. The member of staff then agrees with a colleague that the colleague shall bid up to a certain amount for what appears to be an uninteresting lot, and thus obtains it. If neither the deceased's executors nor the auctioneer is aware of what has been going on, the ruse will probably succeed (in the absence of a sharp-eyed competing dealer). This conduct is likely to amount to a conspiracy to defraud at common law and possibly a statutory conspiracy to obtain property by deception contrary to s 15 of the Theft Act 1968. (The secreting, itself, could also be theft.)

FALSE TRADE DESCRIPTIONS

Descriptions of lots in catalogues supplied by the auctioneer to bidders are of such critical importance that the topic deserves a section to itself. There seems to be evidence of 'folklore' in at least some auctioneering circles that auctioneers are somehow exempt from the penal provisions of, in particular, the Trade Decriptions Act 1968.[23] This is completely untrue and recent, successful and much publicised prosecutions under this Act have perhaps done something to dispel the myth. It should be emphasised, too, that the Act applies to business-to-business transactions as well as business-to-consumer ones. A buyer at auction who is a dealer is therefore transacting business caught by the 1968 Act.

The section most likely to catch a false description of goods specified in a sale catalogue is s1(1) of the Trade Descriptions Act 1968, which runs as follows:

Any person who in the course of a trade or business

(a) applies a false trade description to any goods; or
(b) supplies or offers to supply any goods to which a false trade description is applied, shall, subject to the provisions of this Act, be guilty of an offence.

The clearest way in which this provision can be explained in the context of the Act as a whole,[24] and its applicability to auctioneers considered, is to postulate an imaginary case not noticeably dissimilar to one successfully prosecuted as mentioned above.

Let us assume that an auction of chattels includes a lot thus described: 'A 17th-Century 17″ × 10″ oak joint stool with plain frieze raised on four turned baluster supports and plain cross stretchers'. The 'Standard Con-

---

[23] Relevant sections of this legislation are reproduced in Appendix 2.

[24] The Trade Descriptions Act 1968 is much more extensively explained and analysed in eg Harvey and Parry *The Law of Consumer Protection and Fair Trading* (4th edn, 1992) Butterworths. See also Butterworths' Trading and Consumer Law (a constantly up-dated encyclopaedia).

ditions of Sale' at the end of the catalogue (purchase price £1) state, inter alia, that 'Neither the Auctioneer nor the Vendor(s) are responsible for error in description, authenticity, or genuineness of any lot or for any fault or defect in it, giving no warranty whatsoever, the Buyers being held to have satisfied themselves as to the condition, quantity, quality and description of the lots before bidding.'

On the basis of the catalogue description a private buyer, who states that he buys antiques occasionally at auctions for investment, purchases the item for £200.[25] The facts are investigated by the local trading standards department which ascertains the following:

(a) the buyer, on trying to resell the stool to raise some money urgently, is told that it is a twentieth-century copy. This view is supported by two written statements from expert antique dealers who also state that any expert would recognise the item as a copy for various technical reasons. Its value is put at £40.

(b) On investigating the firm, it is found that a partner, AB, is responsible for chattel auctions, but the description was written by an employee who actively conducted the auction. This employee, CD, has some years of experience but admits to relatively little knowledge in some areas where it is sometimes the practice, if in doubt, to obtain an outside expert opinion. This did not occur here.

The trading standards office in question then decide to bring two charges, one against the partner and one against the firm's employee, as follows:

(i) On the ... day of ... at ..., AB, a partner in the firm of ..., in the course of a business as auctioneers, supplied to [the buyer] a stool to which a false trade description, namely, [as per catalogue] was applied by means of a catalogue, contrary to s 1(1)(b) of the Trade Descriptions Act 1968

(ii) On the ... day of ... at ..., CD, in the course of a business as an auctioneer, applied by means of a catalogue a false trade description, namely, [as per catalogue] to a stool, contrary to s 1(1)(a) of the Trade Descriptions Act 1968.

It will be noticed that the fact that the auctioneers do not 'sell' the goods, not being the owners, is irrelevant. All forms of *supply* are caught. Additionally, although this misdescription was applied by catalogue, section 4(2) states that a trade description may also be made orally, for example from the rostrum.

---

[25] It in fact makes no difference whether the buyer is a private one or a dealer. Nor is it a defence that an experienced dealer should not have been deceived, or even was not actually deceived — see *Chidwick v Beer* (1974) 138 JP Jo 210 (QBD).

POSSIBLE DEFENCES

Reverting to the example, the two defendants, the partner AB and the employee-auctioneer CD, then have to consider their possible defences. In common with many other commercial criminal statutes, the offence in issue here is one of strict liability. There can therefore be no defence that there was no intention to misdescribe (ie no mens rea). The offence will be found proved if in the course of a trade or business a false trade description was actually applied to goods, or goods were 'supplied' (a wider expression than 'sold' and one which includes sales by an agent auctioneer to a buyer)[26] to which a false trade description has been applied and the defendant cannot avail himself of one of the statutory defences considered next. Any doubt in a particular case as to whether a description is false, and there can be no doubt on the facts being considered, may be resolved by reference to s 3(1) of the Trade Descriptions Act 1968 which states that a false trade description is a trade description which is 'false to a material degree' or is similarly misleading (s 3(2)).

The first possible defence is that of 'disclaimer'. Over a series of cases predominantly concerning cars with false odometer readings, it has been held by the courts technically possible to negate a false trade description applied to goods by disclaiming the accuracy of that description. The catalogue here does indeed contain such a disclaimer. However the courts have held, that, to be effective, a disclaimer:[27]

must be as bold, precise and compelling as the trade description itself and must be as effectively brought to the notice of any person to whom the goods may be supplied. In other words, the disclaimer must equal the trade description to the extent to which it is likely to get home to anyone interested in receiving the goods.

Thus a second-hand car may have its false odometer reading zeroised or completely obscured by a notice. There are powerful limitations on the effectiveness of this doctrine. One is that once a trade description has been communicated, a casual remark or 'small print' in a document are not enough to disclaim it.[28] Furthermore, it has been emphasised in a number of cases[29] that a person cannot normally actively falsely describe goods and then purport to disclaim the descriptions — ie disclaim his own fraud.

---

[26] In *British Car Auctions Ltd v Wright* [1972] 3 All ER 462, [1972] 1 WLR 1519 it was held that auctioneers did not 'offer to sell' unroadworthy cars contrary to the Road Traffic Act 1960, s 68. But they would undoubtedly have 'supplied' the vehicles.

[27] *Norman v Bennett* [1974] 3 All ER 351 at 354 per Widgery LCJ.

[28] See generally *R v Hammertons Cars Ltd* [1976] 3 All ER 758, [1976] 1 WLR 1243, CA; *R v McMillan Aviation Ltd and McMillan* [1981] Crim LR 785.

[29] See *Corfield v Starr* [1981] RTR 380; *Hackney London Borough v Measureworth Ltd & Newman* [1981] Crim LR 503 (affirmed by Div Ct (1981) 80 LGR 611, [1982] RTR 296); *R v Southward* [1987] RTR 273; *May v Vincent* (1990) 154 JP 997 [1991] 1 EGLR 27, discussed below.

So, applying these principles to the facts, the partner AB might consider claiming that the Condition of Sale negating misdescriptions disclaimed the false trade description applied by his employee, but since 'small print' of this sort is unlikely to be held to be as 'bold, precise and compelling' as the catalogue description, AB would be unlikely to be successful in sheltering behind such a disclaimer. It would not appear to be an available defence to the employee CD who actually applied the false trade description, since one cannot disclaim one's own wrong. In fact, the standard Conditions of Sale in question may well have been prefaced by a statement along the following lines:

Care is taken to ensure that any statement as to authorisation, attribution, origin, state, age, provenance and condition is reliable and accurate but all such statements are statements of opinion and are not to be taken as statements or representations of fact. The auctioneers reserve the right in forming their opinion to consult and rely upon any expert or authority reasonably considered by them to be reliable.

If this can be regarded as an additional disclaimer, it will stand or fall with the one already considered. It may, in any event, be regarded as itself a false description as to services (contrary to s 14 of the Trade Descriptions Act 1968) if it is known that no care to verify the description of the stool was taken, and can therefore be a double-edged sword.[30] Section 14 of the Trade Descriptions Act 1968 states that it is an offence for any person in the course of any trade or business: (a) to make a statement which he knows to be false; or (b) recklessly to make a statement which is false as to a specified number of matters including 'the provision in the course of any trade or business of any services, accommodation or facilities', or the nature of any such services, or 'the examination, approval or evaluation by any person of any services, accommodation or facilities so provided.' Although the offence requires knowledge of the falsity or recklessness, 'recklessly' has been defined by the courts to catch the trader who does not have regard to the truth or falsity of the statement even though it could not be shown that he was deliberately closing his eyes to the truth, or that he had any kind of dishonest intention.[31]

In *Zawadski v Sleigh*[32] it was accepted that it was *possible* for an auctioneer to make a disclaimer on his own behalf — a rather similar one to that in the above example being set out in Conditions of Sale relating to a car auction — but the court did not authoritatively discuss the issue which it

[30] See *Corfield v Starr*, n 29 above.
[31] See *MFI Warehouses Ltd v Nattrass* [1973] 1 All ER 762, [1973] 1 WLR 307, DC. Section 14 is of importance in the auction business in any circumstances where statements are made, in the catalogue or otherwise, as to the quality of the *service* provided, including the care with which goods are described.
[32] [1975] RTR 113, DC. See also for another case where a car auction was indirectly relevant, *Tarleton Engineering Co Ltd v Nattrass* [1973] 3 All ER 699, [1973] 1 WLR 1261.

regarded as irrelevant. The case was concerned with the correctness of the conviction of the principal-sellers of the cars which had false odometer readings. The court stated that it was not relevant to ask whether such disclaimer was made on behalf of the auctioneers alone or on behalf of both agent and principal. The only test was whether the disclaimer was effective, ie 'potent enough to get through to the buyer and make him disregard the message which the odometer had previously passed on to him.'[33]

The doctrine of 'disclaimer' has been developed by the courts — there is no guidance on it in the Act itself. The fundamental principle is that if the stringent criteria laid down by the courts are met, a false trade description has never been applied at all, and there is therefore no possible mischief to which the Act's provisions can apply.

A slightly, different point arises quite commonly in practice where at or just before the sale the auctioneer discovers a misdescription in the catalogue and makes strenuous efforts to correct the description by announcing it to all bidders (who ought to include all commission bidders). Whilst there is no authority on the point, the court (it is hoped) might either hold that the material description was the corrected one or that the due diligence defence had been established.[34]

Mistake, accident etc

The Trade Descriptions Act 1968 does, however, give to the defendant a two-limbed defence designed to mitigate the underlying no-fault liability imposed by s 1 and s 11, relating to goods and prices respectively. (Section 14, as has been explained, does require knowledge of recklessness in relation to false trade descriptions of services.)

This two-limbed defence is contained in the Trade Descriptions Act 1968, s 24, a section which to a greater or lesser extent appears in many other criminal provisions relating to commerce. It runs:

24. *Defence of mistake, accident, etc.*
(1) In any proceedings for an offence under this Act it shall, subject to subsection
     (2) of this section, be a defence for the person charged to prove —
     (a) that the commission of the offence was due to a mistake or to reliance on
          information supplied to him or to the act or default of another person, an
          accident or some other cause beyond his control; and
     (b) that he took all reasonable precautions and exercised all due diligence to
          avoid the commission of such an offence by himself or any person under his
          control.

---

[33] [1975] RTR 113 at 118 per Lord Widgery.
[34] See *Wings Ltd v Ellis* [1985] AC 272 for a somewhat analogous case, but where due diligence was not argued.

(2) If in any case the defence provided by the last foregoing subsection involves the allegation that the commission of the offence was due to the act or default of another person or to reliance on information supplied by another person, the person charged shall not, without leave of the court, be entitled to rely on that defence unless, within a period ending seven clear days before the hearing, he has served on the prosecutor a notice in writing giving such information identifying or assisting in the identification of that other person as was then in his possession.

(3) In any proceedings for an offence under this Act of supplying or offering to supply goods to which a false trade description is applied it shall be a defence for the person charged to prove that he did not know, and could not with reasonable diligence have ascertained, that the goods did not conform to the description or that the description had been applied to the goods.

The defence involves the *defendant* successfully proving, on the balance of probabilities,[35] that the defendant's commission of the offence was due to (a) a mistake, or (b) reliance on information supplied to him, or (c) the act or default of another person, or an accident or some other course beyond his control, *and* (in any of these cases) he *both* took all reasonable precautions *and* exercised all due diligence to avoid the commission of such an offence by himself or any person under his control.

There are additional points to note. Subsection (2) imposes a pre-condition to relying on pinning the blame on a third party which is self-explanatory. Subsection (3) supplies an additional defence which could be relevant to the auctioneer. Thus, if he offers goods in a chattel sale which bear false or misleading labels or some other false trade description of which he was unaware and could not with *reasonable* diligence have ascertained, this subsection supplies a defence. But it should be noted carefully that the trade description must have been affixed by someone else. When the defendant has himself falsely described the goods in his auction catalogue, the charge would be under s 1(1)(a) of the Trade Descriptions Act 1968, applying a false trade description in the active sense, as opposed to under s 1(1)(b), supplying goods to which a false trade description is applied, in the passive sense. A comparison of the two specimen charges against CD and AB above reveals these respective differences.

There have been many judicial statements on the precise meaning of s 24 of the Trade Descriptions Act 1968. The following are the main points of possible relevance to auctioneers:

(a) Mistake. This must be that of the person charged, not that of an employee or third party.[36]
(b) 'Reliance upon information supplied to him'. This is particularly rel-

---

[35] See *McGuire v Sittingbourne Co-operative Society Ltd* (1976) 140 JP 306, 120 Sol Jo 197.
[36] *Birkenhead and District Co-operative Society Ltd v Roberts* [1970] 3 All ER 391, [1970] 1 WLR 1497.

evant where an auctioneer seeks to rely on reproducing the vendor's description as in the entry form.[37] Reliance cannot be 'blind'. It must be capable of being judged as coming from an informed source which a responsible person would accept and which would stand up to reasonable checking out.[38]

(c) 'The act or default of another person'. In *Tesco Supermarkets Ltd v Nattrass*,[39] it was held that a shop manager employed by the defendant was 'another person'. He was not sufficiently senior to be the *ego* or *alter ego* of the company, which could therefore pin the blame on its subordinate successfully *provided* it could also comply with the second limb of the section and show that its supervisory and training system was such that it could be said to have taken all the precautions to avoid the commission of an offence and shown all due diligence in making the system work (which was held to be the case here). This defence would be much less likely to succeed in the case of auctioneers practising from one place (or a small number of places) where, whilst it is conceivable that an employee responsible for the offence might be regarded as 'another person' from the auctioneering firm, the duty of close and effective supervision is such as to make it unlikely to allow its breakdown to be regarded as consistent with due diligence. In any case where the defence is pleaded, the 'other person' must be identified.[40]

(d) 'An accident' etc. There is little authority on this, but it must clearly be something so unexpected that normal precautions would not have prevented it.

(e) 'All reasonable precautions and exercised all due diligence'. The meaning of these joint requirements has already been indicated under (c) above. The many authorities[41] stress the need for an efficient system actively operated to prevent the offences arising. Thus where watch retailers sold a 'waterproof' watch which filled with water after immersion in a bowl for one hour, it was held when they were charged with selling goods to which a false trade description was applied that they had not taken all due precautions and exercised all due diligence within s 24(1)(b). No precautions at all had been exercised, such as dipping the

---

[37] If this practice is followed, eg in car auctions, trading standards departments are in practice much less likely to prosecute. Such prosecution in any event requires the prior notification of the Director General of Fair Trading under s 130 of the Fair Trading Act 1973. However, the legal basis for this policy seems tenuous. It would be better to regard such auctioneers as having a better chance of successfully using the defence in the Trade Descriptions Act 1968, s 24(3), as explained.

[38] See eg *Barker v Hargreaves* (1981) 125 Sol Jo 165, [1981] RTR 197 (MOT certificate bearing printed warning not sufficient); also *Sutton London Borough v Perry Sanger & Co Ltd* (1971) 135 JP Jo 239 (information relied upon did not stand up to checking out). Note also the *additional* requirement of 'due diligence' in the second limb.

[39] [1972] AC 153, [1971] 2 All ER 127, HL.

[40] *McGuire v Sittingbourne Co-operative Society Ltd* (1976) 140 JP 306, 120 Sol Jo 197.

[41] See Butterworths' Trading and Consumer Law, (3) 250f.

watch in water. The retailer had simply relied on the wholesaler's reputation.[42] On the other hand, if an auctioneer is selling a quantity of used watches some of which may be described on the watch case as 'waterproof', the auctioneer might rely instead on the defence in s 24(3) (discussed above). But this would only cover him if he *himself* had not applied the false trade description — eg by a catalogue description 'waterproof watch'.

Though not strictly another defence, it must be noted for the sake of completeness that s 23 makes provision for any third party whose act or default has caused the commission of the offence to be charged instead of or jointly with the original defendant.

Applying the various principles explained in the points above to the example charges against AB and CD, it seems most unlikely that any statement in the Conditions of Sale would be regarded as a disclaimer. The catalogue description of the lot clearly conveys the false description, and even if the General Conditions are as 'bold, precise and compelling' or as 'potent' as that unequivocal description of the soi-disant seventeenth-century stool, the courts are increasingly tending to deny the possibility of a disclaimer where the defendant has himself applied the false trade description, as is the case with CD, the actual cataloguer and auctioneer. Furthermore, s 24 offers neither defendant much comfort in this situation. Even if a mistake etc could be proved, the evidence showed a lack of any reasonable precautions and due diligence, in that no outside expert opinion was taken. In the case on which the example is founded,[43] the equivalents of AB and CD both pleaded guilty in the event. They were each fined £100 and ordered to pay compensation to the buyer and to pay costs. The case received considerable publicity.

We cannot leave this critical matter without failing to qualify any impression that such cases are necessarily as straightforward as the above. Where reputable auctioneers undertake to sell specialist items such as old master paintings or musical instruments there is normally at least one member of staff highly qualified to assess items or, at least, available for consultation. In order to accommodate doubts, the practice of Sotheby's in their musical instruments catalogue is to include a preliminary Glossary. It is explained that an instrument described as 'by' a named maker means that 'the instrument is in our opinion of the named maker'. Thereafter progressive degrees of doubt are conveyed by the expressions 'ascribed to', 'attributed to', 'School of', 'Workshop of', and 'labelled' — 'the instrument is not in our opinion by the maker indicated'.[44]

---

[42] *Sherratt v Geralds the American Jewellers Ltd* (1970) 114 Sol Jo 147, 68 LGR 256, DC.
[43] See p 220, above.
[44] See also Christie's General Condition 8. For a fuller account of the difficulties of attributing stringed instruments and possible contraventions of the Trade Descriptions Act 1968, see Brian Harvey *Violin Fraud: Deception, Forgery, Theft and the Law* (1992), OUP.

Should it occur that a buyer can establish that such an item has been misattributed in the catalogue,[45] ·it is thought that the defence of 'mistake' etc together with proof of having taken 'all reasonable precautions and exercised all due diligence' is readily available. In addition many auction-eers include a general condition to the effect that any lot which proves to be a 'deliberate forgery' (as defined in those Conditions) may be returned within a specified time (eg five years) to the auctioneers and the sale may then be set aside and the money refunded to the buyer (see eg Sotheby's Condition 16). Whilst this does not in fact negate a trade descriptions offence if committed, it nevertheless renders prosecution less likely if the buyer is treated fairly.

May v Vincent

In *May v Vincent*[46] the Divisional Court of Queen's Bench, on appeal from a decision of the Magistrate's Court, took the opportunity of applying many of the above principles to the sale by auction of a watercolour described in the auction catalogue as 'J. M. W. Turner R. A. A watercolour of moorland, stream, bridge and people, unframed $6\frac{1}{2}'' \times 9\frac{1}{2}''$.' This catalogue descrip-tion was read by the complainant who contracted the auctioneer and au-thorised a bid of up to £700. The sale duly took place and the complainant found that she had been successful at £400. The picture was duly collected and the £400 paid. The picture turned out not to be by J. M. W. Turner R. A. and was virtually worthless.

The catalogue contained a comprehensive disclaimer at the front which included the words that each lot was 'sold with all faults, imperfections and errors of description, and neither the vendor nor the auctioneers are responsible for the authenticity, attribution, genuineness, origin, author-ship, date, age, period, condition or quality of any lot. All statements in the catalogue as to any such matters are statements of opinion . . . purchasers are deemed to have satisfied themselves before bidding by inspection or otherwise as to all such matters, and as to the physical description of any lot.'

The respondent auctioneer was charged under s 1(1)(a) of the Trade Descriptions Act 1968 that he in the course of a trade or business did apply to a watercolour painting a false trade description by means of an entry in his auction catalogue to the effect that the painting was by J. M. W. Turner R. A. The magistrates, whilst accepting that the 1968 Act applied to works

---

[45] This is often difficult, since it involves one expert opinion against another. In the case of antique items the judge can legitimately ask the dissenting expert, 'Were you there when it was made?'

[46] (1990) 154 JP 997.

of art, nevertheless acquitted the respondent on the ground that (inter alia) he was protected by the disclaimer. The respondent also contended that he had only attached to the picture the description which appeared on the 'frame'.

The court had no hesitation in emphasising that, contrary to mythology, auctioneers are covered by s 1(1)(1)(a) as in any other trade or business. It is irrelevant that the auctioneer was only acting as agent in applying a description for the owner.

The other issue in the case was the question of whether the disclaimer was effective to remove potential liability. Applying the cases alluded to previously in this chapter, particularly *Newman and others v Hackney Borough Council*[47] and *R v Southwood*,[48] it was again confirmed that it is not open to a defendant who *applies* a false trade description (as opposed to supplying goods already bearing a false trade description) to disclaim that false trade description.

The disingenuous argument that the Trade Descriptions Act 1968 did not and could not apply to the art world which deals in opinions not facts was also given its quietus. The only fact which disturbed the court was the long delay involved in the prosecution process here. The picture was collected in November 1986, the first complaint was made in April 1988 and the eventual Magistrate's Court hearing was on August 17 1989. The prosecution was therefore argued to be an abuse of the court. Although the Divisional Court decreed that the delay was not a sufficient basis for the magistrates acquitting the auctioneer it was agreed that the auctioneer having been (albeit erroneously) acquitted no purpose would be served in re-opening the matter now that the law had been clarified in the prosecutor's favour.

There are other offences akin to those provided by the Trade Descriptions Act. An example is afforded by the Hallmarking Act 1973, s 1(1) of which provides as follows:

Subject to the provisions of this Act, any person who, in the course of a trade or business —

(a) applies to an unhallmarked article a description indicating that it is wholly or partly made of gold, silver or platinum, or
(b) supplies, or offers to supply, an unhallmarked article to which such a description is applied,

shall be guilty of an offence.

It was decided in *Chilvers v Rayner*[49] that this offence, like that provided by s 1(1) of the Trade Descriptions Act 1968, is an absolute one and that the

---

[47] [1982] RTR 296.   [48] (1987) 151 JP 860; [1987] RTR 273.
[49] [1984] 1 All ER 843, [1984] 1 WLR 328. Unhallmarked silver is often called 'white metal' in auction catalogues.

honest belief that the article was hallmarked is no defence. It should be pointed out that in the Hallmarking Act 1973 there is no equivalent to s 24 of the Trade Descriptions Act 1968.

FALSE ESTIMATES

It is comparatively common in modern auctions for the catalogue to indicate the auctioneer's lower and higher estimate of a lot's saleroom value. Cases are known to the authors where the lower estimate is actually below reserve and hence below the minimum price at which the auctioneer has authority to sell the lot. The motivation seems to be to encourage a good pool of bidders by hinting at a bargain. But bidders attending on this basis will be wasting their time and the practice is widely felt to be unethical. It may also infringe s 20 of the Consumer Protection Act 1977 which prohibits a person in the course of a business (whether acting as principal or agent) giving to consumers an indication which is misleading as to the price at which any goods are available. Section 21 explains that 'misleading' includes an indication that the price is less than in fact it is. If the bottom estimate is, say, £150 and the reserve is £200, the auctioneer is indicating that the goods are capable of being sold at a price less than the minimum at which in fact they are available. However, unlike the offences under the Trade Descriptions Act 1968, this offence does not apply to a business-to-business situation; only to a business-to-consumer one. A consumer is a person who might wish to be supplied with the goods for his own private use or consumption (s 20(6)). It must therefore depend upon the chance of the successful bidder being a consumer, as defined, as to whether the auctioneer actually commits an offence.

It has also been suggested that the buyer should be able to set aside such a contract in civil law on the ground of fraudulent misrepresentation, but it is difficult to see how the misrepresentation could be said to induce the contract in question, which must have been made at a higher bid than the bottom estimate. The real answer is for the professional bodies to give firm guidance to their members that the practice described is unethical, and for buyers or bidders prejudiced by it to ask the enforcement authorities to investigate.

PROHIBITION ON SALES

Whereas the Trade Descriptions Act 1968 and the Hallmarking Act 1973 are aimed essentially at false descriptions, there is in addition a number of statutes which create offences in respect of *what* is sold or to *whom*. A comprehensive treatment of these is beyond the scope of this book, but one or two examples may be mentioned.

WILD BIRDS, ANIMALS AND ENDANGERED SPECIES

The sale or the offering or exposing for sale or possessing for sale of certain live or dead wild birds or part of such or their eggs is made a criminal offence by the Wildlife and Countryside Act 1981. The relevant birds are listed in schedule 3 to the Act. Similarly, by s 9 it is an offence to sell or to offer or expose for sale or to possess those wild animals, whether live or dead, listed in schedule 5 to the Act.

As regards birds there are a number of interlinking provisions within the Act which need to be considered. First s 1(2) provides:

Subject to the provisions of this Part, if any person has in his possession or control —

(a) any live or dead wild bird or any part of or anything derived from, such a bird; or
(b) an egg of a wild bird or any part of such an egg,

he shall be guilty of an offence.

There is then a defence under subsection 3 whereby a person shall not be guilty if he can show that the bird or egg had not been killed or taken, or if it had been killed or taken, such was otherwise than in contravention of the relevant provisions. There are also specific exceptions to s 1 contained in ss 2 and 4.

In addition to the offence in s 1(2) there is an offence provided by s 6 in relation to the sale of live or dead wild birds. Section 6 provides as follows:

(1) Subject to the provisions of this Part, if any person —
    (a) sells, offers or exposes for sale, or has in his possession or transports for the purpose of sale, any live wild bird . . . or an egg of a wild bird or any part of such an egg; or
    (b) publishes or causes to be published any advertisement likely to be understood as conveying that he buys or sells, or intends to buy or sell any of these things,

he shall be guilty of an offence.

Whereas it is relatively unlikely that an auctioneer will sell live wild birds, he may find himself selling or possessing for sale stuffed birds. The sale of such is caught by subsection 2 of s 6 which provides:

Subject to the provisions of this Part, if any person who is not for the time being registered in accordance with regulations made by the Secretary of State —

(a) sells, offers or exposes for sale or has in his possession or transports for the purpose of sale, any dead wild bird other than a bird included in Part 2 or 3 of Schedule 3, or any part of, or anything derived from, such a wild bird; or

(b) publishes or causes to be published any advertisement likely to be understood as conveying that he buys or sells, or intends to buy or sell, any of these things,

he shall be guilty of an offence.

Thus, as regards the sale of dead birds it appears only to be an offence if the person is not registered in accordance with regulations made by the Secretary of State. These regulations are provided by the Wildlife and Countryside (Registration to Sell etc Certain Dead Wild Birds) (Amendment) Regulations 1991.[50]

There has been one reported prosecution of auctioneers under this legislation. In *Robinson* v. *Everett and Another*[51] a taxidermist and auctioneers were both prosecuted with offences under section 1(2)(a) in that they had in their possession or under their control at the auctioneers' premises in Chelsea, a dead Golden Eagle which is a species of wild bird included in Schedule 1 of the Wildlife and Countryside Act 1981. The bird had been found by a tourist in Scotland and subsequently stuffed and mounted in a glass case by the first defendant and then placed with the second defendant for sale by auction. Prosecution was brought before the Stipendiary Magistrate in London and the defendants were acquitted but the prosecutor appealed. On appeal, a number of ingenious defences were run but, oddly, it seems to have been conceded that s 6(2) did not provide a defence to the charge under s 1(2)(a). However, the appeal court had specifically been asked the question whether s 6(2) of the Act had any relevance whatsoever. The judges responded: 'Without finding it necessary to enlarge upon the matter we say it has not.'

On this basis the case was remitted for retrial by another Bench. Subsequently both defendants were convicted and fined. The report of the case is not full and there are a number of uncertainties which remain about the case. However, it seems that both the taxidermist and the auctioneers were registered under the regulations provided for in s 6(2) and whilst the offence under s 1(2)(a) of being in possession or control is clearly separate from the offence of selling or having in one's possession for sale under s 6 it would be unfortunate, to say the least, if the registration of auctioneers under s 6 did not protect them from a charge of an offence contrary to s 1(2)(a).

As regards the import or export of certain species, the Endangered Species (Import and Export) Act 1976, as amended by the Wildlife and Countryside Act 1981, restricts the import and export of certain animals and plants and renders it an offence to sell or offer or expose them for sale to the public unless they have been imported or exported in accordance with the terms of a licence.

A report in The Times, 5 September 1985, indicated that Sotheby's was considering a ban on auctions of all natural history specimens after seven

---

[50] SI 1991/479.   [51] Times, 20 May 1988.

lots of rare butterflies had to be withdrawn from a sale because of suspicions that they might have been imported in contravention of the Convention on International Trade in Endangered Species which is enforced in the United Kingdom under the Wildlife and Countryside Act 1981.

The main difficulty with these offences may lie simply in identification. The average auctioneer may have difficulty in successfully identifying the particular item concerned. He would be wise to take expert advice.

FIREARMS AND OTHER OFFENSIVE WEAPONS

Firearms[52]

Somewhat less esoteric (since there is an established auction tradition in this area) but at least as problematic, may be the legislation relating to the sale of firearms. The possession and sale of firearms is now largely controlled by the Firearms Act 1968.[53] Section 1 of the Act provides that it is an offence to possess certain firearms without a firearms certificate. Section 3 provides two separate offences:

(1) A person commits an offence if, by way of trade or business he —
    (a) manufactures, sells, transfers, . . . any firearm or ammunition to which section 1 of this Act applies, or a shotgun; or
    (b) exposes for sale or transfer or has in his possession for sale, transfer, . . . any such firearm or ammunition or a shotgun,

    without being registered under this Act as a firearms dealer.

(2) It is an offence for a person to sell or transfer to any other person in the United Kingdom, other than a registered firearms dealer, any firearm or ammunition to which section 1 of this Act applies, or a shotgun, unless that other produces a firearms certificate authorising him to purchase or acquire it or, as the case may be, his shotgun certificate, or shows that he is by virtue of this Act entitled to purchase or acquire it without holding a certificate.

Thus it is an offence to sell etc any firearm or shotgun without being registered as a dealer. An auctioneer can quite easily guard against commission of this offence by being so registered. Moreover, if he is not a regular seller of such chattels, he is protected under s 9 of the Firearms Act 1968: first as regards *possession* in the ordinary course of business, and second as regards *sale* or *exposure for sale* even if he is not so registered if he follows the expedient of obtaining a permit therefor from the Chief Officer of Police for the Area.

The real difficulty lies with s 1(2) of the Firearms Act 1968, in that it is an

---

[52] See the definition provided by the Firearms Act 1968 as amended by the Firearms (Amendment) Act 1988. Note that a firearm includes an imitation firearm: Firearms Act 1968, s 57(4) as amended by the Firearms Act 1982.

[53] See Appendix 2.

offence to sell *to* anyone other than a dealer unless that other holds a certificate authorising him to purchase the weapon. Under the Sale of Goods Act 1979 there is a contract of sale where under a contract the property in the goods is transferred to the buyer. However there is no sale but only an agreement to sell where the transfer of the property in the goods is to take place at a future time or subject to some condition to be fulfilled. In the absence of such pre-conditions the sale would normally be complete and the property passed to the buyer on the fall of the hammer, subsequently-imposed conditions not being effective to prevent the property in the goods passing to the buyer.[54] Most auctioneers' general conditions do provide that ownership in property is not to pass to the buyer until the full purchase price has been paid. In the case of sales of firearms and shotguns it would be expedient to include a contractual provision whereby no ownership would pass to the buyer unless and until he produces the requisite certificate.

Section 3(2) of the Firearms Act 1968 also makes it an offence to *transfer* a firearm, ammunition or a shotgun to anyone who fails to show he is entitled to purchase or acquire it. 'Transfer' is defined in s 57(4) of the Act as including 'let on hire, give lend and part with possession'. Thus it would seem that an offence is committed by an auctioneer who returns a firearm to his vendor client who has not a permit to possess it, for example, after an unsuccessful sale; in practice auctioneers should retain such unsold guns until they can find a registered dealer willing to acquire them. Alternatively, with the consent of the vendor, the auctioneer should ensure that the weapon is deactivated before return to the vendor to render it incapable of being discharged. Section 8 of the Firearms (Amendment) Act 1988 details the procedures to be followed. These include that the weapon be provided with a mark made by a body approved by the Secretary of State for that purpose. Presently, the two approved bodies are the Master, Wardens and Society of the Mystery of Gunmakers of the City of London and the Guardians of the Birmingham Proof House or the Rifle Range at Small Heath, Birmingham.

Whilst the auctioneer remains in possession of a firearm or ammunition it is an offence to fail to take reasonable care of such; moreover, it is an offence to fail to report its loss or theft forthwith to the police.[55]

Antiques

Excepted from the rigours of this regulatory statute are antique firearms. Section 58(2) of the Firearms Act 1968 provides: 'Nothing in this Act

---

[54] See *Dennant v Skinner and Collom* [1948] 2 KB 164, [1948] 2 All ER 29.
[55] s 14(1) Firearms (Amendment) Act 1988.

relating to firearms shall apply to an antique firearm which is sold, transferred, purchased, acquired or possessed as a curiosity or ornament.' Thus it would not be an offence to sell an antique firearm for that purpose to a person who failed to produce the requisite certificate, but there are several problems with this exemption.

Honest belief irrelevant

It has been held that s 1 of the Firearms Act 1968 creates an absolute offence. That is to say that if the prosecution proves that a person has in his possession what is in fact a firearm, as defined in s 57 of the Act, then he is guilty of the offence regardless of whether he knew it was such a proscribed weapon.[56] In *R v Howells*,[57] the defendant was charged and convicted of offences under s 1 in respect of a number of firearms including a Colt.31 muzzle-loading percussion revolver which he had bought from a gun dealer as a genuine 1860 Colt. He argued, inter alia, that his conviction was wrong in that the judge had failed to direct the jury that it was a defence to a charge under s 1 if the appellant reasonably and honestly believed the firearm to be an antique and he possessed it as a curiosity or ornament. On this point the Court of Appeal upheld that conviction. The argument that the exemption provided by s 58(2)[58] was necessary to protect *bona fide* dealers and collectors of antique firearms, and that it would be substantially lost if a collector who was the genuine victim of a fake could not escape liability by showing that he honestly and reasonably believed it was an antique, was rejected by the court. Brown LJ said:[59]

This sub-section relates to facts and not beliefs; what is excluded is that which is an antique which is sold or possessed as a curiosity or ornament. There is no room, in our opinion, for any other exclusions such as those firearms that are believed by the possessor to be antiques.

The court took the view that the intention of Parliament in passing this legislation was to provide an absolute prohibition against the possession of lethal firearms without proper authority, and that to allow in a defence of honest belief that the firearm was an antique would defeat this intention.

Although in this case we were concerned with a s 1 offence of possession, the same arguments apply to the offences of sale etc contained in s 3.

---

[56] See *R v Hussain* [1981] 2 All ER 287, [1981] 1 WLR 416, CA; *R v Howells* [1977] QB 614; [1977] 3 All ER 417, CA.

[57] See n 56 above.   [58] This subsection is reproduced above.

[59] [1977] QB 614 at 620, CA.

What is an antique?

Age

If then, whatever the state of mind or belief of an auctioneer, it is an offence to sell or transfer a firearm but there is a defence only if it is, in fact, an antique, it becomes crucially important to determine what is an antique.

Unfortunately Parliament has not seen fit to define an antique, and the judges have been loth to do so themselves. In *Richards v Curwen*[60] a defendant was charged with offences relating to his possession of two revolvers which he bought as antiques and hung on his living-room walls as ornaments. He possessed no firearms certificate for either of them. One revolver was German and had been manufactured sometime after 1891. It could be fired if the hammer was hit hard. The other was Belgian, made after 1893 and was in poor condition but could be rendered capable of being fired. The case against him was brought in 1975 but he was acquitted by the magistrates on the ground that the firearms were antiques and possessed as a curiosity or ornament. The prosecutor appealed but the Divisional Court dismissed the appeal, failing to find that the magistrates had approached the matter improperly. The proper approach in deciding whether a particular item was or was not an antique was, said the court, to recognise that it is 'a question of fact and degree in all the circumstances of the case'.[61] Referring to a dictionary definition might have been of some limited assistance, but essentially it was a matter to be decided by the magistrates or the jury charged with the responsibility of adjudicating upon matters of fact. The judges declined to lay down what age a firearm had to be before it could be regarded as an antique. These weapons were not more than 83 and 85 years old and the court did not accept that to be antiques they needed to be 100 years old.[62]

Decisions holding firearms of that age as antiques must be treated with some caution. They cannot simply be cited as precedents in subsequent cases. In *Bennet v Brown*,[63] the Divisional Court did not disturb a finding by magistrates that a revolver dated circa 1886 was an antique. But it must be stressed that in all these appeals the court's duty was to see whether the tribunal of fact had reached a conclusion properly and the court would only overturn it if it was felt that no reasonable bench or jury could come to that conclusion. It does not by any means follow that the court approved the finding or would itself have found the same way.[64]

[60] [1977] 3 All ER 426, [1977] 1 WLR 747.
[61] [1977] 3 All ER 426 at 430, [1977] 1 WLR 747 at 750, per Wien J.
[62] Although it was recognised that, in auctions of furniture and china, that is generally the test.
[63] (1980) 71 Cr App Rep 109, DC.
[64] See *Bennett v Brown* (1980) 71 Cr App Rep 109, DC, especially per Eveleigh J at 112.

Firing ability

In *Richards v Curwen*[65] both the weapons were capable of being fired. It was suggested by the prosecution that such weapons should not be regarded as antiques. This negative partial definition had been provided in s2 of the Pistols Act 1903, a forerunner of the present Firearms Act but dropped in the Firearms Acts of 1920, 1937 and 1968. In the light of this it was not felt appropriate to adopt such a criterion.

However, usability did feature in the test of antiquity in the subsequent case of *Bennett v Brown*,[66] where the items in question were a post-1905 Mauser rifle in working order and a Mauser pistol, circa 1910, modified but capable of firing a .22 cartridge. The defendant was a genuine collector and it was found that he had these weapons for ornament. The only question was whether they were antiques. Eveleigh LJ observed:[67]

But turning to the weaponry in the present case, what does one find? One finds that the rifle was manufactured post 1905 and the pistol 1910 onwards. Both of these weapons therefore could rightly be envisaged as weapons used in the 1914–1918 war. That I think is not drawing upon any particular judicial knowledge but upon public and general knowledge. One would not expect an army to be equipped with weapons that were only manufactured some six or seven years before the war and would expect even modern armies to use weapons of much greater age than seven, eight or ten years. It seems that it would be quite impossible to say that any weapon that could reasonably be envisaged as available for use in a war in this century could be properly regarded as an antique.[68]

I therefore am of the opinion that the evidence does not support the conclusion that the 8 mm rifle and the Mauser self-loading pistol were antique within the meaning of section 58(2).

Watkins J went further:[69]

Justices must feel entitled to receive practical guidance upon such a difficult matter as whether a firearm is deemed to be of the description antique within the meaning of that word as it is used in the Firearms Act 1968. Whilst it is not possible to be of specific assistance, which can be applied generally when asked a question of the kind that is asked in the instant case, I think this court should be able to say if not what does, then what does not make good sense in attempting to define the word antique. Thus I am prepared to say that no reasonable bench of justices could conclude, regardless of whether or not a firearm could be used in a war at any time, that a firearm which has been manufactured during this century is an antique. To that limited extent I offer with humility some assistance to justices who will continue to be faced with difficulty when called upon to decide the seemingly insoluble problem created by Parliament.

---

[65] [1977] 3 All ER 426, [1977] 1 WLR 747.   [66] (1980) 71 Cr App Rep 109.
[67] (1980) 71 Cr App Rep 109 at 112.
[68] It would seem that this particular limitation is of diminishing significance.
[69] See n 67, above.

In the absence of a willingness on the part either of Parliament or of the courts to grasp this particular nettle, there is little of a positive nature which can be said about identification of antiques in this area; if it is 100 years old it will be; if it is close to that age it may be; if it has been manufactured this century it apparently will not be; and perhaps, its continuing usability as a weapon of war will militate against it being an antique. But it must be reiterated that every case will depend on its own facts and circumstances and expert evidence will be crucial. There is some burden on the defendant to raise the issue that he bought them as antiques but thereafter it is for the prosecution to establish, beyond a reasonable doubt, that they are, in fact, not antiques.[70]

'As a curiosity or ornament'

It will have been seen that for s 58(2) of the Firearms Act 1968 to afford a defence, the firearm must not only be antique but must be possessed, or as far as auctioneers are concerned, sold, as a curiosity or ornament. In *R v Howells* the judge at first instance said to the jury:[71]

Now I'm not going to attempt to go to a dictionary and define for you what keeping something as a curiosity means and what keeping something as an ornament means. I am going to assume that you know perfectly well what it means.

It is obvious that this involves a subjective element and auctioneers might be well advised to stipulate expressly with antique firearms that they are sold for those purposes only.

Other offensive weapons

The 1988 Act details a host of other offensive weapons which it is an offence to sell, hire, lend, import etc.[72] The list includes swordsticks and knives and a number of somewhat exotic oriental martial arts weapons; it also includes more prosaic items such as knuckle-dusters.

There is a general defence in relation to antiques which are simply defined as those over 100 years old at the date of the offence.

OTHER OFFENCES

There is a number of other statutes which create offences relating to the sale of substances or goods which may be harmful.

---

[70] *R v Burke* (1978) 67 Cr App Rep 220, CA.   [71] [1977] QB 614, CA, at 619.

[72] The list is provided by SI 1988/2019 made under the Criminal Justice Act 1988 s 141(2).

These include:

(a) The Food Safety Act 1990, s 8 — sale of food rendered unfit for human consumption.
(b) Agriculture Act 1970, s 73A — sale of material for use as a feeding stuff which is discovered to be unwholesome or dangerous to animals or human beings.
(c) Medicines Act 1968, ss 52 and 53 — proscribing the retailing of drugs.
(d) Safety requirements under (primarily) the Consumer Protection Act 1987 and a large number of Safety Regulations made under the 1987 Act (or earlier legislation) or, as with the General Product Safety Regulations discussed below, under the European Communities Act 1972. These are so extensive that they need to be discussed separately.

SELLING UNSAFE GOODS

In the first edition of this work it was possible to deal with this topic in a few lines which referred the reader briefly to the Consumer Protection Act 1961 and the Consumer Safety Act 1978, and ended with the warning that 'this area of consumer safety law is under review and standards of safety are likely to be tightened up.' There was also the all too prescient statement that the regulations made under this legislation posed potentially a very serious threat to the legality of sales of a wide variety of elderly 'household clutter'.

Alarm was caused in professional circles in 1991 by the report of a prosecution of a firm of auctioneers in Suffolk by the Suffolk County Council who charged them with supplying by auction a second-hand Hoover 'Junior' vacuum cleaner which was not safe in that live parts were accessible, contrary to the Low Voltage Electrical Equipment (Safety) Regulations 1989, SI 1989/728. The firm was fined £500 with costs of £263, having pleaded guilty.

Another recent prosecution, attracting a large fine, has been reported of an auctioneer infringing the Gas Cooking Appliances (Safety) Regulations 1989, SI 1989/149 which are so widely drafted as now to persuade many auctioneers to refuse to accept gas appliances from consignors. These Regulations are two sets of many made under s 11 of the Consumer Protection Act 1987.

Accordingly, one of the professional bodies took counsel's opinion on the seriousness of the threat to the activities of general auctioneers posed by contemporary safety regulations. Counsel gave a written opinion in which he considered the auctioneer's civil liability under Part I of the Consumer

Protection Act 1987 (which imposes strict liability for damage caused by defective products on a wide range of people) and also *criminal* liability under Part II of the 1987 Act for supplying goods which do not comply with the 'General Safety Requirement' there laid down.

This chapter deals with criminal rather than civil liability, but since counsel considered both, the opportunity can be taken of warning auctioneers that in certain, and rather unusual, circumstances the auctioneer might be sued for civil damages by a person subsequently injured by goods sold through the auctioneer. The auctioneer would be liable as 'supplier', but the liability of the supplier under Part I of the 1987 Act is secondary to that of a 'producer', a producer being first in the firing line. This secondary liability is only assumed under s 2(3) of the Act if the auctioneer is unable to meet a request by the plaintiff to name the 'producer' of the goods sold. Because of the technical wording of the relevant provision under the Act, the 'producer' is not normally simply the auctioneer's principal but more likely the manufacturer or importer. This potential risk can be mitigated, as counsel points out, by taking an indemnity from the vendor to cover all claims made against the auctioneer under Part I of the 1987 Act.

Criminal liability is not so easily sidestepped and this needs more comprehensive treatment. The discussion is best followed by realising that there are three possible routes by which a person can attract criminal liability for supplying unsafe goods. These are:

(1) Under Part II of the 1987 Act for supplying goods which do not comply with the 'General Safety Requirement';
(2) Under Safety Regulations made under s 11 of the 1987 Act — in practice the most comprehensive set of prohibitions, and
(3) By contravening the Product Safety Regulations 1994 which implement the EC Directive on General Product Safety (92/59/EEC) and made under s 2(2) of the European Communities Act 1972.

Each will be taken in turn.

The General Safety Requirement under the 1987 Act

In order to deal with the problem that there will always be some goods which, though unsafe, do not actually infringe any specific regulations (because regulations cannot be totally comprehensive) s 10 of the 1987 Act makes it a criminal offence for a person to supply, offer or agree to supply or expose or possess any consumer goods 'which fail to comply with the general safety requirement'. 'Consumer goods' are defined, in subsection (7) as goods ordinarily intended for private use and consumption, but excluding a few specified products such as water, food and motor vehicles.

(These are likely to be covered by other statutes.) Consumer goods will fail to comply with the General Safety Requirement if they are not reasonably safe having regard to all the circumstances including the manner in which and purposes for which they are marketed, their get up, use or marks, instructions and warnings, any published safety standards and the existence of reasonable means for making the goods safer. The section is wide in its scope and is not limited to where there are published standards or where regulations exist.

From the auctioneer's point of view there is one critical exclusion. This is that under s 10(4)(c) it is a defence for a person to show that the terms on which he supplied the goods indicated that the goods were not supplied or to be supplied as new goods. Accordingly, provided the catalogue or, presumably, general circumstances of the sale, amount to an indication that the goods are not being supplied as 'new', there can be no breach of the General Safety Requirement. Whilst the word 'new' is not defined in the Act it is normally taken to be the opposite of 'used'. It is, therefore, only auctions of unused goods, for instance on a liquidation sale, where there remains potential liability on the auctioneer to ensure that, insofar as they are 'consumer goods', those goods comply with the General Safety Requirement as indicated above.

Safety regulations

Safety Regulations themselves do not provide for contravening them to be an offence — see s 11(4). But s 12(1) provides that 'where safety regulations prohibit a person from supplying or offering or agreeing to supply any goods or from exposing or possessing any goods for supply, that person shall be guilty of an offence if he contravenes the prohibition'. Section 39(1) provides a due diligence defence which has been much tested in the courts and which can involve methodical compliance checking, if necessary by way of comprehensive sample, of the goods in question by properly trained staff.

Safety regulations under the 1987 Act and its predecessors are now legion. A list of those most likely to be met together with a summary of their content is contained at the end of this chapter. We have already seen, above, how an auctioneer can easily infringe the Low Voltage Regulations by selling a vacuum cleaner with exposed electrical parts. There are also Regulations dealing with, for instance, toys, ceramics and upholstered furniture, all ostensibly goods commonly consigned to the auction room. It should be particularly appreciated that there is no exemption under the Regulations for goods which are not supplied as 'new'. Whether deliberately or otherwise the Regulations cover all goods in the category specified, whether new or used.

   The only material exclusion is under s 46 of the 1987 Act which states that references in Part VI of the Act (as discussed above) to 'supplying goods' do not include sales to a professional repairer or reconditioner of goods of these description or, by section 46(7)(b), apply to 'a sale of articles as scrap (that is to say, for the value of materials included in the articles rather than the value of the articles themselves).' Some auctioneers have apparently been advised of this 'loophole' by Trading Standards Officers, but if any reliance is to be placed on it evidence will without doubt be needed, either from the catalogue description, or if there is no catalogue, by an overt indication from the rostrum, that the offending article is explicitly sold 'as scrap'.

   What can an auctioneer do to mitigate the possibility of infringing the criminal law in these prolix areas? Firstly, an auctioneer making a practice of selling goods in a particular category, such as electrical goods, upholstered furniture or toys should have the Regulations themselves scrutinised to see whether there are any deliberate 'loopholes' in the legislation. For instance, some Regulations may exempt goods made before a specific date from the full rigour of the compositional requirements, for example upholstered furniture manufactured before 1950, but this can only be ascertained from the text of the Regulations. Secondly it is now becoming widespread practice in the case of, for instance, second-hand electrical goods to require them to be tested by a qualified electrician under the auctioneer's auspices before sale. The electrician should be able to ascertain whether the Regulations are likely to be breached in selling the item and even if this does not occur it is likely that the defence of due diligence would be available in these circumstances. Testing costs a small amount (£4 is currently a typical charge) and this can be passed on to the vendor through the Conditions of Sale or consignment. It is in any event a small price to pay for the protection against possible criminal liability to which the auctioneer is potentially exposed. In the case of other goods, for example, ceramics, it is not possible to make them safe in this manner. The purpose of the protective legislation is to prevent the possibility of consumers coming into contact with harmful substances such as lead. But, of course, antique ceramic ware cannot by definition have been made to comply with safety standards laid down in recent years but, on the other hand, antique ceramics are not excluded from the ambit of the Regulations. The problem was therefore put informally to the Department of Trade and Industry on behalf of one of the professional bodies. The Department stated in writing as follows.[73]

The advice of our lawyers is that antiques are excluded if at the time of supply (rather than when manufactured) they are not intended to come into contact with

[73] This letter is dated 15 June 1992.

foodstuffs. Moreover, the word 'intended' carries an objective meaning, so that goods will be excluded from the 1988 Regulations if at the time of supply no reasonable person would intend them to be used in contact with foodstuffs. In the view of our lawyers the 1988 Regulations clearly cannot have been intended to interfere with the trade in decorated or collectable antiques.

Though the above advice is informal, it may provide a valuable clue to the attitude which is taken, or should be taken, by the prosecuting authorities. Unfortunately it is not possible to state with certainty that all 'antique' glass and ceramics are unlikely to come into contact with food — some buyers might use them for that very purpose. But it is probably sustainable as a general argument that most buyers would buy antiques for display rather than for use and it is on this somewhat tenuous basis that an argument could be mounted that Regulations of this sort do not apply to 'antiques', despite the lack of any express exclusion in the Regulations themselves. Equally, such an implicit exemption could not cover sales of general household clutter where no reasonable person could classify an infringing item as an 'antique' or collectable.

In the light of the uncertainties the only advice that can be given to auctioneers of general household chattels is to consult with their local Trading Standards Office (the enforcement authority) and seek advice. Usually such advice is readily forthcoming and in the occasional case where Trading Standards Officers prove obstructive or unhelpful an approach to a local councillor can often achieve a change of attitude. None of this is any substitute for a better drafted framework for these Regulations which should give proper thought to the exclusion of goods of a certain age when sold by auction in these circumstances. After all, even the most extreme view draws back from making it an offence to own or possess (for enjoyment) infringing articles. To prohibit their sale on, for example, the death of the owner is a serious infringement of property rights, justifiable only if the goods posed a general threat to health or safety, such as a defective gas stove which could explode.

General Product Safety Regulations 1994

In the light of the General Safety Requirement discussed above there might be some surprise that there is a new and additional 'General Safety Requirement' laid down under the 1994 Regulations. This is because the UK was required to implement the General Product Safety Directive (92/59/EEC) and the UK's existing legislation did not quite meet all the requirements of the EU. These Regulations, SI 1994/2328, came into force on 3 October 1994.

The Regulations have two principal effects which are:

(1) to require producers to place only safe products on the market, 'The General Safety Requirement';
(2) to require distributors not to supply products which do not comply with that General Safety Requirement.

Auctioneers are most likely to be concerned with the second of these two principles. This is particularly so as the requirements apply to all products intended for consumers or likely to be used by consumers, whether new, used or reconditioned.

How does the new 'General Safety Requirement' differ from that imposed under the 1987 Act discussed above? The answer is that the application of the new General Safety Requirement is wider because the 1987 Act duty contains a number of sectoral exclusions and does not apply to second-hand goods. Nevertheless, overlap is largely avoided because the Product Safety Regulations 1994 made under the Directive exclude products insofar as they are covered by other Community safety legislation (including the Regulations discussed above), and the Directive does not apply to second-hand products *sold* as antiques or for the purposes of repair or reconditioning.

The duty of a distributor such as an auctioneer is to act with due care in order to help to ensure compliance with the General Safety Requirement and not to supply products that fail to comply with the Requirement. There is the usual due diligence defence.

The interesting exception, referred to above, in favour of 'second-hand products supplied as antiques' (see reg 3(a)) should be particularly noted by auctioneers. Presumably if a catalogue legitimately describes, expressly or by implication, a particular lot as an antique, no question under these 1994 Regulations will arise. It is debatable how far a general condition in the catalogue that all goods are supplied as antiques unless the contrary is stipulated would be held to be an effective exclusion.

Summary of selected Safety Regulations

Regulations made under the Consumer Protection Act 1987

The Benzene in Toys (Safety) Regulations 1987, SI 1987/2116. These regulations prohibit the supply of toys, including balloon-making kits, which contain benzene exceeding the specified concentration.

The Ceramic Ware (Safety) Regulation 1988, SI 1988/1647. These regulations replace earlier regulations and require ceramic ware to satisfy the requirements of BS 6748:1986 concerning the permissible release of lead and cadmium from ceramic ware for use with food.

The Gas Cooking Appliances (Safety) Regulations 1989, SI 1989/149.

These regulations prohibit the supply etc of gas cookers which do not comply with either the requirements specified in the regulations or European Standard EN 30 or BSS 5386: Part 3:1980 or Part 4:1983. The requirements relate to such matters as the safety of burners, surface temperatures of the appliances, the heat emitted from them, the thickness of glass doors, lids etc, and the stability of appliances. There are also provisions covering instructions and warnings to be issued. The Secretary of State may approve amendments or revisions of the standards specified.

The Low Voltage Electrical Equipment (Safety) Regulations 1989, SI 1989/728. These regulations, made under the European Communities Act 1972, s 2(2), apply to any electrical equipment designed or adapted for use with voltages of 50–1,000 (AC) and 75–1,500 (DC), unless excluded by Sch 1 or for export outside the EEC. Electrical equipment is required to be safe and to be made in accordance with engineering practice generally accepted as good within the EEC (reg 5). Compliance with certain harmonised standards, specified international safety provisions or, in the absence of these, with national safety provisions of a member state or with standards approved under the Approval of Safety Standards Regulations 1987[74] will suffice (reg 7). There is provision for the making and certification of goods (reg 10). Enforcement duties and time limits for prosecution are also included.

The Toys (Safety) Regulations 1989, SI 1989/1275.[75] These regulations, made under the European Communities Act 1972, s 2(2), replace the Toys (Safety) Regulations 1974[76] and are designed to provide for the safety of toys by applying European safety standards. The regulations apply to toys other than those supplied for the first time in the Community before 1 January 1990 and not bearing an EC mark (reg 2). Toys are defined in reg 3 as being products or materials designed or clearly intended for use in play by children under 14, providing they are not excluded by Sch 3 which covers, for example, fashion jewellery for children and toy steam engines. Toys are required to satisfy the essential safety requirements as specified in Sch 2. This may be achieved by either compliance with relevant national standards of any Member State and carrying the EC mark (the symbol CE) (reg 5) or compliance with EC-type examination certificates together with the EC mark (reg 6). Provisions are included for approving bodies to test toys (reg 7), application procedures for EC-type examinations certificates (reg 8), for requiring EC marks to be applied (reg 9), for information to be made available by manufacturers and Community importers (reg 12) and for enforcement and prosecutions (regs 13 and 14).

---

[74] SI 1987/1911, see above.
[75] See further 'Toy safety — too important to play around with?' D W Jenkins (1987) 1 *Fair Trader*, Pt 12 p 16; 'Toy safety in the EC' S Weatherill (1989) 86 L S Gaz No 42, p 30; *The Single Market Standards: Toy Safety*, DTI, 1989. See now SI 1995/204.   [76] SI 1974/1367, see below.

Heating Appliances (Fireguards) (Safety) Regulations 1991, SI 1991/
2693. These regulations revoke earlier regulations and impose requirements relating to gas fires and oil heaters. Fireguards may either comply
with BS 1945:1971 or with standards published in EC member states of an
equivalent level of safety.

Summary of selection of current regulations made under the Consumer Protection Act 1961

Regulations made under the Consumer Protection Act 1961 which were
still in force on 1 October 1987 continued to apply as if made under section
11 of the 1987 Act. Those still remaining are as follows.

Stands for Carry-Cots (Safety) Regulations 1966, SI 1966/1610. Carry-cot
stands must have a durable label attached showing maximum length and
width of the carry-cot to be accommodated. The regulations then specify
that the stand should conform to various specifications (eg that the base
shall be wider than the width of the carry-cot and at least as long as 3/4 of
the length of the carry-cot as specified on the label, and the underside must
be not more than 17″ above floor-level, and withstand 60 lb pressure for 12
hours without distortion). (Separate Regulations cover safety of perambu-
lators and pushchairs.)

Electrical Appliances (Colour Code) Regulations 1969, SI 1969/310
(amended by SI 1970/811 and SI 1977/931). The main provision of these
Regulations is that in the case of domestic electrical appliances containing
a mains lead with three wires, these wires must be coloured green and
yellow (earth), brown (live wire) and blue (neutral). A label must be attached explaining the code. This requirement continues indefinitely.

Cooking Utensils (Safety) Regulations 1972, SI 1972/1957. Cooking utensils designed to come into contact with food must not have a metallic
coating containing more than 20 parts in 10,000 of lead content.

Pencils and Graphic Instrument (Safety) Regulation 1974, SI 1974/226.
These Regulations control the proportion of poisonous metals in any part
of pencils, pens and small paint brushes and other writing or drawing
instruments.

Toys (Safety) Regulations 1974, SI 1974/1367. The main features of these
Regulations are (1) that toys (other than table tennis balls) must not be
made of flammable cellulose nitrate; (2) that the paint must not contain
more than a minute specified limit of lead, arsenic, soluble antimony,
barium, mercury, cadmium or chromium; (3) electrical toys must operate at
not more than 24 volts from a separate transformer; (4) pile fabric must not
be inflammable; (5) metal edges and points must generally be protected; (6)
facial features of dolls etc must be safely fastened or embedded, and (7)
plastic bags must be either too thick to cling to a child's face or have a

narrow opening of less than 190 mm dimensions. Although these regulations are repealed by the Toys (Safety) Regulations 1989 (see above), they still apply to toys supplied for the first time in the European Community before 1 January 1990 and which do not bear the EC Mark.

Oil Heaters (Safety) Regulations 1977, SI 1977/167. These Regulations impose controls (based on a re-draft of British Standard 3300) on domestic oil heaters as regards the amount of carbon monoxide emitted, the amount of fuel escaping from overturned heaters, the control of the flame, draught resistance, the performance of the heater when tilted and other matters relating to design, construction and performance. A warning must be affixed to the heater in respect of possible misuses. Tests must be carried out by organisations authorised by the Secretary of State.

Oil Lamps (Safety) Regulations 1979, SI 1979/1125. These Regulations deal with the safe construction and use of domestic paraffin burning oil lamps. Certain warnings and instructions are to be given eg 'Warning: Use only Paraffin', and detailed tests and specifications are laid down to ensure a lamp's strength and safety in use.

The Pedal Bicycles (Safety) Regulations 1984, SI 1984/145 (amended by SI 1984/1057). These Regulations prohibit the supply etc of two-wheeled pedal cycles which are not constructed or adapted for mechanical propulsion unless they comply with BS 6102 Parts 1 and 2 or are of an equivalent standard. Parts for use in two-wheeled pedal cycles must also comply with the British Standard or be of an equivalent standard.

The Asbestos Products (Safety) Regulations 1985, SI 1985/2042 (amended by SI 1987/1979). These Regulations prohibit the supply etc of crocidolite asbestos minerals (blue asbestos) or amosite minerals (brown asbestos) or products containing such minerals other than for research and development or analysis (reg 2). Certain exceptions are made for torque convertors and brake bands for cars containing crocidolite providing warning labels are attached. By reg 3 the supply of further specified asbestos minerals is prohibited unless labelled in accordance with the Schedule to the regulations and, in the case of products specified in reg 4 (eg toys, paints and varnishes), any supply of those specified minerals is prohibited.

Plugs and Sockets etc (Safety) Regulations 1987, SI 1987/603. These Regulations prohibit the supply etc of specified electrical devices such as plugs, sockets, adaptors and fuse links which do not comply with the regulations. The main requirements are conformity with appropriate British Standards or approval by specified persons eg BEAB and BSI. Certain devices specified in reg 3 and Sch 1 are exempted and there are provisions for the granting, refusal, alteration and cancellation of approvals (regs 7 and 8). In addition there are information requirements specified in reg 9.

Bunk Beds (Entrapment Hazards) (Safety) Regulations 1987, SI 1987/1337. These Regulations prohibit the supply etc of bunk beds where there is a risk of a child under six becoming trapped in any part of it, thereby risking strangulation or injury. The Regulations specify permissible gaps between sleeping surfaces and parts of the structure, the Schedule detailing how such gaps are to measured.

Sales of Land by Auction or Tender

AUCTIONS

PRACTICE AND PROCEDURE

The sale of land by auction poses quite different problems of law and practice to those arising in chattel sales.[1] This is partly because a sale of land which is commenced by an auction has to be dovetailed into standard conveyancing practice. Conveyancing practice involves far more careful preliminary enquiries and, usually, much more attention to the details of the description, than in the case of an auction of chattels.

The preliminary decision as to whether to sell land by auction or otherwise involves economic criteria which are outlined in chapter 1. Common cases are sales of investment 'ground rents' (ie the reversion on long leases), commercial property the value of which has to be realised because of liquidation or some other economic imperative and domestic property repossessed by mortgagees or needing realisation because it is the house of an employee relocated by his employer. And where the market is booming (which tends to happen cyclically) an auction may be the only way of establishing and obtaining in hand the market value of a popular property. Further, as remarked at the beginning of this book, auctions tend to work best when the total payable on the day by the buyer is the hammer price and no more. This largely remains the case with land auctions where buyers' premiums are not usually charged and the problems of VAT on goods, by definition, do not arise. This chapter will proceed on the basis that the vendor has accepted the advice of his agent that the most effective way of realizing the value of the land to be sold is by selling it at auction.

So far as the auctioneer is concerned, the preparation for the auction will not be dissimilar to the preparation of land sold by private treaty. Particulars of the land (including, of course, any buildings thereon) to be sold will be carefully prepared for dissemination to all those expressing an interest. The auctioneer will communicate with the solicitor for the vendor who will be charged with the drawing up of the contract. The contract will usually incorporate the Standard Conditions of Sale which are examined later. The successful bidder will normally be required to sign the contract, or possibly

---

[1] See Clive Carpenter and Susan Harris (ed.) *Property Auctions*, (1988) Estates Gazette.

have it signed on his behalf as also explained later, and the transaction then proceeds in a similar way to sales of land by private treaty.

It must be appreciated that the sale of land by auction poses particular problems for potential purchasers. These stem from the fact that the purchaser will not have known whether he has been successful until the auction is held. Meanwhile he must be prepared for the consequences of a successful bid. This will involve, normally, making all the standard local searches preceding the signing of a binding contract and, of course, ensuring that the finance is available for the purchase. It is, therefore, usually impracticable for a purchaser to proceed with a purchase by auction where he is still relying on the possible sale of his existing property unless he is prepared to effect bridging facilities through his bank. This, in itself, can attract heavy, and if the existing property is difficult to sell, perhaps ultimately unsupportable, interest charges. Furthermore many purchasers of domestic property will be dependent upon the provision of a mortgage, and it is not always easy to secure the offer of a mortgage before it is known whether the potential mortgagor has been successful in the auction. It is also not unknown for vendors to use Conditions of Sale far less beneficial to purchasers than those in private treaty sales, perhaps on the theory that at supposedly 'knock-down' auction prices 'punters' will not be so fussy about the normal searching property enquiries and readier to buy a 'pig in a poke'.[2] This policy will ultimately prove counter-productive to the wider use of the auction for land sales and it is strongly suggested that it is high time for the relevant professional bodies of the legal and estate agents' professions to get together and produce a code of practice which removes the danger of abuse by the vendor of the purchaser's position at auction. The vendor and his auctioneer must take these factors into account when deciding whether to employ the auction as the best means of sale.

Some steps can be taken in practice to ease the path of the potential purchaser. For instance, it is quite common for the vendor's solicitors to effect a local search of the vendor's property before the auction and to make the result of this available to potential purchasers. Similarly, standard enquiries before contract may be answered on a pro-forma basis. Occasionally the standard form of contract for land auctions incorporates a provision allowing the purchaser to make his local searches after the auction and rescind if the certificate of search discloses adverse entries which have not been revealed as special conditions in the contract. There is no reason why a survey commissioned by the vendor, and including a timber survey, should not be open for inspection. It has even occurred that a 'Property Title Report' is produced (as a somewhat speculative venture) by an inde-

---

[2] See also B Thornell and G Murphy, 'The Hammer goes down' Law Soc Gaz 91 (1994, 4 May) 19, which reveals some horrifying risks to purchasers including the possibility of damaging special conditions being revealed for the first time when read out at the auction!

pendent solicitor detailing problem areas.[3] However, conveyancing practitioners acting for potential buyers view auctions less than enthusiastically owing to the strong possibility of wasting their time and their client's money on carrying out work which turns out to be fruitless.[4] There are also dangers in acting for vendors. In *Warboys v Cartwrights*[5] it was held that a solicitor who failed to warn his client clearly enough of the danger of incompatible completion dates when the client's existing property was to be sold by auction and the new property purchased by private treaty was negligent.

The auction itself is normally either held on the property to be sold or at premises designated by the auctioneer. The vendor's solicitor will normally be present in order to answer any enquiries which may be made as to the accuracy or completeness of the particulars drawn up by the auctioneer or arising out of General or Special Conditions. It is not normal current practice, as used to be the case, for the whole Conditions to be read out before the auction takes place. It is assumed that all potential purchasers have perused the documentation and, if necessary, obtained a copy of it.

In practice the formal contractual document for sale of land is prepared in duplicate: one copy will be signed by the purchaser and the other, already prepared, will have been signed by the vendor or the auctioneer as his agent though, as explained below, signing is no longer necessary. The purchaser's particulars and the purchase price will, of course, have to be inserted where the documents have been prepared in advance and, in accordance with standard conveyancing practice, the documents are exchanged when signed. The General Conditions applicable to the sale normally state that a ten per cent deposit is payable by the purchaser whose personal cheque is normally necessarily accepted on the occasion. Well drawn Conditions will spell out the consequences if the cheque is dishonoured.

GENERAL STATUTORY REQUIREMENTS

The Law of Property (Miscellaneous Provisions) Act 1989

The former law contained an almost universal requirement that the existence of a properly formed memorandum in writing was essential for there to be an enforcable contract of sale in the case of land. This requirement stemmed from s 40 of the Law of Property Act 1925 (replacing the Statute of Frauds 1677, s 4). Section 40(1) of the Law of Property Act 1925, however, so far as material, provided as follows:

---

[3] See G Murphy and B Thornell, 'Reducing the risk on residential lots' (1993, Aug 14) EG 36. Query, though, whether this might not put the solicitor under an unacceptably wide potential liability for negligence.

[4] See P H Halstead 'Auctions: Suggested Code of Practice' (1984) Law Soc Gaz 2357.

[5] [1992] EGCS 110, Ch D.

No action may be brought upon any contract for the sale or other disposition of land or any interest in land, unless the agreement upon which such action is brought, or some memorandum or note thereof is in writing, and signed by the party to be charged or by some other person thereunto by him lawfully authorised.

When the Law Commission, in its examination of Transfers of Land and Formalities for Contracts for Sale etc of Land (Law Com No 164, 1987), reviewed auction sales, it came to the following conclusions (omitting footnotes):

The present law and practice at auctions is that the vendor and purchaser become contractually bound at the fall of the hammer and that the auctioneer signs a memorandum of the terms of the sale as soon as possible after the sale takes place. He signs as agent of the vendor and may do so also for the purchaser (ie if not ready, able or willing to sign for himself). Thus the requirements of section 40 are fulfilled. The auctioneer's authority to sign cannot be withdrawn or revoked by the vendor or the purchaser after the fall of the hammer. If sales by auction were to be included in our new provisions, there would be no contract at all until the auctioneer had signed, so that it might be open to either party to withdraw. Special provisions could have been devised to ensure that this would not happen, but these would have to be quite complex to ensure that auctions would not become legally hazardous. On further reflection we have decided that it is not necessary to insist on writing to validate a contract made at auction. The present situation where a contract is made at the fall of the hammer has caused no difficulties. We appreciate that the effect of our recommendation is that it will no longer be necessary for any written memorandum to come into being. However, at present the memorandum can come into existence and may be signed without actually involving the parties themselves. It is thus not a formality which necessarily serves the function of warning people what they are doing or making sure they understand the importance of the contract. There is little doubt that in the vast majority of cases the terms of the contract will continue to be put into writing, and if they were not, the courts would readily decide any dispute as to terms as they do now with other oral contracts. However, we propose confining this exception to public auctions since other forms of auction would still seem to call for the protective functions of formalities.

The penultimate sentence of the above perhaps underestimates the difficulties which would arise were the terms of a contract for the sale of land by public auction *not* put into writing. It is open to considerable doubt as to how far the courts would 'readily decide any dispute as to terms' in the far more complex field of transactions in land. Nevertheless, the Law Commission's recommendations were duly incorporated into s2 of the Law of Property (Miscellaneous Provisions) Act 1989. This section (reproduced in Appendix 2) replaced s40 of the Law of Property Act 1925 and instead contains a general requirement that contracts for the sale of interests in land can only be made in writing and only by incorporating, expressly or by reference, all the terms which the parties have expressly agreed in one document or, where contracts are exchanged, in each. This provision removed many of the technicalities associated with litigation on the scope and effect of the former s 40. However, s 2(5) of the Act states 'This section does not apply in relation to — . . . (b) A contract made in the course of a public auction'. The effect of this provision is clearly to abolish any requirement of writing in the case of land sales by public auction. The sale is therefore completed on the fall of the hammer, as with chattels.

However, this does not begin to address some of the difficulties which would arise were there to be no written statement of the terms applying to a specific contract for the sale of land at a public auction. The Law Commission obviously envisaged that there would normally be such a document, although the *signing* of it is no longer required. Nevertheless, a signature virtually eliminates any possible argument as to notice of these written terms and is highly desirable for this reason.

In these circumstances, two possible sets of clauses to be inserted in the statement of written terms, usually in the catalogue, might be envisaged. Firstly, it is perhaps possible to take the view that the contract formed at the fall of the hammer is simply a contract by the vendor to enter into a written contract in the traditional form and by the purchaser to sign that written contract. If this solution is preferred, the General Conditions of Sale in the catalogue or the Particulars of Sale of a specific property will need to include a term along the following lines:

(a) In inviting bids the Vendor is not inviting offers to buy but only offers to enter into a written contract for the purchase of the property described in the particulars on the terms of these provisions and by accepting a bid the Vendor only undertakes to enter into a written contract to sell the property to the bidder in the form prepared and available for inspection and at the price bid.

(b) If after his successful bid the bidder does not then immediately give his name and address to the auctioneer and then sign a written contract (or sign and exchange an identical copy) the Vendor may either require the auctioneer to sign such contract on behalf of that bidder (who by making a bid so irrevocably authorises the auctioneer so to act) or may withdraw his offer and end any obligation to contract with the bidder.

(c) Where the bidder acts for a principal whose identity has not been stated in writing to the auctioneer before the bidding starts or is not so stated after the bid so as to enable it to be included in the contract to be signed the vendor may treat the bidder as acting personally.[6]

Alternatively, and perhaps more simply, the catalogue or particulars could contain a term or 'notice' printed in the catalogue (as is used by one eminent auctioneering firm) requiring the buyer after the hammer has fallen to supply his name and address and sign a prepared standard form contract, along the following lines:

---

[6] See *Precedents for the Conveyancer*, 19–49, and commentary thereon. The form in the text differs in some respects from that precedent.

(1) The property is sold subject to the condition that immediately after the property is knocked down to him the successful bidder shall give to the auctioneer his name and address or, where he is acting as agent, the name and address of the principal on whose behalf he has bid and shall immediately sign on his own behalf or on behalf of any such principal a memorandum setting out the agreed terms and conditions subject to which the bid and acceptance thereof are made and property is to be conveyed to the buyer on the Standard Conditions (which includes the obligation to pay a ten per cent deposit).
(2) Any failure to comply with the above condition shall entitle the auctioneer on behalf of the vendor to treat the contract as repudiated and to put up the property for sale again or withdraw it or to take action against the said bidder to enforce the contract.
(3) Any person bidding should be deemed to have read and accepted these terms and the Standard Conditions referred to above.

It will be seen that in either event the effect is to require the buyer to sign a written contract of sale, incorporating the Standard Conditions (unless some variant is used) and all the Special Conditions specifically applicable to the property, and which is prepared and ready for signature (once the details of price and identity are known) at the time of the sale. This aspect is considered further below.

Sale of Land by Auction Act 1867

This venerable and somewhat obscure statute is discussed in detail in chapter 6.[7] It will be recalled that the mischief against which it was aimed was the possible fraud committed on a purchaser where the vendor of land attended the auction and bid for the property without disclosing his intention of doing so. Alternatively, and perhaps with a little more subtlety, the vendor might employ a puffer to inflate the price on his behalf.

The Act, as will have been seen from the discussion in chapter 6 cannot be regarded as a model of draftsmanship in its attempt at controlling the use of bidding by or on behalf of the vendor. However, the paucity of cases within the last 50 years on the 1867 Act seems to suggest that the obvious incompetence of its draftsmanship has not caused significant problems in practice. This is no doubt attributable to the widespread use of General Conditions of Sale which cater for the Act's provisions satisfactorily.

GENERAL CONDITIONS OF SALE AS TO THE CONDUCT OF LAND AUCTIONS

Where, as is standard practice, the auction of land is by reference to the Standard Conditions of Sale, constituting an amalgam of the formerly

---

[7] See p 185 above.

widely used National Conditions of Sale and the Law Society's General Conditions of Sale, these contain provision for the general conduct of the auction. It follows that there is no need for the auctioneer to have his separate *conditions*, although it is good practice to make it clear in the *particulars* of the property that the sale will be subject to the stipulated General and Special Conditions of Sale in the pro-forma contract[8] and also to announce this at the commencement of the auction. This is because there are some provisions in the above-mentioned General Conditions of Sale which apply to all bidders whether successful or not. The remainder of the contractual document will, however, only bind the purchaser.[9]

The relevant Standard General Conditions are as follows:

2.3 Auctions

2.3.1 On a sale by auction the following conditions apply to the property and, if it is sold in lots, to each lot.

2.3.2 The sale is subject to a reserve price.

2.3.3 The seller, or a person on his behalf, may bid up to the reserve price.

2.3.4 The auctioneer may refuse any bid.

2.3.5 If there is a dispute about a bid, the auctioneer may resolve the dispute or restart the auction at the last undisputed bid.

With regard to these Standard General Conditions, the following points should be noted.

The auctioneer has the right to refuse any bid. In the case of a dispute about a bid, the auctioneer may resolve the dispute or again put up the property at the last undisputed bid. The formerly quite widely used National Conditions, 1(4), gave the auctioneer the option of withdrawing the property but this right is omitted from the Standard Conditions. For what constitutes a 'dispute about a bid' see *Richards v Phillips*[9] discussed elsewhere in this book.

It is specifically stipulated that the sale is subject to a reserve price and

---

[8] A typical clause in the auctioneer's particulars might run: The property will, unless previously withdrawn, be sold subject to General and Special Conditions of Sale which may be inspected during usual office hours at the offices of the vendor's solicitors and the Auctioneers, during the seven days (excluding Saturday and Sunday) immediately before the day of the auction. The Conditions of Sale may also be inspected in the Sale Room but they will not then be read out. Purchasers shall be deemed to have notice of each Condition and all bidders to have bid on the basis that they have inspected the said Conditions (whether they have in fact done so or not). Failure to distinguish between the auctioneer's particulars, which are primarily for information only, and the contract which, apart from the specific General Conditions dealing with the conduct of the auction, is binding but only on the highest accepted bidder, causes some confusion in practice. The clause suggested in the passage above must be given contractual effect as regards *all* bidders if the two complementary documents are to be properly linked. Yet some auctioneers' particulars specifically deny that they constitute 'an offer or a contract'. The clause in the preceding footnote must in fact, be construed as a collateral contract with all bidders.

[9] [1969] 1 Ch 39.

the right to bid up to the reserve price is reserved to the vendor or his agent. The contract being complete on the fall of the hammer, there is no longer any need for the Condition to require the buyer to sign the contract forthwith, though as will be shown below there is considerable merit in maintaining the essence of the former practice and by a special stipulation binding on all bidders require the successful bidder to sign the prepared memorandum which would in circumstances other than the sale of land by public auction constitute the contract.

The Standard Conditions do not contain a clause prohibiting retraction of bids, perhaps because of academic debate as to whether such a provision would contractually bind all bidders. If all bidders were aware of this type of stipulation, however, and in effect were permitted by the auctioneer to participate in the bidding on that basis, there seems little doubt that it would bind.

As may be inferred from above, the deposit of ten per cent of the purchase price is paid by the purchaser on making the contract. Condition 2.2.1 of the Standard Conditions requires this and implicitly allows the public auction buyer to pay (exceptionally) by personal cheque. The Condition also implies that it is normally paid to the vendor's solicitor as stakeholder — see Condition 2.2.3.

The Standard Conditions contain specific provision for errors, misstatements or omissions with regard to descriptions of the property. These conditions are considered specifically under the next heading.

PROBLEMS REGARDING MISREPRESENTATION AND MISDESCRIPTIONS

MISREPRESENTATIONS PRIOR TO THE SALE

As already indicated, in a typical auction-sale of land, particulars of sale will have been prepared initially by the auctioneer. The function of these is to advertise the property to all potential purchasers and the particulars will essentially contain a description of the property, including a detailed description of buildings on the property, facilities and services enjoyed by the property and any other general remarks which may or may not be statements of fact rather than opinion. More often than not the particulars are accompanied by a photograph of the property (showing it in its best light on a sunny day).[10] The difference between land auctions and chattel auctions is that the description of the property which is formally the subject of the sale will not be in the auctioneer's particulars but in the contract normally

---

[10] A misleading photograph can give rise to liability — see *Atlantic Estates v Ezekiel* [1991] EGCS 54 and *St Marylebone Property Co Ltd v Payne* [1994] EG 156 (discussed below).

prepared by the vendor's solicitors. The contractual description of the land will normally be taken from the documents of title. It will not describe in detail the buildings on the land but will, or should, define the area of land to be sold accurately and deal with such matters as the grant and reservation of easements over neighbouring land. The contract will also reveal all matters which under general conveyancing law must be revealed to the purchaser relating to latent defects, incumbrances etc; and, since the auctioneer will not normally include these in his own particulars, it is good practice for the auctioneer's particulars to cross-refer to the more detailed description in the draft contract.

With regard to the auctioneer's particulars, potential liability exists if there is a factual statement which misrepresents the position. In this connection there have been many cases in the law of contract on the difference between a statement of opinion (or 'puff') and a statement of fact. Thus, describing land as 'uncommonly rich watermeadow'[11] or as 'fertile and improvable'[12] were held to be expressions of opinion only. Particulars for the sale of land, whether by private treaty or auction, are renowned for eulogistic descriptions of the property to be sold. The usual type of phrase such as 'a most desirable property' or 'a substantial and convenient dwelling-house' are all likely to be held as merely puffs.[13] However, where the statement is essentially factual, such as that the property is in good repair[14] or, as in the well-known case of *Smith v Land and House Property Corpn*[15] where a hotel was sold by auction and described as let to 'a most desirable tenant' (the tenant being in arrears with rent and generally undesirable), the Court of Appeal held that the purchasers were entitled to rescind the contract, the description being one of fact rather than one of opinion. There was an implicit assertion that nothing had occurred which could be regarded as rendering the tenant undesirable.[16]

In addition to this civil liability, the Property Misdescriptions Act 1991 now imposes criminal liability on the selling agent. It is an offence under s 1 to make a false or misleading statement about a prescribed matter in the course of an estate agency or property development business, otherwise than in providing conveyancing services. 'Prescribed matters' include false or misleading statements as to aspect, view, outlook, or environment, proximity to amenities, size, physical characteristics and history, including age. But the making of such a statement does not affect the validity of the underlying contract and does not give rise to civil (as opposed to criminal) liability.

---

[11] *Scott v Hanson* (1829) 1 Russ & M 128.
[12] *Dimmock v Hallett* (1866) 2 Ch App 21, 36 LJ Ch 146.
[13] See *Johnson v Smart* (1860) 2 Giff 151, 2 LT 307; *Watson v Burton* [1956] 3 All ER 929.
[14] See *Dyer v Hargrove* (1805) 10 Ves 505.   [15] (1884) 28 ChD 7, 51 LT 718.
[16] An 'opinion' implies that the representor believes it to be soundly based. If the 'opinion' is not really held at all, it would give rise to an actionable misrepresentation.

Misrepresentations prior to the sale can also be made by inaccurate replies to the standard form Enquiries Before Contract, submitted by the purchaser's solicitors to the vendor's solicitors. As has been mentioned, it is normal practice to issue interested potential purchasers with prepared forms containing answers to the standard enquiries. This variation from private-treaty sales does not appear to affect the contractual situation, in that anyone proceeding to purchase the property and having been induced to do so by misrepresentations of fact would be in the same position here as if the sale had been by private treaty.

The law of contract governs the situation where a material misrepresentation has been made, and a full discussion of this topic is outside the scope of this book. Suffice it to say here that where a representation is made which is a false statement of fact by one party to the contract to the other, and which does not technically form a term of that contract, but in whole or in part induces the person to whom it is made to enter into the contract, the law permits two remedies. Whether the misrepresentation is fraudulent, negligent or, more commonly, innocent, the purchaser may normally exercise the equitable remedy of rescission. In these circumstances the contract is in effect nullified and the parties returned to their former position. If the misrepresentation is fraudulent or, in some cases, negligent, the purchaser may in addition be entitled to damages. The common law position relating to misrepresentation generally has been radically altered as regards parties to the contract by the Misrepresentation Act 1967 (as amended)[17] and as to the position in tort of those making false statements on which others rely, by the decision of the House of Lords in *Hedley-Byrne & Co Ltd v Heller & Partners Ltd*.[18]

The implications of the *Hedley-Byrne* decision for professional people are wide. Thus, for instance, in *Yianni v Edwin Evans & Sons*[19] a surveyor negligently reported that a house was worth a certain sum of money. The report was to the purchaser's building society which offered to lend that amount of money for the purchase of the house and this was in fact worth much less. The property was subject to serious defects and the report of the surveyors was described by the judge as 'grossly incompetent and negligent'. It was held that the firm of surveyors in this case knew the purpose of their report to the building society and they had a duty of care to the buyers. Damages were awarded against the firm, related to the worth of remedial work (£8,000) which was required. Similar reasoning was employed by the House of Lords in fixing liability on the valuer in favour of the house purchaser in *Smith v Eric S. Bush (a firm)*.[20] The implications of this type of

---

[17] The relevant legislation can be found in Appendix 2.
[18] [1964] AC 465, [1963] 2 All ER 575, HL. See above, p 126f.
[19] [1982] QB 438, [1981] 3 All ER 592.
[20] [1990] 1 AC 831; and see the discussion in Harvey and Parry, *The Law of Consumer Protection and Fair Trading*, (4th edn) Ch 7.

development to auctioneers who make statements negligently to potential purchasers are obvious. Indeed, a case in the High Court of Ireland[21] decided that an auctioneer who misrepresented to the purchaser of leasehold land the price at which the freehold would be available was liable in tort (on *Hedley Byrne* principles) to that purchaser for the difference between the value of the land as bid and its lower, true value. But for present purposes, this part of this chapter will concentrate on the contractual position only and in particular the purchaser's right to rescind the contract as against the vendor through whom the misrepresentation has occurred, particularly where the vendor relies on some sort of disclaimer.

As an illustration of a simple misrepresentation made in the auctioneer's particulars of sale which was held to entitle the purchaser to rescind the sale, the decision of the Court of Appeal in *Brown v Raphael*[22] is helpful (though the facts do not involve a sale of real property). What occurred was that in a sale by auction held in 1955, lot 11 was described as an absolute reversion in a trust fund on the death of an annuitant who was 'believed to have no aggregable estate'. The significance of the latter words is that, at the time, whether or not the annuitant had an aggregable estate would affect the estate duty payable on the absolute reversion and hence its net value. The statement in question was made honestly by the solicitors for the vendor, but they had no reasonable grounds for so believing. Lord Evershed MR emphasised that the purchaser seeking to rescind must establish three things: first, he must show that the language relied upon does import or contain a representation of some material fact; second, he must show that the representation is untrue; and, third, he must show that in entering into the contract he was induced so to do in reliance upon it. The Court of Appeal went on to hold the purchaser entitled to rescind on the ground of an innocent misrepresentation. The statement was one obviously and vitally affecting the subject matter being offered and the vendor was in a far stronger position than the purchaser to ascertain the relevant facts; it must accordingly be imported into the representation that the vendor had reasonable grounds to support his belief. Accordingly the purchaser was entitled to rescind the contract.

Similarly in *Museprime Properties Ltd v Adhill Properties Ltd*[23] Scott J held that a false statement made in auction particulars that certain rentals were still open to negotiation (and this misrepresentation was compounded by an oral statement from the rostrum) entitled the purchaser to rescind the auction contract for misrepresentation.

It must be emphasised that the defendant will be the principal who has expressly or impliedly authorised the misrepresentation. The decision of

---

[21] See *McArney v Hanrahan* (1993) Irish Times, October 11. It is not clear why the purchaser sued in tort rather than contract. It was perhaps tied in with a claim (unsuccessful) for extra damages for mental distress.

[22] [1958] Ch 636, [1958] 2 All ER 79, CA.   [23] [1990] 36 EG 114.

Mustill J in *Resolute Maritime Inc v Nippon Kaiji Kyokai, The Skopas*[24] makes it clear that the agent in this situation incurs no personal liability under s2(1) of the Misrepresentation Act 1967 to the purchaser though he may be so liable in tort or for breach of a collateral warranty.[25]

Exclusion clauses and disclaimers

In modern practice it is common for both auctioneers' and estate agents' particulars and replies to enquiries by solicitors to contain written disclaimers of legal responsibility. Estate agents often use a form of disclaimer which runs in this way:

These Particulars do not constitute any part of an offer or contract and any intending purchaser must satisfy himself by inspection or otherwise as to the correctness of each of the statements contained herein. The vendor and his agents make or give no representation or warranty whatever in relation to this property and no responsibility can be taken for the statements contained in these Particulars which are not to be relied on as statements or representations of fact on the part of either of them.

Printed forms of enquiry sometimes used by solicitors contain a warning that the replies are believed to be correct though their accuracy is not guaranteed and the replies do not obviate the need for the purchaser to make appropriate searches, enquiries and inspections.

These disclaimers must now be read in the light of modern consumer protection legislation. The statutory provisions likely to be most applicable are contained in the Misrepresentation Act 1967, s3, and the Unfair Contract Terms Act 1977, ss2 and 11.[26]

We will take first the position where a misrepresentation is made prior to the contract by the auctioneer.

In these circumstances the vendor's first line of defence might well be to look at any disclaimer incorporated into his particulars. These might include a statement that 'neither the auctioneers nor any person in the employment of the auctioneers has any authority to make or give any representation or warranty in relation to these properties.'[27]

The validity of a somewhat similar disclaimer came before the High Court in *Overbrooke Estates Ltd v Glencombe Properties Ltd*.[28] The issue in this case was whether the disclaimer of authority in the particulars of sale

---

[24] [1983] 2 All ER 1, [1983] 1 WLR 857.   [25] On liability under these heads, see ch 5.
[26] These two sections are reproduced in Appendix 2.
[27] See a similar disclaimer published in October 1981 by the Royal Institution of Chartered Surveyors, reproduced in (1981) Conv 8006/3. The auctioneer's own possible liability under a collateral contract, as in *Shanklin Pier Ltd v Detel Products Ltd* [1951] 2 KB 854, [1951] 2 All ER 471, and a long line of subsequent cases, must also be borne in mind, as also liability for negligence.
[28] [1974] 3 All ER 511, [1974] 1 WLR 1335.

which stated that 'neither the auctioneers nor any person in the employment of the auctioneers has any authority to make or give any representation or warranty' was effective to negate liability for a misrepresentation which would have allowed the defendants to refuse to complete the purchase from the plaintiff-vendors. The misrepresentation alleged was that the defendants, who were the highest bidders at the auction, had asked the auctioneers questions about the development plans of the local authorities to which inaccurate replies had been made. Brightman J held that even if the allegations could be proved, the misrepresentations could not be relied upon. The auctioneers had effectively disclaimed their authority to make such statements. This was so despite the terms of s 3 of the Misrepresentation Act 1967 which, in its current version, runs as follows:[29]

3. If a contract contains a term which would exclude or restrict —
(a) Any liability to which a party to a contract may be subject by reason of any misrepresentation made by him before the contract was made; or
(b) Any remedy available to another party to the contract by reason of such misrepresentation,

that term shall be of no effect except in so far as it satisfies the requirement of reasonableness as stated in section 11(1) of the Unfair Contract Terms Act 1977; and it is for those claiming that the term satisfies the requirement to show that it does.

Brightman J went on to hold that the terms of s 3 of the Misrepresentation Act 1967 were not relevant since the disclaimer in question in the particulars did not 'exclude or restrict any liability'. The disclaimer merely imposed a limitation on the apparent authority of the auctioneers.[30] It should also be noted in this context that s 3 refers to terms in a 'contract'. Disclaimers in auctioneers' or estate agents' particulars are traditionally regarded as a preliminary to, and not a part of, the contract itself. Although Sch 1 of the Unfair Contract Terms Act 1977 excludes 'any contract' relating to the creation or transfer of an interest in land, the 'notice' or disclaimer of the type being discussed here by definition does not appear in a contract but in the preliminary particulars. It is therefore open to possible attack as a 'notice' attempting to exclude negligence liability under s 2 and would then have to comply with the definition of 'reasonableness' in the Unfair Contract Terms Act 1977.

---

[29] The decision in this case was based on an earlier version of s 3, but it is thought that the amendments would have made no difference. See also the similar decision in *Collins v Howell-Jones* (1980) 259 EG 331, CA. See also Murdoch (1981) LQR 522.

[30] This decision was made before the passing of the Unfair Contract Terms Act 1977. Section 2 of that Act refers to 'any contract term or to a notice' excluding or restricting liability for negligence. The decision in *The Skopas* [1983] 2 All ER 1, [1983] 1 WLR 857, discussed above, emphasises that the liability imposed by s 2(1) of the Misrepresentation Act 1967 (damages for innocent misrepresentation) attaches to the *principal* rather than to his authorised agent. An agent may be liable for negligence under the principle in *Hedley Byrne & Co Ltd v Heller & Partners Ltd* [1964] AC 465, [1963] 2 All ER 575, HL, and it is this liability against which any exemption clause will be aimed, as explained in the text.

Quite apart from the question of whether such disclaimers are caught by the Unfair Contract Terms Act 1977, it may be possible for the vendor to show, at the least, that the purchaser did not rely on the misrepresentation. Reliance is a necessary precondition of liability for misrepresentation, but it is for the vendor to show, if the misrepresentation was capable of inducing the contract, that the purchaser did not rely on it.[31] But, this apart, the courts now seen to take a more robust view of such defensive statements, the Court of Appeal in *Cremdean Properties Ltd v Nash*[32] going so far as to suggest that if an exclusion clause in auction particulars is not contractual, it would not help the vendor. If it were contractual, it would be caught by s 3 of the Misrepresentation Act 1967.

MISDESCRIPTIONS IN THE CONTRACT

The distinction between misrepresentations and misdescriptions has some-times been blurred by the courts,[33] but this distinction is that whereas a misrepresentation is made prior to, and induces, the contract, a misdescription is an error in the terms of the contract.[34] A number of cases in conveyancing law contain the situation where the contract itself misdescribes a property. As with misrepresentation, the purchaser potentially has the equitable remedy of rescission available to him in these circumstances.

Since we are now dealing with misdescriptions in the written part of the 'formal' contract, the blame for these will usually lie with the vendor's solicitors rather than the auctioneers. Admittedly the auctioneers, in their capacity as surveyors, may have drawn up an inaccurate plan for which, incidentally, separate liability may lie to the vendor (in contract) or to the purchaser (in tort, under the *Hedley Byrne* principle).[35] But the situation most likely to arise is where the contract contains some material misdescription, omission or error in respect of which the purchaser wishes to exercise his remedy of rescission and if the contractual description takes in, by implication, a photograph of the property taken by the auctioneer and this photograph, for example by the addition of arrows drawn to show the extent of the property, is inaccurate, the fault is obvious — though it must be remembered that the disappointed purchaser will sue the auction-eer's principal (ie the vendor) for rescission.[36]

---

[31] See eg *Smith v Chadwick* (1884) 9 App Cases 187, 196.

[32] [1977] EG 547. See also *St Marylebone Property Co Ltd v Payne* [1994] EG 156, discussed in more detail below.

[33] See *Laurence v Laccourt Holdings Ltd* [1978] 1 WLR 3; for a case of misdescription arising from the auction particulars, see *Watson v Burton* [1957] 1 WLR 19, below.

[34] See per Boggis QC in *St Marylebone Property Co Ltd v Payne* [1994] EG 156.

[35] Explained above, p 258.

[36] This is what occurred in *St Marylebone Property Ltd v Payne* [1994] EG 156. See also John Samson and Jonathan Radgick, 'Misdescription: vendors beware' (1995) EG 28 Jan., 1976.

A contract for the sale of land, unlike the more general particulars drawn up for all potential purchasers by the auctioneers, must be a precise document. The contract will normally contain at least the following matters:

(a) a physical description of the property with its boundaries;
(b) a statement as to the tenure of the property (ie freehold or leasehold, and if leasehold, with particulars of the terms of the lease);
(c) a statement of any easements or other appurtenant rights affecting the property;
(d) a statement as to incumbrances including easements, restrictive covenants and mortgages to which the property is subject;
(e) if the property is let, the terms of the lease subject to which the purchaser must take.

The vendor is under an obligation to prove that the identity of the property matches the description in the document of title. If there is a misdescription of the property, there will be a breach of contract in respect of which the purchaser may either rescind or claim compensation according to the seriousness of the misdescription. In addition, the vendor is under an obligation to disclose all latent defects in his title and in the property. An example of the latter might be a defect which renders the property valueless for the purpose for which the purchasers are likely to require it. It will be seen from this that the vendor is under the dual duty to avoid misdescribing the land and actively to disclose certain matters. Of these two duties, that of description is the most commonly broken. In *Flight v Booth* it was stated that[37]

where the description, although not proceeding from fraud, is in a material and substantial point so far affecting the subject matter of the contract that it may reasonably be supposed, but for the misdescription, the purchaser might never have entered the contract at all, in such a case the contract is voided altogether.

Thus if property is stated in the particulars in the contract to amount to approximately 3,920 square yards, but in fact contains only 2,360 square yards, a misstatement of the area to this extent namely 40 per cent, is likely to be held to be substantial. In *Watson v Burton*,[38] where similar facts arose, the vendor's action for specific performance was dismissed and judgment given for the purchaser for rescission and return of the deposit. Similarly, a misdescription of use such as 'valuable business premises' which was applied to business premises unusable for a number of ordinary trades was held not to be a fair description and to entitle the purchaser to rescission and recovery of the deposit.[39]

Having outlined the general law relating to misdescription and non-disclosure, it is now necessary to examine the position in the context of the auction-room.

[37] (1834) 1 Bing NC 370 at 377.   [38] [1956] 3 All ER 929, [1957] 1 WLR 19.
[39] *Charles Hunt Ltd v Palmer* [1931] 2 Ch 287, 100 LJ Ch 356.

ORAL ATTEMPTS TO MODIFY WRITTEN TERMS

As explained at the beginning of this chapter, it is common practice for the auctioneer and vendor's solicitor to invite questions about properties before they are actually auctioned. This raises the question of whether oral corrections of written terms are likely to be effective. The 'parol evidence' rule serves generally to exclude all evidence which adds to, varies or contradicts a written document. Thus in *Powell v Edmunds*[40] printed Conditions of Sale concerning timber growing in a certain close did not state anything about the quantity. It was held that parol evidence that the auctioneer at the time of sale warranted a certain quantity was not admissible, as varying the written contract.[41]

The practical lesson is that where variations or amendments are found to be desirable prior to the auction, the contract ought to be amended before the auction takes place. However, where this practice is not followed, the fact that the auctioneer or vendor's solicitor has corrected a misleading description or statement, and that the purchaser was aware of this correction, may enable the vendor fully to enforce the contract on the basis that the purchaser was not *induced* to sign the contract on the basis of a misrepresentation,[42] or that an ambiguity has been clarified orally so that the purchasers knew the facts.[43] Equally, the principle will work in reverse, for example when the auctioneer makes a mis-statement, or incorrectly modifies a written statement from the rostrum.[44]

Damping the sale

It is convenient here also briefly to discuss the practice known as '*damping the sale*'. This essentially consists of a bidder or bidders making audible derogatory statements or comments about the lot to be sold, prior to the bidding beginning. Although this can occur in any sale it is, in the authors' experience, more likely to happen in sales of land. This is because, normally, a specific opportunity is given to ask questions and it is not uncommon to find some of those present taking the opportunity of querying such

---

[40] (1810) 12 East 6.

[41] See also *Ogilvie v Foljambe* (1817) 3 Mer 53; *Heywood v Mallalieu* (1883) 25 Ch D 357, 53 LJ Ch 492.

[42] See *Farebrother v Gibson* (1875) 1 De G & J 602; contrast *Manser v Back* (1848) 6 Hare 443 and *Re Hare and O'More's Contract* [1901] 1 Ch 93, 70 LJ Ch 45, where, in neither case, was it thought equitable for the contract to be enforced against the purchaser since the purchaser did not hear or appreciate the corrections.

[43] *Re Edwards to Daniel Sykes & Co Ltd* (1890) 62 LT 445.

[44] See *Museprime Properties Ltd v Adhill Properties Ltd* [1990] EG 144, where Scott J also confirmed that the auctioneer had the vendor's authority to make statements about the rent level position.

matters as the status of the planning permission enjoyed by development land, the feasibility of access to that land, or the structural state of the property as contrasted with the description in the auction particulars. If this process results in either a sale at a price reduced from the true value or no sale at all, the vendor may have remedies.

Where there is a sale, but the purchaser has 'damped' it, he may not be entitled to the equitable remedy of a specific performance. Being a discretionary remedy, the plaintiff's conduct will be in issue, and it seems from the very elderly authorities on this matter that the conduct in question may fall short of actual fraud, though it must presumably be in some way unconscionable.[45]

If a person present maliciously makes statements which are untrue as to the vendor's property and consequently no sale results, the vendor has an action against him for the tort of malicious falsehood (or slander of title).[46] There seems no reason in principle why this should not also be the case where the property is sold at a proven depreciated price as a result of the public pronouncement of untrue and malicious statements or innunendoes.

It might be thought that an agreement between two interested potential purchasers not to bid against each other would be equivalent to 'damping' the sale, since the vendor is unlikely to get the same value as if there were unfettered competition. But it was clearly held in the more modern case of *Harrop v Thompson*[47] that this was not contrary to public policy as being in restraint of trade. In that case the plaintiff had agreed to buy the defendant's farm at a public auction, and applied to the court under RSC Ord 86 for specific performance of the agreement. The defendants resisted the application on the grounds that the plaintiff had acquired the farms cheaply because the plaintiff had agreed with a potential bidder that he should stay away from the auction. The court ruled that the plaintiff was entitled to specific performance, there being no vitiating factor as explained above. Even an agreement for a subsequent 'knock-out' sale has been held not to be illegal,[48] but if the parties to such an agreement are 'dealers' this principle must now be read subject to the Auctions (Bidding Agreements) Acts 1927 and 1969 and the right of the vendor to set such a sale aside for fraud.[49]

[45] See *Twining v Morrice* (1788) 2 Bro CC 326; *Manson v Armitage* (1806) 13 Ves 25; *Fuller v Abrahams* (1821) 3 Brod & Bing 116, 6 Moore CP 316 (a barge was stated by the plaintiff not to have been paid for).

[46] See *Mayer v Pluck* (1971) 223 EG 33, 219 (the defendant, who had unsuccessfully negotiated for the plaintiff's house, publicly asked the auctioneer if he knew the house was built on an underground stream and that the cellar was waterlogged).

[47] [1975] 2 All ER 94, [1975] 1 WLR 545.

[48] *Lepard v Litoun* (1897) 41 Sol Jo 545; *Rawlings v General Trading Co* [1921] 1 KB 635, 90 LJKB 404, CA.

[49] Discussed in ch 8.

WRITTEN STATEMENTS ATTEMPTING TO DISCLAIM MISREPRESENTATIONS AND MISDESCRIPTIONS

These must now be read in the light of s 3 of the Misrepresentation Act 1967 (already considered) and also the material provisions of the Unfair Contract Terms Act 1977. (The EC Directive on Unfair Terms in Consumer Contracts (93/13/EEC), which is discussed in detail in chapter 6, applies only to goods and services.)

As an illustration of the current position, the decision in *Walker v Boyle*[50] provides useful guidance. In that case the vendor of a property, in answering the usual preliminary enquiries before contract, stated to the purchaser that to the vendor's knowledge there were no disputes regarding the boundaries of the property. There was in fact a boundary dispute and the purchaser claimed rescission of the contract against the vendor. The vendor relied on Condition 17(1) of the National Conditions of Sale (19th edn) which then provided that 'no error, mis-statement or omission in any preliminary answer concerning the property . . . shall annul the sale'. Dillon J held that a vendor who made an innocent representation about his property when the true facts were within his knowledge was not entitled to rely on this condition, but even if Condition 17(1) were to apply, it would only exclude the vendor's liability for the misrepresentation if it satisfied the requirement of reasonableness[51] as set out in s 11(1) of the Unfair Contract Terms Act 1977: that 'the term shall have been a fair and reasonable one to be included having regard to the circumstances which were, or ought reasonably to have been, known to or in the contemplation of the parties when the contract was made.' It was held in this case that in all the circumstances Condition 17(1) (which was subsequently redrafted) did not satisfy the requirement of reasonableness. Furthermore, the standard warning on the preliminary enquiries form that the 'replies on behalf of the vendor are believed to be accurate but accuracy is not guaranteed and they do not obviate the need to make appropriate searches, enquiries and inspections' could not prevent the answers given on the form from being *representations of fact.*

Since this decision, Condition 7 of the Standard Conditions has been published. This states 'If any plan or statement in the contract or in the negotiations leading to it, is or was misleading or inaccurate due to an error or omission, the remedies available are as follows . . .' and 7.1.3. limits rescission to cases of fraud or recklessness unless the injured party would otherwise be obliged to accept, to his prejudice, property differing substantially in quantity, quality or tenure from what he was led to expect. For material errors of lesser degree damages may be available in other cases

---

[50] [1982] 1 All ER 634, [1982] 1 WLR 495.
[51] As required by s 3 of the Misrepresentation Act 1967 (see Appendix 2).

under 7.1.2. This statement reflects what the law would probably be if no attempt were made to disclaim liability and represents a substantial shift in favour of the purchaser when compared to earlier widely used conditions.

A further illustration of a purported disclaimer which became a casualty of s 3 of the Misrepresentation Act 1967 is illustrated by the decision of Croom-Johnson J in *South Western General Property Co Ltd v Marton*.[52] In 1979 the plaintiffs sold some land by auction to the defendant. The defendant's action was to rescind the contract on the grounds of innocent misrepresentation. The land was sold by description in the auctioneer's catalogue, lot 82 being described as 'long leasehold building land'. The particulars went on to imply that planning consent for the land had been refused. This was because the proposed development was out of character with the area. In fact it was unlikely that planning consent for a dwelling would ever be given on the site, as this would have been detrimental to visual amenities and to the character of a conservation area. Furthermore, by implication, various other conditions were incorporated into the contract similar to those then found in the Conditions of Sale of the Law Society and the National Conditions. Amongst these conditions was a statement that any error or omission found in the particulars or Conditions of Sale should not annul the sale or entitle the purchaser to be discharged from the purchase. There was a further condition which stated that all statements in the particulars were made without responsibility on the part of the auctioneers or the vendor and were statements of opinion and were not to be taken as or implying a statement or representation of fact and that any intending purchaser must satisfy himself by inspection or otherwise as to the correctness of each statement contained in the particulars.

In fact the purchaser, who was a builder, attended the auction at short notice. He acquired the catalogue only the day before. The only enquiries he made as to the property were informal ones at the auction (the effect of which, if any, the judge ignored).

In the event it was held that the particulars contained a false, though innocent, representation which had been acted upon by the purchaser. The various disclaimer clauses did not in the circumstances satisfy the requirement of reasonableness (as stated in s 11(1) of the Unfair Contract Terms Act 1977) as required by s 3 of the Misrepresentation Act 1967. The judge concluded:[53]

The words of s 11 of the Unfair Contract Terms Act are very wide. I have to deal with this contract, with the parties to this contract and the circumstances in which the contract was made. The conclusion I have come to is that the plaintiffs have not satisfied me that these are terms which are fair and reasonable and have been

[52] (1982) 263 EG 1090.   [53] (1982) 263 EG 1090 at 1092.

included in the contract between the plaintiffs and defendant at the time of the auction. These terms, if they were included, would exclude liability for the failure to tell the purchaser more than only a part of the facts which were among the most material to the whole contract of sale. In the result the plaintiffs are unable to rely upon the condition in the auctioneer's catalogue, and there must be judgment for the defendant [ie the purchaser].

It is not clear how far the facts of this case render the judge's conclusion generally applicable. Some weight appears to have been attached to 'the circumstances in which this contract was made' and these were unusual. The buyer does not normally enter into a contract for the sale of land, even by auction, at such very short notice and without making his own searches and enquiries. Had this purchaser done so it is conceivable that more weight might have been put on the relevant disclaimer clauses. Nevertheless, the case is a salutary warning that the prevailing tendency of the courts is to scrutinise carefully the reasonableness of such disclaimers and where the bargaining powers are unequal or the state of knowledge of the vendor is much greater than that of the purchaser, the court's sympathies seem to lie with the purchaser. The power to negate exclusion and disclaimer clauses is, as the learned judge points out, a very wide one. In practice, though, solicitors and auctioneers will no doubt take the view that nothing is lost by putting them in if in some circumstances they could remain effective.

As mentioned above, Standard Condition 7 (Second Edition, 1992) restores much more of an even balance between vendor and purchaser than was previously the case. It is arguable that it is declaratory of the existing law rather than an attempt to modify it. The only possible problem would seem to be where an error is regarded as non-fraudulent or reckless but *material* rather than *substantial*. Here the Condition seeks to limit the purchaser's remedy to damages rather than rescission. But some auctioneers continue to use far more vendor-biased liabilities for a wide range of blunders, perhaps on the basis that the auction atmosphere will attract purchasers who will take a gamble despite the 'small print' being legally hazardous.

These remarks gain some support from the circumstances of and decision in *St Marylebone Property Co Ltd v Payne*.[54] This case, transferred from the High Court to the County Court, involved the sale by auction of commercial property whose description relied partly on a photograph on which was endorsed a black line and two arrowheads, showing the lateral extent of the property and erroneously including a doorway. The professional buyer, who inspected the property externally only (from his car), satisfied the court that he would not have bought the property for the £190,000 in question, had he known the property's true dimensions. The contract contained the

[54] [1994] EG 156.

blanket exemption clauses of the sort described above, including one negating liability for arrows on photographs. The buyer brought an action for rescission and return of the 10 per cent deposit for misrepresentation, misdescription and under the court's general discretion to do justice in deposit disputes under s 49(2) of the Law of Property Act 1925.

Assistant Recorder Boggis QC in an exceptionally comprehensive judgment found that this amounted to a material misdescription which could not be excluded by an exemption clause. Insofar as the photograph also amounted to a misrepresentation, it was held that it did induce the contract and that the exclusion clauses were not fair and reasonable within s 11 of the Misrepresentation Act 1977. Repayment of the deposit was therefore ordered under s 49(2) of the 1925 Act.

TENDERS

PRACTICE AND PROCEDURE

The background and contractual situation where the sale of land takes place by tender has already been explained in chapter 1. That chapter also contains a brief description of the advantages and disadvantages of adopting this method of sale, and proceeds on the assumption that such sales are not by *public* auction and not therefore exempted from the formalities of the 1989 Act relating to a comprehensively written and signed contract.

Whilst there is no 'standard' procedure, the following describes the practice that is often adopted.

The auctioneers in this instance will fulfil approximately the same function as if the sale were at auction. In other words, their function is to disseminate the tender documents to all potential tenderers, and generally act as agents for the vendor. Tenders sent in reponse to the invitation to tender may either be sent to the auctioneers or to the vendor's solicitors or, in some cases, to the vendor direct. The auctioneers will be responsible for drawing up the tender documentation in conjunction with the vendor's solicitors. Essentially the transaction takes place in three stages. The first stage involves dissemination of the invitation to tender to all potential purchasers, notice being given therein that tenders must be submitted by a stipulated date. The second stage involves consideration of the tenders and notification of acceptance by the vendor to the successful tenderer by a further stipulated date. The third stage will be handled by the vendor's solicitors and will involve the normal post-contractual conveyancing procedure with completion taking place by a further stipulated date.

THE CONTENT OF TENDER DOCUMENTS[55]

The tender documentation — which is prepared by the auctioneers in conjunction with the vendor's solicitors — normally commences with a detailed description of the property. Particulars here will be similar to those involved in a sale by private treaty or by auction. Information with regard to services, rateable value, town planning, fixtures and fittings and viewing arrangements is normally included together with a standard disclaimer as to absence of responsibility for statements made in the particulars or as to the authority of the auctioneers to make or give warranties in relation to the property. The status of this type of disclaimer in a contract for the sale of land by tender was discussed by the Court of Appeal in *Cremdean Properties Ltd v Nash*,[56] and this case is discussed below. Accompanying the particulars prepared by the agents there will often be a detailed plan.

There then is likely to follow a statement of the conditions of tender and sale. The purpose of these conditions is to explain the procedure to be adopted for the sale. Standard Conditions of Tender will contain the following clauses:

(a) A condition that each tenderer will send his tender on the appropriate form. This will contain his name, address, the amount of his offer and other relevant details. The condition will also stipulate that the completed form must be placed in a sealed envelope and addressed to the stipulated recipient — ie the vendor's agent or the vendor personally. The envelope should be appropriately marked to make it clear that it is a tender, and if sent by post, it should be sent by recorded delivery. The condition also imposes the deadline by which tenders must have arrived — eg 'to arrive [at the stipulated address] at or before noon on the Tender Date' (the latter being defined as a particular date).

(b) The second condition may make specific provision for tenders being made jointly, in which case full names of those involved should be given; or where the tender is made on behalf of a company, the full name and registered office of the company should be stipulated. If made on behalf of a partnership, the tender should be signed by a duly authorised signatory. If an offer is made by an agent, he should be required to give the full name and address of his principal or principals as well as his own and it can be made clear that no tender will be accepted from undisclosed principals. The purpose of this condition is to give the vendor the fullest information as to the nature and standing of the potential purchaser.

---

[55] There is a convenient precedent in *The Conveyancer and Property Lawyer*, vol 2: *Precedents for the Conveyancer*, 16–24.

[56] (1977) 244 EG 547, CA.

(c) The next condition may stipulate that the amount tendered should be a fixed sum in sterling and not eg a reference to a stipulated amount above other offers.[57]

(d) As explained in chapter 1, the invitation to tender is not normally regarded as an offer. The vendor can therefore reserve the right not to accept a Tender, even though it be the highest bid. This condition may thus state: 'The Vendor does not undertake to accept the highest or any Tender'. In some circumstances the court will infer a contractual duty to consider all tenders.[58]

(e) The next condition may make arrangements for the payment of the deposit. This will normally be ten per cent of the amount of the tender payable by cheque or banker's draft. In the case of cheques it is wise to provide that the vendor may present the cheque prior to the date on which he undertakes to notify the successful bidder. If the cheque is not met upon first presentation, provision may be made for the vendor to reject the tender forthwith.

(f) Next, a condition is necessary to settle the situation with regard to notification of the successful tenderer. This condition will stipulate that by a certain date (usually approximately fourteen days after the deadline for tenders) the vendor or his agent will indicate acceptance of the tender to the successful tenderer by letter sent by recorded delivery at the address inserted in the tender form. The cheque or banker's draft accompanying the successful tender will then be retained by the vendor as a deposit on account of the purchase price in accordance with the above conditions. This condition will also stipulate that the cheques or banker's drafts of unsuccessful tenderers will then be returned forthwith.

(g) Finally, a condition should be inserted making it clear that each person who submits a tender is deemed to accept the Conditions of Tender and Sale contained in the documentation and to undertake that his tender will remain unvaried and open for acceptance until, and will not be withdrawn before, a stipulated time (usually two days) after the date specified for notification of the successful bid. Although there must be some doubt as to the validity of this provision in the absence of consideration supplied by the tenderer, it is conceivable it could be upheld as a collateral contract.

The next part of the document will contain the 'Conditions of Sale'. These will correspond to the Special Conditions inserted in normal standard form contracts for the sale of land, and will be prepared by the vendor's solicitors.

---

[57] 'If the offeror wishes to rule out referential bids, he should say so' — per Waller LJ in *Harvela v Royal Trust Co* [1985] 1 All ER 261 at 267.

[58] See *Blackpool & Fylde Aero Club Ltd v Blackpool Borough Council* [1990] 3 All ER 25, CA.

The Conditions will deal with such matters as the date for completion, the position if there is delay on completion, the title of the vendor to the property, the matters subject to which the property is sold and, often, a further disclaimer with regard to errors, omissions or misdescriptions of the property whether contained in the Conditions of Tender or of Sale. The Special Conditions will also normally indicate whether or not vacant possession is to be given on completion. The Conditions of Sale are then normally followed by a schedule describing the land by reference to its description in the documents of title. In addition it is normal practice to 'fill the gaps' by incorporating by reference one of the two standard sets of General Conditions discussed above, the contractual position being that these General Conditions will apply except in so far as they may be varied by the Special Conditions, here entitled 'Conditions of Sale'.

Finally, a form of tender attached to the documentation and returned by tenderers will be appended. This takes the form of a simple statement that 'the Tenderer hereby submits a Tender to purchase the [property in question], the Tender being in the sum of £ . . .' (usually in figures and words to avoid possible ambiguities) and a statement that a banker's draft or cheque for ten per cent of the sum tendered is enclosed.

It is wise also to append a formal acknowledgement that the tender is submitted in accordance with the 'Conditions of Tender and Sale' annexed. It is essential that the tender is signed by the tenderer and that it should contain his address and be dated. The form of tender should indicate to whom cheques or banker's drafts should be payable.

In principle the combination of the signed offer to purchase by the successful bidder together with the vendor's notification of acceptance will jointly comply with the requirements of s 2 of the Law of Property (Miscellaneous Provisions) Act 1989, which requires, in essence, each party to sign a document incorporating all the terms, expressly or by reference. There have been queries in practice as to whether either the vendor or purchaser may change his mind after this stage, but since there is from this stage onwards a binding contract (if the form discussed above is used), there can then be no question of going back. This point was reaffirmed by Goff J in *Michael Richards Properties Ltd v Corporation of Wardens of St Saviour's Parish Church, Southwark*[59] where the vendors mistakenly accepted the successful tender 'subject to contract'. Goff J rejected the latter words as meaningless. The learned judge emphasised that the tender documents set out all the terms of the contract and nothing further needed to be negotiated.

Mention was made above of the decision in *Cremdean Properties Ltd v Nash.*[60] The decision involved consideration of a tender, and the judge

[59] [1975] 3 All ER 416.
[60] (1977) 244 EG 547, CA. See also J. E. Adams [1981] Conv 326.

described at some length the documents involved which are similar to those described above.

The facts were that the appellants decided to sell an important block of property in Bristol for redevelopment mainly as offices, outline planning permission having been secured. The position was slightly complicated by the fact that there were two vendors; one was the owner of part of the property and the other was a body of trustees of a charity who owned the remaining part. They instructed agents jointly, and the agents invited prospective purchasers to tender for the whole block. The stipulated date by which tenders had to be received was 14 November 1973. On 13 November 1973 the plaintiffs put in a tender for £552,500, which was accepted. This represented the price based on values at the height of the then property boom. The acceptance of the plaintiffs' tender resulted in the conclusion of two separate contracts, the tendered sum being apportioned between the two vendors. One contract was completed by conveyance; the other contract (with the charity trustees) was never completed but this part of the action was compromised.

The plaintiffs claimed rescission of both contracts on the ground of misrepresentation. The misrepresentation alleged was that the agent's particulars described the property as consisting of 'approximately 17,900 square feet of offices, a new Church Hall and 8 car parking spaces'. The document also incorporated a plan. Two pages of the document were then headed 'Special Conditions of Sale by Tender' and these consisted of 18 numbered clauses and two schedules. A footnote to the Special Conditions of Sale by Tender read as follows:

Messrs . . . [the agents acting for the defendants in relation to the sale] for themselves, for the vendors or landlords whose agents they are give notice that (a) these particulars are prepared for the convenience of an intending purchaser or tenant and although they are believed to be correct their accuracy is not guaranteed and any error, omission or misdescription shall not annul the sale or be grounds on which compensation may be claimed and neither do they constitute any part of an offer of a contract; (b) any intending purchaser or tenant must satisfy himself by inspection or otherwise as to the correctness of each of the statements contained in these particulars.

The main issue in the case was the consequences of the alleged misrepresentation, in that the amount of office-space permitted was much less than the 17,900 square feet, in the light of the purported disclaimers. Bridge LJ stated that the statement in the Conditions of Sale that 'any error, omission or misdescription shall not annul the sale or be grounds on which compensation may be claimed' was nothing more or less than a purported exclusion of liability which would otherwise accrue on the ground of the misrepresentations in the statements to be found in the document. Bridge LJ regarded the decision in the *Overbrooke Estates Ltd* case[61] as not material to this issue. The agents had the full authority of their principals to say what they did in the document. As already discussed above, s 3 of the Misrepresentation Act 1967 makes any purported disclaimer of liability of this sort subject to a test of reasonableness.

The court was in fact concerned with trying the preliminary issue as to whether the existence of the condition in question conclusively negated any misrepresentation. The Court of Appeal rejected this view. Section 3 of the Misrepresentation Act 1967 applied to the purported disclaimer and at the trial proper the court would have to decide whether it was fair and reasonable to allow the defendants, in the circumstances of the case, to rely on their disclaimer.

The court also dealt with another problem. It is not always clear whether disclaimers such as these are part of the contract (as will normally be the case in tender documents) or merely a preliminary misrepresentation not being a term of the contract. Bridge LJ summarised the position in this case by saying that if the disclaimer was a term of the contract binding as between the parties, then it was a term which was counter to s 3 of the Act and therefore ineffective, unless the court trying the action thought it fair and reasonable to give it effect. If it was not part of the contract, then it was not binding on the purchaser and it would therefore not help the vendor in any case.

The issue in this case is of general importance in property sales, whether they take place by auction, tender or private treaty. It again emphasises the modern judicial tendency to view with great suspicion attempts by the vendor or his agents to disclaim responsibility for matters which are within their knowledge and within their power to control. If the purchaser is induced by a misrepresentation to enter into a contract, whether formed at an auction, as a result of a tender or by private treaty, s 3 of the Misrepresentation Act 1967 is a formidable hurdle for the vendor to jump, in so far as he hopes to rely on this type of disclaimer. Where sales of chattels are concerned, the same type of issue arises and is discussed in some detail in chapter 6.

[61] [1974] 3 All ER 511, [1974] 1 WLR 1335, discussed above.

10

Vehicle Auctions and Specialised Auctions of Other Property

VEHICLE AUCTIONS

Sales by auction of motor vehicles have rapidly increased in popularity in recent years. The biggest specialist car auctioneer in the UK, ADT Auctions Ltd, now produces an Annual Report, and specific information in this chapter has been provided by courtesy of that company. The 1994 Report shows that about 6.2 million second-hand vehicles were sold in 1993, and although vendors disposed of 44 per cent of these privately, 40 per cent by way of part-exchange to dealers and only 6 per cent were disposed of by auction, ADT (which operates auction centres in the USA and on the European mainland as well as in the UK) handled over 2.5 million vehicles in 1993, selling vehicles at the rate of one every 20 seconds of every business day. Vendors include motor dealers anxious to mitigate cash-flow difficulties by selling within a 90 day period, owners of fleet vehicles and private vendors. In addition to specialist auctioneers, non-specialist ones may find that, for instance, a deceased's chattels to be disposed of by auction include a car. Auctions of motor vehicles give rise to specific problems, whatever the status of the auctioneer. Some of these problems concern the laxity with which some Conditions of Sale are drawn up. Others concern possible infringements of the criminal law, particularly under s 75 of the Road Traffic Act 1988 (formerly s 60 of the Road Traffic Act 1972) (selling unroadworthy vehicles) or under s 1 of the Trade Descriptions Act 1968 (fully discussed in chapter 8).[1]

CONDITIONS OF SALE

The first consideration here is whether the Conditions bind the purchasers of the vehicles sold and bind bidders generally. The same considerations apply here as were fully discussed in chapter 6, and the party seeking to rely on the conditions will need to show that the actual or potential defendant has notice of the Conditions. Much will depend on the circumstances. For

---

[1] See Appendix 2 for the full text of these sections.

instance, it is quite common for less formal vehicle auctions to accept entries up to a few minutes before the start of the auction, not to issue catalogues (scarcely practicable in these circumstances) and to print Conditions of Sale on the *entry* form. This obviously does not as such affect buyers with notice of relevant protective and exclusion clauses unless the Conditions of Sale are also on prominent display at the auction site. It is also common to find Conditions affecting sellers (eg rates of commission) intermingled with Conditions of Sale affecting bidders and buyers. It is with the latter type of condition that problems of this character could arise; for example, a buyer purporting to reject an 'unsatisfactory', formerly 'unmerchantable' car where its 'merchantability' has been purportedlly excluded by a non-binding clause.

The content of the Conditions of Sale affecting *buyers* is dissimilar only in a few important details to conditions appropriate for the sale of chattels generally, but it is suggested that specific clauses should be added, namely:

(a) A clause giving purchasers the right to reject a materially defective vehicle purchased within one hour (or other appropriate time) of the sale of it to him *if* the vehicle is specifically sold by the auctioneer on 'pre-trial' terms. It is sensible to qualify the right to reject by excluding from consideration defects specifically revealed by the seller on the entry form.[2] Examples have been seen of very loosely-drawn clauses along these lines and used in practice, but it is nevertheless likely that disputes could arise, even with the above qualification, as to whether a vehicle is 'materially defective'. However, this phrase is an improvement on an unqualified right to reject 'trial before payment' cars, which gives ample scope for purchasers to reject for no good reason in law.

(b) A clause excluding all express and implied conditions and warranties relating to the vehicle. In some of the more sophisticated vehicle auctions intending purchasers can have the vehicle inspected by an engineer before bidding. This should largely remove the need for any guarantees by the seller who may or may not be in a position to have given them. The 'pre-trial' terms above would be similar in effect.

(c) A clause making it clear that any written or oral reference to the year of a motor vehicle refers to the date of its first registration in the UK. The reason for this is that there can be discrepancies between the date of manufacture and date of registration, the latter being the only date readily discoverable from the registration documents. There has been litigation under the Trade Descriptions Act 1968 on this point. Thus in

---

[2] The clause could thus run: 'The Purchaser shall have the right to reject vehicles specifically sold by the Auctioneer on "Pre-Trial" terms if found to be materially defective, such rejection taking place within one hour of the Purchaser's successful bid, except that there is no right to reject in respect of defects revealed on the Entry Form relating to a vehicle available for inspection by the Purchaser in advance.'

Routledge v Ansa Motors (Chester le Street) Ltd[3] a Ford manufactured in 1972 was converted into a caravanette and registered on 1 August 1975. In November 1975 it was sold and described as 'one used 1975 Ford Escort Fiesta'. In allowing an appeal against the justices' finding that there was no case to answer to a charge under ss 1 and 2(1)(h) of the Trade Descriptions Act 1968,[4] the court stated that the justices should have considered whether '1975' was likely to be taken as an indication of the *age* of the vehicle and if so whether this was false or misleading to a material degree under s 3 of the Trade Descriptions Act 1968.

(d) A clause making it clear that vehicles are sold with the benefit of any unexpired vehicle excise licences attached thereto and current MOT certificate relating thereto.

(e) A clause stating that the purchaser of any motor vehicle is responsible for complying with all legal requirements as to the roadworthiness, construction and use of that vehicle and for obtaining all certificates, permits or other authorisation necessary before that vehicle can be used on any road. The purpose of this clause is to mitigate the possibility of prosecution of the auctioneer for contravention of s 75 of the Road Traffic Act 1988, and for other legislative provisions requiring current excise licences, MOT certificates etc. The clause should be tied in with a clause on the entry form affecting sellers under which all sellers are required to warrant that, unless previously disclosed to the auctioneer, any vehicle consigned by the seller for sale is in a roadworthy condition and complies with the regulations made under s 41 of the Road Traffic Act 1988 (relating to construction and use). (An additional clause relating to the currency of licences will be required if the auctioneer or his staff will need to drive the vehicle on a highway.)

(f) A clause indemnifying the auctioneer against the cost of insurance, the desirability of which is explained below.

Some conditions refer to 'as seen' vehicles, for example Condition 7 of the standard ADT Auctions Conditions. The only assertion under this type of condition is that the vehicle has not been treated by an insurance company as a total loss. Otherwise all express or implied conditions as to age, description, fitness for purpose, merchantability or roadworthiness are excluded.

The discussion of the legality of this very broad disclaimer contained in chapter 6 will not be repeated here. Suffice it to say that such a clause is vulnerable to being held unreasonable under the Unfair Contract Terms Act 1977 or 'unfair' under the EC Directive.

Sellers should be required to confirm that the car is their own, unencumbered, property free from any hire-purchase agreement.

---

[3] (1979) 123 Sol Jo 735, [1980] RTR 1.   [4] See Appendix 2.

SOME SPECIAL FEATURES OF MOTOR AUCTIONS

Vehicle auctions seem to be the main type to employ the use of the 'provisional bid' which is in effect a fall-back procedure where a vehicle attracts a bid less than its reserve. The practice was examined in *RH Willis & Son v British Car Auctions Ltd*,[5] and during the course of his judgment Lord Denning MR described the provisional bid system as an established feature of the vehicle auction trade. The case also highlights problems of title to vehicles subject to hire-purchase agreements or not otherwise owned by the seller.

The facts were that RHW, the plaintiffs, were car dealers who 'sold' a car to C on hire-purchase terms, a deposit being paid. The hire-purchase agreement contained the usual warning that the goods could not be sold before all instalments were paid. Instead, C took the car to the defendant auctioneers BCA, with a reserve agreed of £450. The highest bid, made by W, was £410. BCA then contacted C, either by telephone or through their 'provisional bid office' and having ascertained that W would 'stand by' the bid of £410 (ie not withdraw it) asked C if he would accept it. C agreed provided BCA reduced their commission, which they did. The auctioneers checked with Hire Purchase Information (HPI)[6] who stated that no information was registered against that vehicle. The deal therefore went through, and shortly afterward C became bankrupt and the facts came to light.

The issue was whether the loss (the £275 balance on the hire-purchase agreement) should fall on RHW, the dealers, or BCA, the auctioneers. The auctioneers could only be liable if they had committed the tort of conversion.[7] Lord Denning had no doubt that under the present state of the law, sales under the hammer of goods to which the vendor has no title give rise to liability in conversion, on behalf of both the auctioneer and the buyer, to the true owner.[8] The question was whether a sale by 'provisional bid' was any different. The Court of Appeal was satisfied that it was not different. Decisive factors included the auctioneer's own evidence that the 'provisional bid' system was to facilitate sales 'because we are in commerce to make money and we are delighted if a sale can be agreed so that we can earn the negotiating fee'.[9] The court equated the negotiating fee with conventional commission. In addition, each purchaser under the 'provisional bid' system was required, under clause 20 of the relevant Conditions of Sale

---

[5] [1978] 2 All ER 392, [1978] 1 WLR 438, CA.

[6] HPI and the status of answers supplied by HPI to enquiries were discussed in *Moorgate Mercantile Co Ltd v Twitchings* [1977] AC 890, [1976] 2 All ER 641, HL; see also discussion in Harvey and Parry *Law of Consumer Protection and Fair Trading* (4th edn, 1992) Butterworths, ch 10.

[7] This aspect of *R H Willis & Son v British Car Auctions Ltd* [1978] 2 All ER 392, [1978] 1 WLR 438, CA, is discussed further in ch 5.

[8] See *Barker v Furlong* [1891] 2 Ch 172 at 181.   [9] [1978] 2 All ER 392 at 398.

for auctions, to pay £2 premium to an insurance company associated with the auctioneers against losses suffered through any defect in title of the seller. Since this was a system applying to hammer sales as well as provisional bid sales, the same consequences should ensue in either case. Lord Denning was particularly swayed by the policy point that the innocent acquirer (here, W) and the innocent handler (here, the auctioneers BCA) were both protected against claims by the true owner through the insurance policy 'so that the loss is not borne by any single individual but is spread through the community at large'.[10] But even if the vehicle auctioneer did not avail himself and purchasers of insurance protection, it is to be assumed that the provisional bid procedure would still be indistinguishable in its essential nature and legal consequences from sales under the hammer. The decision underlines the good sense of such auctioneers taking out insurance against the consequences of the vendor's vehicle having been stolen or being subject to an undischarged hire-purchase agreement, and purchasers at such sales checking that valid insurance exists.[11]

SELLING UNROADWORTHY CARS

Criminal liability

Criminal liability now depends on s 75 of the Road Traffic Act 1988 which makes it an offence for a person to supply vehicles in an unroadworthy condition or altered so as to be unroadworthy. (The word 'supply' is defined so as to cover selling, offering to sell or supply and to expose for sale.)

Section 75(6) excepts cases where the defendant proves

(a) that the vehicle was supplied for export from Great Britain or
(b) that he had reasonable cause to believe it would not be used on a road in Great Britain or would not be so used until it had been put into a condition in which it might lawfully be so used.

Section 75(6)(A) now imposes the additional obligation on sellers who expose for sale such vehicles in the course of a business to prove that they took all reasonable steps to make prospective purchasers aware that such use would be unlawful, or if offering to sell such vehicles, to ensure that the offeree was made aware of this fact before the defence in s 75(6)(b) (above

---

[10] [1978] 2 All ER 392 at 397.
[11] The court did not analyse the provisional bid procedure in terms of offer and acceptance, but presumably the 'provisional bid' is a conditional offer which must first be made unconditional by the buyer. The auctioneer then accepts or rejects it having received fresh instructions from the vendor. See also Condition 6 of ADT Auctions Standard Conditions which categorises this procedure as a private treaty sale.

— reasonable belief) can be used. This is a very important point for vehicle auctioneers to heed.

A number of points may be made about the above.

(a) In *British Car Auctions Ltd v Wright*[12] it was held that an auctioneer, when he stood on his rostrum, does not make an 'offer to sell' the goods in question; he merely invites those present at the auction to make offers to buy them. Accordingly the auctioneers were not guilty of an offence under the predecessor of this section, which referred to its being unlawful 'to sell, or to supply, or to offer to sell or supply' unroadworthy vehicles. The current legislation adds the significant words 'or to expose for sale'. Vehicles in the course of being auctioned are clearly exposed for sale. (The possiblity that the auctioneer had nevertheless 'sold' the car was not examined.)

(b) If an auctioneer does 'expose for sale' an unroadworthy vehicle, the offence is of 'strict liability'. Absence of knowledge of the defects is irrelevant.[13] The defence to the charge is likely to be under s 75(6)(B) of the Road Traffic Act 1988. The auctioneer must show that he had reasonable cause to believe that the vehicle would not be used on a road in Great Britain, or would not be so used until it had been put into a condition in which it might lawfully be so used. In this latter connection, a clause such as Condition (e) above (putting the onus on the purchaser to ensure that the vehicle is roadworthy before using it on any road) will be helpful. The question of whether the auctioneer did have 'reasonable cause to believe' involves satisfying the court that he did so actually believe and had reasonable cause so to do.[14] In addition, as explained above, business dealers are required to bring s 75(6)(A) unroadworthiness to the attention of prospective or actual purchasers.

(c) Section 75(7) of the Road Traffic Act 1988 (as amended) makes it clear that infringement of this section does not invalidate, by reason of illegality, any civil contract made between seller and buyer for the sale of the car. The purchaser will still be bound to pay the price, though in any consequential criminal proceedings the court has discretion to make a compensation order under s 35 of the Powers of Criminal Courts Act 1973 (as amended) in addition to or instead of a fine. Compensation is limited to £5,000 (in 1994) in magistrates' courts.

---

[12] [1972] 3 All ER 462, [1972] 1 WLR 1519, QBD, following *Fisher v Bell* [1961] 1 QB 394, [1960] 3 All ER 731 and *Partridge v Crittenden* [1968] 2 All ER 421, [1968] 1 WLR 1204. The more colloquial meaning was rejected in this particular context.

[13] *Sandford Motor Sales v Habgood* [1962] Crim LR 487; see also the note following the report which questions the Divisional Court's assumption that no mens rea is necessary in these circumstances. The question is whether the section's wording clearly or by implication rules out the requirement of guilty knowledge.

[14] See *Nakkuda Ali v M F de S Jayaratne* [1951] AC 56; *McArdle v Egan* (1933) 150 LT 412, 98 JP 103, CA; and *R v Harrison* [1938] 3 All ER 134, 159 LT 95.

(d) The offence is a summary one carrying a maximum fine of level 5 on the standard scale (see s 46(1) of the Criminal Justice Act 1982).

Civil liability

Contract

It is not proposed to repeat in detail here the analysis provided in chapter 6 of the conditions of fitness for purpose and satisfactory quality contained in s 14 of the Sale of Goods Act 1979 (as amended), and the validity of any clause attempting to exclude these implied terms. Suffice it to say that an unroadworthy car is, on the face of it, likely neither to be fit for the purpose of the buyer nor of satisfactory quality. But these statements must be qualified by re-emphasising that the term of satisfactory quality does not apply as regards defects first drawn to the buyer's attention, or as regards defects which ought to have been revealed on the examination made by the buyer; the condition as to fitness for purpose may equally not be implied if, for instance, the buyer's purpose is purely to buy the car for spares or to 'cannibalise' (see *Hurley v Dyke*,[15] discussed below).

Even if such a sale is in breach of one or both these terms, the Conditions of Sale are likely to contain an exemption clause. Assuming that this clause has been effectively brought to the notice of the buyer or is otherwise contractually binding, the buyer's only line of attack could be that the exemption clause does not satisfy the requirement of reasonableness as laid down by s 6 of the Unfair Contract Terms Act 1977 (discussed in chapter 6) or is 'unfair' under the regulations implementing the relevant EC directive also discussed in chapter 6.

Tort

Suppose that a buyer of a car at auction drives it away and is injured as a result of an accident caused by the car's unroadworthy condition. Most defendants would prefer to sue the seller on the basis of a breach of the implied terms in s 14 of the Sale of Goods Act 1979, as amended, since if a breach can be proved, the seller's liability is strict, ie there is no need to prove that the seller was negligent.[16]

However, as shown above, a contractually-based action may not be available to the plaintiff either because there is in fact no breach of contract or because there is no privity of contract between the buyer of the car who is injured and the seller at auction. This latter situation occurred in *Hurley v*

---

[15] [1979] RTR 265, HL.
[16] See *Randall v Newsom* (1876) 45 LJQB, 364; and generally, Harvey and Parry *Law of Consumer Protection and Fair Trading* (4th edn, 1992) Butterworths, ch 5.

Dyke[17] which is worth careful study in this area and will now be examined. It illustrates the possibilities of and limitations surrounding a possible action in tort against the seller, and this in turn can have implications for the auctioneer.

The facts were that D, a small-garage owner, bought a Reliant three-seater car from an owner when it broke down near his garage. He paid £10 for it (in 1971) and though it was obvious that the car was in very bad structural condition, the House of Lords found as a fact that the extent of D's knowledge of the defects was that he 'was aware of the very real danger of driving the car without further examination and the doing of any necessary repairs which that examination revealed'.[18]

Some days later, without any material work being done on the car, it was driven by D's mechanic to a local auction held by British Car Auctions Ltd. D also drove over and entered the car at a reserve of £40 and subject to the auctioneer's conditions. There was both an entry condition and Condition of Sale stipulating that vehicles offered 'as seen' or realising £200 or less 'are sold and bought for what they are and with all their faults' and all conditions and warranties were excluded. In addition, Condition of Sale 16(a) stipulated that if a vehicle sold was in a condition to make its use on the road unlawful 'there shall be deemed to be incorporated in the contract between the seller and the purchaser an undertaking on the part of the purchaser that it will not be used on a road until a valid Test Certificate has been obtained' or it was otherwise made roadworthy.

When the car was sold, the auctioneer repeated what was written on the entry form: namely, that it was sold 'As seen and with all its faults and without warranty'.

The car was knocked down to J for £40, J's intention being to cannibalise it. C had also attended the auction, but had been an unsuccessful bidder. But he succeeded in getting J to re-sell it to him (C) for a slightly enhanced price. Having driven the car apparently without serious incident for eight days, C was then involved in a catastrophic accident when the chassis snapped due to corrosion beneath the passenger seat. C was killed and the plaintiff, H, was seriously injured. H would have been entitled to claim £45,000 damages if he could show D was responsible in negligence (there being no passenger insurance). D would be liable for the tort of negligence if it could be shown that he was in breach of his duty of care to a foreseeable purchaser. Lord Denning had found D so liable in a dissenting judgment in the Court of Appeal,[19] the essence of his judgment being that (a) clearly a duty of care was owed, (b) D knew the car to be a 'death-trap' and (c) in these circumstances the auctioneer's warning was insufficient.

---

[17] [1979] RTR 265, HL.   [18] [1979] RTR 265, HL, at 302.
[19] [1979] RTR 265 at 276.

Although the House of Lords disagreed with Lord Denning (and Jones J at first instance) in finding D liable, there seems to have been general agreement at all levels that the vendor at an auction of an article which he knows to be dangerous owes a duty of care to potential buyers of the article.[20] The nub of the issue was whether D had discharged this duty of care by the giving of the warning at the auction. Having regard to the fact of D's limited knowledge of the fatal defect, the House of Lords held that he had.[21]

The hypothetical question then arises: what would the position have been if it could have been established that the seller knew the car to be dangerous? Both Viscount Dilhorne and Lord Scarman agreed that it should not be assumed that the seller had discharged such duty as lay upon him by selling it 'as seen and with all its faults and without warranty'.

Although the position of the *auctioneer* was nowhere discussed in this litigation, it is apparent that there is a strong likelihood of his incurring civil liability, jointly with the vendor or exclusively, in a variety of circumstances. For instance, if the auctioneer was *aware* of the dangerous condition of the vehicle and had not given any effective warning to the buyer, there seems no reason in principle why the buyer should not succeed against the auctioneer in negligence — a duty of care clearly exists in this situation, as explained in *Hurley v Dyke*.[22] An attempted negation of this duty of care via a Condition of Sale or notice would be nullified by s 2(1) of the Unfair Contract Terms Act 1977, which states: 'A person cannot by reference to any contract term or to a notice given to persons generally or to particular persons exclude or restrict his liability for death or personal injury resulting from negligence.'[23] The obvious moral is that auctioneers should be scrupulous in: (a) requiring a full declaration by the seller as to any feature of the vehicle rendering it unroadworthy, and if this is so, (b) passing on explicitly an appropriate warning to all bidders in the form found adequate in *Hurley v Dyke*.[24]

---

[20] See per Lord Diplock [1979] RTR 265, HL, at 301.

[21] *Ward v Hobbs* (1878) 4 App Cas 13, 48 LJQB 281, HL, where a similar warning held by the House of Lords to be effective in the case of the sale of pigs known by the seller to be diseased, was considered. There is some doubt whether this 'shocking decision' (Lord Denning's words in *Hurley v Dyke* [1979] RTR 265 at 281) would be followed today in the light of the development of the law of negligence after *Donoghue v Stevenson* [1932] AC 562, 101 LJPC 119, HL.

[22] [1979] RTR 265, HL.

[23] There is also the possibility of an action for breach of statutory duty. There is no authority on whether such an action would lie in these circumstances, but there is a presumption against its availability where the statute does not expressly confer the right to sue. Section 75 the Road Traffic Act 1988 merely confirms that the civil *contract* is not vitiated by the criminal illegality of the sale.

[24] Above, n 22.

TRADE DESCRIPTIONS

Offences capable of being committed by auctioneers under the Trade Descriptions Act 1968 are extensively discussed in chapter 8. Here we concentrate purely on the position of the vehicle auctioneer.

Prima facie any materially false description of a vehicle sold (or exposed for sale) at an auction, and which is not effectively disclaimed, constitutes an offence under s 1 of the Trade Descriptions Act 1968. A false trade description can relate purely to the catalogue description, or be made orally, or can be applied by means of a false odometer reading — there being an abundance of authority on this point.

The offence may be committeed by the auctioneer or by the seller via the entry form.

As an example of the first, in the Scottish case of *Aitchison v Reith & Anderson (Dingwall & Tain) Ltd*,[25] the respondents were long-established auctioneers but had not before auctioned a motor vehicle. They described the vehicle in writing as in 'Good Condition' without taking any technical advice. The description was false. The qualified auctioneer who conducted the sale checked the particulars from the registration book, and relying on the presence of an MOT certificate and its good external appearance assumed it was roadworthy. The High Court of Justiciary instructed the conviction of the respondents under s 1(1)(a) of the Trade Descriptions Act 1968, finding that there was no valid defence to the charge under this section by virtue of s 24 of that Act — taking all reasonable precautions and exercising all due diligence. An MOT certificate did not cover the defects from which the car suffered, and it was important to take technical advice on a sale outside the auctioneers' normal competence and experience. Although a director had apparently instructed that no descriptions should be issued, he had not ensured that these instructions were carried out.

The second situation, where a false trade description can be applied by the seller, is illustrated by *Zawadski v Sleigh*.[26] This decision also illustrates the principle, discussed in chapter 8, that a trader can avoid commission of an offence by an effective disclaimer of what would otherwise be a false trade description applied to goods contrary to s 1(1)(b) of the Trade Descriptions Act 1968. In the case of vehicles, the most common case of this is the display of a false odometer reading, and it has been held in *Norman v Bennett*[27] that in order to negative such a false trade description the disclaimer must be as bold, precise and compelling as the odometer reading itself.

---

[25] (1973) unreported, High Court of Justiciary; see O'Keefe *Law Relating to Trade Descriptions*, Butterworths, 3/80.

[26] [1975] 119 Sol Jo 318, [1975] RTR 113, DC.

[27] [1974] 3 All ER 351, [1974] 1 WLR 1229, followed and refined in numerous other decisions.

In *Zawadski v Sleigh*[28] the defendants were not the auctioneers but the motor dealers who had entered through British Car Auctions at Measham three cars whose odometer readings were incorrect, the mileage being substantially in excess of that indicated. The auctioneers used a comprehensive exemption clause in their Conditions of Sale which negated any warranty, condition, description or representation on the part of the auctioneers affecting any vehicle sold through them together with all statutory or other warranties as to condition, roadworthiness or mileages otherwise given on the part of the auctioneers. The auctioneers' practice was to give regular oral warnings that mileage was not guaranteed, but no specific disclaimer was made as to the three cars in question.

The Divisional Court upheld the justices' conviction of the defendant dealers on a charge under s 1 of the Trade Descriptions Act 1968 on the basis that the disclaimers made by the auctioneers were on these facts insufficiently potent to remove the false impression given by the mileometer readings. Lord Widgery CJ emphasised that the correct question was not whether the disclaimer was made on the defendants' behalf by the auctioneers. It was 'whether the disclaimer would be potent enough to get through to the buyer and make him disregard the message which the odometer had previously passed on to him.'[29]

This case has some unsatisfactory features as regards the potential liability of the auctioneers. Their position was not clearly considered, but the possibility of an effective disclaimer as to their own potential liability under the Trade Descriptions Act 1968 was clearly accepted.

MISCELLANEOUS AUCTIONS OF OTHER COMMODITIES

INTRODUCTION

Auctions of commodities other than those specifically considered in this book, such as motor cars, are many and various. Sales by auction of fruit, vegetables and fish are a world-wide phenomenon. The same applies to auctions of other commodities in which there is a daily market such as tea, coffee and certain minerals. Each commodity auction is likely to have some special features, but to deal with them specifically is beyond the scope of this book. We do, however, now consider briefly three additional types of auction which take place in the UK and discuss their special features.

---

[28] Above, n 26.   [29] [1975] RTR 113 at 118.

PLANT AND MACHINERY

Sales of factory or commercial plant and machinery by auction have increased in frequency over recent years, no doubt owing to economic problems caused by the recession and the need for liquidators and receivers to turn plant into cash as quickly and efficiently as possible.

With regard to the General Conditions which could be applicable in these circumstances, the Royal Institution of Chartered Surveyors has published recommended Conditions of Sale for auctions of plant and machinery held on the vendor's premises.[30] It is not proposed, therefore, to discuss the form which these conditions might otherwise take since the professionally-approved model is readily available.

There are, however, a few specific problems concerned with the nature of the commodity sold which can only be guarded against if properly appreciated.

Firstly, plant and machinery can be very heavy (eg grinding machines, lathes, milling machines) and may be firmly affixed to the factory floor. The situation may arise where the land and factory building either belongs to a landlord or a creditor-mortgagee has a charge over the same. There can then arise a distinction between that land and premises which the owner of the business may not sell, and those items of plant and machinery which, being separate chattels, the business owner or his agent may be free to sell. To decide whether heavy plant fixed to the floor is a 'fixture' going with the land, or a chattel, depends upon the law of fixtures as developed as part of the law of real property. A general test involves consideration of both the *degree* of annexation and the *purpose* of that annexation. An article fixed to the floor is prima facie a fixture — the more so if it would cause difficulty to remove. But machinery standing by its own weight normally remains a chattel.[31] The 'purpose' test sometimes removes from the category of what would otherwise be a fixture an article affixed to the land because there is no other way to 'enjoy' it — eg a tapestry nailed to the wall.[32] But the courts have not been entirely consistent in applying either of these tests and the following, for example, have been held to be fixtures: looms in a worsted mill fixed by nails to wooden beams in the floor,[33] seats in a cinema,[34] machinery fixed by bolts,[35] and an electric light generating machine fixed by bolts.[36]

[30] (Sept. 1991) Royal Institution of Chartered Surveyors.
[31] *Hulme v Brigham* [1943] KB 152, [1943] 1 All ER 204 see also p. 77.
[32] *Leigh v Taylor* [1902] AC 157, 71 LJ Ch 272, HL.
[33] *Holland v Hodgson* (1872) LP 7CP 328, 41 LJCP 146.
[34] *Vaudeville Electric Cinema Ltd v Muriset* [1923] 2 Ch 74, 92 LJ Ch 558; but contrast *Lyon & Co v London City and Midland Bank* [1903] 2 KB 135, 72 LJKB 465 (seats fixed for temporary use held to be chattels).
[35] *Reynolds v Ashby & Son* [1904] AC 466, 73 LJKB 946, HL.
[36] *Jordan v May* [1947] KB 427, [1947] LJR 653, CA (but the batteries were chattels).

If it is apparent that a piece of machinery is a fixture (the fact that it has been installed by the business owner being, of course, irrelevant), the law must again be examined to see if the business proprietor nevertheless has the right to remove the fixture. This right attaches in particular to tenants of factories or other land where the fixture has been attached by the tenant for the purpose of his trade or business. A number of fixtures such as vats, fixed steam engines and boilers have come into this category of 'tenant's fixtures'. But if the fixture is to be removed, this must occur during the currency of the lease or, if the lease has not been forfeited or surrended, within a reasonable time after expiry.[37] Once this time elapses, the fixture becomes the absolute property of the landlord and may, therefore, not properly be sold without his consent.

There are special rules relating to the removal of agricultural fixtures where the tenant may, subject to certain conditions, remove fixtures within two months after the determination of the term.[38]

Enough has been stated to show that great care must be taken by the auctioneer to ensure that the machinery and plant in question is the vendor's unencumbered property. This includes consideration of Romalpa[39] clauses under which the vendor of goods delivered to the purchaser reserves, or purports to reserve, his title to those goods until some condition (usually full payment) has been met. Difficult problems of priority can also arise where, for instance, hired machinery is fixed to a mortgaged factory,[40] but whoever may then have the best title to the machinery, it is certainly not the hirer's property to sell.

Problems can also arise with machinery not complying with safety legislation, such as the Health and Safety at Work etc. Act 1974, either with regard to its safe functioning or because it contains toxic chemicals such as asbestos. The best that can be done here is to emphasise by notice in the Conditions of Sale that such machinery may not comply with current safety legislation and is sold on the basis that it is the buyer's responsibility to ensure that the machine's subsequent use is in compliance with this legislation. Auctions of farm machinery, to which numerous safety regulations apply, incur similar risks and a specific duty should be put on purchasers to check items and secure compliance before use. Alternatively, a condition could state that lots are sold on the basis that they are not for use 'at work' (and therefore not within the 1974 Act above), but the efficacy of this device remains to be tested. In either case it is legitimate for the auctioneer

[37] See *Lavies, ex p Stephens* (1877) 7 Ch D 127, 47 LJ Bcy 22, CA.

[38] Agricultural Holdings Act 1986, s 10.

[39] See *Aluminium Industrie Vaassen BV v Romalpa Aluminium Ltd* [1976] 2 All ER 552, [1976] 1 WLR 676. Creditors of a company may not be bound by such a clause unless it is registered as a charge under Companies Act 1985, s 395.

[40] See generally, Megarry and Wade *The Law of Real Property* (5th edn, 1984) Stevens, p 738.

to require an indemnity from the seller, though no one can be 'indemnified' against a criminal conviction.

The sale of large, heavy plant may cause serious administrative problems with regard to its removal. Again, Conditions of Sale should deal with the buyer's obligations on this point and bind him to reinstate any damage after removal at his own expense within a reasonable time. The buyer may need police or other permission to transport wide loads on a public highway and a warning as to this could be a wise precaution.

SALES OF REVERSIONS AND FUTURE PROPERTY INTERESTS

As Messrs H E Foster and Cranfield[41] state in their Conditions of Sale:

H E Foster & Cranfield's periodical sales of absolute or contingent reversions to funded property, annuities, policies of assurance, life interests, . . . and all descriptions of present or prospective property were established in the year 1843 and have been continued successfully since that date.

The auctions in question take place normally twice a month throughout the year in London.

There is clearly a market for sales and purchases of reversions — or more accurately 'remainders' in most cases[42] — and other property to which there is a present right to future enjoyment (ie a vested future interest) or a contingent right to future enjoyment (contingent future interest). A straightforward example of a vested future interest is where a testator has left his estate to his wife for life with remainder to his only son. The son's interest is a vested one to which he will either succeed on the death of the mother, or if he predeceases his mother the remainder then falls to be distributed amongst those entitled to the son's estate. The value of the remainder (or 'reversion' as it is loosely called) will depend on such factors as: (a) the present capital value of the fund; (b) liability, if any, to inheritance tax on the death of the mother as it affects the fund; (c) the trustee's future investment policy; and (d) the life expectation of the mother. The greater the latter is, the more the value of the 'reversion' will be discounted. The attraction of an immediate sale to the son is the capital prematurely in hand. The attraction to a purchaser is that the difference between the price immediately paid and the value of the interest when it falls in could represent a considerable capital gain, though the factors enumerated above

---

[41] Auctioneers, Valuers and Estate Agents, 29 Britton St., London EC1.
[42] A reversion technically reverts to the original donor — eg a gift by X to A for life, X retaining the reversionary interest. A remainder is illustrated in the example in the text.

introduce a heavy element of chance. A *contingent* interest is considerably more risky.

Similarly there is a burgeoning market for life policies not yet matured and whose surrender value is likely to be less than its saleroom value, annuities which the annuitant wishes to sell in return for a capital sum (and in this case the annuitant's longevity is at a premium for the buyer) and other property interests of this sort which the owner wishes to convert into a capital sum in possession.

There can be very considerable legal complexities in these transactions and it is interesting to note that in Messrs H E Foster and Cranfield's General Conditions of Sale there are included conditions which entitle the purchasers to proof of the vendor's title and all proper conveyances, transfers, and assignments, the cost of the latter falling on the purchaser. Under these conditions, ten per cent deposit is payable at the successful bid (evidenced by a signed memorandum), the remaining money being payable on completion of the transaction.

LIVESTOCK SALES

The selling of livestock, from the regular market sales of cattle and sheep for slaughter, to the more specialised annual sales of thoroughbred horses is almost exclusively effected by auction. Indeed, in the case of prime stock or slaughter stock sales it is difficult to see how they might otherwise be organised. The value of the trade runs to something currently approaching £2 billion per year. These auction market sales have certain particular features which should be noted. There exist statutory controls, and detailed specialist Conditions of Sale are normally employed.[43]

It should be noted in addition, that there exists European Community led regulation in respect of the care and also transportation of livestock, particularly internationally. The Welfare of Livestock Regulations, SI 1994/2126 are operative from 10 August 1994 and implement Council Directives 88/166 and 91/630 EEC in connection with care of battery hens, calves and pigs.

---

[43] The Livestock Auctioneers' Association has produced a standard set of Conditions of Sale for Cattle, Calves, Sheep and Pigs at Livestock Auction Market. At the time of writing of this edition the current conditions are those issued in 1987. However a new set is in the course of preparation. Grateful thanks are offered to John Martin, the Secretary of the Livestock Auctioneers' Association for his many valuable comments on the industry. These Conditions are in general use in such auctions and are registered with the Office of Fair Trading in accordance with the Restrictive Practices Act 1976. The authors are grateful to the Association for its kind permission to utilise and reproduce these Conditions.

Statutory controls

The main statutory control of livestock auction markets is in the field of
weighing cattle. An auctioneer must not sell cattle[44] at any market where
such are habitually sold unless facilities for weighing them are provided at
the market. Fines of up to £500[45] may be levied and if the offence is a
continuing one, the penalty is £10 per day for every day it continues.

If an auctioneer sells cattle[46] fit for slaughter where such weighing facilities are provided and he fails either to weigh them or to notify the bidder of
their weight at the time the cattle are offered for sale, he commits an
offence under s 2 of the Markets and Fairs (Weighing of Cattle) Act 1926.
The penalty for breach of this provision is £2 per head of cattle so sold.

The penalties for infringement of these provisions are not very great.
However the controls are effective. Stock is normally sold by weight[47]
(today, prices usually being calculated per kilogram) and the organisers of
the market ensure that proper and accurate weighing machines are used. If,
as is usually the case, the market is run by the local authority for the area,
the authority will ensure compliance by installing and inspecting machines.
Alternatively, if, as the case in Hereford, for example, the market is run by
a company formed by a consortium of auctioneer firms, the company will
obtain annual certification as to the accuracy of the machines from the local
authority's trading standards department.

Conduct of the sale

As we have already observed, livestock auctioneers are well served by
standard Conditions of Sale and we do not attempt to provide our own
alternative terms. However it might be useful to consider a few of the
conditions commonly utilised.

Diseased etc animals

As we have seen in chapter 5, an auctioneer may be under a duty to care for
the goods of his vendor as bailee, and possibly also those of the purchaser

---

[44] 'In this Act the word "cattle" includes ram, ewe, wether, lamb, and swine': Markets and
Fairs (Weighing of Cattle) Act 1887, s 3. But seen n 46, below.

[45] Markets and Fairs (Weighing of Cattle) Act 1891, s 4, as amended by the Criminal Justice
Act 1982, s 37 and the Criminal Justice Act 1991, s 17(1). The scale corresponds to level 2: ss
37 and 46 of the Criminal Justice Act 1982.

[46] The Markets and Fairs (Weighing of Cattle) Act 1926, s 1(3): 'In this section [Disclosure
of weight of fat cattle on sale by auction] the expression "cattle" means bulls, cows, oxen and
heifers.'

[47] Though sheep, albeit weighed, may he sold 'per head'.

either in a similar capacity or generally in negligence. One obvious risk in livestock auctions is that a diseased animal may infect those belonging to others whilst under the care and control of the auctioneer. It is sensible to guard against this potential liability and an appropriate condition is that supplied by Condition 4 of the Standard Conditions recommended by the Livestock Auctioneers' Association. The condition places the liability for losses occasioned directly upon the person bringing such diseased animal onto the auction premises. It also permits the auctioneer at his discretion to exclude or dispose of any such animal.

Dangerous animals

An auctioneer will also be potentially liable in negligence for any injury to other animals or persons caused by an animal under his control. Whilst the female of the species may sometimes be regarded as being deadlier than the male[48] there is obviously a particular risk in relation to bulls. The Standard Conditions provide[49] that no bull over ten months of age is to be brought onto the auction premises unless properly ringed and haltered.

Sales of heifers by weight

Heifers and other animals sold for slaughter are sold by weight. It is obvious that if sold as warranted free of calf or lamb as the case may be and it transpires that the animal was not so free, the purchaser will have paid an excessive price for the fatstock. He will be entitled to damages for misdescription and conditions are included to ensure that the purchaser's rights under the contract of sale are exercised promptly and reasonably. Thus Condition 43 of the Standard Conditions provides:[50]

Unless stated to the contrary in the catalogue or at the time of sale all heifers are warranted to be free of calf. If:

(a) within 48 hours after the slaughter of a heifer to which the aforegoing warranty applies notice in writing is given to the auctioneers that she was carrying a calf weighing at the time of slaughter more than 9 kg, and

(b) such notice is supported by a certificate signed by the slaughter-house manager or a veterinary surgeon or other competent person and stating the identity number of the heifer, the date of slaughter and the weight of the calf at that date,

---

[48] See the Scottish case *Cameron v Hamilton's Auction Marts Ltd* ((1955) Scots Law Times 74) where an auctioneer was held not liable for damage caused by a cow he had allowed to escape whilst being delivered to the auction mart. The cow had been seen to be in an excited condition, had escaped into a shop, mounted the stairs and collapsed through the floor turning on a tap in the process. The water damage to the goods below was held to be too remote, not being a provable result of their negligence.

[49] See Condition 4(e).

[50] Conditions of Sale for Cattle, Calves, Sheep and Pigs at Livestock Auction Market, Livestock Auctioneers' Association.

then the vendor shall pay to the purchaser, as and for ascertained and agreed liquidated damages, to cover all expenses, depreciation in value and other damages whatsoever, a sum equal to one-and-a-half times the value of the calf alone, calculated as a proportionate part of the value of the heifer ascertained from its purchase price per live kg at the sale. No compensation for damages shall be payable in respect of a calf weighing, at the time of slaughter, 9 kg or less.

The restrictions on the right to reject are thus of two kinds: one relates to the time in which notice is to be given, and the other limits the right to those cases where the calf is at the relevant time in excess of 9 kg in weight. Moreover the clause goes on to provide what is known as a liquidated damages provision which will be upheld only if it is found to represent a reasonable pre-estimate of the loss likely to flow from the breach. Such a clause does not come within the ambit of the Unfair Contract Terms Act 1977. The provision excluding compensation for calves of less than 9 kg is an exclusion clause within the Unfair Contract Terms Act 1977, but apart from the probability that it would be regarded as not unreasonable, it is not likely to be a matter on which litigation would be pursued.

On the other hand, Condition 28 (quoted below)[51] which amounts to an omnibus exclusion clause, will be subject to the test of reasonableness under the Unfair Contract Terms Act 1977 and fairness under the Unfair Terms in Consumer Contracts Regulations, SI 1994/3159. The ramifications of this are discussed fully in chapter 6.

Milking of cows

An unusual 'perk' is provided for in Condition 72, namely that, unless the owner wishes to do so, the auctioneers shall authorise the milking of cows on the sale premises and the milk in that event shall belong to the auctioneers.

Conditions relating to fatstock premium schemes

The European Community introduced regimes whereby member states could establish systems for the payment of premiums for producers of certain animals. There were in operation schemes relating to beef and sheep

---

[51] See below, p 295.
[52] The relevant Regulations and Statutory Provisions are as follows:

    (a) *Beef*
        EEC Regulation 714/89; Beef Special Premium (Protection of Payments) Order, SI 1989/574. See also the relatively recent Suckler Cow Premium Scheme: Suckler Cow Premium (Amendment) Regulations, SI 1994/1528.

meat.[52] The essence of these schemes was that a weekly target price was fixed, and when the average market price (calculated from live-weight auction sales) fell below the target or guide price, a premium was paid.

These schemes have, largely, been phased out over recent years and the subsidy is now provided not on slaughter but 'on farm', ie to the breeder or fattener.

There are several general requirements as to the keeping of records relating to sales of particular commodities and wide powers are vested in the Intervention Board for Agricultural Produce to enter premises and inspect books etc. Failure to comply with these regulations renders a person liable to criminal penalties.[53]

Meat and Livestock Commission schemes

The Meat and Livestock Commission is a statutory corporation having members appointed by the Minister of Agriculture, Fisheries and Food and the Secretary of State for Wales whose function is to promote greater efficiency in the livestock industry. The commission is partly financed by levy schemes which from time to time are instituted. Currently there is a levy scheme relating to cattle, sheep and pigs whereby charges are levied on the slaughter of such livestock. The scheme is set out in the Meat and Livestock Commission Levy Scheme (Confirmation) Order 1979, as amended.[54]

The levy is initially payable by slaughterers of the livestock, but where a slaughterer slaughters livestock on the instructions of the owner, he can recover the whole of the levy from the latter. Where on the other hand, the slaughterer kills livestock which he has in whole or in part purchased himself, he can recover half of the levy from the vendor.

How does all this affect auctioneers? The answer is provided in art 5 of the Principal Order, the proviso to sub-para (2)(a)(i) of which provides that where the slaughterer purchases the livestock slaughtered at auction he

---

(b) *Sheep*
EEC Regulation 1837/80 of 27 June 1980; EEC Regulation 2661/80 of 17 October 1980; EEC Regulation 1238/82 of 20 May 1982; EEC Regulation 1689/83 of 24 June 1983; Sheep Variable Premium (Protection of Payments) (2) Order 1980, SI 1980/1811; Sheep Variable Premium (Protection of Payments) (Amendment) Order 1981, SI 1981/751; Sheep Variable Premium (Protection of Payments) (Amendment) Order 1982, SI 1982/726; Sheep Variable Premium (Protection of Payments) (Amendment) Order 1983, SI 1983/1009.

[53] The Regulations are laid down by the Common Agricultural Policy (Protection of Community Arrangements) Regulations, SI 1992/314. Art 8 provides a number of offences which may be committed in respect of breaches of these regulations; the most serious attracting fines of up to the statutory maximum on summary conviction, or, on indictment such a fine or imprisonment for up to two years, or both — see art 8(12).

[54] SI 1979/393 as amended. The latest statutory instrument (SI 1993/1899) gives effect to the 1993 order.

may recover half of the levy from the auctioneer. In addition, if the slaughterer defaults, the Commission may recover the levy directly from the person from whom the slaughterer could have recovered it — including the auctioneer where appropriate (sub-para (iv)).

Thus auctioneers should ensure that they have the right to recover the levy or part of it where livestock sold for slaughter is within the scheme. Condition 16 of the Livestock Auctioneers' Association provides for this situation. This is normally done in practice by designating a sale or part of it as a 'slaughter sale'; half of the levy is passed on to the abbatoir buyers who then account in full to the Commission.

Sales outside the ring

The above matters have all concerned slaughter stock sales. Pedigree cattle and horses are also commonly sent to auction for sale. Not infrequently in such cases (and occasionally in respect of slaughter stock too) a vendor may effect a sale of the livestock 'outside the ring', that is to say, within the auction premises but either before the goods have gone under the hammer or after an abortive auction sale. In such a case the practice is that the sale is 'booked' through the auctioneer.

The legal significance of this procedure was explained by Diplock J (as he then was) in *Murphy v Jonathan Howlett (a firm)* as follows:[55]

The seller and the intending buyer, ... agree upon the price and agree to book the sale with the auctioneer ... The auctioneer is entitled either to accept or to reject the booking ... If the auctioneer accepts the booking he pays the seller ... the amount of the price agreed between the seller and the intending buyer ... As regards the cattle, the subject-matter of the booked sale, the seller upon receiving his cheque or cash from the auctioneer is no longer interested in the transaction [and] the auctioneer ... exercises all the rights of the owner ... including the right of retaking possession if he has parted with it, and the right of resale ... The evidence as to the practice upon the booking of a sale suggests strongly that what the parties in fact do is to exercise rights and perform obligations which are identical with the legal rights and obligations which would flow from concurrent sales of the cattle (1) by the seller to the auctioneer at the agreed price less commission and (2) by the auctioneer to the buyer at the agreed price. It is the simplest explanation of the way in which the parties act after the booking and I think it is the correct legal analysis.

The significance of this analysis, that there are two concurrent sales, would seem to be that the auctioneer in law sells his *own* goods to the purchaser. He acts not as agent but as principal. In consequence the auctioneer in

---

[55] (1960) 176 EG 311 at 312. This case has also been considered above in chs 4 and 5.

respect of these sales is liable *qua* seller for breaches of the terms as to title, and as regards satisfactory quality and fitness for purpose and the like implied by the Sale of Goods Act 1979, as amended.

In this context one must consider again the effectiveness of any purported exclusion of these implied terms. We have seen in chapter 6 that these terms cannot be excluded in any consumer sale (and that the implied terms as to title cannot be excluded in *any* sale) but that for various reasons sales by auctions are deemed not to be consumer sales. In non-consumer sales, exclusion of the terms is permitted to the extent that it is regarded as reasonable, and certain criteria are supplied by statute. However the question arises whether a sale booked with the auctioneer is a 'sale by auction' within s 12(2) of the Unfair Contract Terms Act 1977 and it is argued that it is not; there is no element of competitive bidding involved. However, and in any event, it is ultimately unlikely that many such sales would be regarded as consumer sales because, save perhaps for certain horses, the goods are not 'of a type ordinarily supplied for private use or consumption' within s 12(1)(c) of the Act. If therefore the implied terms are excludable then one must consider the aptness of the particular exclusion clause. Let us take the exclusion clause provided by the Livestock Auctioneers' Association by way of example. Condition 28 provides:

The auctioneers act in all respects only as agents for the vendor and it shall be deemed that no condition or warranty expressed or implied has in any circumstance been given by the auctioneers, or any servant of the auctioneers, whether as to title, description, the quality of any lot sold or otherwise. The auctioneers and their servants shall not incur any liability to the purchaser in respect of any defect of title, error of description or imperfection or in respect of any announcement or statement relating to or affecting any lot offered for sale whether made orally or in writing and whether given before, during or after the auction, nor shall they incur any liability in relation to any dispute between any purchaser and vendors.

The opening words present an immediate difficulty. The assertion that the auctioneer acts only as agent is false in law in so far as these sales are concerned. It might be open to a court therefore to construe this condition as only applying when the auctioneer *does* act as agent. For the avoidance of doubt it might be safer for auctioneers to insert an exclusion provision directed specifically to private sales booked with them where they acknowledge that they act *qua* sellers and then purport to exclude their liability as appropriate. If auctioneers fail to exclude liability for eg misdescriptions or unsatisfactory quality, then these private sales booked with the auctioneer may render the auctioneer exposed to legal risks to which, as agent, he is normally immune.

The major advantage enuring to the benefit of auctioneers out of the 'booking' procedure, is that it provides them with commission in respect of a private treaty sale which factually they have not effected (though the presence a market has of course facilitated it).

Moreover, as we have pointed out in chapter 4, the auctioneers can sue the buyer for the price as sellers in their own right, but if for any reason the sale to the buyer is vitiated (eg by mistake or otherwise) and the auctioneers are unable to recover against the buyer, this in no way affects the first contract of sale between the seller and the auctioneer. In *Murphy v Howlett*[56] therefore the auctioneers were held unable to avoid their contract with the vendor when doubts arose as to the identity (not to mention the solvency) of the buyer.

[56] Above, n 55.

Sales by Vendors in Special Positions

INTRODUCTION

In normal cases there is a choice open to the buyer. He may either proceed to dispose of his goods by private treaty or by auction. For the vendor who is in a fiduciary or quasi-fiduciary position, this choice may not exist, or, if it does, the choice may be circumscribed. In some cases a sale by auction may be prescribed by statute. Trustees, mortgagees, pawnbrokers and public and court authorities are all examples of vendors who do not own the property beneficially (at least in its entirety) and may be under a fiduciary duty to obtain the best price reasonably obtainable.[1] Each will be taken in turn.

TRUSTEES AND OTHER FIDUCIARIES

Trustees are under an overriding duty to obtain for their beneficiaries the best price reasonably obtainable. Under modern law trustees are not, however, obliged to sell by auction. For instance, s 12 of the Trustee Act 1925 states that trustees may 'sell or concur with any other person in selling all or any part of the property, either subject to prior charges or not, and either together or in lots, by public auction or by private contract.' Nevertheless, particularly in the case of collections of chattels which are trust property, trustees (and executors and administrators) will be likely to choose the auction method so as to demonstrate that they have obtained the best possible price. This applies both to trustees of private trusts and of charitable trusts.

There is an important corollary to the above. This arises from the principle that a purchase of trust property by a trustee from himself and any co-trustee is voidable at the instance of any beneficiary.[2] There is even elderly authority to the effect that the principle includes the case where the sale is at a public auction.[3] If the sale is voidable in these circumstances, any

---

[1] See eg *Buttle v Saunders* [1950] 2 All ER 193.

[2] See Snell's *Equity* (28th edn, 1982) Sweet & Maxwell, 248; *Holder v Holder* [1968] Ch 353, [1968] 1 All ER 665, CA. The purchase by the trustee of the beneficiary's interest is, however, unimpeachable in the absence of some form of fraud or undue influence.

[3] *Ex p Lacey* (1802) 6 Ves 625 at 629. The reason given appears to be that the trustee-vendor might be recognised and thus discourage bidding by others. This hardly seems convincing.

beneficiary has the right to set it aside within a reasonable time after discovery of the facts. The rule will not apply where the trustee has long been retired from the trust,[4] nor to an executor (who is in a similar fiduciary position to that of a trustee for present purposes) who has renounced executorship or disassociated himself from the management of the deceased's estate. Thus, in *Holder v Holder*,[5] a testator appointed his widow, a daughter and his third son Victor to be his executors. The testator died leaving his landed estate to be equally divided between his widow and his children. Victor purported to renounce his executorship, but this renunciation was ineffective since he had intermeddled with the estate. However, he took no part in instructing the valuer who fixed the reserves for the farmland which was to be sold by auction. Victor's bid was successful at the auction and the farms were knocked down to him at a fair price. It was held by the Court of Appeal that in the special circumstances of the case Victor, although an executor, was not precluded from purchasing the property.

Similar principles apply to all persons in a fiduciary position. The rule arises from the fundamental rule that a fiduciary should not profit from his position and his special knowledge. Such persons include agents, solicitors, company directors, employees, guardians, partners, receivers, and members of a Committee of Inspection in Bankruptcy.[6]

There are exceptions to the rule. For instance the trust instrument may expressly authorise a trustee to purchase, and the court has jurisdiction to give the trustee leave to bid at an auction.[7] Under the Settled Land Act 1925, s 68, there is specific provision for a tenant for life of settled land to purchase property which he holds on trust.

MORTGAGEES

A mortgagee of land has a statutory power of sale conferred upon him by s 101 of the Law of Property Act 1925 provided the mortgage has been made by deed. The power is, when the mortgage money has become due, to sell, or to concur with any other person in selling, the mortgaged property or any part thereof, either subject to prior charges or not, and either together or in lots, by public auction or by private contract. The power may not be exercised until the conditions specified in s 103 have been satisfied. These are:

(a) notice requiring payment of the mortgage money has been served on the mortgagor and default has been made for three months after such service; or

---

[4] *Re Boles and British Land Co's Contract* [1902] 1 Ch 244, 71 LJ Ch 130.
[5] [1968] Ch 353, [1968] 1 All ER 665, CA.
[6] See generally Snell (n 2 above) pp 250–51.   [7] See RSC Ord 85, r 2.

(b) interest under the mortgage is in arrear and unpaid for two months after becoming due; or
(c) there has been a breach of some other provision in the mortgage deed imposed by the Law of Property Act 1925 (as amended) 'other than and besides a covenant for payment of the mortgage money or interest thereon'.

The mortgagee exercising his power of sale is in a less onerous position than the trustee considered above. He is not regarded as a trustee for the mortgagor, though he owes a duty to the mortgagor to act in good faith and take reasonable care to obtain the true market value of the mortgaged property on the date that he decides to sell it. The position was summarized cogently by Salmon LJ in *Cuckmere Brick Co Ltd v Mutual Finance Ltd* where it was said:[8]

It is well settled that a mortgage is not a trustee of the power of sale for the mortgagor. Once the power has accrued, the mortgagee is entitled to exercise it for his own purposes whenever he chooses to do so. It matters not that the moment may be unpropitious and that by waiting a higher price could be obtained. He has the right to realise his security by turning it into money when he likes. Nor, in my view, is there anything to prevent a mortgagee from accepting the best bid he can get at an auction, even though the auction is badly attended and the bidding exceptionally low. Provided none of those adverse factors is due to any fault of the mortgagee, he can do as he likes.

However this case is a warning that the mortgagee must still take reasonable care. Here, the plaintiffs had mortgaged 2.6 acres of land to the defendants. The defendants put the property up for sale by public auction without advertising the fact that there existed planning permission for 100 flats, and as a result the sale fetched some £21,000 less than the trial judge estimated the land to be worth. The majority of the Court of Appeal held that there had been a breach of the mortgagee's duty to take reasonable precautions to obtain the true market value of the mortgaged property at the date on which it was decided to sell it.

An example of where an auction of mortgaged land took place in such extraordinary circumstances that the court would have set the sale aside had not the mortgagor inordinately delayed in pursuing the remedies occurred in *Tse Kwong Lam v Wong Chit Sen*.[9] Here, commercial property in Hong Kong was mortgaged and on the default of the mortgagor the mortgagee exercised his power of sale by auction. The property was somewhat modestly advertised and the conditions of sale gave notice that there would be a reserve price and that the vendor-mortgagee reserved the right to bid. The auctioneer was informed of the reserve figure on the day of the auction.

[8] [1971] Ch 949 at 965.   [9] [1983] 3 All ER 54, [1983] 1 WLR 1349, PC.

At the auction the only bidder was the mortgagee's wife, bidding on behalf of the mortgagee's family company. She put in a single bid at the reserve price and the property was knocked down to her. The borrower, with 'inexcusable delay', eventually applied for the sale to be set aside.

The Judicial Committee of the Privy Council held that whilst the mortgagee's company was not debarred from purchasing the property in the present case, the sale could 'only be supported if the mortgagee proves that he took reasonable precautions to obtain the best price reasonably obtainable at the time of sale'. Lord Templeman added: 'An auction which only produces one bid is not necessarily an indication that the true market value has been achieved.' He continued by stating that expert advice ought to have been taken as to the method of sale, as to the steps which ought reasonably to have been taken to make the sale a success, and as to the amount of the reserve.[10] Because of the mortgagor's delay the sale was not set aside, but the borrower's right to sue the mortgagee for damages for failure of the mortgagee to secure the best price was confirmed.

Building society mortgagees have a specific *statutory* duty to take reasonable care to ensure that the price is the best price which can be reasonably obtained.[11]

PAWNBROKERS

For many years the sale of unredeemed pledges in respect of loans not exceeding £50 had been governed by the Pawnbrokers Act 1872 as amended by the Pawnbrokers Act 1960. These statutory provisions required that a pledge pawned for above £2, when disposed of by the pawnbroker, should be disposed of by sale by public auction and not otherwise; and the regulations prescribed by the Act should be observed with reference to the sale. A pawnbroker was permitted to bid for and purchase at a sale by auction, and on such purchase was deemed to be the absolute owner of the pledge purchased. The regulations required by the Act as to the conducting of auctions included that all pledges had to be exposed to public view, the catalogue had to show the pawnbroker's name and business address etc, advertisements in newspapers had to be placed, and valuable items had to be sold as separate lots.

The Pawnbrokers Acts 1872 and 1960 were prospectively repealed by s 121 of the Consumer Credit Act 1974. This section is set out below and it will be seen that as regards those transactions within the ambit of the

---

[10] [1983] 3 All ER 54 at 60, 63.   [11] Building Societies Act 1962, s 36.

section there is no particular method of sale prescribed. Those transactions not within the section will be governed by the ordinary law of contract in this respect. Regulations which have a commencement date of 19 May 1985 have been made pursuant to this section.[12] The section runs as follows:

121. Realisation of pawn

(1) When a pawn has become realisable by him, the pawnee may sell it, after giving to the pawnor (except in such cases as may be prescribed) not less than the prescribed period of notice of the intention to sell, indicating in the notice the asking price and such other particulars as may be prescribed.

(2) Within the prescribed period after the sale takes place, the pawnee shall give the pawnor the prescribed information in writing as to the sale, its proceeds and expenses.

(3) Where the net proceeds of sale are not less than the sum which, if the pawn had been redeemed on the date of the sale, would have been payable for its redemption, the debt secured by the pawn is discharged and any surplus shall be paid by the pawnee to the pawnor.

(4) Where subsection (3) does not apply, the debt shall be treated as from the date of sale as equal to the amount by which the net proceeds of sale fall short of the sum which would have been payable for the redemption of the pawn on that date.

(5) In this section the 'net proceeds of sale' is the amount realised (the 'gross amount') less the expenses (if any) of the sale.

(6) If the pawnor alleges that the gross amount is less than the true market value of the pawn on the date of sale, it is for the pawnee to prove that he and any agents employed by him in the sale used reasonable care to ensure that the true market value was obtained, and if he fails to do so subsections (3) and (4) shall have effect as if the reference in subsection (5) to the gross amount were a reference to the true market value.

(7) If the pawnor alleges that the expenses of the sale were unreasonably high, it is for the pawnee to prove that they were reasonable, and if he fails to do so subsections (3) and (4) shall have effect as if the reference in subsection (5) to expenses were a reference to reasonable expenses.

Note on the above section

In subs(1) above, the 'prescribed period' is fourteen days, and in subs(2) it is twenty working days. Furthermore, the section only applies to articles taken in pawn under a regulated consumer credit agreement, so the financial limits prescribed from time to time under the Act (£50 to £15,000 as from 20 May 1985) must be borne in mind. See generally the Consumer Credit (Realisation of Pawns) Regulations, SI 1983/1568.

---

[12] See Commencement Order No 8.

SALES UNDER WRIT OF FIERI FACIAS

Where a creditor has obtained judgment in the High Court against a debtor there are a number of ways in which the money judgment may be enforced. For present purposes we are concerned with the case where it is decided to levy execution against chattels belonging to the debtor.

In these circumstances, the practice in respect of a High Court judgment is to issue a writ of fieri facias (fi fa). A form of request known as a praecipe is delivered to the court together with copies of the judgment and two copies of the writ of fieri facias. The writ is sealed and sent to the under sheriff for the county in which the debtor has goods to be seized, together with the appropriate sheriff's fee. The under sheriff's officer then executes the writ. He is empowered to take possession of sufficient goods belonging to the debtor to cover the amount for which the writ is issued plus his charges and costs of sale. The technicalities of the seizure of the debtor's goods by the sheriff's officer are beyond the scope of this book.[13]

With regard to the sale of the goods seized, the Supreme Court Act 1981, s 138A provides that

> where any goods seized under a writ of execution issued from the High Court are to be sold for a sum exceeding £20 (including legal incidental expenses), the sale shall, unless the court otherwise orders, be made by public auction and not by bill of sale or private contract, and shall be publicly advertised by the Sheriff on, and during days preceding, the day of sale.[14]

If the sheriff desires to sell otherwise than by auction he may apply to the court under RSC Ord 47, r 6. Such an application must be made by summons and is attended by various other formalities. It is the sheriff's duty to get the best price possible for the goods and it is he that must make the application for sale otherwise than by auction on the basis that he is in the best position to know how to maximise the sale proceeds.

In the county court similar rules apply to the enforcement by the county court of a warrant of execution.[15] Section 97 of the County Courts Act 1984 makes similar provision for goods sold under an execution for a sum exceeding £20 (including legal incidental expenses), to be sold by public auction publicly advertised by the Registrar on, and during three days next preceding, the day of sale. The court has power to order otherwise.

---

[13] For the procedure, see RSC Ords 46 and 47. In the USA it is understood that sales in such circumstances are normally by auction with, in effect, the reserve placed at the amount of the judgment debt.

[14] This section was inserted by the Statute Law (Revision) Act 1989 s 1(2), Sch 2 Part 1, para 4 consequent upon the repeal of the Bankruptcy Act 1883, s 145.

[15] See CCR 1981, Ord 25, r 11; also County Courts Act 1984, s 85 as amended by the High Court and County Court Jurisdiction Order 1991, art 8, and CCR 1981, Ord 25.

A sale not in conformity with the section is voidable only; it stands until set aside.[16]

SALES OF LAND BY ORDER OF THE COURT

By virtue of RSC Ord 31, where in any cause or matter in the Chancery Division relating to land it appears necessary or expedient for the purposes of the cause or matter that the land or any part thereof should be sold, the court may order that land or part to be sold. In carrying out the sale the court may permit the party or person having the conduct of the sale to sell the land in such manner as he thinks fit, or may direct that the land be sold in such manner as the court may either by the order or subsequent directions lay down, for the best price that can be obtained. The usual practice is to order a sale of land out of court, with liberty to apply to the court for any necessary directions should there be disagreement. Depending on the state of the property market, an auction may well be dispensed with, particularly if a price below which the property should not be sold is agreed between the parties.

With regard to the remuneration of the auctioneer, the Vice-Chancellor and judges of the Chancery Division have approved a scale of remuneration. The position is set out in the following Practice Direction:[17]

PRACTICE DIRECTION

Chancery Division
Family Division

1. The charges of estate agents and auctioneers selling freehold or leasehold property pursuant to orders of the Chancery Division, the Family Division, the Court of Protection or divorce county courts will normally be considered reasonable by the court if they do not exceed the rate of commission which that agent would normally charge on a sole agency basis, and they do not exceed $2\frac{1}{2}$% of the sale price, exclusive of value added tax.
2. These charges are to include all commission, valuations, expenses and other disbursements, including making affidavits, the cost of advertising and all other work except surveys. The allowance for a survey will be at the court's discretion.
3. If (a) an agent's charges do not fall within the limits set out in para 1 or (b) there is a sale of any investment property, business property or farm property or (c) a property is sold in lots or by valuation, an application must be made to the court to authorise the fee to be charged.

---

[16] See *Crawshaw v Harrison* [1894] 1 QB 79, 63 LJQB 94.
[17] [1983] 1 All ER 160, [1983] 1 WLR 86.

4. The limits set out in paras 1 and 2 above do not apply to sales of property for patients of the Court of Protection where an agreement has been concluded with the estate agent before the jurisdiction of the court has been invoked.
5. In matrimonial cases, either where the party who has been condemned in these costs has not agreed to the increased rate or where the costs fall to be paid out of the legal aid fund, the higher charges will be subject to the discretion of the taxing officer.
6. This Practice Direction applies to all instructions for sale which are placed with estate agents and auctioneers after 1 January 1983.

The Practice Directions of 26 July 1972 ([1972] 3 All ER 256, [1972] 1 WLR 1431) and 18 October 1972 ([1972] 3 All ER 910, [1972] 1 WLR 1471) are hereby revoked.

By direction of the Vice-Chancellor and the President of the Family Division and with the concurrence of the Lord Chancellor.

E R Heward
Chief Chancery Master
A B McFarlane
Master, Court of Protection
B P Tickle

22 December 1982   Senior Registrar, Family Division.

If there is a dispute as to the auctioneer's remuneration, the auctioneer is entitled to be represented before the master when the amount of the remuneration is fixed.[18] Under a sale directed by the court, if the solicitor to the auction or any party thereto desires to participate as a bidder at the auction, he must obtain leave to bid before the sale. No special conditions of sale are laid down for the sale by auction of land pursuant to a court order. Normally one of the forms of General Conditions discussed in chapter 9 will be appropriate.[19]

Similar provisions exist in the County Court by virtue of Ord 22, r 11 of the County Court Rules 1981. This rule applies the same provisions as the rules of the Supreme Court considered above.

SALES UNDER DISTRESS FOR RENT

The right of distress has its origin in feudal times and was used by a lord to enforce the rendering of services by his tenant, subject to which services the tenant held the land. The remedy is now limited to when a landlord and tenant relationship exists as to land and where the rent is in arrear.

---

[18] *Re Wolfe, Heller v Wolfe* [1952] 2 TLR 388.
[19] In *Re Walford, Walford v Walford* (1889) 5 TLR 251, CA, where a testator's land was sold by auction under a power of sale in the mortgage but the mortgagees had taken directions from the chief clerk the sale was regarded as if directed by the court and the auctioneer limited to the appropriate scale charge.

Although the remedy has not fallen into complete desuetude, and although in 1975 the government announced that it had no intention of abolishing it,[20] this area of law is rightly regarded as 'highly complex, technical and archaic'.[21]

Distress is essentially a self-help remedy by the landlord, no court order being necessary unless the tenant is protected by the Rents Acts. Essentially, either the landlord or, in practice, a duly certificated bailiff, enters onto the tenant's land and takes possession of a sufficient amount of the tenant's non-privileged goods to provide reasonable security for outstanding rent and expenses. The bailiff is certificated by the County Court and should be given a distress warrant by the landlord authorising him to levy the distress. The goods may not be sold for five days, and this period can be extended to fifteen days if the tenant so applies in writing. Until the sale the tenant has the right to 'replevy' them ie tender the rent owing and expenses.

If the goods are sold, there is an ancient duty to sell at the best price obtainable for the goods. Thus a public auction is desirable if not essential. The tenant may expressly request in writing that the goods be removed to a public auction room or some other fit and proper place to be there sold.[22]

SALES UNDER OTHER MISCELLANEOUS POWERS

The following persons have powers of sale over goods in their possession, though these powers may not necessarily be exercised by auctions:

(a) A repairer who has expended money on uncollected goods. The position here is that following the 18th Report of the Law Reform Committee (Conversion and Detinue) the Disposal of Uncollected Goods Act 1952 (which prescribed sale by public auction) was repealed and replaced by the Torts (Interference With Goods) Act 1977. The bailee-repairer now has a general power to sell the goods by the best method of sale reasonably available in the circumstances. Various obligations are imposed upon him, particularly as to notice to the owner, before this right may be exercised.

(b) Innkeepers. An innkeeper enjoys the right, by virtue of the Innkeepers Act 1878, to detain under a lien a guest's goods brought to the hotel until the cost of food and lodging is met. If the goods are detained for six weeks the goods may be sold if the sale is advertised as specified by

[20] HC Official Report (5th series) written answer.
[21] See Report of Payne Committee on the Enforcement of Judgment Debts (1969) Cmnd 3909, paras 912–32 — abolition was recommended; also similar remarks of Lord Denning MR in *Abingdon RDC v O'Gorman* [1968] 2 QB 811, CA, at 819.
[22] Law of Distress Amendment Act 1888.

the Act at least a month beforehand. Section 1 of the Act specifically prescribes that the sale shall be by public auction.[23]

(c) Certain warehousemen. Hitherto, under ss 497 and 498 of the Merchant Shipping Act 1894, wharfingers and warehousemen mentioned in these sections were permitted to sell either perishable goods, or in other cases, after ninety days, general goods on which they had an undischarged lien for storage charges, by public auction. The sections imposed preconditions including the giving of notice by advertisement and specific notice to the owner, though the title of a bona fide purchaser was not affected by omission to send the latter notice.[24] These powers were abolished by the Statute Law (Revision) Act 1993, s 1(1), Sch 1 Part XV.

(d) Trustees in bankruptcy have power to sell the bankrupt's property by virtue of s 314(1)(b) of and Sch 8 para 9 to the Insolvency Act 1986.

(e) Liquidators of companies are empowered to sell the company's property under s 539(2) of the Companies Act 1985.

PROPERTY IN THE POSSESSION OF THE POLICE

Property can come into the possession of the police either because it is being used or is intended for use for purposes of crime or, more usually, because it is connected with the investigation of a suspected offence.

In the former case, s 43 of the Powers of Criminal Courts Act 1973 empowers the court to make an order depriving an offender of such property, and if it is claimed that the offender does not own the property, no claim may be made to it after six months from the date of such order. In the latter case, above, the Police (Property) Act 1897 empowers the Secretary of State to make regulations for the disposal of such property. There is also a general power to sell perishable property or property whose custody involves unreasonable expense and inconvenience. In this case, the proceeds of sale must be kept for a year; in other cases, the goods must be retained for a year.

The Police (Disposal of Property) Regulations 1975[25] provide that property in the possession of the police either by virtue of s 43 of the Powers of Criminal Courts Act 1973, or when the owner has not been ascertained and no court order is made, 'shall be sold'. No method of sale is specified but, again, a public auction is normally chosen. The regulations go on to deal with the application of the proceeds of sale which are kept in the Police

[23] The definitions of 'Innkeeper' and 'Hotel' are now contained in the Hotel Proprietors Act 1956.

[24] Agents of necessity also have common law powers of sale in limited cases of emergency.

[25] Made primarily under the Police (Property) Act 1897 mentioned above.

Property Act Fund, but these details are not relevant to the subject matter of this book.[26]

PROBLEMS OF TITLE

Section 21 of the Sale of Goods Act 1979 makes specific provision for sales under statutory powers. Having stated the *nemo dat* rule (that the buyer acquires no better title than the seller), s 21(2) goes on to state that 'nothing in this Act affects . . . the validity of any contract of sale under any special common law or statutory power of sale or under the order of a court of competent jurisdiction.'

Specific statutes also protect bona fide purchasers in limited circumstances. Thus in the case of sales by distraining landlords. where the goods are unprotected from distress, the purchaser from the distraining landlord gets a good title as against the true owner — eg where the tenant possessed the goods on hire-purchase.[27]

Sales by trustees in bankruptcy pass a good title to the purchaser, even if the goods are only in the reputed ownership of the bankrupt (with the owner's consent). Here the true owner must prove in the bankruptcy for their value.[28]

---

[26] In the case of stolen property whose owner cannot be traced, it will be seen that there can be no identifiable person with a direct interest in obtaining the best possible price. Nevertheless, auction sales of 'unclaimed property by direction of the Police' are commonplace and offer the best proof of a bona fide sale should this ever be questioned.

[27] Law of Distress Amendment Act 1908, s 4.

[28] *Re Button, ex p Haviside* [1907] 2 KB 180, 76 JKB 833, CA.

Value Added Tax

HISTORY

The implementation on 14 February 1994 of the 7th VAT Directive (94/5/EC) has greatly complicated the VAT position of auction sales. In order to understand the philosophy behind and working of the new system, some knowledge of the old system is required.

GOODS SOLD OUTSIDE THE 'SPECIAL SCHEME'

Briefly, where vendors of lots are registered for VAT and wish to pass on the VAT on the eventual hammer price to the buyer, Conditions of Sale may entitle them to do so and, traditionally, auctioneers indicate lots subject to VAT on the hammer price by a 'dagger' or asterisk sign. The buyer is then liable to pay VAT at the applicable rate prevailing on the day of the auction on both the hammer price and the premium. Where there is no indication that the hammer price was subject to VAT (as was most commonly the case prior to 1995), the buyer was under no obligation to pay VAT on the hammer price (but did have to pay VAT on the premium) and the seller, if registered for VAT, had to treat the net proceeds of sales as including VAT.

Because of the intrinsic unfairness of taxing second-hand goods twice, the Treasury made orders under which, subject to certain conditions, the amount of the price on resale of relevant goods which attracted VAT was limited to the *dealer's margin* as opposed to the whole of the sale price. The 'special scheme' in question applied particularly to used motor cars, antiques, second-hand works of art, and scientific collections. So, for example, if the rate of VAT was 15 per cent and an item cost £600 and was then resold for £692, the selling margin amounts to £92. VAT included in the margin is represented by the fraction 15/115 (3/23). Accordingly, the VAT due to Customs and Excise on that transaction was $3/23 \times 92 = £12$.

Most items sold by VAT registered dealers in chattel auctions normally fell within the special scheme, but items such as plant and machinery sold on behalf of VAT registered commercial organisations did not and were (and are) likely to be auctioned subject to VAT. If buyers are registered for

VAT, they could (and can) treat VAT so paid as input tax. Other articles sold outside the special scheme by VAT registered dealers included paintings created after 1 April 1973, including those sold by or on behalf of the painter, and modern jewellery.

Looking at the situation through the buyer's eyes, unless the lot was 'daggered' or 'starred' the buyer was formerly in the position of paying no separate amount of VAT on the hammer price. On the introduction by most auctioneers of the buyer's premium, VAT was also charged on that premium. This proved quite controversial. It was argued by some that the auctioneers supplied no service to the *buyer* and since VAT was a tax (inter alia) on services supplied, no VAT was exigible. This argument was considered by the London VAT Tribunal. In *Jocelyn Feilding Fine Arts Ltd v Customs and Excise Comr.*[1] the appellants carried on business as dealers in fine art and sold articles through Christie's and Sotheby's subject to the buyer's premium. The Customs and Excise contended that on sale the buyer's premium formed part of the sale consideration and accordingly was liable to VAT even though the seller never received it. Under both Christie's and Sotheby's Conditions, the buyer's premium was stated to be part of the purchase price. The tribunal, however, considered that the buyer's premium was not part of the purchase price as it was expressly retained by the auctioneer. Instead, the tribunal analysed the transaction as consisting of:

(a) the consideration for which the goods are supplied by the seller, this being the *final bid price*;
(b) the buyer's premium, being the consideration not for the supply of goods by the seller but for the services provided by the auctioneer.

Accordingly, the consideration for the supply of goods would exclude the buyer's premium. Following this decision the Commissioners of Customs and Excise decided to treat the final bid price as the buying price for all sales by auction, whether outside or under the special scheme. Accordingly, the following principles applied:

(a) VAT was charged at the standard rate on any buyer's premium applicable (s 3 of the Value Added Tax Act 1983, replacing previous similar provisions).
(b) Any VAT paid on the buyer's premium by a registered dealer could be treated as input tax under the normal rules.
(c) The final bid price is the consideration for which goods sold under the special scheme were supplied by the seller and acquired by the buyer. This was therefore the figure to be entered in either the seller's or

---

[1] [1978] VAT TR 164.

buyer's special scheme stock-book, and the margin had to be calculated on that basis.

SEVENTH DIRECTIVE

The Seventh Directive, for the many years in which it was in draft, was the subject of considerable apprehension by the UK art and auctioneering world. Prior to 1995, qualifying works of art and antiques could flow in and out of London free of any tax. It was for this reason that London established its reputation as a great *entrepot*. This position attracted jealous eyes from elsewhere in the EU because the UK was seen to be trading at a competitive advantage. (The interesting assumption was made that it was not open to other countries to reduce or eliminate the taxation in issue.) In 1991 art valued at around £700 million or approximately 50 per cent of all imports, came into the UK from the US, Japan, Switzerland and elsewhere. The lack of bureaucratic hurdles obviously appealed to foreign sellers. In some important sales of fine art as a consequence about 90 per cent of the lots might come from abroad, mainly from outside what is now the EU, and departed in a similar fashion. The obvious fear was that London, if the UK were subjected to a uniform rate of VAT on such sales, would lose its competitive advantage to other non-EU cities such as New York and Geneva.

In the event, helpful concessions were made to the UK's position in the scheme which was eventually agreed. The Commission understood the principle that most second-hand goods had already been subject to VAT when sold new. To tax them a second time on their total value (as was the case in some Member States) when they were re-introduced in the trade circuit was tantamount to double taxation. This surcharge could grow in cases of successive re-sales between professional re-sellers and individuals, which could be frequent, especially for works of art. The EU therefore adopted the principles of the UK's 'special scheme' whereby sales of second-hand goods and works of art throughout the Community can be taxed in the country of the seller and at that country's VAT rate on the seller's profit margin (being the difference between the price at which the seller bought the goods and the price at which he sold them) and not on the total value. The Seventh Directive also confirmed that sales of second-hand goods and works of art from private individuals to private individuals anywhere in the EU were not subject to VAT and they could therefore move freely in the internal market.

The Directive also provides for common terms of taxation on imports of art into the EU. Member States are empowered to apply a reduced rate equal to at least 5 per cent to the hammer or selling price of any item imported from outside the EU. However, a special derogation was made in the case of the UK since works of art acquired before 1973, antiques and certain collectors' items had hitherto been exempted from VAT. The UK was empowered to apply an effective rate of VAT of 2.5 per cent to imports of works of art during the VAT transition period, ie up to 30 June 1999. The implication is that thereafter there will be a uniform rate throughout the EU. However there will be a review in 1996 of the impact of the new regulations on the European art market and it is a fair bet that there will be considerable resistance to any increase in the rate in the UK from affected interests and on the basis of the arguments outlined above. Post 1 April 1973 art works sold by the artist (and other non-qualifying items) continue to attract VAT at the full rate.

At the time of writing it is hoped by auctioneers that any VAT due on import can be deferred until the goods are sold and then discharged out of the proceeds of sale. If the lot is returned to the vendor unsold, no VAT would be payable. Limited deferral provision for the temporary import of second-hand goods imported with a view to their sale by auction is, in fact, made by H M Customs and Excise, Notice 200, January 1988, but the profession finds the maximum of six months too short a period during which they may remain in the EU, and the provisions for security for VAT by way of a cash deposit, guarantee or bond financially and administratively burdensome. This period may now be extended to two years.

In practical terms the major changes to the VAT system on second-hand goods are as follows:

(1) The special margin scheme of accounting for VAT becomes available to dealers in many more types of second-hand goods. For practical purposes all second-hand goods from within the EU are now covered, including works of art, antiques and collector's items, except precious metals and (loose) gemstones.

(2) Because dealers may handle a considerable volume of low value goods about which it would be impossible to keep detailed records of purchases and sales, a system of 'global accounting' has been introduced whereby dealers account for VAT on the difference between the buying and selling prices of all eligible goods bought and sold in each accounting period, without the need to maintain a detailed record of individual items dealt with under the margin schemes.

(3) Goods sold under the margin scheme are subject to VAT only in the Member State where the sale takes place, even where they are sold to a VAT registered dealer from another Member State. Sales to countries outside the EU are unaffected and continue to be zero rated if items are sold outside the margin scheme.[2] If sold within the scheme,

---

[2] As currently, VAT on the premium is not, however, recoverable.

the non-EU buyer will be unable to reclaim any VAT because it will be unidentifiable.

(4) Before 1995, most works of art, antiques and collector's items were exempt from VAT at import into the UK from non-EU countries. These now become subject to an effective rate of 2.5 per cent (as mentioned above). An important point as far as auctions are concerned is that VAT at 2.5 per cent now on the hammer price and on the premium will produce a total amount payable by the buyer which is very nearly the same as the amount previously paid by the buyer of goods when paying 17.5 per cent VAT on the buyer's premium but without VAT on the hammer price.

IMPLEMENTATION

Although the Seventh Directive was meant to be implemented by 1 January 1995, this was only partially achieved in the UK. In particular those provisions directly affecting auction sales were deferred until the passing of the then current Finance Bill. In fact the proposed new system took many firms by surprise and it was found, amongst other things, that commonly used computer programmes were unsuitable for the new invoicing system required. At the legislative level there were important details still subject to negotiation with Customs and Excise who were reported to have found the terms in which the Directive was expressed difficult to apply in legislative form. The new Scheme in fact applies from 1 June 1995.

As this book went to press Customs and Excise produced a draft of Notice 718 which will effect the necessary legal changes in VAT Margin Schemes.

SPECIAL POSITION OF AUCTIONEERS

After the Budget in November 1994 Customs and Excise announced that from Royal Assent to the then current Finance Bill supplies of goods through agents, including auctioneers, who act in their own names will be treated for VAT purposes as supplies both to them and by them. A special accounting scheme was introduced for auctioneers who organise sales by public auction, acting in their own names, under a contract on which commission is payable. This scheme allows auctioneers selling second-hand goods, works of art, antiques and collector's items to calculate VAT on a notional margin basis. Under this scheme, effectively the auctioneer is deemed to be a principal who buys the relevant goods at the hammer price after subtracting commission, insurance and any other sale-related costs. A split second later the auctioneer is treated as selling those goods at the hammer price plus buyer's premium thereon (if applicable).

Invoices under this system must not show any VAT because the margin scheme applies and amounts are shown gross inclusive of VAT. So as far as the buyer and the buyer's premium is concerned, this is shown as a VAT inclusive price, as is the vendor's commission and other vendor charges. Customs and Excise announced that, generally speaking, the amount of output tax due would be largely unchanged in comparison with the former treatment of supplies by auctioneers.

The practical effect on dealers buying at auction is, therefore, that the selling dealer will show the net amount received from the auctioneer as the selling price in their stock books, and the buyer the gross amount paid as their purchase price. No VAT invoice will be issued, though the hammer price in most cases is likely to be given for information.

The position with regard to the calculation necessary to arrive at the new VAT inclusive premium, assuming that a buyer's premium of 15 per cent is to be currently charged and this, in turn, attracts VAT at $17\frac{1}{2}$ per cent thereon, is as follows, assuming a hammer price of £500:

	£	£
Hammer Price		500.00
Plus 15% Premium	75.00	
VAT thereon	13.125	
		88.125
Total payable		588.125

The figure of £88.125 as a fraction of £500 = 17.625 per cent. This figure, possibly rounded up or down, will therefore be shown as the new VAT inclusive premium.

Assume now that a work of art is sold for £5,000 and it is desired to compare the old and new systems from both the buyer's and seller's point of view. (An adjusted rate of selling commission on a VAT inclusive bill of 11.75 per cent and a similar insurance rate of 1.175 per cent is assumed.) The position is as follows:

Buyer

		Old		New
Hammer Price		5,000.00		5,000.00
Premium	(15%)	750.00	(17.625%)	881.25
VAT		131.25		
Total Payable		5,881.25		5,881.25

Seller

		Old		New
Hammer Price		5,000.00		5,000.00
Commission	(10%)	500.00	(11.752%)	587.50
VAT thereon		87.50		
Insurance	(1%)	50.00	(1.175%)	58.75
VAT thereon		8.75		
Net		4,353.75		4,353.75

These calculations apply where the seller is either a private individual or registered under the margin scheme. Where the seller operates not under the margin scheme but is registered for VAT, the buyer will pay 17½ per cent on the hammer price as at present.

Under the new arrangements, the auctioneer will be treated for VAT purposes as having bought the item from the seller for £4,353.75 and then having sold it on to the buyer for £5,881.25. His margin of £1,527.50 is inclusive of VAT of £227.50 (7/47 × £1,527.50) which will be payable to Customs and Excise.[3]

---

[3] 7/47 is the appropriate fraction where VAT is 17.5 per cent (see p 308). As to insurance, unless recharged to the exact amount (in which case it is an exempt supply), it attracts VAT as an additional service of the auctioneer.

Appendix 1

Conditions of Sale

Conditions of Sale of Sotheby's
Conditions of Sale of Christie Manson & Woods Ltd

CONDITIONS OF SALE OF SOTHEBY'S[1]

SOTHEBY'S
FOUNDED 1744
CONDITIONS OF BUSINESS

Sotheby's carries on business (whether with actual or prospective buyers and sellers or consignors requiring inspection, appraisal or valuation of property or persons reading catalogues, or otherwise) on the following terms and conditions and on such other terms, conditions and notices as may be set out in any relevant catalogue. The definition of words and phrases with special meanings appear in Condition 40.

Conditions mainly concerning buyers

1 The buyer
The highest bidder shall be the buyer at the 'hammer price' and any dispute shall be settled at the auctioneer's absolute discretion. Any bidder acting for any person who is not bidding shall be jointly and severally liable with that person for satisfaction of all obligations and liabilities hereunder.

2 Minimum increment
The auctioneer shall have the right to refuse any bid which does not exceed the previous bid by at least 5 per cent, or by such other proportion as the auctioneer shall in his absolute discretion direct.

3 The buyer's premium
The buyer shall pay to Sotheby's a premium at the 'stated rates' on the 'hammer price' together with Value Added Tax at the standard rate on the premium and agrees that Sotheby's, when acting as agent for the seller, may also receive commission from the seller in accordance with Condition 19.

4 Value Added Tax (VAT)
Lots on which Value Added Tax is payable by the buyer on the 'hammer price' are indicated in the catalogue with a sign — see Important Information for Buyers.

---

[1] These 1993 Conditions are the copyright of Sotheby's and are reproduced by their kind permission.

Value Added Tax, the rates of which are subject to alteration by law, is payable at the rates prevailing on the day of the auction.

5 Currency converter
A currency converter will be operated at some auctions but only for the guidance of bidders. Sotheby's will not accept any responsibility in the event of error on the currency converter whether in the foreign currency equivalent of bids in pounds sterling or otherwise.

6 Payment
Immediately after a lot is sold the buyer shall: —
(a) give to Sotheby's his name and address and, if so requested, proof of identity; and (b) pay to Sotheby's the 'total amount due' (unless credit terms have been agreed with Sotheby's before the auction).

7 Sotheby's may, at its absolute discretion, agree to provide credit terms to a buyer under which the buyer will be entitled to take possession of lots purchased up to an agreed amount in value with payment of the 'total amount due' on a determined future date(s).

8 Any payments by a buyer to Sotheby's may be applied by Sotheby's towards any sums owing from that buyer to Sotheby's on any account whatever without regard to any directions of the buyer or his agent, whether express or implied as to how that payment should be applied.

9 Ownership of purchases
The ownership of the lot purchased shall not pass to the buyer until he has made payment in full to Sotheby's of the 'total amount due'.

10 Collection of purchases
(a) The buyer shall at his own expense take away the lot purchased not later than 5 working days after the day of the auction but (unless credit terms have been agreed in accordance with Condition 7) not before payment to Sotheby's of the 'total amount due'.
(b) The buyer shall be responsible for any removal and storage of any lot not taken away within 5 working days after the day of the auction.
(c) The packing and handling of purchased lots by Sotheby's staff is undertaken solely as a courtesy to clients, and in the case of fragile articles, will be undertaken only at Sotheby's discretion. In no event will Sotheby's be liable for damage to glass or frames, regardless of cause. (While Sotheby's may recommend packers and shippers, Sotheby's are not responsible for their errors and omissions).

11 For wines, spirits and cigars not available for collection from Sotheby's premises, the supply of a release order authorising the release of the lot to the buyer will constitute delivery by Sotheby's.

12 Buyers responsibilities for lots purchased
The buyer will be responsible for loss or damage to lots purchased from the time of collection or the expiry of 5 working days after the day of the auction, whichever is

the sooner, and neither Sotheby's nor its servants or agents shall thereafter be responsible for any loss or damage of any kind, whether caused by negligence or otherwise, while any lot is in its custody or under its control.

13 The buyer of a 'motor vehicle' is responsible for complying with the provision of the Road Traffic Act 1972 and all relevant regulations made under section 40 thereof (including the Motor Vehicles [Construction and Use] Regulations 1973) and any statutory modification thereof.

14 The buyer of a firearm is responsible for obtaining a valid firearm certificate, shot gun certificate or certificate of registration as a firearms dealer and for conforming with the regulations in force in Great Britain relating to firearms, notice of which is published in catalogues of firearms. Sotheby's will not deliver lots to buyers without production of evidence of compliance with this condition.

15 Remedies for non-payment or failure to collect purchases
If any lot is not paid for in full and taken away in accordance with Conditions 6 and 10, or if there is any other breach of either of those Conditions, Sotheby's as agent of the seller and for itself, as appropriate, shall, at its absolute discretion and without prejudice to any other rights it may have, be entitled to exercise one or more of the following rights and remedies: —
(a) to proceed against the buyer for damages for breach of contract;
(b) to rescind the sale of that or any other lots sold to the defaulting buyer at the same or any other auction;
(c) to re-sell the lot or cause it to be re-sold by public auction or private sale and the defaulting buyer shall pay to Sotheby's any resulting deficiency in the 'total amount due' (after deduction of any part payment and addition of re-sale costs and Sotheby's commission and buyer's premium at the stated rates) and any surplus shall belong to the seller;
(d) to remove, store and insure the lot at the expense of the defaulting buyer and, in the case of storage, either at Sotheby's premises or elsewhere:
(e) to charge interest at a rate not exceeding 2% per month on the 'total amount due' to the extent it remains unpaid for more than 5 working days after the day of the auction;
(f) to retain that or any other lot of the same buyer whether held by Sotheby's or by any Sotheby's company, and release any such lot(s) only after payment of the 'total amount due';
(g) to reject or ignore any bids made by or on behalf of the defaulting buyer at any future auctions or obtain a deposit before accepting any bids in future;
(h) to apply any proceeds of sale then due or at any time thereafter becoming due to the defaulting buyer towards settlement of the 'total amount due', to exercise a lien on any property of the defaulting buyer which is in the possession of Sotheby's or any Sotheby's company for any purpose, and to sell that property.

16 Liability of Sotheby's and sellers
(a) Goods auctioned are usually of some age. All goods are sold with all faults and imperfections and errors of description. Illustrations in catalogues are for identification only. Buyers should satisfy themselves prior to sale as to the condition of each

lot and should exercise and rely on their own judgement as to whether the lot accords with its description. Subject to the obligations accepted by Sotheby's under this Condition, none of the seller, Sotheby's, its servants or agents is responsible for errors of descriptions or for the genuineness or authenticity of any lot, no warranty whatever is given by Sotheby's, its servants or agents, or any seller to any buyer in respect of any lot and any express or implied conditions or warranties are hereby excluded.

(b) Any lot which proves to be a 'deliberate forgery' may be returned by the buyer to Sotheby's within 5 years of the date of the auction in the same condition in which it was at the time of the auction, accompanied by a statement of defects, the number of the lot, and the date of the auction at which it was purchased. If Sotheby's is satisfied that the item is a 'deliberate forgery' and that the buyer has and is able to transfer a good and marketable title to the lot free from any third party claims, the sale will be set aside and any amount paid in respect of the lot will be refunded; provided that the buyer shall have no rights under this Condition if:

(i) the description in the catalogue at the date of the sale was in accordance with the then generally accepted opinion of scholars and experts or fairly indicated that there was a conflict of such opinion; or

(ii) the only method of establishing at the date of publication of the catalogue that the lot was a 'deliberate forgery' was by means of scientific processes not generally accepted for use until after publication of the catalogue or a process which was unreasonably expensive or impractical; or

(iii) in the case of musical instrument bows, where it is established on removal of the lapping that the bow is a composite piece.

(c) A buyer's claim under this Condition shall be limited to any amount paid in respect of the lot and shall not extend to any loss, interest or damage suffered or expense incurred by him.

(d) The benefit of this Condition shall not be assignable and shall rest solely and exclusively in the buyer who, for the purpose of this Condition, shall be and only be the person to whom the original invoice is made out by Sotheby's in respect of the lot sold.

(e) Neither Sotheby's nor the seller make any representations or warranties, implied or express, as to whether any lot is subject to copyrights, nor whether the purchaser acquires any copyrights, including but not limited to any reproduction rights, in any lot sold.

Conditions mainly concerning sellers and consignors

17 Warranty of title and availability.

(a) The seller warrants to Sotheby's and to the buyer that he is the true owner of the property or is properly authorised to sell the property by the true owner and is able to transfer good and marketable title to the property free from any third party claims, liens or encumbrances, that there are no claims of governments or governmental agencies with respect to the property and that the seller has provided Sotheby's with all information the seller has concerning the provenance of the property.

(b) The seller of a cultural object falling within the catagories and value limits in the E.C. Regulations (EEC 3911/92) declares that to the best of his knowledge that item was either in the UK before 1.1.93 or, if exported, directly or indirectly, from a member state to another member state of the European Community after 1.1.93, was lawfully removed from that state and that he will provide such available documentation as necessary.

(c) The seller of property not held by Sotheby's on its premises or under its control, warrants and undertakes to Sotheby's and the buyer that the property will be available and in a deliverable state on demand by the buyer.

(d) The seller will indemnify Sotheby's, its servants and agents and the buyer against any loss or damage suffered by either in consequence or any breach or alleged breach of (a) or (b) above or otherwise, of these Conditions on the part of the seller.

18 Reserves

The seller shall be entitled to place prior to the auction a reserve on any lot, being the minimum 'hammer price' at which that lot may be treated as sold. A reserve once placed by the seller shall not be changed without the consent of Sotheby's. Sotheby's may at its option sell at a 'hammer price' below the reserve, but in any such case the sale proceeds to which the seller is entitled shall be the same as if the lot had sold on the reserve. No seller may bid, nor may any third party bid, on a seller's behalf. Where a reserve has been placed, Sotheby's may, on behalf of the seller, bid up to that reserve.

19 Authority to deduct commission, buyer's premium and expenses

The Seller authorises Sotheby's to deduct commission at the 'stated rates' and 'expenses' from the 'hammer price' and acknowledges Sotheby's right to retain the buyer's premium payable by the buyer in accordance with Condition 3.

The insurance premium will be charged as an expense to the seller on the 'hammer price' (or if unsold, the reserve price, or if no reserve, Sotheby's low saleroom estimate) at a rate of 1% plus VAT thereon regardless of the nature of the property.

20 Risk of loss of damage

Unless otherwise instructed, Sotheby's will assume risk of loss or damage to property (other than 'motor vehicles') consigned to it or put under its control for sale until whichever is the earlier of the ownership of the property passing from the seller, or the seller or consignor becoming bound to collect the property. Sotheby's may, at its discretion, assume risk of loss or damage to property put under its control for any other purpose.

If Sotheby's is to assume such risk, this will be at the expense of the seller or consignor and Sotheby's liability for loss or damage to any property will not exceed the amount estimated by Sotheby's to be, from time to time, the current value of the property at auction, less Sotheby's commission and expenses, nor in any event will it exceed:

(a) the 'hammer price' less Sotheby's commission and expenses if the property has been sold;

(b) the reserve, less Sotheby's commission and expenses if the property has not been sold after being offered for sale and the reserve has been determined;
(c) the mid saleroom estimate, less Sotheby's commission and expenses in any other case.

In no event will Sotheby's be liable for damage to glass or picture frames. Sotheby's, its servants and agents shall have no liability in connection with loss or damage to property caused by (i) any third party instructed to deal with the property with the seller's or consignor's consent; (ii) changes in humidity or temperature; (iii) inherent conditions or defects; (iv) errors in processing; (v) war, nuclear radiation or radioactive contamination.

In all cases, save where Sotheby's is to assume risk of loss or damage, the property shall remain at all times at the risk of the seller or consignor and neither Sotheby's, nor its servants or agents will be responsible for any loss or damage, whether caused by negligence or otherwise.

If the seller instructs Sotheby's not to assume risk of loss or damage for a lot, and following expiry of any period of risk assumed by Sotheby's pursuant to the above, it shall at all times remain at the risk of the seller who hereby undertakes:

(1) to indemnify Sotheby's against all claims made or proceedings brought against Sotheby's in respect of loss or damage to the lot of whatever nature, howsoever and wheresoever occurring, and in any circumstances even where negligence is alleged or proven;

(2) to reimburse Sotheby's on demand for all payments, costs or expenses, including legal fees made, incurred or suffered by Sotheby's in consequence thereof or arising therefrom. Any payment which Sotheby's shall make in respect of such loss or damage or payments, costs or expenses shall be binding upon the seller and shall be accepted by the seller as conclusive evidence that Sotheby's was liable to make such payment.

(3) to waive all rights and claims he may have against Sotheby's, its servants and agents in connection with such loss or damage referred to in Condition 20(1).

(4) to notify any insurer of the existence of the indemnity contained in this Condition, and to procure a waiver of subrogation by such insurer of all rights and claims they may have against Sotheby's in connection with loss or damage referred to in Condition 20(1).

21 Electrical and mechanical goods

The seller or consignor of electrical or mechanical goods warrants and undertakes to Sotheby's that at the date on which the same are consigned to Sotheby's or put under Sotheby's control, and except as previously disclosed to Sotheby's, the same are safe if reasonably used for the purpose for which they were designed and free from any defect not obvious on external inspection which could prove dangerous to human life or health, and will indemnify Sotheby's its servants and agents against any loss or damage suffered by any of them in consequence of any breach or alleged breach of the above warranty and undertaking.

22 Rescission of the sale

If the buyer makes a claim to rescind the sale under Condition 16, and Sotheby's is of the opinion that the claim is justified, Sotheby's is authorised to rescind the sale and refund to the buyer any amount paid to Sotheby's in respect of the lot. The seller or consignor will return to Sotheby's any sale proceeds paid by Sotheby's to the seller or consignor for such lot. When the sale proceeds, together with Sotheby's expenses in connection with the rescinded sale, have been repaid to Sotheby's, Sotheby's will return the lot to the seller or consignor.

23 Payment of sale proceeds
Sotheby's shall remit the 'sale proceeds' to the seller 35 days after the auction, but if by that date Sotheby's has not received the 'total amount due' from the buyer, then Sotheby's will remit the 'sale proceeds' within 5 working days after the date on which the 'total amount due' is received from the buyer. If credit terms in excess of 35 days have been agreed between Sotheby's and the buyer, Sotheby's shall remit to the seller the sale proceeds not later than 35 days after the auction, unless otherwise agreed by the seller; provided that where in the case of postage stamps Sotheby's has granted an extension, it shall remit the 'sale proceeds' when a certificate of genuineness is received by Sotheby's or 65 days after the auction, whichever is the sooner, but if by then Sotheby's has not received the 'total amount due' from the buyer, then Sotheby's will remit the 'sale proceeds' within 5 working days after the day on which the 'total amount due' is received from the buyer.
A charge at the 'stated rate' will be made for each payment to a seller in any form other than a sterling cheque.

24 If the buyer fails to pay to Sotheby's the 'total amount due' within 35 days after the auction, Sotheby's will endeavour to notify the seller and take the seller's instructions as to the appropriate course of action, provided that Sotheby's has no obligation to undertake legal proceedings. The seller authorises Sotheby's at the seller's expense to agree special terms for payment of the 'total amount due', to remove, store and insure the lot sold, to settle claims made by or against the buyer on such terms as Sotheby's shall in its absolute discretion think fit, to take such steps as are necessary to collect monies due by the buyer to the seller and Sotheby's and if necessary, to rescind the sale and refund money to the buyer.

25 If, notwithstanding that the buyer fails to pay to Sotheby's the 'total amount due' within 35 days after the auction, Sotheby's remits the 'sale proceeds' to the seller, the ownership of the lot shall pass to Sotheby's.

26 Charges for withdrawn lots
Where a seller cancels instructions for sale, or where a lot is withdrawn for any reason other than misattribution or authenticity, Sotheby's reserves the right to charge a fee equal to the vendor's commission and buyer's premium calculated on Sotheby's then mid saleroom estimate of the property withdrawn, together with Value Added Tax thereon and 'expenses' incurred in relation to the property.

27 Rights to photographs and illustrations
The seller gives Sotheby's full and absolute right to photograph and illustrate any lot placed in its hands for sale and to use such photographs and illustrations and any photographs and illustrations provided by the seller at any time and in any manner

at its absolute discretion, whether or not in connection with the auction. Except where the seller has informed Sotheby's to the contrary, the seller represents and warrants that no lot is subject to any copyright restrictions.

28 Unsold lots

Where any lot fails to sell, Sotheby's shall notify the seller accordingly. The seller shall make arrangements either to reoffer the lot for sale or to collect the lot and to pay the reduced commission under Condition 30 and 'expenses'. If such arrangements are not made: —

(a) within 7 days of notification, the seller shall be responsible for any removal, storage and insurance expenses;

(b) within 3 months of notification, Sotheby's shall have the right to sell the lot at public auction without reserve and to deduct from the 'hammer price' any sum owing to Sotheby's including (without limitation) removal, storage and insurance expenses, the 'expenses' of both auctions, reduced commission under Condition 30 in respect of the first auction as well as commission at the 'stated rates' on the sale and all other reasonable expenses before remitting the balance to the seller or, if he cannot be traced, placing it in a bank account in the name of Sotheby's for the seller.

29 Private sales

If any lot fails to reach its reserve and is bought-in for the seller's account, the seller authorises Sotheby's, as the seller's exclusive agent, for a period of sixty days following the auction to sell the lot privately for a price that will result in a payment to the seller of not less than the net amount (after Sotheby's commissions and expenses) to which the seller would have been entitled had the lot been sold at a price equal to the agreed reserve. In such event, the seller's obligations to Sotheby's and the buyer hereunder with respect to such lot are the same as if it had been sold at auction.

30 Sotheby's reserves the right to charge commission up to one-half of the 'stated rates' calculated on the reserve and in addition 'expenses' in respect of any unsold lots.

31 The seller authorises Sotheby's to undertake any tests, or any searches or enquiries in relation to the property as Sotheby's may in its absolute discretion deem appropriate.

General conditions and definitions

32 Sotheby's sells as agent for the seller (except where it is stated wholly or partly to own any lot as principal) and as such is not responsible for any default by seller or buyer.

33 Any representation or statement by Sotheby's in any Catalogue as to authorship, attribution, genuineness, origin, date, age, provenance, condition, reserve price or estimated selling price is a statement of opinion only. Sotheby's reserve the right in forming its opinion to consult and rely on any expert or authority of their choice. Every person interested should exercise and rely on his own judgement as to such matters and neither Sotheby's nor its servants or agents are responsible for the correctness of such opinions.

34 Whilst the interests of prospective buyers are best served by attendance at the auction, Sotheby's will, if so instructed execute bids on their behalf, neither Sotheby's nor its servants or agents being responsible for any neglect or default relating to bids made in doing so or for failing to do so, or for any failure of telecommunications relating to bids made.

35 Sotheby's shall have the right, at its discretion, to refuse admission to its premises or attendance at its auctions by any person.

36 Sotheby's has absolute discretion without giving any reason to refuse any bid, to divide any lot, to combine any two or more lots, to withdraw any lot from the auction and in case of dispute to put up any lot for auction again.

37 (a) Any indemnity under these Conditions shall extend to all actions, proceedings, costs including legal costs, expenses, claims and demands whatever incurred or suffered by the person entitled to the benefit of the indemnity.
(b) Sotheby's declares itself to be a trustee for its relevant servants and agents of the benefit of every indemnity under these Conditions to the extent that such indemnity is expressed to be for the benefit of its servants and agents.
(c) Sotheby's reserve the right to pay out of its commission, a fee to any agent introducing property.

38 Any notice by Sotheby's to a seller, consignor, prospective bidder or buyer may be given by first class mail or airmail and if so given shall be deemed to have been duly received by the addressee 48 hours after posting.

39 These Conditions shall be governed by and construed in accordance with English law. All transactions to which these Conditions apply and all matters connected therewith shall also be governed by English law. Sotheby's hereby submits to the exclusive jurisdiction of the English courts and all other parties concerned hereby submit in favour of Sotheby's to the non-exclusive jurisdiction of the English courts.

40 In these Conditions: —
(a) 'catalogue' includes any advertisement, brochure, estimate, price list and other publication;
(b) 'hammer price' means the price at which a lot is knocked down by the auctioneer to the buyer;
(c) 'total amount due' means the 'hammer price' in respect of the lot sold, together with any buyer's premium, Value Added Tax chargeable and additional charges and expenses due from a defaulting buyer under Condition 15, in pounds sterling;

(d) 'book' means any item included or proposed to be included in a sale of books and includes a manuscript or print;

(e) 'deliberate forgery' means an imitation made with the intention of deceiving as to authorship, origin, date, age, period, culture or source which is not shown to be such in the description in the catalogue and which at the date of the sale had a value materially less than it would have had if it had been in accordance with that description;

(f) 'sale proceeds' means the net amount due to the seller being the 'hammer price' of the lot sold less commission at the 'stated rates' and 'expenses' and any other amounts due to Sotheby's by the seller in whatever capacity and howsoever arising;

(g) 'stated rates' means Sotheby's published rates of commission, buyer's premium and other charges from time to time applicable to the relevant sale, plus Value Added Tax thereon;

(h) 'expenses' in relation to the sale of any lot means Sotheby's charges and expenses for insurance, illustrations, special advertising, packing and freight of that lot, reproduction rights, costs of testing, searches or enquiries relating to any lot and any Value Added Tax thereon;

(i) 'motor vehicle' means any item included or proposed to be included in a sale of motor vehicles;

(j) 'mid saleroom estimate' means the average of the latest low and high saleroom estimates of the auction price stated or published by Sotheby's.

(k) Sotheby's company means any company being a member of the Sotheby's group of companies.

41 Special terms may be used in catalogues in the description of a lot. Where terms are not self-explanatory and have special meanings ascribed to them, a glossary will appear before Lot 1 in the catalogue of the auction.

42 The headings in these Conditions do not form part of the Conditions but are for convenience only.

(i) Alternative Condition 16 for Catalogues for sales of Impressionist, Modern and Contemporary Art.

16. Liability of Sotheby's and Sellers
(a) Goods auctioned are usually of some age. All goods are sold with all faults and imperfections and errors of description. Illustrations in catalogues are for identification only. Buyers should satisfy themselves prior to sale as to the condition of each lot and should exercise and rely on their own judgement as to whether the lot accords with its description. Subject to the obligation accepted by Sotheby's under this Condition, none of the seller, Sotheby's, its servants or agents is responsible for errors of descriptions or for the genuineness or authenticity of any lot, no warranty whatever is given by Sotheby's, its servants or agents, or any seller to any buyer in respect of any lot and any express or implied conditions or warranties are hereby excluded.

(b) Any lot which was executed by someone other than the person described in the catalogue as the artist may be returned by the buyer to Sotheby's within five years of the date of the auction, in the same condition in which it was at the time of the auction, accompanied by a statement of defects, the number of the lot and the date of the auction at which it was purchased. If Sotheby's is satisfied that the lot was so executed and that the buyer has and is able to transfer a good and marketable title to the lot free from any third party claims the sale will be set aside and any amount paid in respect of the lot will be refunded. Provided that the buyer shall have no rights under this Condition if the description in the catalogue at the date of the sale was in accordance with the then generally accepted opinion of scholars and experts or fairly indicated that there was a conflict of such opinion.

(c) A buyer's claim under this Condition shall be limited to any amount paid in respect of the lot and shall not extend to any loss, interest or damage suffered or expense incurred by him.

(d) The benefit of this Condition shall not be assignable and shall rest solely and exclusively in the buyer who, for the purpose of this Condition, shall be and only be the person to whom the original invoice is made out by Sotheby's in respect of the lot sold.

(e) Neither Sotheby's nor the seller make any representations or warranties, implied or express, as to whether any lot is subject to copyrights, nor whether the purchaser acquires any copyrights, including but not limited to any reproduction rights, in any lot sold.

(ii) Alternative Condition 16 for Catalogues for sales of 'Books'.

16. Liability of Sotheby's and Sellers
(a) Goods auctioned are usually of some age. All goods are sold with all faults and imperfections and errors of description. Illustrations in catalogues are for identification only. Buyers should satisfy themselves prior to sale as to the condition of each lot and should exercise and rely on their own judgement as to whether the lot accords with its description. Subject to the obligation accepted by Sotheby's under this Condition, none of the seller, Sotheby's, its servants or agents is responsible for errors of descriptions or for the genuineness or authenticity of any lot, no warranty whatever is given by Sotheby's, its servants or agents, or any seller to any buyer in respect of any lot and any express or implied conditions or warranties are hereby excluded.

(b) If within 21 days of the auction, the buyer gives notice to Sotheby's in writing that an item is a forgery or defective in text or illustration and returns the lot to Sotheby's in the same condition in which it was at the time of the auction indicating the number of the lot and the date of the auction at which it was purchased, and it is established that the lot is defective, or a forgery Sotheby's will rescind the sale and refund any amount paid in respect of the lot:

Provided that such an item may not be returned nor will its sale be set aside or refund made if: —

(i) it is described in the catalogue as sold not subject to return; or

(ii) it is sold un-named in a lot; or

(iii) it comprises an atlas, an extra-illustrated book, a volume with fore-edge paintings, a periodical publication or a print or drawing; or

(iv) in the case of a manuscript, it was not described in the catalogue as complete; or

(v) the defect in question was mentioned in the catalogue; or

(vi) the defect complained of is other than in text or illustration. For example (but without limitation) an item may not be returned nor will its sale be set aside on account of damage to bindings, stains, foxing, marginal wormholes, lack of blank leaves, or other conditions not affecting the completeness of the text or illustration, lack of list of plates, inserted advertisements, cancels or any subsequently published volume, supplement, appendix or plates or error in the enumeration of the plates.

(c) A buyer's claim under this Condition shall be limited to any amount paid in respect of the lot and shall not extend to any loss, interest or damage suffered or expense incurred by him.

(d) The benefit of this Condition shall not be assignable and shall rest solely and exclusively in the buyer who, for the purpose of this Condition, shall be and only be the person to whom the original invoice is made out by Sotheby's in respect of the lot sold.

(e) Neither Sotheby's nor the seller make any representations or warranties, implied or express, as to whether any lot is subject to copyrights, nor whether the purchaser acquires any copyrights, including but not limited to any reproduction rights, in any lot sold.

(iii) Alternative Condition 16 for Catalogues for sales of Gemstones and Pearls.

16. Liability of Sotheby's and Sellers

(a) Goods auctioned are usually of some age. All goods are sold with all faults and imperfections and errors of description. Illustrations in catalogues are for identification only. Buyers should satisfy themselves prior to sale as to the condition of each lot and should exercise and rely on their own judgement as to whether the lot accords with its description. Subject to the obligations accepted by Sotheby's under this Condition, none of the seller, Sotheby's, its servants or agents is responsible for errors of descriptions or for the genuineness or authenticity of any lot, no warranty whatever is given by Sotheby's, its servants or agents, or any seller to any buyer in respect of any lot and any express or implied conditions or warranties are hereby excluded.

(b) Gemstones and pearls are sold as genuine, untreated and of natural origin, unless stated to be otherwise in the catalogue or by the auctioneer at the sale. If within 21 days of an auction the buyer of a gemstone or pearl gives notice in writing to Sotheby's that an item purchased is not genuine, untreated, or of natural origin, and returns the lot to Sotheby's in the same condition as it was at the date of the sale, and it is established by a test carried out by a competent authority that the defect complained of is justified, Sotheby's will rescind the sale and refund any amount paid in respect of the lot, together with the testing fee, if paid by the buyer:

(c) A buyer's claim under this Condition shall be limited to any amount paid in respect of the lot and shall not extend to any loss, interest or damage suffered or expense incurred by him.

(d) The benefit of this Condition shall not be assignable and shall rest solely and exclusively in the buyer who, for the purpose of this Condition, shall be and only be the person to whom the original invoice is made out by Sotheby's in respect of the lot sold.

(e) Neither Sotheby's nor the seller make any representations or warranties, implied or express, as to whether any lot is subject to copyrights, nor whether the purchaser acquires any copyrights, including but not limited to any reproduction rights, in any lot sold.

(iv) Alternative Condition 16 for Catalogues for sales of Numismatic items.

16. Liability of Sotheby's and Sellers
(a) Goods auctioned are usually of some age. All goods are sold with all faults and imperfections and errors of description. Illustrations in catalogues are for identification only. Buyers should satisfy themselves prior to sale as to the condition of each lot and should exercise and rely on their own judgement as to whether the lot accords with its description. Subject to the obligation accepted by Sotheby's under this Condition, none of the seller, Sotheby's, its servants or agents is responsible for errors of descriptions or for the genuineness or authenticity of any lot, no warranty whatever is given by Sotheby's, its servants or agents, or any seller to any buyer in respect of any lot and any express or implied conditions or warranties are hereby excluded.

(b) If within eight days of the auction the buyer gives notice in writing to Sotheby's that an item purchased is a "deliberate forgery" and returns the lot to Sotheby's in the same condition as it was at the date of the sale and it is established that the item is a "deliberate forgery", Sotheby's will rescind the sale and refund any amount paid in respect of the lot.

(c) A buyer's claim under this Condition shall be limited to any amount paid in respect of the lot and shall not extend to any loss, interest or damage suffered or expense incurred by him.

(d) The benefit of this Condition shall not be assignable and shall rest solely and exclusively in the buyer who, for the purpose of this Condition, shall be and only be the person to whom the original invoice is made out by Sotheby's in respect of the lot sold.

(e) Neither Sotheby's nor the seller make any representations or warranties, implied or express, as to whether any lot is subject to copyrights, nor whether the purchaser acquires any copyrights, including but not limited to any reproduction rights, in any lot sold.

(v) Alternative Condition 16 for Catalogues for sales of Postage Stamps.

16. Liability of Sotheby's and Sellers
(a) Subject to the obligations accepted by Sotheby's under this Condition, none of the seller, Sotheby's, its servants or agents is responsible for errors of description or

for the genuineness or authenticity of any lot, no warranty whatever is given by Sotheby's, its servants or agents, or any seller to any buyer in respect of any lot and any express or implied conditions or warranties are hereby excluded.

(b) If within 21 days of the auction Sotheby's receives notice in writing from the buyer of a postage stamp lot claiming that an item is not genuine or does not correspond with the description in the catalogue and the lot is returned to Sotheby's by a date agreed by Sotheby's in the same condition as it was at the time of sale and on the original lot folder and Sotheby's agrees that the buyer's claim is justified, Sotheby's will rescind the sale and refund any amount paid to Sotheby's in respect of the lot: Provided that no return will be accepted nor sale rescinded nor refund made if: —

(i) the lot is described in the catalogue or is announced by the auctioneer at the sale as being not subject to return or as being defective; or

(ii) the lot is a collection or mixed lot containing more than four items, in which case the lot is purchased by the buyer with all (if any) faults, lack of genuineness and errors of description including the number of stamps in the lot; or

(iii) the lot has been illustrated and the defect complained of is apparent in the illustrations; or

(iv) there is a conflict of opinion between the Royal Philatelic Society London and B.P.A. Expertising Limited or either is unable to express a conclusive opinion.

(c) Where an extension has been granted under (d) below on an item which is proved not to be genuine then Sotheby's will rescind the sale and refund any amount paid to Sotheby's in respect of that item; Provided that: —

(i) within the extension period of 60 days Sotheby's receives back the item together with the certificate stating that it is not genuine; and (ii) the buyer has paid for the lot in accordance with Conditions 6 or 7.

(d) if Sotheby's receives a written application for an extension on a lot not later than 24 hours before an auction from an intending buyer, Sotheby's may grant an extension for a maximum of 60 days from the date of the auction during which the buyer may obtain a certificate of genuineness or non-genuineness from the Royal Philatelic Society of London or B.P.A. Expertising Limited: Provided that no extension will be granted on: —

(i) a collection or mixed lot containing more than four items or a single item contained in such a lot; or

(ii) an item which is described as accompanied by a specified certificate of opinion dated within ten years of the sale.

(e) Sotheby's reserves the right on behalf of the seller to withdraw a lot on which an extension has been requested under (d) above.

(f) (i) The certificate of either the Royal Philatelic Society London or B.P.A. Expertising Limited obtained under (d) above is conclusive; (ii) All costs in connection with obtaining such certificate are the responsibility of the buyer regardless of the opinion received.

(g) A buyer's claim under this Condition shall be limited to any amount paid in respect of the lot and shall not extend to any loss, interest or damage suffered or expense incurred by him.

(h) The benefit of this Condition shall not be assignable and shall rest solely and exclusively in the buyer who, for the purpose of this Condition, shall be and only be the person to whom the original invoice is made out by Sotheby's in respect of the lot sold.

(i) Neither Sotheby's nor the seller make any representations or warranties, implied or express, as to whether any lot is subject to copyrights, nor whether the purchaser acquires any copyrights, including but not limited to any reproduction rights, in any lot sold.

(vi) Alternative Condition 16 for Sales of Wines, Spirits and Cigars, and for Sales of Motor Vehicles.

16. Liability of Sotheby's and Sellers
Goods auctioned are usually of some age. All goods are sold with all faults and imperfections and errors of description. Illustrations in catalogues are for identification only. Buyers should satisfy themselves prior to sale as to the condition of each lot and should exercise and rely on their own judgement as to whether the lot accords with its description. None of the seller, Sotheby's, its servants or agents is responsible for errors of descriptions or for the genuineness or authenticity of any lot, no warranty whatever is given by Sotheby's, its servants or agents, or any seller to any buyer in respect of any lot and any express or implied conditions or warranties are hereby excluded.

(vii) Alternative Condition 16 for Catalogues for sales of Musical Instruments.

16. Liability of Sotheby's and Sellers
(a) Goods auctioned are usually of some age. All goods are sold with all faults and imperfections and errors of description. Illustrations in catalogues are for identification only. Buyers should satisfy themselves prior to sale as to the condition of each lot and should exercise and rely on their own judgement as to whether the lot accords with its description. Subject to the obligation accepted by Sotheby's under this Condition, none of the seller, Sotheby's, its servants or agents is responsible for errors of descriptions or for the genuineness or authenticity of any lot, no warranty whatever is given by Sotheby's, its servants or agents, or any seller to any buyer in respect of any lot and any express or implied conditions or warranties are hereby excluded.

(b) Any lot which proves to be a 'deliberate forgery' may be returned by the buyer to Sotheby's within 5 years of the date of the auction in the same condition in which it was at the time of the auction, accompanied by a statement of defects, the number of the lot, and the date of the auction at which it was purchased. If Sotheby's is satisfied that the item is a 'deliberate forgery' and that the buyer has and is able to transfer a good and marketable title to the lot free from any third party claims, the sale will be set aside and any amount paid in respect of the lot will be refunded: Provided that the buyer shall have no rights under this Condition if:

(i) the description in the catalogue at the date of the sale was in accordance with the then generally accepted opinion of scholars and experts or fairly indicated that there was a conflict of such opinion; or

(ii) the only method of establishing at the date of publication of the catalogue that the lot was a 'deliberate forgery' was by means of scientific processes not generally accepted for use until after publication of the catalogue or a process which was unreasonably expensive or impractical; or

(iii) in the case of musical instrument bows, where it is established on removal of the lapping that the bow is a composite piece.

(c) In the case of musical instrument bows if within 21 days of the auction the buyer gives notice to Sotheby's in writing that at the time of the auction the bow was broken in a place other than underneath the lapping and returns the bow to Sotheby's in the same condition in which it was at the time of the auction and it is established that such a claim is justified, Sotheby's will rescind the sale and refund any amount paid in respect of such bow: Provided that such a bow may not be returned nor will its sale be set aside or refund made if: (i) it is described in the catalogue as having been repaired; (ii) the lot also contains items other than musical instrument bows.

(d) A buyer's claim under this Condition shall be limited to any amount paid in respect of the lot and shall not extend to any loss, interest or damage suffered or expense incurred by him.

(e) The benefit of this Condition shall not be assignable and shall rest solely and exclusively in the buyer who, for the purpose of this Condition, shall be and only be the person to whom the original invoice is made out by Sotheby's in respect of the lot sold.

(f) Neither Sotheby's nor the seller make any representations or warranties, implied or express, as to whether any lot is subject to copyrights, nor whether the purchaser acquires any copyrights, including but not limited to any reproduction rights, in any lot sold.

(viii) Alternative Condition 20 for Motor Vehicle Catalogues.

20. Risk of loss or damage

The 'motor vehicle' shall remain at all times at the risk of the seller or consignor until the ownership of the property passes from the seller and neither Sotheby's nor its servants or agents will be responsible for any loss or damage whether caused by negligence or otherwise. The seller or consignor of a 'motor vehicle' warrants and undertakes to Sotheby's that at the date at which it is consigned to Sotheby's or put under Sotheby's control either:

(i) The vehicle can lawfully be used on the road, complies with the provisions of the Road Traffic Act 1972 and all relevant regulations made thereunder (including the Motor Vehicles (Construction and Use) Regulations 1978) and any statutory modifications thereof and there is in force any test certificate required in relation to such use and insurance complying with the said Act such as will enable the vehicle to be driven lawfully by servants and agents of Sotheby's and with an indemnity against all loss or damage; or

(ii) the seller or consignor has notified Sotheby's that the vehicle cannot lawfully be used on the road.

In all cases, save where Sotheby's is to assume risk of loss or damage, the property shall remain at all times at the risk of the seller or consignor and neither Sotheby's, nor its servants or agents will be responsible for any loss or damage, whether caused by negligence or otherwise.

If the seller instructs Sotheby's not to assume risk of loss or damage for a lot, and following expiry of any period of risk assumed by Sotheby's pursuant to the above, it shall at all times remain at the risk of the seller who hereby undertakes:

(a) to indemnify Sotheby's against all claims made or proceedings brought against Sotheby's in respect of loss or damage to the lot of whatever nature, howsoever and wheresoever occurring, and in any circumstances even where negligence is alleged or proven;

(b) to reimburse Sotheby's on demand for all payments, costs or expenses, including legal fees made, incurred or suffered by Sotheby's in consequence thereof or arising therefrom. Any payment which Sotheby's shall make in respect of such loss or damage or payments, costs or expenses shall be binding upon the seller and shall be accepted by the seller as conclusive evidence that Sotheby's was liable to make such payments;

(c) to waive all rights and claims he may have against Sotheby's, its servants and agents in connection with any loss or damage to, or caused by, the lot;

(d) to notify any insurer of the existence of the indemnity contained in this Condition, and to procure a waiver of subrogation by such insurer of all rights and claims they may have against Sotheby's in connection with loss or damage referred to above.

CONDITIONS OF SALE OF CHRISTIE MANSON & WOODS LTD[2]

CONDITIONS OF BUSINESS

These Conditions of Business represent the terms upon which Christie's, the fine art auctioneers, contracts with Sellers and, acting in its capacity as agent on behalf of Sellers, contracts with Buyers. These Conditions of Business shall supersede and take precedence over any Conditions of Business previously entered into or otherwise agreed between Christie's and the Seller.

Buyers and Sellers are advised to read carefully the Conditions of Business and the explanation of cataloguing practice set out below which contain the terms on which Christie's conducts sales and handles other related matters. Conditions A.1 to 12 inclusive and the explanation of cataloguing practice, where applicable, are of particular relevance to Buyers and Conditions B.1 to 14 inclusive to Sellers. Definitions of words and phrases with special meanings appear in Condition C.8.

A. The Buyer

1. Christie's as agent

Save as otherwise appears, Christie's acts only as agent for the Seller.

[2] These 1993 Conditions are the copyright of Christie, Manson & Woods Ltd and are reproduced by their kind permission.

2. The Buyer

(a) The Buyer shall be the highest bidder acceptable to Christie's and Christie's shall have absolute discretion to settle any dispute;

(b) every bidder shall be deemed to act as principal unless Christie's has, before the date of the auction, acknowledged in writing that the bidder is acting as agent on behalf of a disclosed principal;

(c) every bidder shall, if required by Christie's, complete and sign a Registration Form and provide identification before making any bid at the auction.

3. Catalogue Descriptions

(a) Any representation or statement by Christie's whether in the catalogue or other publication or in a condition report as to the authorship, origin, date, age, size, medium, attribution, genuineness, provenance, condition or estimated selling price of any Lot is a statement of opinion only. Any illustrations in the catalogue are solely for guidance and are not to be relied upon in terms of tone or colour or necessarily to reveal imperfections in any Lot;

(b) in addition, many Lots are of an age or nature which precludes their being in pristine condition and some descriptions in the catalogue or given by way of condition report make reference to damage and/or restoration. Such information is given for guidance only and the absence of such a reference does not imply that a Lot is free from defects nor does any reference to particular defects imply the absence of others;

(c) Buyers must satisfy themselves as to all matters referred to in (a) and (b) above by inspection or otherwise prior to the date of the auction. The attention of Buyers is also drawn to the explanation of cataloguing practice contained in the catalogue.

4. Premium

The Buyer shall pay to Christie's a Premium at the Rates of Premium set out in Condition C.8 together with VAT at the standard rate and the Buyer acknowledges that Christie's may also receive commission from the Seller in accordance with Condition B.4.

5. Value Added Tax

In the case of a lot marked with a dagger (†) in the catalogue, VAT is payable by the Buyer on the Hammer Price at the rate prevailing on the date of the auction which may be refundable in certain circumstances where the lot is removed from the United Kingdom.

6. Currency Converter and Video

For the guidance of Buyers:

(a) a currency converter will be operated at some auctions based on the one month forward rates of exchange quoted to Christie's by Lloyds Bank Plc at opening on the date of the auction. Christie's shall not accept any responsibility in the event of error on the currency converter as to the accuracy of the Lot number displayed or as to the foreign currency equivalent of bids in pounds sterling or otherwise; and

(b) videoed or other images of Lots will be screened in connection with some auctions. Christie's shall not accept any responsibility in the event of error in the screening whether to the relevance or accuracy of any such image or otherwise.

7. Payment
(a) Upon sale of a Lot, the Buyer shall:
  (i) unless he has already done so, give to Christie's his name and address and, if so required by Christie's, his bank or other suitable references; and
  (ii) pay to Christie's the Purchase Price within seven days from the date of sale, notwithstanding that, where the Buyer wishes to export the Lot, an export licence may be required.
(b) Christie's may, at its absolute discretion, agree terms for credit with the Buyer under which the Buyer will be entitled to take possession of the Lot before payment is made in full.
(c) The property in a Lot shall not pass to the Buyer until he has paid the Purchase Price in full.

8. Collection of Purchases
(a) Subject to Condition 7(b) above, no Lot may be taken away during the auction, nor may any Lot be taken away until the Purchase Price has been paid in full;
(b) the Buyer shall remove all purchased lots within seven days of the date of the sale;
(c) in the event that Lots remain uncollected, the Buyer shall be responsible for all storage charges from day 28 after the sale;
(d) any packing and handling of purchased Lots by Christie's staff is undertaken solely as a service to Buyers, and will only be undertaken at Christie's discretion and at the Buyer's risk. Christie's shall not be liable in any event for any damage to glass or frames, irrespective of cause. In addition, Christie's shall not be liable for any errors or omissions or damage caused by packers and shippers that Christie's has recommended to Buyers.

9. Responsibility for purchased Lots
The purchased Lot(s) shall be at the Buyer's risk in all respects from the time of collection or the expiry of seven days from the date of sale, whichever is the sooner, and neither Christie's nor its employees nor agents shall thereafter be liable for any loss or damage of any kind, whether caused by negligence or otherwise, while any Lot is in or under their respective custody or control.

10. Remedies for non-payment or failure to collect purchases
If a Buyer fails either to pay for or to take away any Lot, Christie's shall, without further notice to the Buyer and at its absolute discretion and without prejudice to any other rights or remedies it may have, be entitled to exercise one or more of the following rights or remedies:
(a) to issue proceedings against the Buyer for damages for breach of contract together with the costs of such proceedings on a full indemnity basis;
(b) to rescind the sale of that or any other Lots sold to the Buyer at the same or any other auction;

(c) to resell the Lot or cause it to be resold by public or private sale. Any deficiency in the Purchase Price resulting from such resale (after giving credit for any payment) together with full costs incurred in connection with the Lot shall be paid to Christie's by the Buyer and any surplus over the Proceeds of Sale shall belong to the Seller and in this Condition the expression 'Proceeds of Sale' shall have the same meaning in relation to a sale by private treaty as it has in relation to a sale by auction:

(d) to store the Lot or cause it to be stored whether at its own premises or elsewhere at the sole expense of the Buyer, and to release the Lot only after payment in full of the Purchase Price, the accrued cost of removal, storage and insurance and all other costs incurred in connection with the Lot;

(e) to charge interest on the Purchase Price at the rate of 4 per cent above Lloyds Bank Plc base rate to the extent that it remains unpaid for more than seven days from the date of sale, or, after judgment shall have been entered, at a rate of whichever is the higher of 4 per cent above Lloyds Bank Plc base rate and any statutory rate for the time being in force in relation to unpaid judgment debts;

(f) to retain that or any other Lot sold to the Buyer at the same or any other auction and release the same only after payment of the Purchase Price;

(g) to apply any proceeds of sale of any Lot then due or at any time thereafter becoming due to the Buyer towards settlement of the Purchase Price and Expenses, and Christie's shall be entitled to a lien on any property of the Buyer which is in Christie's possession for any purpose;

(h) to apply any payments by the Buyer to Christie's towards any sums owing from the Buyer to Christie's or to any associated company of Christie's without regard to any directions of the Buyer or his agent, whether express or implied.

11. Guarantee

(a) Subject to the obligations accepted by Christie's under this Condition, none of the Seller, Christie's, its employees or agents is responsible for the correctness of any statement as to the authorship, origin, date, age, size, medium, attribution, genuineness or provenance of any Lot, for any other errors of description or for any faults or defects in any Lot and no warranty whatsoever is given by the Seller, Christie's, its employees or agents in respect of any Lot and any express or implied conditions or warranties are hereby excluded;

(b) if, within five years of the date of the auction (1) Christie's has received notice in writing from the Buyer of any Lot that in his view the Lot is a Forgery, (2) within fourteen days of such notice, Christie's has the Lot in its possession in the same condition as at the date of the auction and (3) within a reasonable time thereafter, the Buyer satisfies Christie's that the Lot is a Forgery and that the Buyer is able to transfer a good and marketable title to the Lot free from any liens or encumbrances, Christie's will set aside the sale and refund to the Buyer any amount paid by the Buyer in respect of the Lot provided that the Buyer shall have no rights under this Condition if:

   (i) the catalogue description at the date of the auction was in accordance with the then generally accepted opinion of scholars or experts or fairly indicated there to be a conflict of such opinion; or

   (ii) it can be established that the Lot is a Forgery only by means of a scientific

process not generally accepted for use until after publication of the catalogue or by means of a process which at the date of the auction was
unreasonably expensive or impracticable or likely to have caused damage
to the Lot;
(c) the Buyer shall not be entitled to claim under this Condition for more than the
amount paid by him for the Lot and in particular shall have no claim for any
loss, consequential loss or damage whether direct or indirect suffered by him;
(d) the benefits of this guarantee shall not be assignable and shall rest solely and
exclusively in the Buyer who shall be the person to whom the original invoice
was made out by Christie's in respect of the Lot when sold and who has since the
sale retained uninterrupted, unencumbered ownership thereof.

12. Commission bids
(a) Prospective Buyers are advised to attend at the auction. Christie's will, however, if so instructed, execute bids provided in writing in advance of the auction
or bids by telephone (at Christie's discretion) on their behalf, but neither
Christie's nor its employees nor agents shall be liable to either the Buyer or the
Seller for any neglect or default in so doing or for failure to do so;
(b) in the event that Christie's has received commission bids on a Lot for identical
amounts and at auction those commission bids are the highest bids for that Lot,
the Lot shall be knocked down to the person whose commission bid (for the
relevant amount) was received first.
Note: Clause A.11(b) does not apply to Coins and Medals, or Jewellery.

13. Buyer's VAT status
The buyer shall give Christie's prior to the auction all relevant information as to
his VAT status which he warrants shall be correct and on which Christie's shall
be able to rely. Once a Lot has been purchased on the basis of such information,
no alteration so as to affect liability to VAT shall be made.

B. The Seller

1. Christie's discretion
(a) Christie's shall have absolute discretion as to:
   (i) whether the Lot is suitable for sale by Christie's, and if so as to the place
   and date of sale, the conditions of sale and the manner in which such sale
   is conducted;
   (ii) the description of any Lot in the catalogue;
   (iii) whether the views of any expert shall be obtained (including the submission
   of items of precious metal to the Worshipful Company of Goldsmiths and/
   or the London Assay Office); and
   (iv) the illustration of any Lot in the catalogue which will be at the Seller's
   expense up to a maximum of £90 for black and white and £500 for colour
   (together with any VAT chargeable thereon);
(b) Christie's reserves the right to withdraw any property at any time before the
actual sale if, in Christie's sole judgement:

(i) there is doubt as to its attribution or to its authenticity;

(ii) there is doubt as to the accuracy of the Seller's representations or warranties set forth herein in any respect;

(iii) the Seller has breached or is about to breach any provision of these Conditions of Business; or

(iv) any other just cause exists.

In the event of a withdrawal pursuant to Condition (ii) or (iii) above, the Seller shall pay a charge as provided in Condition B.9.

2.   Warranties and Indemnities

(a) The Seller warrants to Christie's and to the Buyer that he has and will be able to transfer good and marketable title to the Lot free from all third party rights or claims;

(b) the Seller shall indemnify Christie's, its employees and agents and the Buyer against all claims made or proceedings brought by persons entitled or purporting to be entitled to the Lot;

(c) the Seller warrants to Christie's and to the Buyer that he has complied in all respects with any applicable laws, regulations and requirements relating to any export of any of the Lots from any country or any intermediary country and also to the import of any such Lot into the United Kingdom, including (without limitation) payment of any duties or taxes relating to, and obtaining all licences, permits or other authorisations necessary for, such export and import; the Seller shall provide such available documentation as necessary;

(d) the Seller shall indemnify Christie's, its employees and agents and the Buyer against all claims made or proceedings brought due to any default of the Seller in complying with any applicable requisite export and/or import legislation, regulations or requirements; and

(e) the Seller shall reimburse Christie's in full and on demand for all payments, costs, expenses or any other loss or damage whatsoever made, incurred or suffered as a result of any breach by the Seller of (a) and/or (c) above.

3.   Reserves

(a) All Lots will be offered subject to a reserve as agreed in writing between Christie's and the Seller and, once a reserve has been agreed, it may be changed only with the consent of Christie's;

(b) the Seller shall not bid for his property nor employ any person to bid for him and Christie's alone shall have the right to bid on behalf of the Seller up to the amount of the reserve;

(c) if a reserve is placed in a currency other than sterling, such a reserve will be calculated at the one month forward rate of exchange quoted to Christie's by Lloyds Bank Plc at opening on the date of the auction, the certificate in writing of Christie's as to such rate to be conclusive except in the case of manifest error;

(d) the sterling equivalent of the foreign currency reserve calculated in accordance with (c) above may at Christie's absolute discretion be increased or reduced during the course of bidding to the nearest multiple of pounds sterling by which the bidding is being advanced;

(e) the Seller authorises Christie's to accept bids of less than the amount of the agreed reserve provided that for the sole purpose of determining any amounts due to or from the Seller under these Conditions the Hammer Price for any Lot sold at less than the agreed reserve will be deemed to have been the full amount of the agreed reserve and not the lower price at which the Lot was actually sold.

4. Commission and Expenses

(a) The Seller authorises Christie's to deduct commission at the Published Rates and Expenses from the Hammer Price and, notwithstanding that Christie's is his agent, acknowledges that Christie's may retain the Premium payable by the Buyer in accordance with Condition A.4;

(b) if a Lot fails to reach its reserve, the Seller authorises Christie's to deduct unsold commission at the Published Rates calculated on the last bid for the Lot and Expenses.

(c) The Seller shall pay, and/or authorise Christie's to deduct, an administration charge of ten per cent of all costs incurred on behalf of the Seller together with any VAT thereon.

5. Insurance

(a) Unless otherwise instructed by the Seller, all Lots will automatically be covered by insurance under Christie's own Fine Arts Policy for such sum as Christie's shall from time to time in its absolute discretion estimate;

(b) the rate of insurance premium payable by the Seller is 1 per cent of the Hammer Price plus VAT and the Seller shall also pay to Christie's any applicable charge for transit insurance together with any VAT thereon. The sum for which a Lot is covered for insurance under this Condition will not constitute and shall not be relied upon by the Seller as a representation, warranty or guarantee as to the value of the Lot or that it will, if and when sold by Christie's, be sold for such amount. Such insurance will subsist until payment is due from the Buyer or, in the case of Lots bought in or otherwise unsold, until the expiry of seven days after the receipt by the Seller of notice from Christie's requiring the Seller to collect;

(c) if the Seller instructs Christie's not to insure a Lot, it shall at all times remain at the risk of the Seller who hereby undertakes (1) to indemnify Christie's against all claims made or proceedings brought against Christie's in respect of loss or damage to the Lot of whatever nature howsoever and wheresoever occurring and in any circumstances even where negligence is alleged or proven (2) to reimburse Christie's on demand for all payments, costs or expenses made, incurred or suffered by Christie's in consequence thereof or arising therefrom. Any payment which Christie's shall make in respect of such loss or damage or payments, costs or expenses shall be binding upon the Seller and shall be accepted by the Seller as conclusive evidence that Christie's was liable to make such payment (3) to notify any insurer of the existence of the indemnity contained in this Condition;

(d) Christie's does not accept responsibility for Lots damaged by woodworm or by changes in atmospheric conditions and Christie's shall not be liable for such damage nor for any other damage to picture frames or to glass in picture frames;

(e) the sum for which a Lot is insured under Christie's own Fine Arts Policy in accordance with subclause (a) above shall be the total amount due to the Seller in the event of a successful claim being made under the Fine Arts Policy.

6. Rescission of the Sale
If before the Proceeds of Sale have been paid to the Seller, Christie's receives notice from the Buyer under Condition A.11(b) that, in the Buyer's view, the Lot is a Forgery, and Christie's agrees with that view, Christie's will rescind the sale and refund to the Buyer any amount paid to Christie's in respect of the Lot.

7. Payment of Proceeds of Sale
(a) Christie's shall pay the Proceeds of Sale to the Seller thirty-five days after the date of sale if Christie's has by then been paid the Purchase Price in full by the Buyer and Christie's has not received any notice from the Buyer under Condition A.11(b);
(b) if by the due date Christie's has not received the Purchase Price in full from the Buyer, then Christie's will pay the Proceeds of Sale within seven working days after the date on which the Purchase Price in full is received from the Buyer;
(c) if before the Purchase Price is paid in full by the Buyer, Christie's pays the Seller an amount equal to the Proceeds of Sale, property in the Lot shall pass to Christie's;
(d) the Proceeds of Sale will be paid to the Seller in such currency available to Christie's as may be agreed provided that the Seller specifies to Christie's in writing before the date of the auction the currency required. A charge of £25 (together with VAT thereon) may be deducted from the Proceeds of Sale in the event the Seller elects for payment to be made in a currency other than sterling, such sum representing costs and expenses incurred by Christie's. The sum to be paid to the Seller shall be calculated at the one month forward rate of exchange for the Proceeds of Sale quoted to Christie's by Lloyds Bank Plc prevailing on the next working day after the date of the auction, the certificate in writing of Christie's as to such rate being conclusive. If no currency is specified and agreed, the Proceeds of Sale will be paid in sterling.

8. Collection of the Purchase Price
If the Buyer fails to pay to Christie's the Purchase Price within one month after the date of sale, Christie's will endeavour to take the Seller's instructions as to the appropriate course of action to be taken and, so far as in Christie's opinion is practicable, will assist the Seller to recover the Purchase Price from the Buyer save that Christie's shall not be obliged to issue proceedings against the Buyer in its own name. Notwithstanding the foregoing, Christie's reserves the right and is hereby authorised at the Seller's expense, and in each case at Christie's absolute discretion, to agree special terms for payment of the Purchase Price, to remove, store and insure the Lot sold, to settle claims made by or against the Buyer on such terms as Christie's shall think fit, to take such steps as are necessary to collect monies due from the Buyer to the Seller and, if appropriate, to set aside the sale and refund money to the Buyer.

9. Charges for withdrawn Lots

The Seller may not withdraw the Lot prior to the auction without the consent of Christie's. In the event that such consent is given, or in the event of a withdrawal pursuant to Condition B.1(b)(ii) or (iii), a charge of 20 per cent of the reserve together with any VAT chargeable thereon and Expenses shall become payable or, if no reserve has yet been agreed, a charge of 20 per cent of the figure at which the Lot has been valued for insurance (as determined by Christie's) together with any VAT chargeable thereon and Expenses.

10. Unsold Lots

(a) Lots bought in or otherwise unsold by auction must be collected at the Seller's expense within the period of two months after receipt by the Seller of notice from Christie's requiring him to collect. Upon the expiry of such period Christie's shall have the right to sell such Lots by public or private sale and on such terms as it thinks fit and to deduct from the Proceeds of Sale any sum owing to Christie's or to any associated company of Christie's including (without limitation) removal, storage and insurance expenses, expenses with regard to the prior auction, unsold commission at the Published Rates in respect of the prior auction, commission at the Published Rates and expenses on the sale of the Lots and all other reasonable expenses before remitting the balance to the Seller or, if he cannot be traced, placing it in a bank account in the name of Christie's for the Seller. Lots returned at the Seller's request shall be returned at his risk and expense and will not be insured in transit unless Christie's is otherwise instructed by the Seller. In this Condition the word 'Seller' includes a consignor of property and the expression 'Proceeds of Sale' shall have the same meaning in relation to a sale by private treaty as it has in relation to a sale by auction.

(b) If any Lot is bought in or otherwise unsold by auction, Christie's is authorised as the exclusive agent for the Seller for a period of two months following the auction to sell such Lot privately for a price that will result in a payment to the Seller of not less than the net amount — ie after deduction of Christie's Commission and Expenses — to which the Seller would have been entitled had the Lot been sold at a price equal to the agreed reserve, or for such lesser amount as Christie's and the Seller shall agree. In such event the Seller's obligations to Christie's hereunder with respect to such a Lot are the same as if it had been sold at auction.

11. Firearms

Supplement, available on request.

12. Seller's VAT status

The Seller shall give to Christie's all relevant information as to his VAT status within the EC with regard to the Lot to be sold which he warrants is and will be correct and upon which Christie's shall be entitled to rely. Once a lot has been designated in the catalogue on the basis of such information no alteration so as to affect liability to VAT shall be made.

13. Photographs and Illustrations

The Seller hereby grants to Christie's the right to illustrate and photograph any Lot given to Christie's by the Seller for sale and to use such photographs, illustrations or images therefrom, and any illustrations, photographs or images provided by the Seller to Christie's, at any time and for such purposes as it sees fit whether such purposes are related to the sale of the Lot in question or not.

14. Electrical and Mechanical Goods

The Seller of electrical and mechanical goods warrants and undertakes to Christie's and to the Buyer that, except as previously disclosed to Christie's, the same are safe if reasonably used for the purpose for which they were designed and free from any defect not obvious on external inspection which could prove dangerous to human life or health, and will indemnify Christie's, its employees and agents against any loss or damage suffered by any of them in consequence of any breach of the above warranty and undertaking.

C. General Conditions

1. Christie's as agent for the Seller is not responsible for any default by the Seller or the Buyer.

2. Christie's shall have the right at its absolute discretion to refuse admission to its premises or attendance at its auctions by any person.

3. Christie's has the right at its absolute discretion to refuse any bid, to advance the bidding as it may decide, to withdraw or divide any Lot, to combine any two or more Lots and in the case of dispute to put up any Lot for auction again.

4. (a) Any indemnity hereunder shall extend to all actions, proceedings, costs, claims and demands whatsoever incurred or suffered by the person for whose benefit the indemnity is given;
   (b) Christie's shall hold any indemnity on trust for its employees and agents where it is expressed to be for their benefit.

5. Any notice given hereunder shall be in writing and if given by post shall be deemed to have been duly received by the addressee in the ordinary course of post.

6. The copyright in all illustrations and written matter relating to the Lots shall be and will remain at all times the absolute property of Christie's and shall not without the prior written consent of Christie's be used by any person.

7. These Conditions of Business shall be governed by and construed in accordance with English Law and all parties concerned hereby submit to the non-exclusive jurisdiction of the English Courts.

8. In these Conditions of Business the following words and expressions shall have the following meanings:

'Bought in'
Those Lots which fail to reach their reserve.

'Christie's'
Christie, Manson & Woods Limited.

'Expenses'
Christie's charges for insurance, illustrations, special advertising, packing storage, import and freight and any VAT thereon.

'Forgery'
A Lot made or substantially made with an intention to deceive as to authorship, origin, date, age, period, culture or source which is not shown to be such in the description in the catalogue and which at the date of the auction had a value materially less than it would have had if it had been in accordance with the description.

'Hammer Price'
The price at which a Lot is knocked down to the Buyer.

'Lot'
Any item deposited with Christie's with a view to its sale at auction whether on its premises or elsewhere and, in particular, the item or items described against any lot number in any catalogue.

'Rates of Premium'
Christie's rates of Premium which are 15 per cent of the first £30,000 of the Hammer Price of each Lot and 10 per cent of the excess of the Hammer Price above £30,000 except for coins, medals and wine where the Premium is 10 per cent of the Hammer Price of each Lot. VAT at the standard rate is payable on all Premiums.

'Proceeds of Sale'
The net amount due to the Seller being the Hammer Price less commission at the Published Rates and Expenses and any other amounts due to Christie's or to any associated company of Christie's from the Seller in whatever capacity and howsoever arising.

'Published Rates'
Christie's rates of commission which are 10 per cent of the Hammer Price on Lots selling for £2,501 and above and 15 per cent on Lots selling for £2,500 or less, except for (a) wine where the commission is 10 per cent of the Hammer Price on each consignment of Lots selling for £1,001 and above and 15 per cent on each consignment of Lots selling for £1,000 or less and (b) stamps and coins and medals where the commission is 10 per cent of the Hammer Price on Lots selling for £1,001 and above and 15 per cent on Lots selling for £1,000 or less. In the case of Lots failing to reach their reserve, a charge of 5 per cent may be made on the last bid for all Lots. There shall be a minimum commission of £50 levied on all

Lots, except for wine where the minimum commission shall be £30, for coins and medals where the minimum commission shall be £15 and for stamps where the minimum commission shall be £1. VAT at the standard rate is payable on all Seller's commission.

'Purchase Price'

The Hammer Price plus any premium, VAT chargeable and additional charges and expenses due from a defaulting Buyer under Condition A.10, in pounds sterling.

Appendix 2

Statutory and Other Material: Selected Extracts

Appendix 2 is in four parts, as follows:
Sale of goods
Criminal law
Land
Supplies of a service

SALE OF GOODS

This section of Appendix 2 contains individual sections etc of Acts, as follows:
Sale of Goods Act 1979, (as amended by the Sale and Supply of Goods Act 1994)
ss 12–15, 20–26 and 57
Factors Acts 1889, s 2(1)
Misrepresentation Act 1967, ss 1–3
Unfair Contract Terms Act 1977, ss 2, 3, 6, 10–12 and Sch 2
Unfair Terms in Consumer Contracts Regulations, SI 1994/3159
Torts (Interference with Goods) Act 1977, s 8
Civil Liability (Contribution) Act 1978, ss 1–8

SALE OF GOODS ACT 1979

12. Implied terms about title, etc.
(1) In a contract of sale, other than one to which subsection (3) below applies, there is an implied term on the part of the seller that in the case of a sale he has a right to sell the goods, and in the case of an agreement to sell he will have such a right at the time when the property is to pass.

(2) In a contract of sale, other than one to which subsection (3) below applies, there is also an implied term that —

(a) the goods are free, and will remain free until the time when the property is to pass, from any charge or encumbrance not disclosed or known to the buyer before the contract is made, and
(b) the buyer will enjoy quiet possession of the goods except so far as it may be disturbed by the owner or other person entitled to the benefit of any charge or encumbrance so disclosed or known.

(3) This subsection applies to a contract of sale in the case of which there appears from the contract or is to be inferred from its circumstances an intention that the seller should transfer only such title as he or a third person may have.

(4) In a contract to which subsection (3) above applies there is an implied term that all charges or encumbrances known to the seller and not known to the buyer have been disclosed to the buyer before the contract is made.

(5) In a contract to which subsection (3) above applies there is also an implied term that none of the following will disturb the buyer's quiet possession of the goods, namely —

(a) the seller;
(b) in a case where the parties to the contract intend that the seller should transfer only such title as a third person may have, that person;
(c) anyone claiming through or under the seller or that third person otherwise than under a charge or encumbrance disclosed or known to the buyer before the contract is made.

(5A) As regards England and Wales and Northern Ireland, the term implied by subsection (1) above is a condition and the terms implied by subsections (2), (4) and (5) above are warranties.

13. Sale by description
(1) Where there is a contract for the sale of goods by description, there is an implied term that the goods will correspond with the description.

(1A) As regards England and Wales and Northern Ireland, the term implied by subsection (1) above is a condition.

(2) If the sale is by sample as well as by description it is not sufficient that the bulk of the goods corresponds with the sample if the goods do not also correspond with the description.

(3) A sale of goods is not prevented from being a sale by description by reason only that, being exposed for sale or hire, they are selected by the buyer.

14. Implied terms about quality or fitness
(1) Except as provided by this section and section 15 below and subject to any other enactment, there is no implied term about the quality or fitness for any particular purpose of goods supplied under a contract of sale.

(2) Where the seller sells goods in the course of a business, there is an implied term that the goods supplied under the contract are of satisfactory quality.

(2A) For the purposes of this Act, goods are of satisfactory quality if they meet the standard that a reasonable person would regard as satisfactory, taking account of any description of the goods, the price (if relevant) and all other relevant circumstances.

(2B) For the purposes of this Act, the quality of goods includes their state and condition and the following (among others) are in appropriate cases aspects of the quality of goods —

(a) fitness for all the purposes for which goods of the kind in question are commonly supplied,
(b) appearance and finish,
(c) freedom from minor defects,
(d) safety, and
(e) durability.

(2C) The term implied by subsection (2) above does not extend to any matter making the quality of goods unsatisfactory —

(a) which is specifically drawn to the buyer's attention before the contract is made,
(b) where the buyer examines the goods before the contract is made, which that examination ought to reveal, or
(c) in the case of a contract for sale by sample, which would have been apparent on a reasonable examination of the sample.

(3) Where the seller sells goods in the course of a business and the buyer, expressly or by implication, makes known —

(a) to the seller, or
(b) where the purchase price or part of it is payable by instalments and the goods were previously sold by a credit-broker to the seller, to that credit-broker,

any particular purpose for which the goods are being bought, there is an implied term that the goods supplied under the contract are reasonably fit for that purpose, whether or not that is a purpose for which such goods are commonly supplied, except where the circumstances show that the buyer does not rely, or that it is unreasonable for him to rely, on the skill or judgment of the seller or credit-broker.

(4) An implied term about quality or fitness for a particular purpose may be annexed to a contract of sale by usage.

(5) The preceding provisions of this section apply to a sale by a person who in the course of a business is acting as agent for another as they apply to a sale by a principal in the course of a business, except where that other is not selling in the course of a business and either the buyer knows that fact or reasonable steps are taken to bring it to the notice of the buyer before the contract is made.

(6) As regards England and Wales and Northern Ireland, the terms implied by subsections (2) and (3) above are conditions.

15. Sale by sample

(1) A contract of sale is a contract for sale by sample where there is an express or implied term to that effect in the contract.

(2) In the case of a contract for sale by sample there is an implied term —

(a) that the bulk will correspond with the sample in quality;
(b) [Repealed by the Sale and Supply of Goods Act 1994, Schedule 2]
(c) that the goods will be free from any defect, making their quality unsatisfactory, which would not be apparent on reasonable examination of the sample.

(3) As regards England and Wales and Northern Ireland, the term implied by subsection (2) above is a condition.

15A(1) Where in the case of a contract of sale —

(a) the buyer would, apart from this subsection, have the right to reject goods by reason of a breach on the part of the seller of a term implied by section 13, 14 or 15 above, but
(b) the breach is so slight that it would be unreasonable for him to reject them,

then, if the buyer does not deal as consumer, the breach is not to be treated as a breach of condition but may be treated as a breach of warranty.

(2) This section applies unless a contrary intention appears in, or is to be implied from, the contract.

(3) It is for the seller to show that a breach fell within subsection (1)(b) above.

(4) This section does not apply to Scotland.

15B [Applies only in Scotland]

20. Risk prima facie passes with property

(1) Unless otherwise agreed, the goods remain at the seller's risk until the property in them is transferred to the buyer, but when the property in them is transferred to the buyer the goods are at the buyer's risk whether delivery has been made or not.

(2) But where delivery has been delayed through the fault of either buyer or seller the goods are at the risk of the party at fault as regards any loss which might not have occurred but for such fault.

(3) Nothing in this section affects the duties or liabilities of either seller or buyer as a bailee or custodier of the goods of the other party.

21. Sale by person not the owner

(1) Subject to the Act, where goods are sold by a person who is not their owner, and who does not sell them under the authority or with the consent of the owner, the

buyer acquires no better title to the goods than the seller had, unless the owner of the goods is by his conduct precluded from denying the seller's authority to sell.

(2) Nothing in this Act affects —

(a) the provisions of the Factors Acts or any enactment enabling the apparent owner of goods to dispose of them as if he were their true owner;
(b) the validity of any contract of sale under any special common law or statutory power of sale or under the order of a court of competent jurisdiction.

22. Market overt
[Repealed by Sale of Goods (Amendment) Act 1994 with effect from 3 January 1995. The market overt doctrine is abolished in relation to any contract for sale of goods made after the 1994 Act comes into force.]

23. Sale under voidable title
When the seller of goods has a voidable title to them, but his title has not been avoided at the time of the sale, the buyer acquires a good title to the goods, provided he buys them in good faith and without notice of the seller's defect of title.

24. Seller in possession after sale
Where a person having sold goods continues or is in possession of the goods, or of the documents of title to the goods, the delivery of transfer by that person, or by a mercantile agent acting for him, of the goods or documents of title under any sale, pledge, or other disposition thereof, to any person receiving the same in good faith and without notice of the previous sale, has the same effect as if the person making the delivery or transfer were expressly authorised by the owner of the goods to make the same.

25. Buyer in possession after sale
(1) Where a person having bought or agreed to buy goods obtains, with the consent of the seller, possession of the goods or the documents of title to the goods, the delivery or transfer by that person, or by a mercantile agent acting for him, of the goods or documents of title, under any sale, pledge, or other disposition thereof, to any person receiving the same in good faith and without notice of any lien or other right of the original seller in respect of the goods, has the same effect as if the person making the delivery or transfer were a mercantile agent in possession of the goods or documents of title with the consent of the owner.

(2) For the purposes of subsection (1) above —

(a) the buyer under a conditional sale agreement is to be taken not to be a person who has bought or agreed to buy goods, and
(b) 'conditional sale agreement' means an agreement for the sale of goods which is a consumer credit agreement within the meaning of the Consumer Credit Act 1974 under which the purchase price or part of it is payable by instalments, and

the property in the goods is to remain in the seller (notwithstanding that the buyer is to be in possession of the goods) until such conditions as to the payment of instalments or until such conditions as to the payment of instalments or otherwise as may be specified in the agreement are fulfilled.

26. Supplementary to sections 24 and 25

In sections 24 and 25 above 'mercantile agent' means a mercantile agent having in the customary course of his business as such agent authority either —

(a) to sell goods, or
(b) to consign goods for the purpose of sale, or
(c) to buy goods, or
(d) to raise money on the security of goods.

57. Auction sales

(1) Where the goods are put up for sale by auction in lots, each lot is prima facie deemed to be the subject of a separate contract of sale.

(2) A sale by auction is complete when the auctioneer announces its completion by the fall of the hammer, or in other customary manner; and until the announcement is made any bidder may retract his bid.

(3) A sale by auction may be notified to be subject to a reserve or upset price, and a right to bid may also be reserved expressly by or on behalf of the seller.

(4) Where a sale by auction is not notified to be subject to a right to bid by or on behalf of the seller, it is not lawful for the seller to bid himself or to employ any person to bid at the sale, or for the auctioneer knowingly to take any bid from the seller or any such person.

(5) A sale contravening subsection (4) above may be treated as fraudulent by the buyer.

(6) Where, in respect of a sale by auction, a right to bid is expressly reserved (but not otherwise) the seller or any one person on his behalf may bid at the auction.

FACTORS ACT 1889

2. Powers of mercantile agent with respect to disposition of goods

(1) Where a mercantile agent is, with the consent of the owner, in possession of goods or of the documents of title to goods, any sale, pledge, or other disposition of the goods, made by him when acting in the ordinary course of business of a mercantile agent, shall, subject to the provisions of this Act, be as valid as if he were expressly authorised by the owner of the goods to make the same; provided that the person taking under the disposition acts in good faith, and has not at the time of the disposition notice that the person making the disposition has not authority to make the same.

(2) ...

(3) ...

(4) ...

MISREPRESENTATION ACT 1967

1. Removal of certain bars to rescission for innocent misrepresentation
Where a person has entered into a contract after a misrepresentation has been made to him, and

(a) the misrepresentation has become a term of the contract; or
(b) the contract has been performed; or both,
   then, if otherwise he would be entitled to rescind the contract without alleging fraud, he shall be so entitled, notwithstanding the matters mentioned in paragraphs (a) and (b) of this section.

2. Damages for misrepresentation
(1) Where a person has entered into a contract after a misrepresentation has been made to him by another party thereto and as a result thereof he has suffered loss, then, if the person making the misrepresentation would be liable to damages in respect thereof had the misrepresentation been made fraudulently, that person shall be so liable notwithstanding that the misrepresentation was not made fraudulently, unless he proves that he had reasonable grounds, to believe and did believe up to the time the contract was made that the facts represented were true.

(2) Where a person has entered into a contract after a misrepresentation has been made to him otherwise than fraudulently, and he would be entitled, by reason of the misrepresentation, to rescind the contract, then, if it is claimed, in any proceedings arising out of the contract, that the contract ought to be or has been rescinded, the court or arbitrator may declare the contract subsisting and award damages in lieu of rescission, if of opinion that it would be equitable so to do, having regard to the nature of the misrepresentation and the loss that would be caused by it if the contract were upheld, as well as to the loss that rescission would cause to the other party.

(3) Damages may be awarded against a person under subsection (2) of this section whether or not he is liable to damages under subsection (1) thereof, but where he is so liable any award under the subsection (2) shall be taken into account in assessing his liability under the said subsection (1).

3. Avoidance of certain provisions excluding liability for misrepresentation
If a contract contains a term which would exclude or restrict —

(a) Any liability to which a party to a contract may be subject by reason of any misrepresentation made by him before the contract was made; or

(b) Any remedy available to another party to the contract by reason of such a misrepresentation,

that term shall be of no effect except in so far as it satisfies the requirement of reasonableness as stated in section 11(1) of the Unfair Contract Terms Act 1977; and it is for those claiming that the term satisfies the requirement to show that it does.

UNFAIR CONTRACT TERMS ACT 1977

2. Negligence liability
(1) A person cannot by reference to any contract term or to a notice given to persons generally or to particular persons exclude or restrict his liability for death or personal injury resulting from negligence.

(2) In the case of other loss or damage, a person cannot so exclude or restrict his liability for negligence except in so far as the term or notice satisfies the requirement of reasonableness.

(3) Where a contract term or notice purports to exclude or restrict liability for negligence a person's agreement to or awareness of it is not of itself to be taken as indicating his voluntary acceptance of any risk.

3. Liability arising in contract
(1) This section applies as between contracting parties where one of them deals as consumer or on the other's written standard terms of business.

(2) As against that party, the other cannot by reference to any contract term —

(a) when himself in breach of contract, exclude or restrict any liability of his in respect of the breach; or
(b) claim to be entitled —
    (i) to render a contractual performance substantially different from that which was reasonably expected of him, or
    (ii) in respect of the whole or any part of his contractual obligation, to render no performance at all,

except in so far as (in any of these cases mentioned above in this subsection) the contract term satisfies the requirement of reasonableness.

6. Sale and hire-purchase
(1) Liability for breach of the obligations arising from —

(a) section 12 of the Sale of Goods Act 1979 (seller's implied undertakings as to title etc);
(b) section 8 of the Supply of Goods (Implied Terms) Act 1973 (the corresponding thing in relation to hire-purchase),

cannot be excluded or restricted by reference to any contract term.

(2) As against a person dealing as a consumer, liability for breach of the obligations arising from —

(a) section 13, 14, or 15 of the 1979 Act (seller's implied undertakings as to conformity of goods with description or sample, or as to their quality or fitness for a particular purpose);

(b) section 9, 10 or 11 of the 1973 Act (the corresponding things in relation to hire-purchase),

cannot be excluded or restricted by reference to any contract term.

(3) As against a person dealing otherwise than as consumer, the liability specified in subsection (2) above can be excluded or restricted by reference to a contract term, but only in so far as the term satisfies the requirement of reasonableness.

(4) The liabilities referred to in this section are not only the business liabilities defined by section 1(3), but include those arising under any contract of sale of goods or hire-purchase agreement.

10. Evasion by means of secondary contract

A person is not bound by any contract term prejudicing or taking away rights of his which arise under or in connection with the performance of, another contract, so far as those rights extend to the enforcement of another's liability which this Part of this Act prevents that other from excluding or restricting.

11. The 'reasonableness' test

(1) In relation to a contract term, the requirement of reasonableness for the purposes of this Part of this Act, section 3 of the Misrepresentation Act 1967 and section 3 of the Misrepresentation Act (Northern Ireland) 1967 is that the term shall have been a fair and reasonable one to be included having regard to the circumstances which were, or ought reasonably to have been, known to or in the contemplation of the parties when the contract was made.

(2) In determining for the purposes of section 6 or 7 above whether a contract term satisfies the requirement of reasonableness, regard shall be had in particular to the matters specified in Schedule 2 of this Act; but this subsection does not prevent the court or arbitrator from holding, in accordance with any rule of law, that a term which purports to exclude or restrict any relevant liability is not a term of the contract.

(3) In relation to a notice (not being a notice having contractual effect) the requirement of reasonableness under this Act is that it should be fair and reasonable to allow reliance on it, having regard to all the circumstances obtaining when the liability arose or (but for the notice) would have arisen.

(4) Where by reference to a contract term or notice a person seeks to restrict liability to a specified sum of money, and the question arises (under this or any other Act) whether the term or notice satisfies the requirement of reasonableness, regard shall be had in particular (but without prejudice to subsection (2) above in the case of contract terms) to —

(a) the resources which he could expect to be available to him for the purposes of meeting the liability should it arise; and
(b) how far it was open to him to cover himself by insurance.

(5) It is for those claiming that a contract term or notice satisfies the requirement of reasonableness to show that it does.

12. 'Dealing as consumer'

(1) A party to a contract 'deals as consumer' in relation to another party if —

(a) he neither makes the contract in the course of a business nor holds himself out as doing so; and
(b) the other party does make the contract in the course of a business; and
(c) in the case of a contract governed by the law of sale of goods or hire-purchase, or by section 7 of this Act, the goods passing under or in pursuance of the contract are of a type ordinarily supplied for private use or consumption.

(2) But on a sale by auction or by competitive tender the buyer is not in any circumstances to be regarded as dealing as consumer.

(3) Subject to this, it is for those claiming that a party does not deal as consumer to show that he does not.

Schedule 2
'Guidelines' for application of reasonableness test

The matters to which regard is to be had in particular for the purposes of section 6(3), 7(3) and (4), 20 and 21 are any of the following which appear to be relevant —

(a) the strength of the bargaining positions of the parties relative to each other, taking into account (among other things) alternative means by which the customer's requirements could have been met;
(b) whether the customer received an inducement to agree to the term or in accepting it had an opportunity of entering into a similar contract with other persons, but without having to accept a similar term;
(c) whether the customer knew or ought reasonably to have known of the existence and extent of the term (having regard, among other things, to any custom of the trade and any previous course of dealing between the parties);
(d) where the term excludes or restricts any relevant liability if some condition is not complied with, whether it was reasonable at the time of the contract to expect that compliance with that condition would be practicable;

(e) whether the goods were manufactured, processed or adapted to the special order of the customer.

UNFAIR TERMS IN CONSUMER CONTRACTS REGULATIONS, SI 1994/3159

1. Citation and commencement
These Regulations may be cited as the Unfair Terms in Consumer Contracts Regulations 1994 and shall come into force on 1st July 1995.

2. Interpretation
(1) In these Regulations —

'business' includes a trade or profession and the activities of any government department or local or public authority;

'the Community' means the European Economic Community and the other States in the European Economic Area;

'consumer' means a natural person who, in making a contract to which these Regulations apply, is acting for purposes which are outside his business;

'court' in relation to England and Wales and Northern Ireland means the High Court, and in relation to Scotland, the Court of Session;

'Director' means the Director General of Fair Trading;

'EEA Agreement' means the Agreement on the European Economic Area signed at Oporto on 2 May 1992 as adjusted by the protocol signed at Brussels on 17 March 1993;

'member State' shall mean a State which is a contracting party to the EEA Agreement but until the EEA Agreement comes into force in relation to Liechtenstein does not include the State of Liechtenstein;

'seller' means a person who sells goods and who, in making a contract to which these Regulations apply, is acting for purposes relating to his business; and

'supplier' means a person who supplies goods or services and who, in making a contract to which these Regulations apply, is acting for purposes relating to his business.

(2) In the application of these Regulations to Scotland for references to an 'injunction' or an 'interlocutory injunction' there shall be substituted references to an 'interdict' or 'interim interdict' respectively.

3. Terms to which these Regulations apply
(1) Subject to the provisions of Schedule 1, these Regulations apply to any term in a contract concluded between a seller or supplier and a consumer where the said term has not been individually negotiated.

(2) In so far as it is in plain, intelligible language, no assessment shall be made of the fairness of any term which —

(a) defines the main subject matter of the contract, or
(b) concerns the adequacy of the price or remuneration, as against the goods or services sold or supplied.

(3) For the purposes of these Regulations, a term shall always be regarded as not having been individually negotiated where it has been drafted in advance and the consumer has not been able to influence the substance of the term.

(4) Notwithstanding that a specific term or certain aspects of it in a contract has been individually negotiated, these Regulations shall apply to the rest of a contract if an overall assessment of the contract indicates that it is a pre-formulated standard contract.

(5) It shall be for any seller or supplier who claims that a term was individually negotiated to show that it was.

4. Unfair terms
(1) In these Regulations, subject to paragraphs (2) and (3) below, 'unfair term' means any term which contrary to the requirement of good faith causes a significant imbalance in the parties' rights and obligations under the contract to the detriment of the consumer.

(2) An assessment of the unfair nature of a term shall be made taking into account the nature of the goods or services for which the contract was concluded and referring, as at the time of the conclusion of the contract, to all circumstances attending the conclusion of the contract and to all the other terms of the contract or of another contract on which it is dependent.

(3) In determining whether a term satisfies the requirement of good faith, regard shall be had in particular to the matters specified in Schedule 2 to these Regulations.

(4) Schedule 3 to these Regulations contains an indicative and non-exhaustive list of the terms which may be regarded as unfair.

5. Consequence of inclusion of unfair terms in contracts
(1) An unfair term in a contract concluded with a consumer by a seller of supplier shall not be binding on the consumer.

(2) The contract shall continue to bind the parties if it is capable of continuing in existence without the unfair term.

6. Construction of written contracts
A seller or supplier shall ensure that any written term of a contract is expressed in plain, intelligible language, and if there is doubt about the meaning of a written term, the interpretation most favourable to the consumer shall prevail.

7. Choice of law clauses
These Regulations shall apply notwithstanding any contract term which applies or purports to apply the law of a non member State, if the contract has a close connection with the territory of the member States.

8. Prevention of continued use of unfair terms
(1) It shall be the duty of the Director to consider any complaint made to him that any contract term drawn up for general use is unfair, unless the complaint appears to the Director to be frivolous or vexatious.

(2) If having considered a complaint about any contract term pursuant to paragraph (1) above the Director considers that the contract term is unfair he may, if he considers it appropriate to do so, bring proceedings for an injunction (in which proceedings he may also apply for an interlocutory injunction) against any person appearing to him to be using or recommending use of such a term in contracts concluded with consumers.

(3) The Director may, if he considers it appropriate to do so, have regard to any undertakings given to him by or on behalf of any person as to the continued use of such a term in contracts concluded with consumers.

(4) The Director shall give reasons for his decision to apply or not to apply, as the case may be, for an injunction in relation to any complaint which these Regulations require him to consider.

(5) The court on an application by the Director may grant an injunction on such terms as it thinks fit.

(6) An injunction may relate not only to use of a particular contract term drawn up for general use but to any similar term, or a term having like effect, used or recommended for use by any party to the proceedings.

(7) The Director may arrange for the dissemination in such form and manner as he considers appropriate of such information and advice concerning the operation of these Regulations as may appear to him to be expedient to give to the public and to all persons likely to be affected by these Regulations.

Schedule 1
Contracts and particular terms excluded from the scope of these Regulations
These Regulations do not apply to —

(a) any contract relating to employment;
(b) any contract relating to succession rights;
(c) any contract relating to rights under family law;
(d) any contract relating to the incorporation and organisation of companies or partnerships; and
(e) any term incorporated in order to comply with or which reflects —

    (i) statutory or regulatory provisions of the United Kingdom; or

    (ii) the provisions or principles of international conventions to which the member States or the Community are party.

Schedule 2
Assessment of good faith

In making an assessment of good faith, regard shall be had in particular to —

(a) the strength of the bargaining positions of the parties;

(b) whether the consumer had an inducement to agree to the term;

(c) whether the goods or services were sold or supplied to the special order of the consumer, and

(d) the extent to which the seller or supplier has dealt fairly and equitably with the consumer.

Schedule 3
Indicative and illustrative list of terms which may be regarded as unfair

1. Terms which have the object or effect of —

(a) excluding or limiting the legal liability of a seller or supplier in the event of the death of a consumer or personal injury to the latter resulting from an act or omission of that seller or supplier;

(b) inappropriately excluding or limiting the legal rights of the consumer vis-à-vis the seller or supplier or another party in the event of total or partial non-performance or inadequate performance by the seller or supplier of any of the contractual obligations, including the option of offsetting a debt owed to the seller or supplier against any claim which the consumer may have against him;

(c) making an agreement binding on the consumer whereas provision of services by the seller or supplier is subject to a condition whose realisation depends on his own will alone;

(d) permitting the seller or supplier to retain sums paid by the consumer where the latter decides not to conclude or perform the contract, without providing for the consumer to receive compensation of an equivalent amount from the seller or supplier where the latter is the party cancelling the contract;

(e) requiring any consumer who fails to fulfil his obligation to pay a disproportionately high sum in compensation;

(f) authorising the seller or supplier to dissolve the contract on a discretionary basis where the same facility is not granted to the consumer, or permitting the seller or supplier to retain the sums paid for services not yet supplied by him where it is the seller or supplier himself who dissolves the contract;

(g) enabling the seller or supplier to terminate a contract of indeterminate duration without reasonable notice except where there are serious grounds for doing so;

(h) automatically extending a contract of fixed duration where the consumer does not indicate otherwise, when the deadline fixed for the consumer to express this desire not to extend the contract is unreasonably early;

(i) irrevocably binding the consumer to terms with which he had no real opportunity of becoming acquainted before the conclusion of the contract;

(j) enabling the seller or supplier to alter the terms of the contract unilaterally without a valid reason which is specified in the contract;
(k) enabling the seller or supplier to alter unilaterally without a valid reason any characteristics of the product or service to be provided;
(l) providing for the price of goods to be determined at the time of delivery or allowing a seller of goods or supplier of services to increase their price without in both cases giving the consumer the corresponding right to cancel the contract if the final price is too high in relation to the price agreed when the contract was concluded;
(m) giving the seller or supplier the right to determine whether the goods or services supplied are in conformity with the contract, or giving him the exclusive right to interpret any term of the contract;
(n) limiting the seller's or supplier's obligation to respect commitments undertaken by his agents or making his commitments subject to compliance with a particular formality;
(o) obliging the consumer to fulfil all his obligations where the seller or supplier does not perform his;
(p) giving the seller or supplier the possibility of transferring his rights and obligations under the contract, where this may serve to reduce the guarantees for the consumer, without the latter's agreement;
(q) excluding or hindering the consumer's right to take legal action or exercise any other legal remedy, particularly by requiring the consumer to take disputes exclusively to arbitration not covered by legal provisions, unduly restricting the evidence available to him or imposing on him a burden of proof which, according to the applicable law, should lie with another party to the contract.

2. Scope of subparagraphs 1(g), (j) and (l)

(a) Subparagraph 1(g) is without hindrance to terms by which a supplier of financial services reserves the right to terminate unilaterally a contract of indeterminate duration without notice where there is a valid reason, provided that the supplier is required to inform the other contracting party or parties thereof immediately.
(b) Subparagraph 1(j) is without hindrance to terms under which a supplier of financial services reserves the right to alter the rate of interest payable by the consumer or due to the latter, or the amount of other charges for financial services without notice where there is a valid reason, provided that the supplier is required to inform the other contracting party or parties thereof at the earliest opportunity and that the latter are free to dissolve the contract immediately.

Subparagraph 1(j) is also without hindrance to terms under which a seller or supplier reserves the right to alter unilaterally the conditions of a contract of indeterminate duration, provided that he is required to inform the consumer with reasonable notice and that the consumer is free to dissolve the contract.
(c) Subparagraphs 1(g), (j) and (l) do not apply to:
— transactions in transferable securities, financial instruments and other products or services where the price is linked to fluctuations in a stock exchange quotation or index or a financial market rate that the seller or supplier does not control;

— contracts for the purchase or sale of foreign currency, traveller's cheques or international money orders denominated in foreign currency;

(d) Subparagraph 1(l) is without hindrance to price indexation clauses, where lawful, provided that the method by which prices vary is explicitly described.

TORTS (INTERFERENCE WITH GOODS) ACT 1977

8. Competing rights to the goods

(1) The defendant in an action for wrongful interference shall be entitled to show, in accordance with rules of court, that a third party has a better right than the plaintiff as respects all or any part of the interest claimed by the plaintiff, or in right of which he sues, and any rule of law (sometimes called jus tertii) to the contrary is abolished.

(2) Rules of court relating to proceedings for wrongful interference may —

(a) require the plaintiff to give particulars of his title,

(b) require the plaintiff to identify any person who, to his knowledge, has or claims any interest in the goods.

(c) authorise the defendant to apply for directions as to whether any person should be joined with a view to establishing whether he has a better right than the plaintiff, or has a claim as a result of which the defendant might be doubly liable,

(d) where a party fails to appear on an application within paragraph (c), or to comply with any direction given by the court on such an application, authorise the court to deprive him of any right of action against the defendant for the wrong either unconditionally, or subject to such terms or conditions as may be specified.

(3) Subsection (2) is without prejudice to any other power of making rules of court.

CIVIL LIABILITY (CONTRIBUTION) ACT 1978

1. Entitlement to contribution

(1) Subject to the following provisions of this section, any person liable in respect of any damage suffered by another person may recover contribution from any other person liable in respect of the same damage (whether jointly with him or otherwise).

(2) A person shall be entitled to recover contribution by virtue of subsection (1) above notwithstanding that he has ceased to be liable in respect of the damage in question since the time when the damage occurred, provided that he was so liable immediately before he made or was ordered or agreed to make the payment in respect of which the contribution is sought.

(3) A person shall be liable to make contribution by virtue of subsection (1) above notwithstanding that he has ceased to be liable in respect of the damage in question since the time when the damage occurred, unless he ceased to be liable by virtue of the expiry of a period of limitation or prescription which extinguished the right on which the claim against him in respect of the damage was based.

(4) A person who has made or agreed to make any payment in bona fide settlement or compromise of any claim made against him in respect of any damage (including a payment into court which has been accepted) shall be entitled to recover contribution in accordance with this section without regard to whether or not he himself is or ever was liable in respect of the damage, provided, however, that he would have been liable assuming that the factual basis of the claim against him could be established.

(5) A judgment given in any action brought in any part of the United Kingdom by or on behalf of the person who suffered the damage in question against any person from whom contribution is sought under this section shall be conclusive in the proceedings for contribution as to any issue determined by that judgment in favour of the person from whom the contribution is sought.

(6) References in this section to a person's liability in respect of any damage are references to any such liability which has been or could be established in an action brought against him in England and Wales by or on behalf of the person who suffered the damage; but it is immaterial whether any issue arising in any such action was or would be determined (in accordance with the rules of private international law) by reference to the law of a country outside England and Wales.

2. Assessment of contribution

(1) Subject to subsection (3) below, in any proceedings for contribution under section 1 above the amount of the contribution recoverable from any person shall be such as may be found by the court to be just and equitable having regard to the extent of that person's responsibility for the damage in question.

(2) Subject to subsection (3) below, the court shall have power in any such proceedings, to exempt any person from liability to make contribution, or to direct that the contribution to be recovered from any person shall amount to a complete indemnity.

(3) Where the amount of the damages which have or might have been awarded in respect of the damage in question in any action brought in England and Wales by or on behalf of the person who suffered it against the person from whom the contribution is sought was or would have been subject to —

(a) any limit imposed by or under any enactment or by any agreement made before the damage occurred;
(b) any reduction by virtue of section 1 of the Law Reform (Contributory Negligence) Act 1945 or section 5 of the Fatal Accidents Act 1976; or

(c) any corresponding limit or reduction under the law of a country outside England and Wales;

the person from whom the contribution is sought shall not by virtue of any contribution awarded under section 1 above be required to pay in respect of the damage a greater amount than the amount of those damages as so limited or reduced.

3. Proceedings against persons jointly liable for the same debt or damage
Judgment recovered against any person liable in respect of any debt or damage shall not be a bar to an action, or to the continuance of an action, against any other person who is (apart from any such bar) jointly liable with him in respect of the same debt or damage.

4. Successive actions against persons liable (jointly or otherwise) for the same damage
If more than one action is brought in respect of any damage by or on behalf of the person by whom it was suffered against persons liable in respect of the damage (whether jointly or otherwise) the plaintiff shall not be entitled to costs in any of those actions, other than that in which judgment is first given, unless the court is of the opinion that there was reasonable ground for bringing the action.

5. Application to the Crown
Without prejudice to section 4(1) of the Crown Proceedings Act 1947 (indemnity and contribution), this Act shall bind the Crown, but nothing in this Act shall be construed as in any way affecting Her Majesty in Her private capacity (including in right of Her Duchy of Lancaster) or the Duchy of Cornwall.

6. Interpretation
(1) A person is liable in respect of any damage for the purposes of this Act if the person who suffered it (or anyone representing his estate or dependants) is entitled to recover compensation from him in respect of that damage (whatever the legal basis of his liability, whether tort, breach of contract, breach of trust or otherwise).

(2) References in this Act to an action brought by or on behalf of the person who suffered any damage include references to an action brought for the benefit of his estate or dependants.

(3) In this Act 'dependants' has the same meaning as in the Fatal Accidents Act 1976.

(4) In this Act, except in section 1(5) above, 'action' means an action brought in England and Wales.

7. Savings
(1) Nothing in this Act shall affect any case where the debt in question became due or (as the case may be) the damage in question occurred before the date on which it comes into force.

(2) A person shall not be entitled to recover contribution or liable to make contribution in accordance with section 1 above by reference to any liability based on breach of any obligation assumed by him before the date on which this Act comes into force.

(3) The right to recover contribution in accordance with section 1 above supersedes any right, other than an express contractual right, to recover contribution (as distinct from indemnity) otherwise than under this Act in corresponding circumstances; but nothing in this Act shall affect —

(a) any express or implied contractual or other right to indemnity; or
(b) any express contractual provision regulating or excluding contribution;

which would be enforceable apart from this Act (or render enforceable any agreement for indemnity or contribution which would not be enforceable apart from this Act).

8. Application to Northern Ireland
In the application of this Act to Northern Ireland —

(a) the reference in section 2(3)(b) to section 1 of the Law Reform (Contributory Negligence) Act 1945 or section 5 of the Fatal Accidents Act 1976 shall be construed as a reference to section 2 of the Law Reform (Miscellaneous Provisions) Act (Northern Ireland) 1948 or Article 7 of the Fatal Accidents (Northern Ireland) Order 1977;
(b) the reference in section 5 to section 4(1) of the Crown Proceedings Act 1947 shall be construed as a reference to section 4(1) of that Act as it applies in Northern Ireland;
(c) the reference in section 6(3) to the Fatal Accidents Act 1976 shall be construed as a reference to the Fatal Accidents (Northern Ireland) Order 1977;
(d) references to England and Wales shall be construed as references to Northern Ireland; and
(e) any reference to an enactment shall be construed as including a reference to an enactment of the Parliament of Northern Ireland and a Measure of the Northern Ireland Assembly.

CRIMINAL LAW

This section of Appendix 2 contains individual sections etc of Acts, as follows:

Auctions (Bidding Agreements) Act 1927, ss 1–4
Auctions (Bidding Agreements) Act 1969, ss 1–5
Theft Act 1968, s 15
Trade Descriptions Act 1968, ss 1–6, 13, 14 and 23–25
Firearms Act 1968 as amended, ss 1–3 and 57

AUCTIONS (BIDDING AGREEMENTS) ACT 1927

1. Certain bidding agreements to be illegal

(1) If any dealer agrees to give, or gives, or offers any gift or consideration to any other person as an inducement or reward for abstaining, or for having abstained, from bidding at a sale by auction either generally or for any particular lot, or if any person agrees to accept, or accepts, or attempts to obtain from any dealer any such gift or consideration as aforesaid, he shall be guilty of an offence under this Act, and shall be liable on summary conviction to a fine not exceeding the statutory maximum, or to a term of imprisonment for any period not exceeding six months, or to both such fine and such imprisonment:

Provided that, where it is proved that a dealer has previously to an auction entered into an agreement in writing with one or more persons to purchase goods at the auction bonâ fide on a joint account and has before the goods were purchased at the auction deposited a copy of the agreement with the auctioneer, such an agreement shall not be treated as an agreement made in contravention of this section.

(2) For the purposes of this section the expression 'dealer' means a person who in the normal course of his business attends sales by auction for the purpose of purchasing goods with a view to reselling them.

(3) In England and Wales a prosecution for an offence under this section shall not be instituted without the consent of the Attorney-General or the Solicitor-General.

2. [Repealed]

3. Copy of Act to be exhibited at sale

The particulars which under section seven of the Auctioneers Act 1845, are required to be affixed or suspended in some conspicuous part of the room or place where the auction is held shall include a copy of this Act, and that section shall have effect accordingly.

4. Short title, commencement and extent

(1) This Act may be cited as the Auctions (Bidding Agreements) Act 1927...

(2) This Act shall not extend to Northern Ireland.

AUCTIONS (BIDDING AGREEMENTS) ACT 1969

1. Offences under Auctions (Bidding Agreements) Act 1927 to be indictable as well as triable summarily, and extension of time for bringing summary proceedings

(1) Offences under section 1 of the Auctions (Bidding Agreements) Act 1927 (which, as amended by the Criminal Justice Act 1967, renders a dealer who agrees to give, or gives, or offers a gift or consideration to another as an inducement or reward for abstaining, or for having abstained, from bidding at a sale by auction

punishable on summary conviction with a fine not exceeding the statutory maximum or imprisonment for a term not exceeding six months, or both, and renders similarly punishable a person who agrees to accept, or accepts, or attempts to obtain from a dealer any such gift or consideration as aforesaid) shall be triable on indictment as well as summarily; and the penalty that may be imposed on a person on conviction on indictment of an offence under that section shall be imprisonment for a term not exceeding two years or a fine or both.

. . .

(5) This section applies only to offences committed after the commencement of this Act.

2. Persons convicted not to attend or participate in auctions
(1) On any such summary conviction or conviction on indictment as is mentioned in section 1 above, the court may order that the person so convicted or that person and any representative of him shall not (without leave of the court) for a period from the date of such conviction —

(a) in the case of a summary conviction, of not more than one year, or
(b) in the case of a conviction on indictment, of not more than three years,

enter upon any premises where goods intended for sale by auction are on display or to attend or participate in any way in any sale by auction.

(2) In the event of a contravention of an order under this section, the person who contravenes it (and, if he is the representative of another, that other also) shall be guilty of an offence and liable —

(a) on summary conviction, to a fine not exceeding the statutory maximum;
(b) on conviction on indictment, to imprisonment for a term not exceeding two years or to a fine or to both.

(3) In any proceedings against a person in respect of a contravention of an order under this section consisting in the entry upon premises where goods intended for sale by auction were on display, it shall be a defence for him to prove that he did not know, and had no reason to suspect, that goods so intended were on display on the premises, and in any proceedings against a person in respect of a contravention of such an order consisting in his having done something as the representative of another, it shall be a defence for him to prove that he did not know, and had no reason to suspect, that that other was the subject of such an order.

(4) A person shall not be guilty of an offence under this section by reason only of his selling property by auction or causing it to be so sold.

3. Rights of seller of goods by auction where agreement subsists that some person shall abstain from bidding for the goods
(1) Where goods are purchased at an auction by a person who has entered into an agreement with another or others that the other or the others (or some of them)

shall abstain from bidding for the goods (not being an agreement to purchase the goods bona fide on a joint account) and he or the other party, or one of the other parties, to the agreement is a dealer, the seller may avoid the contract under which the goods are purchased.

(2) Where a contract is avoided by virtue of the foregoing subsection, then, if the purchaser has obtained possession of the goods and restitution thereof is not made, the persons who were parties to the agreement that one or some of them should abstain from bidding for the goods the subject of the contract shall be jointly and severally liable to make good to the seller the loss (if any) he sustained by reason of the operation of the agreement.

(3) Subsection (1) above applies to a contract made after the commencement of this Act whether the agreement as to the abstention of a person or persons from bidding for the goods the subject of the contract was made before or after that commencement.

(4) Section 2 of the Auctions (Bidding Agreements) Act 1927 (right of vendors to treat certain sales as fraudulent) shall not apply to a sale the contract for which is made after the commencement of this Act.

(5) In this section, 'dealer' has the meaning assigned to it by section 1(2) of the Auctions (Bidding Agreements) Act 1927.

4. Copy of Act to be exhibited at sale
Section 3 of the Auctions (Bidding Agreements) Act 1927 (copy of Act to be exhibited at sale) shall have effect as if the reference to that Act included a reference to this Act.

5. Short title, commencement and extent
(1) This Act may be cited as the Auctions (Bidding Agreements) Act 1969.

(2) This Act shall come into force at the expiration of one month beginning with the day on which it is passed.

(3) This Act shall not extend to Northern Ireland.

THEFT ACT 1968

15. Obtaining property by deception
(1) A person who by any deception dishonestly obtains property belonging to another, with the intention of permanently depriving the other of it, shall on conviction on indictment be liable to imprisonment for a term not exceeding ten years.

(2) For purposes of this section a person is to be treated as obtaining property if he obtains ownership, possession or control of it, and 'obtain' includes obtaining for another or enabling another to obtain or to retain.

(3) Section 6 above shall apply for purposes of this section, with the necessary adaptation of the reference to appropriating, as it applies for purposes of section 1.

(4) For purposes of this section 'deception' means any deception (whether deliberate or reckless) by words or conduct as to fact or as to law, including a deception as to the present intentions of the person using the deception or any other person.

TRADE DESCRIPTIONS ACT 1968

1. Prohibition of false trade descriptions

(1) Any person who, in the course of a trade or business —

(a) applies a false trade description to any goods; or
(b) supplies or offers to supply any goods to which a false trade description is applied;

shall, subject to the provisions of this Act, be guilty of an offence.

(2) Sections 2 to 6 of this Act shall have effect for the purposes of this section and for the interpretation of expressions used in this section, wherever they occur in this Act.

2. Trade description

(1) A trade description is an indication, direct or indirect, and by whatever means given, of any of the following matters with respect to any goods or parts of goods, that is to say —

(a) quantity, size or gauge;
(b) method of manufacture, production, processing or reconditioning;
(c) composition;
(d) fitness for purpose, strength, performance, behaviour or accuracy;
(e) any physical characteristics not included in the preceding paragraphs;
(f) testing by any person and results thereof;
(g) approval by any person or conformity with a type approved by any person;
(h) place or date of manufacture, production, processing or reconditioning;
(i) person by whom manufactured, produced, processed or reconditioned;
(j) other history, including previous ownership or use.

(2) The matters specified in subsection (1) of this section shall be taken —

(a) in relation to any animal, to include sex, breed or cross, fertility and soundness;
(b) in relation to any semen, to include the identity and characteristics of the animal from which it was taken and measure of dilution.

(3) In this section 'quantity' includes length, width, height, area, volume, capacity, weight and number.

. . .

3. False trade description

(1) A false trade description is a trade description which is false to a material degree.

(2) A trade description which, though not false, is misleading, that is to say, likely to be taken for such an indication of any of the matters specified in section 2 of this Act as would be false to a material degree, shall be deemed to be a false trade description.

(3) Anything which, though not a trade description, is likely to be taken for an indication of any of those matters and, as such an indication, would be false to a material degree, shall be deemed to be a false trade description.

(4) A false indication, or anything likely to be taken as an indication which would be false, that any goods comply with a standard specified or recognised by any person or implied by the approval of any person shall be deemed to be a false trade description, if there is no such person or no standard so specified, recognised or implied.

4. Applying a trade description to goods

(1) A person applies a trade description to goods if he —

(a) affixes or annexes it to or in any manner marks it on or incorporates it with —
  (i) the goods themselves or
  (ii) anything in, on or with which the goods are supplied; or
(b) places the goods in, on or with anything which the trade description has been affixed or annexed to, marked on or incorporated with, or places any such thing with the goods; or
(c) uses the trade description in any manner likely to be taken as referring to the goods.

(2) An oral statement may amount to the use of a trade description.

(3) Where goods are supplied in pursuance of a request in which a trade description is used and the circumstances are such as to make it reasonable to infer that the goods are supplied as goods corresponding to that trade description, the person supplying the goods shall be deemed to have applied that trade description to the goods.

5. Trade descriptions used in advertisements

(1) The following provisions of this section shall have effect where in an advertisement a trade description is used in relation to any class of goods.

(2) The trade description shall be taken as referring to all goods of the class, whether or not in existence at the time the advertisement is published —

(a) for the purpose of determining whether an offence has been committed under paragraph (a) of section 1(1) of this Act; and

(b) where goods of the class are supplied or offered to be supplied by a person publishing or displaying the advertisement, also for the purpose of determining whether an offence has been committed under paragraph (b) of the said section 1(1).

(3) In determining for the purposes of this section whether any goods are of a class to which a trade description used in an advertisement relates regard shall be had not only to the form and content of the advertisement but also to the time, place, manner and frequency of its publication and all other matters making it likely or unlikely that a person to whom the goods are supplied would think of the goods as belonging to the class in relation to which the trade description is used in the advertisement.

6. Offer to supply
A person exposing goods for supply or having goods in his possession for supply shall be deemed to offer to supply them.

13. False representations as to supply of goods or services
If any person, in the course of any trade or business, gives, by whatever means, any false indication, direct or indirect, that any goods or services supplied by him are of a kind supplied to any person he shall, subject to the provisions of this Act, be guilty of an offence.

14. False or misleading statements as to services etc
(1) It shall be an offence for any person in the course of any trade or business —

(a) to make a statement which he knows to be false; or
(b) recklessly to make a statement which is false; as to any of the following matters, that is to say —
   (i) the provision in the course of any trade or business of any services, accommodation or facilities,
   (ii) the nature of any services, accommodation or facilities provided in the course of any trade or business;
   (iii) the time at which, manner in which or persons by whom any services, accommodation or facilities are so provided;
   (iv) the examination, approval or evaluation by a person of any services, accommodation or facilities so provided; or
   (v) the location or amenities of any accommodation so provided.

(2) For the purposes of this section —

(a) anything (whether or not a statement as to any of the matters specified in the preceding subsection) likely to be taken for such a statement as to any of those matters as would be false shall be deemed to be a false statement as to that matter; and
(b) a statement made regardless of whether it is true or false shall be deemed to be made recklessly, whether or not the person making it had reasons for believing that it might be false.

(3) In relation to any services consisting of or including the application of any treatment or process or the carrying out of any repair, the matters specified in subsection (1) of this section shall be taken to include the effect of the treatment, process or repair.

(4) In this section 'false' means false to a material degree and 'services' does not include anything done under a contract of service.

23. Offences due to fault of other person
Where the commission by any person of an offence under this Act is due to the act or default of some other person that other person shall be guilty of the offence, and a person may be charged with and convicted of the offence by virtue of this section whether or not proceedings are taken against the first-mentioned person.

24. Defence of mistake, accident etc
(1) In any proceedings for an offence under this Act it shall, subject to subsection (2) of this section, be a defence for the person charged to prove —

(a) that the commission of the offence was due to a mistake or to reliance on information supplied to him or to the act or default of another person, an accident or some other cause beyond his control; and
(b) that he took all reasonable precautions and exercised all due diligence to avoid the commission of such an offence by himself or any person under his control.

(2) If in any case the defence provided by the last foregoing subsection involves the allegation that the commission of the offence was due to the act or default of another person or to reliance on information supplied by another person, the person charged shall not, without leave of the court, be entitled to rely on that defence unless, within a period ending seven clear days before the hearing, he has served on the prosecutor a notice in writing giving such information identifying or assisting in the identification of that other person as was then in his possession.

(3) In any proceedings for an offence under this Act of supplying or offering to supply goods to which a false trade description is applied it shall be a defence for the person charged to prove that he did not know, and could not with reasonable diligence have ascertained, that the goods did not conform to the description or that the description had been applied to the goods.

25. Innocent publication of advertisement
In proceedings for an offence under this Act committed by the publication of an advertisement it shall be a defence for the person charged to prove that he is a person whose business it is to publish or arrange for the publication of advertisements and that he received the advertisement for publication in the ordinary course of business and did not know and had no reason to suspect that its publication would amount to an offence under this Act.

FIREARMS ACT 1968 (as amended)

1. Requirement of firearm certificate
(1) Subject to any exemption under this Act, it is an offence for a person —

(a) to have in his possession, or to purchase or acquire a firearm to which this section applies without holding a firearm certificate in force at the time, or otherwise than as authorised by such a certificate;
(b) to have in his possession or to purchase or acquire, any ammunition to which this section applies without holding a firearm certificate in force at the time, or otherwise than as authorised by such a certificate, or in quantities in excess of those so authorised.

(2) It is an offence for a person to fail to comply with a condition subject to which a firearm certificate is held by him.

(3) This section applies to every firearm except —

(a) a shot gun within the meaning of this Act, that is to say a smooth-bore gun (not being an air gun) which —
    (i) has a barrel not less than 24 inches in length and does not have any barrel with a bore exceeding 2 inches in diameter;
    (ii) either has no magazine or has a non-detachable magazine incapable of holding more than two cartridges; and
    (iii) is not a revolver gun; and
(b) an air weapon (that is to say, an air rifle, air gun or air pistol not of a type declared by rules made by the Secretary of State under section 53 of this Act to be specially dangerous).

(3A) A gun which has been adapted to have such a magazine as is mentioned in subsection (3)(a)(ii) above shall not be regarded as falling within that provision unless the magazine bears a mark approved by the Secretary of State for denoting that fact and that mark has been made, and the adaptation has been certified in writing as having been carried out in a manner approved by him, either by one of the two companies mentioned in section 58(1) of this Act or by such other person as may be approved by him for that purpose.

(4) This section applies to any ammunition for a firearm, except the following articles, namely:

(a) cartridges containing five or more shot, none of which exceeds .36 inch in diameter;
(b) ammunition for an air gun, air rifle or air pistol; and
(c) blank cartridges not more than one inch in diameter measured immediately in front of the rim or cannelure of the base of the cartridge.

2. Requirement of certificate for possession of shot guns

(1) Subject to any exemption under this Act, it is an offence for a person to have in his possession, or to purchase or acquire, a shot gun without holding a certificate under this Act authorising him to possess shot guns.

(2) It is an offence for a person to fail to comply with a condition subject to which a shot gun certificate is held by him.

3. Business and other transactions with firearms and ammunitions

(1) A person commits an offence if, by way of trade or business, he —

(a) manufactures, sells, transfers, repairs, tests or proves any firearm or ammunition to which section 1 of this Act applies, or a shot gun; or
(b) exposes for sale or transfer, or has in his possession for sale, transfer, repair, test or proof any such firearm or ammunition, or a shot gun,

without being registered under this Act as a firearms dealer.

(2) It is an offence for a person to sell or transfer to any other person in the United Kingdom, other than a registered firearms dealer, any firearm or ammunition to which section 1 of this Act applies, or a shot gun, unless that other produces a firearm certificate authorising him to purchase or acquire it or, as the case may be, his shot gun certificate, or shows that he is by virtue of this Act entitled to purchase or acquire it without holding a certificate.

(3) It is an offence for a person to undertake the repair, test or proof of a firearm or ammunition to which section 1 of this Act applies, or of a shot gun, for any other person in the United Kingdom other than a registered firearm dealer as such, unless that other produces or causes to be produced a firearm certificate authorising him to have possession of the firearm or ammunition or, as the case may be, his shot gun certificate, or shows that he is by virtue of this Act entitled to have possession of it without holding a certificate.

(4) Subsections (1) to (3) above have effect subject to any exemption under subsequent provisions of this Part of this Act.

(5) A person commits an offence if, with a view to purchasing or acquiring, or procuring the repair, test or proof of, any firearm or ammunition to which section 1 of this Act applies, or a shot gun, he produces a false certificate or a certificate in which any false entry has been made, or personates a person to whom a certificate has been granted, or makes any false statement.

(6) It is an offence for a pawnbroker to take in pawn any firearm or ammunition to which section 1 of this Act applies, or a shot gun.

57. Interpretation

(1) In this Act, the expression 'firearm' means a lethal barrelled weapon of any description from which any shot, bullet or other missile can be discharged and includes —

(a) any prohibited weapon, whether it is such a lethal weapon as aforesaid or not; and

(b) any component part of such a lethal or prohibited weapon; and

(c) any accessory to any such weapon designed or adapted to diminish the noise or flash caused by firing the weapon;

and so much of section 1 of this Act as excludes any description of firearm from the category of firearms to which that section applies shall be construed as also excluding component parts of, and accessories to, firearms of that description.

(2) In this Act, the expression 'ammunition' means ammunition for any firearm and includes grenades, bombs and other like missiles, whether capable of use with a firearm or not, and also includes prohibited ammunition.

(2A) In this Act 'self-loading' and 'pump action' in relation to any weapon mean respectively that it is designed or adapted (otherwise than as mentioned in section 5(1)(a)) so that it is automatically re-loaded or that it is so designed or adapted that it is re-loaded by the manual operation of the fore-end or forestock of the weapon.

(2B) In this Act 'revolver', in relation to a smooth-bore gun, means a gun containing a series of chambers which revolve when the gun is fired.

(3) For purposes of sections 45, 46, 50, 51(4) and 52 of this Act, the offences under this Act relating specifically to air weapons are those under sections 22(4), 22(5), 23(1) and 24(4).

(4) In this Act —
'acquire' means hire, accept as a gift or borrow and 'acquisition' shall be construed accordingly;
'air weapon' has the meaning assigned to it by section 1(3)(b) of this Act;
'another member State' means a member State other than the United Kingdom, and 'other member States' shall be construed accordingly;
'area' means a police area;
'Article 7 authority' means a document issued by virtue of section 32A(1)(b) or (2) of this Act;
'certificate' (except in a context relating to the registration of firearms dealers) and 'certificate under this Act' mean a firearm certificate or a shot gun certificate and —

(a) 'firearm certificate' means a certificate granted by a chief officer of police under this Act in respect of any firearm or ammunition to which section 1 of this Act applies and includes a certificate granted in Northern Ireland under section 1 of the Firearms Act 1920, or under an enactment of the Parliament of Northern Ireland amending or substituted for that section; and

(b) 'shot gun certificate' means a certificate granted by a chief officer of police under this act and authorising a person to possess shot guns;

'European firearms pass' means a document to which the holder of a certificate under this Act is entitled by virtue of section 32A(1)(a) of this Act;

'European weapons directive' means the directive of the Council of the European Communities No 91/477/EEC (directive on the control of the acquisition and possession of weapons);

'firearms dealer' means a person who, by way of trade or business, manufactures, sells, transfers, repairs, tests or proves firearms or ammunition to which section 1 of this Act applies, or shot guns;

'imitation firearm' means any thing which has the appearance of being a firearm (other than such a weapon as is mentioned in section 5(1)(b) of this Act) whether or not it is capable of discharging any shot, bullet or other missile;

'premises' includes any land;

'prescribed' means prescribed by rules made by the Secretary of State under section 53 of this Act;

'prohibited weapon' and 'prohibited ammunition' have the meanings assigned to them by section 5(2) of this Act;

'public place' includes any highway and any other premises or place to which at the material time the public have or are permitted to have access, whether on payment or otherwise;

'registered', in relation to a firearms dealer, means registered either —

(a) in Great Britain, under section 33 of this Act, or
(b) in Northern Ireland, under section 8 of the Firearms Act 1920, or any enactment of the Parliament of Northern Ireland amending or substituted for that section,

and references to 'the register', 'registration' and a 'certificate of registration' shall be construed accordingly, except in section 40;

'rifle' includes carbine;

'shot gun' has the meaning assigned to it by section 1(3)(a) of this Act and, in sections 3(1) and 45(2) of this Act and in the definition of 'firearms dealer', includes any component part of a shot gun and any accessory to a shot gun designed or adapted to diminish the noise or flash caused by firing the gun;

'slaughtering instruments' means a firearm which is specially designed or adapted for the instantaneous slaughter of animals or for the instantaneous stunning of animals with a view to slaughtering them; and

'transfer' includes let on hire, give, lend and part with possession, and 'transferee' and 'transferor' shall be construed accordingly.

(4A) For the purposes of any reference in this Act to the use of any firearm or ammunition for a purpose not authorised by the European weapons directive, the directive shall be taken to authorise the use of a firearm or ammunition as or with a slaughtering instrument and the use of a firearm and ammunition —

(a) for sporting purposes;
(b) for the shooting of vermin, or, in the course of carrying on activities in connection with the management of any estate, of other wildlife; and
(c) for competition purposes and target shooting outside competitions.

(5) The definitions in subsections (1) to (3) above apply to the provisions of this Act except where the context otherwise requires.

(6) For purposes of this Act —

(a) the length of the barrel of a firearm shall be measured from the muzzle to the point at which the charge is exploded on firing; and
(b) a shot gun or an air weapon shall be deemed to be loaded if there is ammunition in the chamber or barrel or in any magazine or other device which is in such a position that the ammunition can be fed into the chamber or barrel by the manual or automatic operation of some part of the gun or weapon.

LAND

This section of Appendix 2 contains individual sections etc of Acts as follows:

Sale of Land by Auction Act 1867, ss 4–6
Estate Agents Act 1979, ss 12–15
Law of Property (Miscellaneous Provisions) Act 1989, s 2

SALE OF LAND BY AUCTION ACT 1867

4. Sales of land invalid in law from employment of a puffer to be also invalid in equity

And whereas there is at present a conflict between Her Majesty's court of law and equity in respect of the validity of sales by auction of land where a puffer has bid, although no right of bidding on behalf of the owner was reserved, the courts of law holding that all such sales are absolutely illegal, and the courts of equity under some circumstances giving effect to them but even in courts of equity the rule is unsettled: And whereas it is expedient that an end should be put to such conflicting and unsettled opinions: Be it therefore enacted, that from and after the passing of this Act whenever a sale by auction of land would be invalid at law by reason of the employment of a puffer, the same shall be deemed invalid in equity as well as at law.

5. Rule respecting sale without reserve etc

... The particulars or conditions of sale by auction of any land shall state whether such land will be sold without reserve, or subject to a reserved price, or whether a right to bid is reserved; if it is stated that such land will be sold without reserve, or to that effect, then it shall not be lawful for the seller to employ any person to bid at such sale, or for the auctioneer to take knowingly any bidding from any such person.

6. Rule respecting sale subject to right of seller to bid

And where any sale by auction of land is declared either in the particulars or conditions of such sale to be subject to a right for the seller to bid, it shall be lawful for the seller or any one person on his behalf to bid at such auction in such manner as he may think proper.

ESTATE AGENTS ACT 1979

12. Meaning of 'clients' money' etc

(1) In this Act 'clients' money', in relation to a person engaged in estate agency work, means any money received by him in the course of that work which is a contract or pre-contract deposit —

(a) in respect of the acquisition of an interest in land in the United Kingdom, or
(b) in respect of a connected contract,

whether that money is held or received by him as agent, bailee, stakeholder or in any other capacity.

(2) In this Act 'contract deposit' means any sum paid by a purchaser —

(a) which in whole or in part is, or is intended to form part of the consideration for acquiring such an interest as is referred to in subsection (1)(a) above or for a connected contract; and
(b) which is paid by him at or after the time at which he acquires the interest or enters into an enforceable contract to acquire it.

(3) In this Act 'pre-contract deposit' means any sum paid by any person —

(a) in whole or in part as an earnest of his intention to acquire such an interest as is referred to in subsection (1)(a) above, or
(b) in whole or in part towards meeting any liability of his in respect of the consideration for the acquisition of such an interest which will arise if he acquires or enters into an enforceable contract to acquire the interest or
(c) in respect of a connected contract,

and which is paid by him at a time before he either acquires the interest or enters into an enforceable contract to acquire it.

(4) In this Act 'connected contract', in relation to the acquisition of an interest in land, means a contract which is conditional upon such an acquisition or upon entering into an enforceable contract for such an acquisition (whether or not it is also conditional on other matters).

13. Clients' money held on trust or as agent

(1) It is hereby declared that clients' money received by any person in the course of estate agency work in England, Wales or Northern Ireland —

(a) is held by him on trust for the person who is entitled to call for it to be paid over to him or to be paid on his direction or to have it otherwise credited to him, or

(b) if it is received by him as stakeholder, is held by him on trust for the person who may become so entitled on the occurence of the event against which the money is held.

(2) It is hereby declared that clients' money received by any person in the course of estate agency work in Scotland is held by him as agent for the person who is entitled to call for it to be paid over to him or to be paid on his discretion or to have it otherwise credited to him.

(3) The provisions of sections 14 and 15 below as to the investment of clients' money, the keeping of accounts and records and accounting for interest shall have effect in place of the corresponding duties which would be owed by a person holding clients' money as trustee, or in Scotland as agent, under the general law.

(4) Where an order of the Director under section 3 above has the effect of prohibiting a person from holding client's money the order may contain provision —

(a) appointing another person as trustee, or in Scotland as agent, in place of the person to whom the order relates to hold and deal with clients' money held by that person when the order comes into effect; and
(b) requiring the expenses and such reasonable remuneration of the new trustee or agent as may be specified in the order to be paid by the person to whom the order relates, or if the order provides, out of the clients' money;

but nothing in this subsection shall affect the power conferred by section 41 of the Trustee Act 1925 or section 40 of the Trustee Act (Northern Ireland) 1958 to appoint a new trustee to hold clients' money.

(5) For the avoidance of doubt it is hereby declared that the fact that any person has or may have a lien on clients' money held by him does not affect the operation of this section and also that nothing in this section shall prevent such a lien from being given effect.

14. Keeping of client accounts
(1) Subject to such provision as may be made by accounts regulations, every person who receives clients' money in the course of estate agency work shall, without delay, pay the money into a client account maintained by him or by a person in whose employment he is.

(2) In this Act a 'client account' means a current or deposit account which —

(a) is with an institution authorised for the purposes of this section, and
(b) is in the name of a person who is or has been engaged in estate agency work; and
(c) contains in its title the word 'client'.

(3) The Secretary of State may make provision by regulations (in this section referred to as 'accounts regulations') as to the opening and keeping of client ac-

counts, the keeping of accounts and records relating to clients' money and the auditing of those accounts; and such regulations shall be made by statutory instrument which shall be subject to annulment in pursuance of a resolution of either House of Parliament.

(4) As to the opening and keeping of client accounts, accounts regulations may in particular specify —

(a) the institutions which are authorised for the purposes of this section;
(b) any persons or classes of persons to whom, or any circumstances in which, the obligation imposed by subsection (1) above does not apply;
(c) any circumstances in which money other than clients' money may be paid into a client account; and
(d) the occasions on which, and the persons to whom, money held in a client account may be paid out.

(5) As to the auditing of accounts relating to clients' money, accounts regulations may in particular make provision

(a) requiring such accounts to be drawn up in respect of specified accounting periods and to be audited by a qualified auditor within a specified time after the end of each period;
(b) requiring the auditor to report whether in his opinion the requirements of this Act and of the accounts regulations have been complied with or have been substantially complied with;
(c) as to the matters to which such a report is to relate and the circumstances in which a report of substantial compliance may be given; and
(d) requiring a person who maintains a client account to produce on demand to a duly authorised officer of an enforcement authority the latest auditor's report.

. . .

(8) A person who —

(a) contravenes any provision of this Act or of accounts regulations as to the manner in which clients' money is to be dealt with or accounts and records relating to such money are to be kept, or
(b) fails to produce an auditor's report when required to do so by accounts regulations,

shall be liable on summary conviction to a fine not exceeding level 4 on the standard scale.

15. Interest on clients' money
(1) Accounts regulations may make provision for requiring a person who has received any clients' money to account, in such cases as may be prescribed by the regulations, to the person who is or becomes entitled to the money for the interest

which was, or could have been, earned by putting the money in a separate deposit account at an institution authorised for the purposes of section 14 above.

LAW OF PROPERTY (MISCELLANEOUS PROVISIONS) ACT 1989

2. Contracts for sale etc of land to be made by signed writing

(1) A contract for the sale or other disposition of an interest in land can only be made in writing and only by incorporating all the terms which the parties have expressly agreed in one document or, where contracts are exchanged, in each.

(2) The terms may be incorporated in a document either by being set out in it or by reference to some other document.

(3) The document incorporating the terms or, where contracts are exchanged, one of the documents incorporating them (but not necessarily the same one) must be signed by or on behalf of each party to the contract.

(4) Where a contract for the sale or other disposition of an interest in land satisfies the conditions of this section by reason only of the rectification of one or more documents in pursuance of an order of a court, the contract shall come into being, or be deemed to have come into being, at such time as may be specified in the order.

(5) This section does not apply in relation to —

(a) a contract to grant such a lease as is mentioned in section 54(2) of the Law of Property Act 1925 (short leases);
(b) a contract made in the course of a public auction; or
(c) a contract regulated under the Financial Services Act 1986;

and nothing in this section affects the creation or operation of resulting, implied or constructive trusts.

(6) In this section —

'disposition' has the same meaning as in the Law of Property Act 1925;
'interest in land' means any estate, interest or charge in or over land or in or over the proceeds of sale of land.

(7) Nothing in this section shall apply in relation to contracts made before this section comes into force.

(8) Section 40 of the Law of Property Act 1925 (which is superseded by this section) shall cease to have effect.

SUPPLIES OF A SERVICE

SUPPLY OF GOODS AND SERVICES ACT 1982

12. The contracts concerned
(1) In this Act 'contract for the supply of a service' means, subject to subsection (2) below, a contract under which a person ('the supplier') agrees to carry out a service.

(2) For the purposes of this Act, a contract of service or apprenticeship is not a contract for the supply of a service.

(3) Subject to subsection (2) above, a contract is a contract for the supply of a service for the purposes of this Act whether or not goods are also —

(a) transferred or to be transferred, or
(b) bailed or to be bailed by way of hire,

under the contract, and whatever is the nature of the consideration for which the service is to be carried out.

(4) The Secretary of State may by order provide that one or more of sections 13 to 15 below shall not apply to services of a description specified in the order, and such an order may make different provision for different circumstances.

(5) The power to make an order under subsection (4) above shall be exercisable by statutory instrument subject to annulment in pursuance of a resolution of either House of Parliament.

13. Implied term about care and skill
In a contract for the supply of a service where the supplier is acting in the course of a business, there is an implied term that the supplier will carry out the service with reasonable care and skill.

14. Implied term about time for performance
(1) Where, under a contract for the supply of a service by a supplier acting in the course of a business, the time for the service to be carried out is not fixed by the contract, left to be fixed in a manner agreed by the contract or determined by the course of dealing between the parties, there is an implied term that the supplier will carry out the service within a reasonable time.

(2) What is a reasonable time is a question of fact.

15. Implied term about consideration
(1) Where, under a contract for the supply of a service, the consideration for the service is not determined by the contract, left to be determined in a manner agreed

by the contract or determined by the course of dealing between the parties, there is an implied term that the party contracting with the supplier will pay a reasonable charge.

(2) What is a reasonable charge is a question of fact.

Appendix 3

Rules of Procedure: Selected Extracts

The rules given below are those applicable to procedure in the High Court. By virtue of the High Court and County Courts Jurisdiction Order 1991, usually cases involving under £25,000 will be heard in the County Court and those over £50,000 in the High Court. In practice, many intermediate cases are heard in the County Court, as are many cases relating to land title disputes. We have given the appropriate County Court Rule in the footnotes to the text of the Supreme Court Rule.

Appendix 3 contains the following:
RSC Ord 15, r 4
RSC Ord 16, rr 1, 2, 6–8, 10(1) and 11
RSC Ord 17, rr 1–3, 5, 7 and 8
RSC Ord 29, rr 2A, 4 and 6
RSC Ord 43, rr 1–8

ORDER 15. CAUSES OF ACTIONS, COUNTERCLAIMS AND PARTIES

4. Joinder of parties[1]
(1) Subject to rule 5(1), two or more persons may be joined together in one action as plaintiffs or as defendants with the leave of the Court or where —

(a) if separate actions were brought by or against each of them, as the case may be, some common question of law or fact would arise in all the actions, and
(b) all rights to relief claimed in the action (whether they are joint, several or alternative) are in respect of or arise out of the same transaction or series of transactions.

(2) Where the plaintiff in any action claims any relief to which any other person is entitled jointly with him, all persons so entitled must, subject to the provisions of any Act and unless the Court gives leave to the contrary, be parties to the action and any of them who does not consent to being joined as a plaintiff must, subject to any order made by the Court on an application for leave under this paragraph, be made a defendant.

This paragraph shall not apply to a probate action.

---

[1] The corresponding County Court Rule to RSC Ord 15, r 4 is CCR 1981, Ord 5, r 2.

ORDER 16. THIRD PARTY AND SIMILAR PROCEEDINGS[2]

1. Third party notice
Where in any action a defendant who has given notice of intention to defend —

(a) claims against a person not already a party to the action any contribution or indemnity; or
(b) claims against such a person any relief or remedy relating to or connected with the original subject-matter of the action and substantially the same as some relief or remedy claimed by the plaintiff; or
(c) requires that any question or issue relating to or connected with the original subject-matter of the action should be determined not only as between the plaintiff and the defendant but also as between either or both of them and a person not already a party to the action;

then, subject to paragraph (2), the defendant may issue a notice in Form No. 20 or 21 in Appendix A, whichever is appropriate (in this Order referred to as a third party notice), containing a statement of the nature of the claim made against him and, as the case may be, either of the nature and grounds of the claim made by him or of the question or issue required to be determined.

(2) A defendant to an action may not issue a third party notice without the leave of the Court unless the action was begun by writ and he issues the notice before serving his defence on the plaintiff.

(3) Where a third party notice is served on the person against whom it is issued, he shall as from the time of service be a party to the action (in this Order referred to as a third party) with the same rights in respect of his defence against any claim made against him in the notice and otherwise as if he had been duly sued in the ordinary way by the defendant by whom the notice is issued.

2. Application for leave to issue third party notice
(1) Application for leave to issue a third party notice may be made ex parte but the Court may direct a summons for leave to be issued.

(2) An application for leave to issue a third party notice must be supported by an affidavit stating —

(a) the nature of the claim made by the plaintiff in the action;
(b) the stage which proceedings in the action have reached;
(c) the nature of the claim made by the applicant or particulars of the question or issue required to be determined, as the case may be, and the facts on which the proposed third party notice is based; and
(d) the name and address of the person against whom the third party notice is to be issued

---

[2] The corresponding County Court Rule to RSC Ord 16 is CCR 1981, Ord 12.

6. Setting aside third party proceedings
Proceedings on a third party notice may, at any stage of the proceedings, be set aside by the Court.

7. Judgment between defendant and third party
(1) Where in any action a defendant has served a third party notice, the Court may at or after the trial of the action or, if the action is decided otherwise than by trial, on an application by summons or motion, order such judgment as the nature of the case may require to be entered for the defendant against the third party or for the third party against the defendant.

(2) Where judgment is given for the payment of any contribution or indemnity to a person who is under a liability to make a payment in respect of the same debt or damage, execution shall not issue on the judgment without the leave of the Court until that liability has been discharged.

(3) For the purpose of paragraph (2) 'liability' includes liability under a judgment in the same or other proceedings and liability under an agreement to which section 1(4) of the Civil Liability (Contribution) Act 1978 applies.

8. Claims and issues between a defendant and some other party
(1) Where in any action a defendant who has given notice of intention to defend —

(a) claims against a person who is already a party to the action any contribution or indemnity; or
(b) claims against such a person any relief or remedy relating to or connected with the original subject-matter of the action and substantially the same as some relief or remedy claimed by the plaintiff; or
(c) requires that any question or issue relating to or connected with the original subject-matter of the action should be determined not only as between the plaintiff and himself but also as between either or both of them and some other person who is already a party to the action;

then, subject to paragraph (2), the defendant may, without leave, issue and serve on that person a notice containing a statement of the nature and grounds of his claim or, as the case may be, of the question or issue required to be determined.

(2) Where a defendant makes such a claim as is mentioned in paragraph (1) and that claim could be made by him by counterclaim in the action, paragraph (1) shall not apply in relation to the claim.

(3) No acknowlegement of service of such a notice shall be necessary if the person on whom it is served has acknowledged service of the writ or originating summons in the action or is a plaintiff therein, and the same procedure shall be adopted for the determination between the defendant by whom, and the person on whom, such a notice is served of the claim, question or issue stated in the notice as would be appropriate under this Order if the person served with the notice were a third party and (where he has given notice of intention to defend the action or is a plaintiff) had given notice of intention to defend the claim, question or issue.

(4) Rule 4(2) shall have effect in relation to proceedings on a notice issued under this rule as if for the words '7 days after giving notice of intention to defend' there were substituted the words '14 days after service of the notice on him'.

10. Offer of contribution

(1) If, at any time after he has acknowledged service, a party to an action who, stands to be held liable in the action to another party to contribute towards any debt or damages which may be recovered against that other party in the action, makes (without prejudice to his defence) a written offer to that other party to contribute to a specified extent to the debt or damages, then, notwithstanding that he reserves the right to bring the offer to the attention of the Judge at the trial, the offer shall not be brought to the attention of the Judge until after all questions of liability and amount of debt or damages have been decided.

11. Counterclaim by defendant

Where in any action a counterclaim is made by a defendant, the foregoing provisions of this Order shall apply in relation to the counterclaim as if the subject-matter of the counterclaim were the original subject-matter of the action, and as if the person making the counterclaim were the plaintiff and the person against whom it is made a defendant.

ORDER 17. INTERPLEADER[3]

1. Entitlement to relief by way of interpleader

(1) Where —

(a) a person is under a liability in respect of a debt or in respect of any money, goods or chattels and he is, or expects to be, sued for or in respect of that debt or money or those goods or chattels by two or more persons making adverse claims thereto, or
(b) claim is made to any money, goods or chattels taken or intended to be taken by a sheriff in execution under any process, or to the proceeds or value of any such goods or chattels, by a person other than the person against whom the process is issued,

the person under liability as mentioned in sub-paragraph (a) or (subject to rule 2) the sheriff, may apply to the Court for relief by way of interpleader.

(2) References in this Order to a sheriff shall be construed as including references to any other officer charged with the execution of process by or under the authority of the High Court.

2. Claim to goods etc taken in execution

(1) Any person making a claim to or in respect of any money, goods or chattels taken or intended to be taken in execution under process of the Court, or to the proceeds or value of any such goods or chattels, must give notice of his claim to the

---

[3] The corresponding County Court Rule to RSC Ord 17 is CCR 1981, Ord 33.

sheriff charged with the execution of the process and must include in his notice a statement of his address, and that address shall be his address for service.

(2) On receipt of a claim made under this rule the sheriff must forthwith give notice thereof to the execution creditor and the execution creditor must, within 4 days after receiving the notice, give notice to the sheriff informing him whether he admits or disputes the claim.

An execution creditor who gives notice in accordance with this paragraph admitting a claim shall only be liable to the sheriff for any fees and expenses incurred by the sheriff before receipt of that notice.

(3) Where —

(a) the sheriff receives a notice from an execution creditor under paragraph (2) disputing a claim, or the execution creditor fails, within the period mentioned in that paragraph, to give the required notice, and
(b) the claim made under this rule is not withdrawn,

the sheriff may apply to the Court for relief under this Order.

(4) A sheriff who receives a notice from an execution creditor under paragraph (2) admitting a claim made under this rule shall withdraw from possession of the money, goods or chattels claimed and may apply to the Court for relief under this Order of the following kind, that is to say, an order restraining the bringing of an action against him for or in respect of his having taken possession of that money or those goods or chattels.

3. Mode of application
(1) An application for relief under this Order must be made by originating summons unless made in a pending action, in which case it must be made by summons in the action.

. . .

(3) An originating summons under this rule shall be in Form No. 10 in Appendix A.

(4) Subject to paragraph (5), a summons under this rule must be supported by evidence that the applicant —

(a) claims no interest in the subject-matter in dispute other than for charges or costs,
(b) does not collude with any of the claimants to that subject-matter, and
(c) is willing to pay or transfer that subject-matter into court or to dispose of it as the Court may direct.

. . .

5. Powers of Court hearing summons
(1) Where on the hearing of a summons under this Order all the persons by whom

adverse claims to the subject-matter in dispute (hereafter in this Order referred to as 'the claimants') appear, the Court may order —

(a) that any claimant be made a defendant in any action pending with respect to the subject-matter in dispute in substitution for or in addition to the applicant for relief under this Order, or
(b) that an issue between the claimants be stated and tried and may direct which of the claimants is to be plaintiff and which defendant.

(2) Where —

(a) the applicant on a summons under this Order is a sheriff, or
(b) all the claimants consent or any of them so requests, or
(c) the question at issue between the claimants is a question of law and the facts are not in dispute,

the Court may summarily determine the question at issue between the claimants and make an order accordingly on such terms as may be just.

(3) Where a claimant, having been duly served with a summons for relief under this Order, does not appear on the hearing of the summons or, having appeared, fails or refuses to comply with an order made in the proceedings, the Court may make an order declaring the claimant, and all persons claiming under him, for ever barred from prosecuting his claim against the applicant for such relief and all persons claiming under him, but such an order shall not affect the rights of the claimants as between themselves.

7. Power to stay proceedings
Where a defendant to an action applies for relief under this Order in the action, the Court may by order stay all further proceedings in the action.

8. Other powers
Subject to the foregoing rules of this Order, the Court may in or for the purposes of any interpleader proceedings make such order as to costs or any other matter as it thinks just.

ORDER 29. INTERLOCUTORY INJUNCTIONS, INTERIM PRESERVATION OF PROPERTY, INTERIM PAYMENTS ETC

2A. Delivery of goods under s4 of Torts (Interference with Goods) Act 1977[4]
(1) Without prejudice to rule 2, the Court may, on the application of any party to a cause or matter, make an order under section 4 of the Torts (Interference with Goods) Act 1977 for the delivery up of any goods which are the subject-matter of the cause or matter or as to which any question may arise therein.

---

[4] There is no corresponding County Court Rule to RSC Ord 29, r 2A but it is applied directly by virtue of CCR 1981, Ord 13, r 7(1)(d).

(2) Paragraphs (2) and (3) of rule 1 shall have effect in relation to an application for such an order as they have effect in relation to an application for the grant of an injunction.

4. Sale of perishable property[5]
(1) The Court may, on the application of any party to a cause or matter, make an order for the sale by such person, in such manner and on such terms (if any) as may be specified in the order of any property (other than land) which is the subject-matter of the cause or matter or as to which any question arises therein and which is of a perishable nature or likely to deteriorate if kept or which for any other good reason it is desirable to sell forthwith.

In this paragraph 'land' includes any interest in, or right over, land.

6. Recovery of personal property subject to lien etc[6]
Where the plaintiff, or the defendant by way of counterclaim, claims the recovery of specific property (other than land) and the party from whom recovery is sought does not dispute the title of the party making the claim but claims to be entitled to retain the property by virtue of a lien or otherwise as security for any sum of money, the Court, at any time after the claim to be so entitled appears from the pleadings (if any) or by affidavit or otherwise to its satisfaction, may order that the party seeking to recover the property be at liberty to pay into court, to abide the event of the action, the amount of money in respect of which the security is claimed and such further sum (if any) for interest and costs as the Court may direct and that, upon such payment being made, the property claimed be given up to the party claiming it.

ORDER 43. ACCOUNTS AND INQUIRIES

1. Summary order for account
(1) Where a writ is endorsed with a claim for an account or a claim which necessarily involves taking an account, the plaintiff may, at any time after the defendant has acknowledged service of the writ or after the time limited for acknowledging service, apply for an order under this rule.

(1A) A defendant to an action begun by writ who has served a counterclaim, which includes a claim for an account or a claim which necessarily involves taking an account, on —

(a) the plaintiff, or
(b) any other party, or
(c) any person who becomes a party by virtue of such service may apply for an order under this rule.

---

[5] The corresponding County Court Rule to RSC Ord 29, r 4 is CCR 1981, Ord 13, r 7.
[6] The corresponding County Court Rule to RSC Ord 29, r 6 is CCR 1981, Ord 13, r 7.

(2) An application under this rule must be made by summons and, if the Court so directs, must be supported by affidavit or other evidence.

(3) On the hearing of the application, the Court may, unless satisfied that there is some preliminary question to be tried, order that an account be taken and may also order that any amount certified on taking the account to be due to either party be paid to him within a time specified in the order.

2. Court may direct taking of accounts etc[7]

(1) The Court may, on an application made by summons at any stage of the proceedings in a cause or matter, direct any necessary accounts or inquiries to be taken or made.

(2) Every direction for the taking of an account or the making of an inquiry shall be numbered in the judgment or order so that, as far as may be, each distinct account and inquiry may be designated by a number.

3. Directions as to manner of taking account or making inquiry[7]

(1) Where the Court orders an account to be taken or inquiry to be made it may by the same or a subsequent order give directions with regard to the manner in which the account is to be taken or vouched or the inquiry is to be made.

(2) Without prejudice to the generality of paragraph (1) the Court may direct that in taking an account the relevant books of account shall be evidence of the matters contained therein with liberty to the parties interested to take such objections thereto as they think fit.

4. Account to be made, verified etc

(1) Where an account has been ordered to be taken, the accounting party must make out his account and, unless the Court otherwise directs, verify it by an affidavit to which the account must be exhibited.

(2) The items on each side of the account must be numbered consecutively.

(3) Unless the order for the taking of the account otherwise directs, the accounting party must lodge the account with the Court and must at that same time notify the other parties that he has done so and of the filing of any affidavit verifying the account and of any supporting affidavit.

5. Notice to be given of alleged omissions etc in account

Any party who seeks to charge an accounting party with an amount beyond that which he has by his account admitted to have received or who alleges that any item

---

[7] RSC Ord 43, rr 2 and 3 are expressly incorporated into the County Court Rules 1981 by virtue of the County Courts Act 1984, s 76.

in his account is erroneous in respect of amount or in any other respect must give him notice thereof stating, so far as he is able, the amount sought to be charged with brief particulars thereof or, as the case may be, the grounds for alleging that the item is erroneous.

6. Allowances

In taking any account directed by any judgment or order all just allowances shall be made without any direction to that effect.

7. Delay in prosecution of accounts etc

(1) If it appears to the Court that there is undue delay in the prosecution of any accounts or inquiries, or in any other proceedings under any judgment or order, the Court may require the party having the conduct of the proceedings or any other party to explain the delay and may then make such order for staying the proceedings or for expediting them or for the conduct thereof and for costs as the circumstances require.

(2) The Court may direct any party or the official solicitor to take over the conduct of the proceedings in question and to carry out any directions made by an order under this rule and may make such order as it thinks fit as to the payment of the official solicitor's costs.

8. Distribution of fund before persons entitled are ascertained

Where some of the persons entitled to share in a fund are ascertained, and difficulty or delay has occurred or is likely to occur in ascertaining the other persons so entitled, the Court may order or allow immediate payment of their shares to the persons ascertained without reserving any part of those shares to meet the subsequent costs of ascertaining those other persons.

Appendix 4

Title in Cases of Theft of Goods in the UK[1]

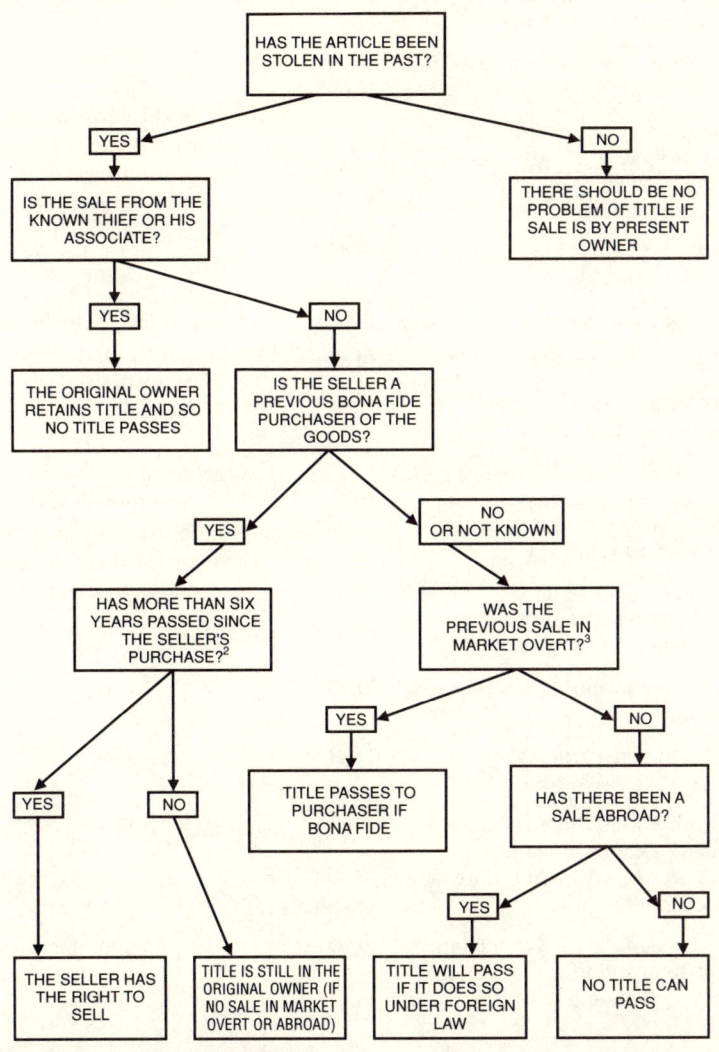

---

[1] See B W Harvey, 'Theft of Goods in the UK and the International Dimension', *Croner's Buying and Selling Law Bulletin*, Sept 1992, p 13.

[2] See the Limitation Act 1980, s 4.

[3] 'Market overt' was abolished from 3 January 1995 by the Sale of Goods (Amendment) Act 1994.

Values at or above which an export licence is required (from 1 April 1993)

	UK LICENCE (£)	EC LICENCE (£)
Any antique item not shown below, more than 50 years old	39,600	39,600
Archaeological material found in UK soil or UK territorial waters	zero	zero
Archaeological material from outside the UK[1]	39,600	zero
Elements forming an integral part of artistic, historical or religious monuments, which have been dismembered, and which are:		
— more than 50 years old but less than 100 years old	39,600	no EC licence required
— more than 100 years old	39,600	zero
Incunabula more than 50 years old	39,600	zero
Manuscripts more than 50 years old, including maps and musical scores, singly or collections	zero	zero
Archives, and any elements thereof, of any kind, on any medium, which are more than 50 years old	zero	zero
Architectural, scientific and engineering drawings produced by hand, more than 50 years old	zero	11,900
Arms and armour, more than 50 years old	20,000	39,600
Textiles (excluding carpets and tapestries)	6,000	39,600
Mosaics (other than those falling in the archaeological or monument categories above), which are more than 50 years old	39,600	11,900
Drawings executed entirely by hand on any medium and in any material, more than 50 years old	39,600	11,900

[1] There is a discretion under the EC Regulation which allows Member States not to require EC export licences for objects of limited archaeological or scientific interest. Guidance on this can be obtained from the Department of National Heritage.

Continued

	UK LICENCE (£)	EC LICENCE (£)
Original engravings, prints, serigraphs and lithographs, and their respective plates, and original posters, more than 50 years old	39,600	11,900
Photographs, films and negatives thereof, which are more than 50 years old	6,000	11,900
Printed maps which are:		
— more than 50 years old but less than 200 years old	39,600	no EC licence required
— more than 200 years old	39,600	11,900
Original sculptures or statuary, and copies produced by the same process as the original, which are more than 50 years old (other than those which fall within the archaeological category)	39,600	39,600
Books which are:		
— more than 50 years old but less than 100 years old	39,600	no EC licence required
— more than 100 years old	39,600	39,600
Collections and specimens from zoological, botanical, mineralogical or anatomical collections	no UK licence required	39,600
Collections of historical, palaentological, ethnographic or numismatic interest	no UK licence required	39,600
Means of transport which are:		
— more than 50 years old but less than 75 years old	39,600	no EC licence required
— more than 75 years old	39,600	39,600
Portraits or likenesses which are more than 50 years old, of British Historic Persons	6,000	119,000
Paintings in oil or tempera, which are more than 50 years old (excluding portraits of British Historic Persons)	119,000	119,000
Paintings in other media, which are more than 50 years old (excluding portraits of British Historic Persons)	39,600	119,000

APPLICATION FOR EC EXPORT LICENCE — SAMPLE COPY[1]

European Community — Cultural Goods Sample Copy

1 Application 1

1 Applicant (Name and address) A. N. Other 4 Walk Way Chestertown	**2 Export Licence** No Valid until / / / Definitive [x] Temporary ☐ Date for reimportation / / /
3 Applicant's Representative (Name and address) Fly Sky PLC Smith Street London	**4 Issuing Authority** (Name and address) Department Of National Heritage 2–4 Cockspor Street London SW1Y 5DH
5A Country of Destination or of Temporary Stay United States of America	**6 Member State of Consignment** United Kingdom
5B Consignee Apple Gallery, Maryville, USA	

7 Description in Terms of the Annex to EC Regulation (EEC) No 3911/92 Category of the Cultural Goods
Paintings in other media, which are more than 50 years old (excluding portraits of British Historic Persons).

8 Description of Cultural Object or Objects 'The Meadows' Watercolour by Mr Smith	**9 Commodity Code** 9701 **10 Mass** 1 Kg
If the space is insufficient you may continue on one or more supplementary pages which should be copied in triplicate and should contain the information required in boxes 8 to 18 (see note in box 23)	**11 Estimated Value** £170,000

Criteria to be used for identification

12 Measurements	**13 Title or Subject**	**14 Dating**	**15 Other Characteristics**
30 × 40 cms	'The Meadows'	1880	

16 Artist, Period or Workshop	**17 Medium or Technique**
Mr Smith, Pink Period	Watercolour

18 Documents submitted/specific indications relating to identification
☑ photograph ☐ list ☑ bibliography ☐ catalogue

Provenance:
Purchased by Mr Jones 1885
Purchased by I.M. Other 1910
Then by Descent.

Application	
19A I hereby apply for an export licence in respect of the cultural object described above and declare in good faith that the information in this application and the supporting documents is true.	**20** Signature and stamp of issuing authority

[1] This form, the preceding chart and the Annex following are copyright and are reproduced by permission of the Controller, HMSO.

ANNEXE TO APPLICATION FOR EC EXPORT LICENCE.

Please ensure that this form is completed and returned with every application for an EC export licence.

1. Your reference — quote in correspondence

2. Telephone number for queries

3. Have the goods been imported into the UK or the Isle of Man in the last 50 years? If 'Yes' supply available evidence (NB For items which have been licensed previously for temporary exportation only and return but which otherwise had been in the UK or Isle of Man for more than 50 years the answer should be 'No').

4. State the official reference number(s) of any previous application(s) for export licence(s) for the goods

WARNING

Penalties may be imposed for false statements in connection with applications for export licences.

DECLARATION

1. The goods to be exported are my/our property of the owner(s) named above for whom I am authorised to act in this transaction as the sole responsible representative.

2. I am aware that the exporter or shipper of the goods may be required to provide to Customs and Excise, within such time as they allow, proof to their satisfaction that the goods covered by this licence were delivered at the destination named in the licence.

Signed .... Owner of goods* proprietor* partner*
director* company secretary*
(*Delete those which do not apply)

Date .... *Official number of authorised signatory*

Other signatories may be authorised upon written application to the Department of National Heritage.

Index